SONGS

#

1	23 Years Too Late	WIRE
2	#135 Muckefuck	STROTTER INST.
3	⁒	SCHNELLERTOLLERMEIER

A

4	A Perspective with No End	TOMAGA
5	About Farewell	ALELA DIANE
6	Acid Rat	EGOPUSHER
7	All Kings Do Confess	SHABAZZ PALACES
8	All the People Sleep	TOPS
9	An Ocean in Between the Waves	THE WAR ON DRUGS
10	Anchored in Love (the Carter Family)	PRUNO TRUMAN AND FRIENDS
11	And Sing While Thou on Pressed Flowers Dost Sleep	MAJA RATKJE
12	Arthur Russell's Instrumentals	PETER GORDON, PETER ZUMMO, ERNIE BROOKS, RHYS CHATHAM, BILL RUYLE, GAVIN RUSSOM, MAX GORDON, GERRY O'BEIRNE
13	Asylum	JESSICA93
14	At the Seams	KIMYA DAWSON

B

15	Back in the Tall Grass	FUTURE ISLANDS
16	Bad Bonn Raag	AL COMET
17	Baldomero	FUMAÇA PRETA
18	Berberian Wedding	ACID ARAB
19	Big MAC	TIM FITE
20	Black Grease	THE BLACK ANGELS
21	Bloodsucker	MOZES AND THE FIRSTBORN
22	Bloom	OSCAR AND THE WOLF
23	Blue Skies	RÖKKURRÓ
24	Boulder (Ογκόλιθος)	LARRY GUS
25	Bronx in a Six	SLEAFORD MODS
26	Burred Lens	ABSOLUTELY FREE

SONGS

SONGS

	54	Grand Canyon	TIMBER TIMBRE
	55	Green Eyes	AMEN DUNES
	56	Guaracha U.F.O.	MERIDIAN BROTHERS
H	57	Hands Up	EAUX
	58	Hang of Summer	SAMARA LUBELSKI
	59	Headlines	WARM GRAVES
	60	Her Tenere	BOMBINO
I	61	I Know It's Pathetic but That Was the Greatest Night of My Life	SUN KIL MOON
	62	I Love Lou (Song for Lou Reed)	BLACK YAYA
	63	I Miss Your Bones	HOSPITALITY
	64	I Will	SEBADOH
	65	Imaginary Spheres	MONOSKI
	66	In Conflict	OWEN PALLETT
	67	Innocent	HUNDRED WATERS
	68	Iota	ANGEL OLSEN
	69	Is in the House Ya, Is in My Mouth Ya	PUTS MARIE
	70	It's Alive	LA LUZ
J	71	Jude	DAN MANGAN
	72	Jungle Riot	SKIP&DIE
K	73	Kali Yuga Blues	BARDO POND
	74	Key of It All	BRAHMA-LOKA
	75	Kopter	TOY
L	76	Lay and Love	BONNIE "PRINCE" BILLY
	77	Le Léthé	PHILIPPE PETIT
	78	Les Véliplanchistes	FLAVIEN BERGER
	79	Let It Bleed	GOAT
	80	Lilac Garden	JANDEK

SONGS

	No.	Song	Artist
	81	Little Pony	ARTO LINDSAY
	82	Lookin' to Get Right	MASTERS OF REALITY
	83	Looperdate_write_sample	DIEB13
	84	Lucky You, Lucky Me	THE SLOW SHOW
	85	Lurker	STEVE GUNN
M	86	Many Weathers Apart	MERZ
	87	March of Progress	VIET CONG
	88	Me & You & Jackie Mittoo	SUPERCHUNK
	89	Mir schaded de Wirtschaft	MANUEL STAHLBERGER
	90	Mirage Year	STRAND OF OAKS
	91	Modern Art	BLACK LIPS
	92	Mogwai Fear Satan	MOGWAI
	93	Morning Sun	THE UNDERGROUND YOUTH
	94	Motel Money a Way	BIRTH OF JOY
	95	Mother	MERIL WUBSLIN
	96	Motorbike	WOODEN SHJIPS
	97	Mr. Carbon Copy	MORGAN DELT
	98	Muchacho's Tune	PHOSPHORESCENT
N	99	Nada Em Vão	RODRIGO AMARANTE
	100	Never Were the Way She Was	COLIN STETSON & SARAH NEUFELD
	101	New Calm Pt. 2	OUGHT
	102	No Go!	CHELSEA LIGHT MOVING
O	103	Ocean Death	BATHS
	104	Old Gold and Loose Diamonds	JEF BARBARA
	105	On the Water	PALL JENKINS
	106	Opposite of Afternoon	UNKNOWN MORTAL ORCHESTRA
	107	Over the River and Through the Woods	LIGHTNING BOLT
P	108	Power to the Women of the Morning Shift	OUM SHATT

SONGS

	109	Principe Real	PANDA BEAR
	110	Progression	VELMA
R	111	Raptus	LEON
	112	Reach a Bit Further	WILD BEASTS
	113	Ready or Not	KASSETTE
	114	Red Apples 2 (for Tom Scharpling)	KURT VILE
	115	Red Ford Radio	U.S. GIRLS
	116	Reverend Beat Man Sings Bad Bonn	REVEREND BEAT MAN
	117	Rework of John Cage 4'33"	NILS FRAHM
	118	The Ride	CAVE
	119	Rock'n'Roll ehr Wichser	KNÖPPEL
S	120	Sad Song for Jandek	THE FLAMING LIPS
	121	Saturday Bride	QUILT
	122	Shampoo	ELVIS PERKINS
	123	She Might Get Shot	JUAN WAUTERS
	124	Shipbreakers	MOANING CITIES
	125	Slider	BO NINGEN
	126	Sort of Way	R. STEVIE MOORE
	127	The Stars Keep On Calling My Name	MAC DEMARCO
	128	Still	EVJE
	129	Strobohobo	JOCHEN DISTELMEYER
	130	Summer's Game	JACCO GARDNER
	131	Sweet Sweet South	FRESCHARD
T	132	Tenshinhan	ROBBING MILLIONS
	133	The High Heeled Shoe Guitar	CHICKS ON SPEED
	134	This Is My Hand	MY BRIGHTEST DIAMOND
	135	Tiptoes	DAEDELUS
	136	Tom's Diner	SUZANNE VEGA
	137	Too Many Lashes	PHÈDRE

SONGS

BANDS

BANDS

BANDS

BANDS

BANDS

BANDS

	No.	Band	Title
	90	STRAND OF OAKS	Mirage Year
	2	STROTTER INST.	#135 Muckefuck
	33	SUN GLITTERS	Clouds in Your Eyes
	61	SUN KIL MOON	I Know It's Pathetic but That Was the Greatest Night of My Life
	88	SUPERCHUNK	Me & You & Jackie Mittoo
	136	SUZANNE VEGA	Tom's Diner
T	148	TANYA TAGAQ	Untitled
	19	TIM FITE	Big MAC
	54	TIMBER TIMBRE	Grand Canyon
	4	TOMAGA	A Perspective with No End
	8	TOPS	All the People Sleep
	34	TORONAUT	Colors
	75	TOY	Kopter
	36	TWO GALLANTS	Cradle Pyre
U	115	U.S. GIRLS	Red Ford Radio
	93	THE UNDERGROUND YOUTH	Morning Sun
	106	UNKNOWN MORTAL ORCHESTRA	Opposite of Afternoon
V	110	VELMA	Progression
	87	VIET CONG	March of Progress
W	9	THE WAR ON DRUGS	An Ocean in Between the Waves
	149	THE WARLOCKS	Untitled
	59	WARM GRAVES	Headlines
	46	WE ARE THE CITY	Everything Changes
	112	WILD BEASTS	Reach a Bit Further
	1	WIRE	23 Years Too Late
	96	WOODEN SHJIPS	Motorbike

#

23 YEARS TOO LATE

VERSE - E/G/A/Am

CHORUS - E/A

1

23 Years Too Late

WIRE

① WIRE – 23 YEARS TOO LATE

20 DAY PERCH SELECTED
WE SNAIL THROUGH STREETS
OF SMOKE

TILO AND HARDCORE
MASSIVE ATTACK
AND TRANSFER PRINTS
FRESH FROM THE STATES
WITH EXTRA FEAR
EACH SUIT TAILORED FOR
SILOHETTE PROMISE
COPYISTS TARGET THE
SUN-STUNG PIER
AN UNEGAGED JACK
DEMOLISHES WALLS
OF CAREFUL CONSTRUCTION
23 YEARS LATE

1

2.

SMITH & WRIGHT SHOOT IN
FROM BALLISTIC BERLIN
FUELLED BY THE FINNISH
RUDE-BOY ENGINEERING FRONT
IN PLUM-BLACK KNIT-LOVE
THEY OFFICIATE
OPEN-PLAN TENDENCIES
ENGULF THE ROOM
ENTHUSIASTICALLY EMBRACING
THE ZIGGERAT BEAT
HEADLOCKED IN GRIDLOCK
OOZING THROUGH FLANDERS
WHITE KICKER MAGIC PLANTS
POPPIES OF REMEMBRANCE
POPEYE REMEMBERS A CYCLOPTI
MONSTER

23 YEARS LATE
23 YEARS LATE

1

3.

RE-INVENTING THE SCHEDULE
FUN-FILLED FIREMEN
VISIT THE MUSEUM OF
BACKWARD HATS
TOTALLY OSCARED, THE
NETHERLANDS ARE UNTETHERED
RHIZOMIC GASTROPODS
INTERWEAVE SLENDER TAILS
GREY HAIRS GENUFLECT
AS PERFORATED ANARCHISTS
LEAD THE SCREW-TOP REVOLUTION

23 YEARS LATE
23 YEARS LATE

1

WE ENTER THE HASHISH KASBAH
WITH MILLIMETRES TO SPARE
CITIZENS OF CRISTIANIA
THE CANNABIS CASTAWAYS
VICTIMS OF THE COOKIE CUTTER
CRUCIFIXION

23 YEARS LATE
23 YEARS TOO LATE

BECALMED IN GREEN FOG BANKS
OVER BAKED PASTRIES
GOODBYE GOODBYE
GOODBYE GOODBYE

1

CHORUS

23 YEARS TOO LATE
CHISEL JUMPING, LAID-BACK PASTRY
NAKED PUNKS AND STONE HARD PAGANS
SONIC PARAMEDICS WEEP
HARNESS SHORT DELAYS
FUELLED BY FINNISH RUDE FAMILIARS
LEAD THE SCREWTOP REVOLUTIONARIES
IN THE LAND OF HATS
AIRBRUSH CAMOFLAGE
CLOAKED BY NIGHT, WE SLIP THE BORDER
COLLABORATIVE PACTS, THE FERRY
SPURNED WE HIT THE RAMPS,
CHAOS JUNCTIONS CRASH,
UPON A CROWD OF LOST CONSTRUCTION
RUSSIAN HOTEL CHECKIN KITCHEN
EXPECTATIONS, BLACK-KNIT LOVE

---

23 YEARS LATE by WIRE

1

FOR THE

BAD BOY

SONG BOOK

MIX & PLAY

THE

STROTTER-WAY

2
#135 Muckefuck
STROTTER INST.

- min. 2 TURNTABLES
- 2 CLAMPS PER TURNTABLE
- RUBBER-BANDS
- BAD VINYL-RECOROS
- MIXING DESK

3.) PREPARATION OF THE RECORDS

a.) BEAT

NIPPERS OF RUBBERBANDS

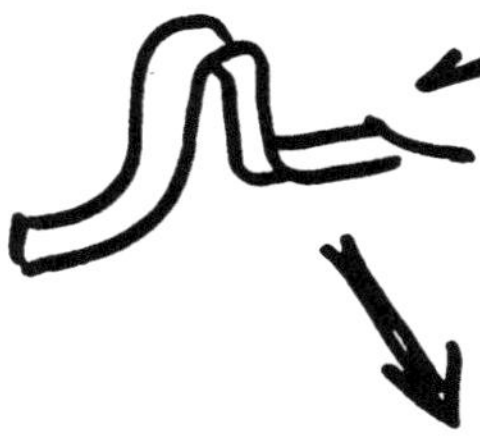

SCOTCH ON BAD POP-RECORDS

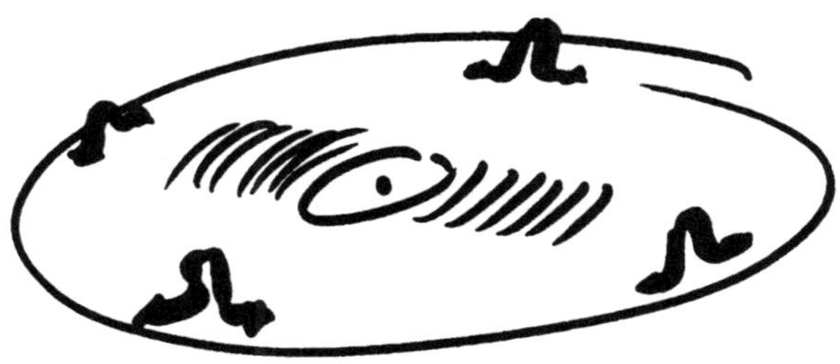

4-QUARTER

b.) DRONES

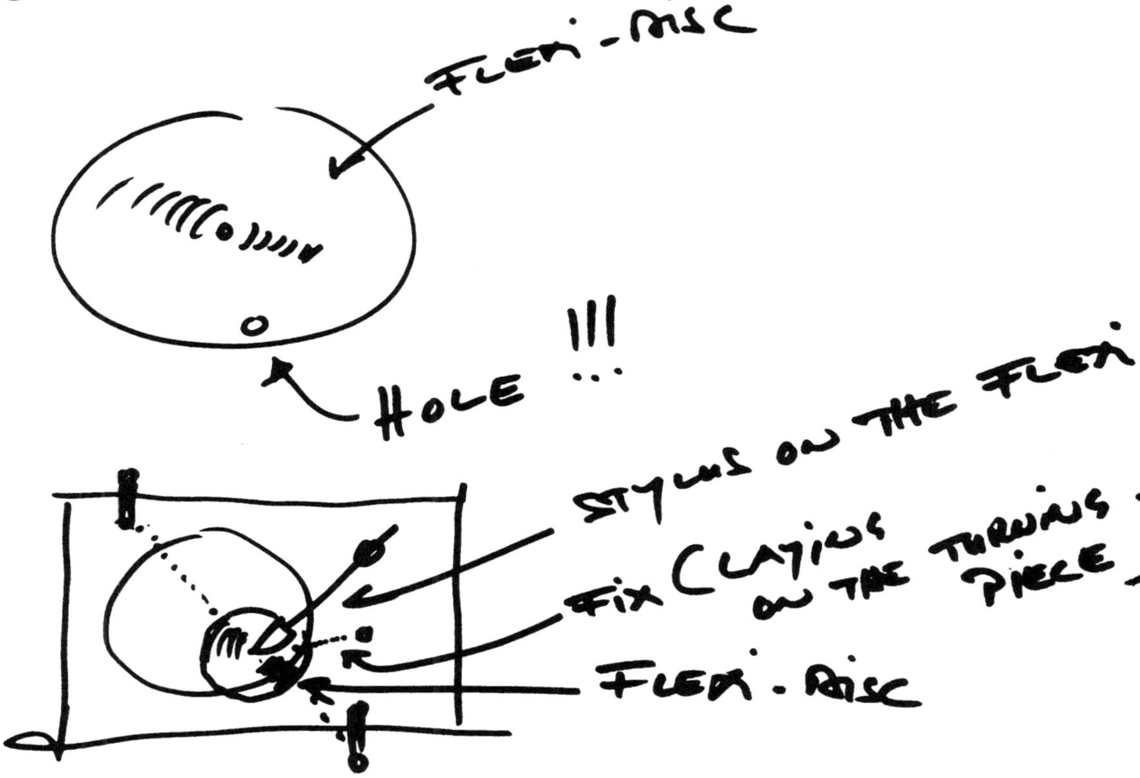

c.) SCRAPES

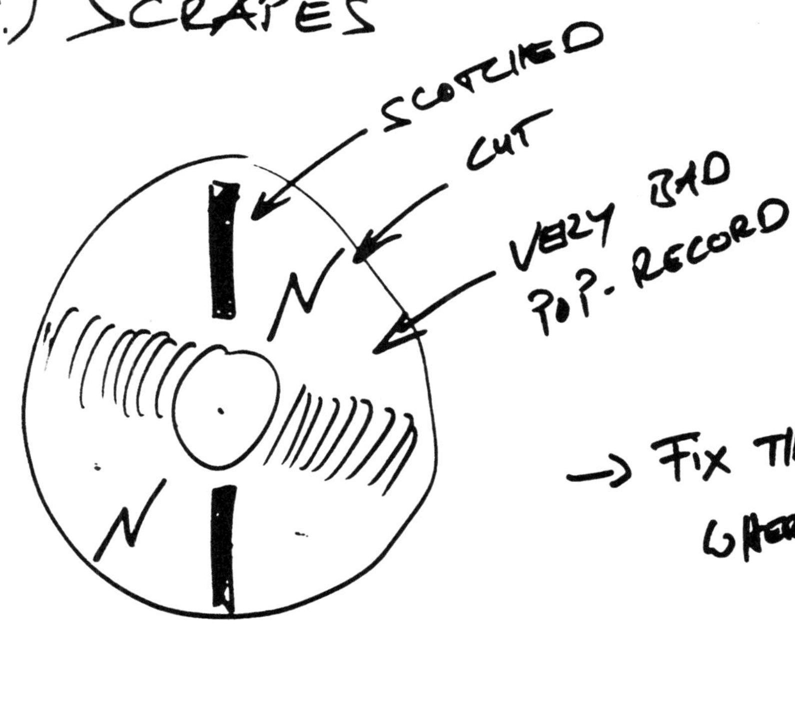

→ FIX THE CARTRIDGE/STYLUS WHEREVER YOU WANT

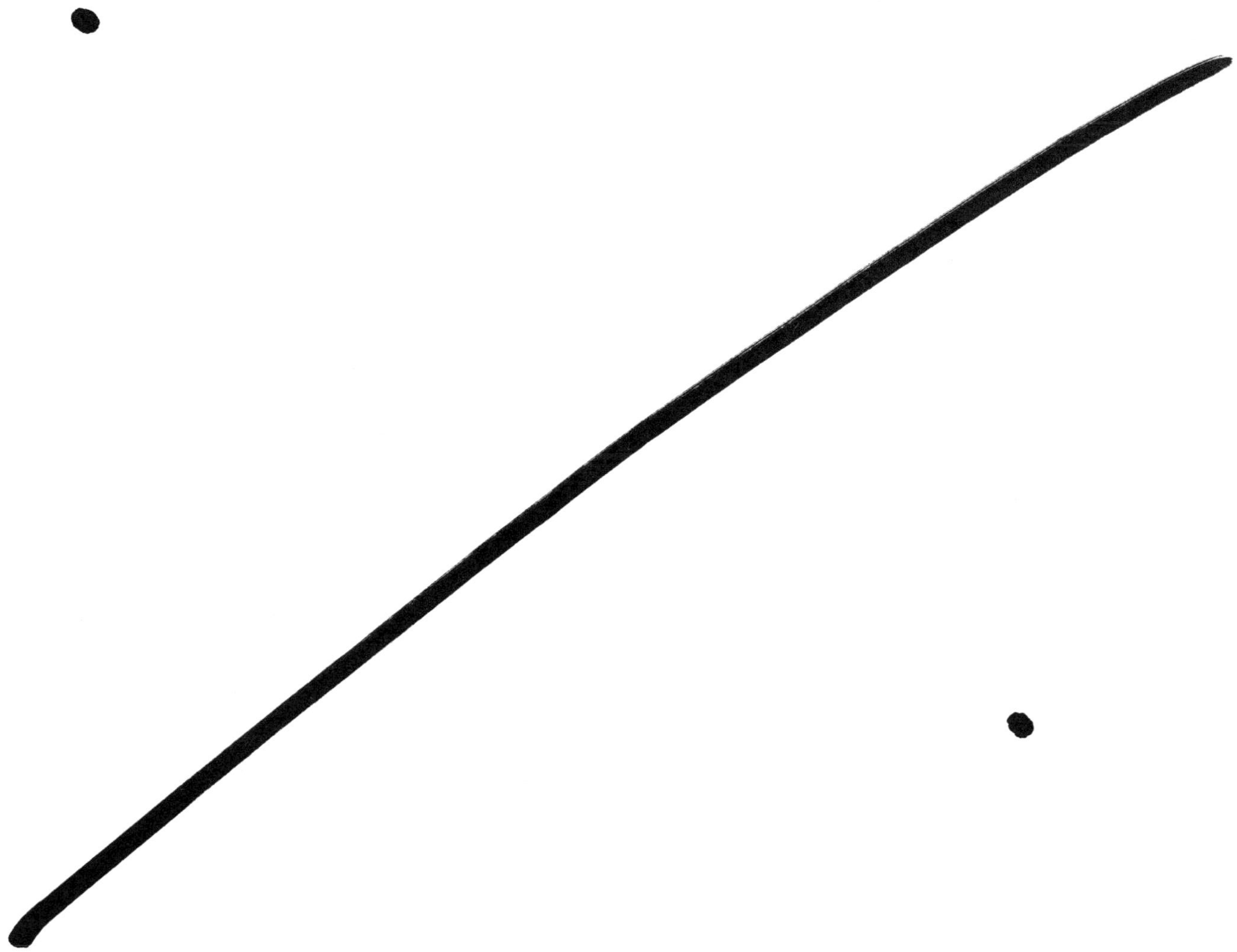

SCHNELLERTOLLERMEIER

3

⁄.

SCHNELLERTOLLERMEIER

A

TOMAGA

A PERSPECTIVE WITH NO END

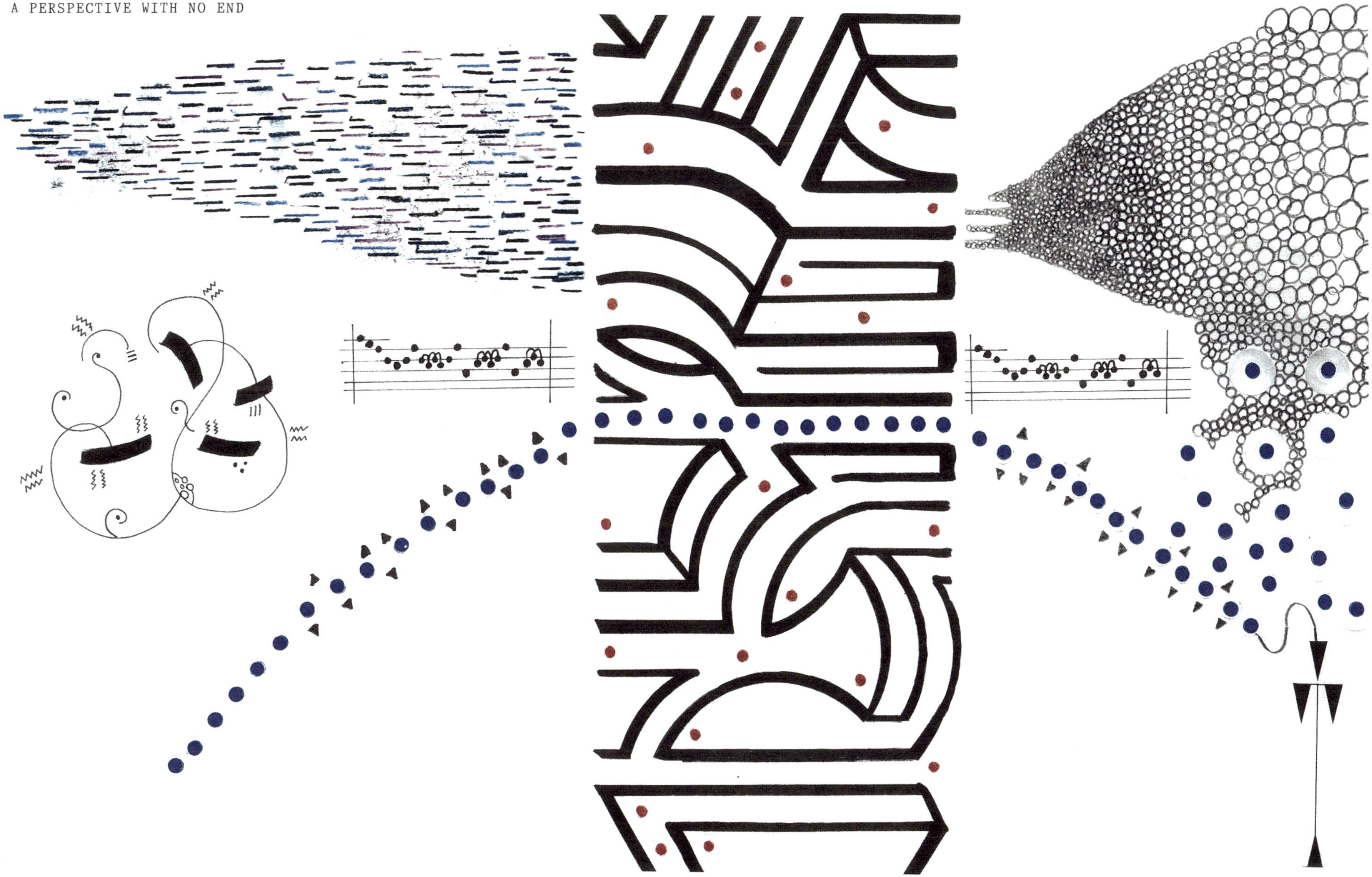

0min | 5min | 8min | 11min | 15min

T-----tones, synthesizer
M---------metal, friction harmonics
-------pulse

T-----bass, repeat
M--triplets
----------pulse

T---maze, vibraphone
M---
-----pulse

T--hiss, white noise
-------bass, repeat
M------triplets
------pulse

fragmentation

4

A Perspective with No End

TOMAGA

About Farewell

It is plain to see that I have one foot
out the door
And I know that your dear heart is
telling you to run
Deep down somewhere
Deep down somewhere
I heard somebody say that
"The brightest lights cast the biggest shadows"
So, honey. I've got to let you go.

Seven years to you, dear heart,
is all that I can give
And I know that without me you'll
find just what you need
Deep down somewhere
Deep down somewhere
I heard somebody say that
"The brightest lights cast the biggest shadows"
So, honey, I've got to let you go.

Leaving is the hardest part,
thats what we've always said
Once upon the other side,
its best not to look back
That's what we say about farewell
That's what we say about farewell..

~ Alela
Diane

5

About Farewell

ALELA DIANE

Egopusher – Acid Rat

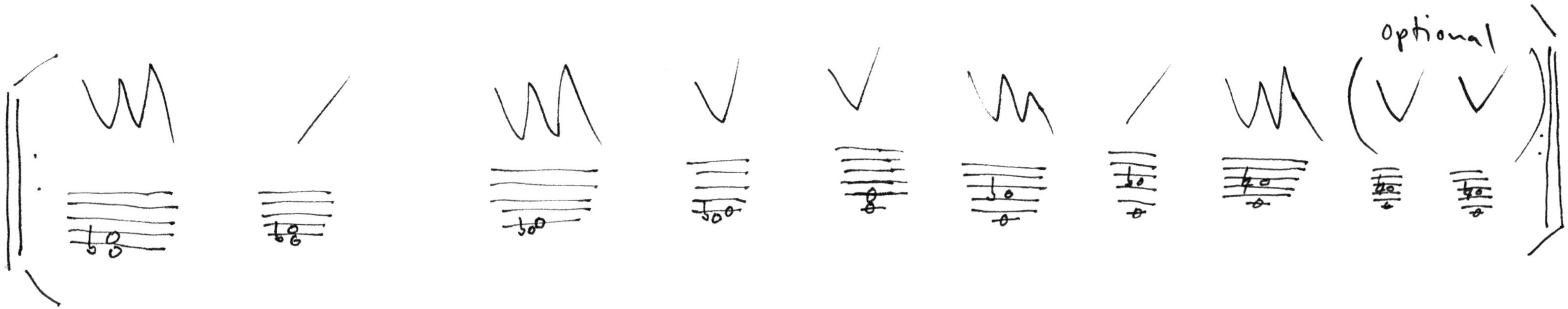

6

Acid Rat

EGOPUSHER

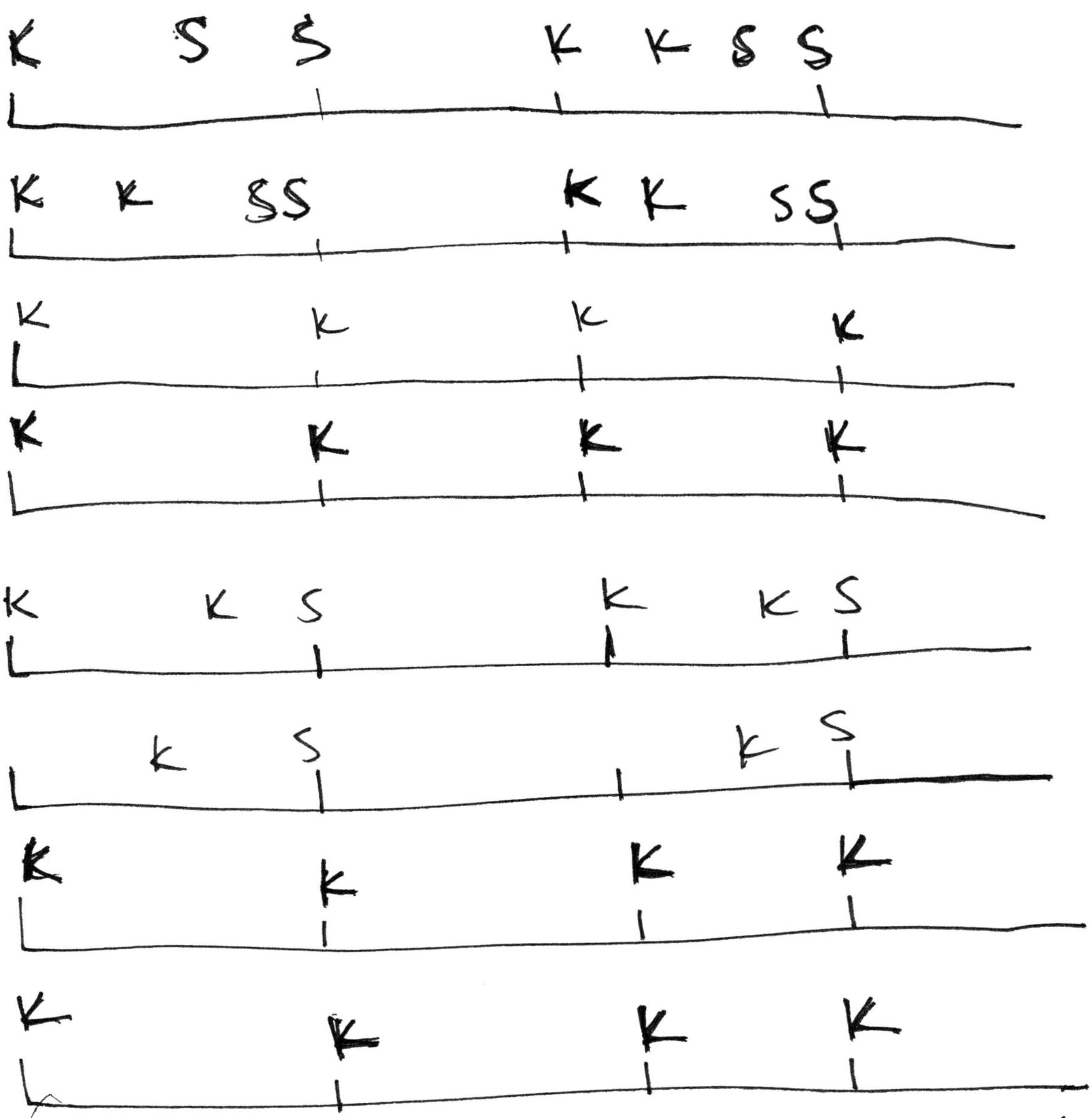

we hold these truths to be self evident…

Smiles are the best
All Kings DO confess
Despite All the rest
From above they are blessed

7

All Kings Do Confess

SHABAZZ PALACES

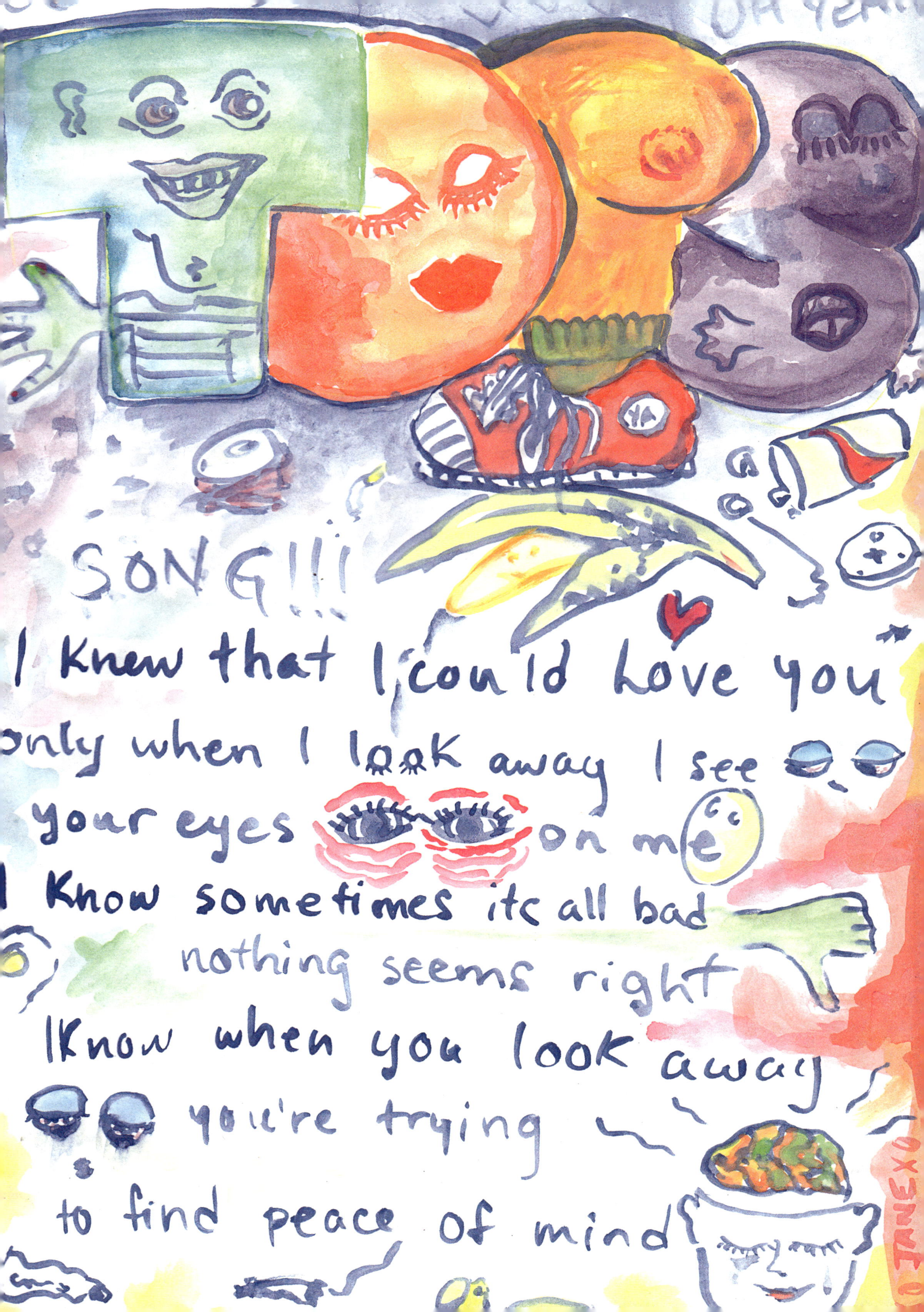
SONG!!!
I Knew that I could Love you
only when I look away I see
your eyes on me
I Know sometimes its all bad
nothing seems right
I Know when you look away
you're trying
to find peace of mind

8

All the People Sleep

TOPS

An Ocean in between The Waves ..

Adam Grandaciel.

Capo on Fret #3

D   Emin

Run away I'm a travellin' man
been workin' everyday.
I watch you as you hesitate.
walkin through the rain
I bet against the company again.
They try to redefine
everything that i know n love
gotta know yr mine. yeah.

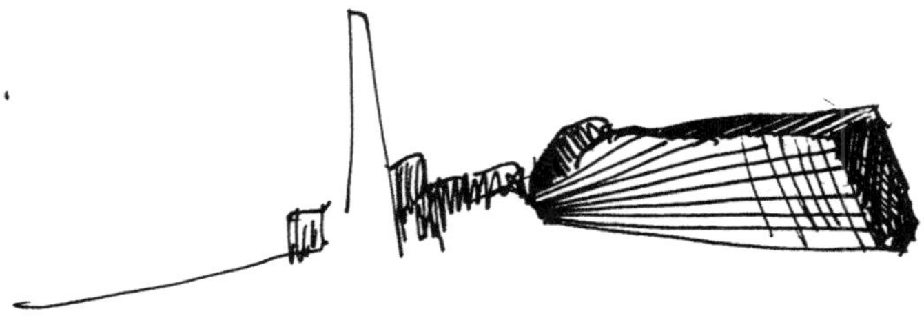

gotta know yr mine. yeah.
feel the way that the wild wind blows through the room
like a nail down through the heart
just don't beat the same anymore
might as well be gone

C   Emin   D   Em

(I'm in my finest hour can i be more than just a fool
it always gets so hard to see right before the morn. [D, C, Em]

SOLO [D, Em, D, A, Bmin, A, G, Em, D, C, Em]

D   Em

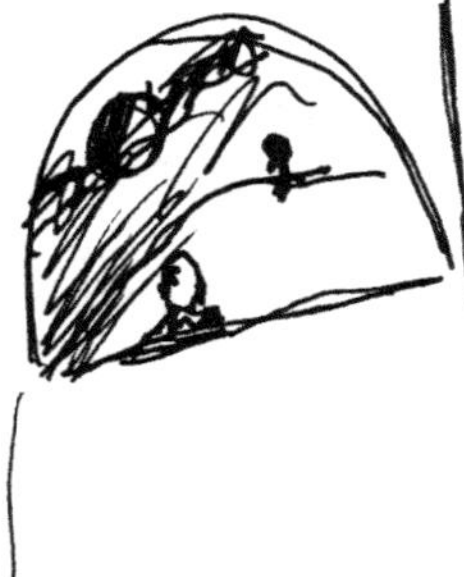

far away ma there's a black sun risin' overhead
there's a moon through the midnight rain
how can i summon your body in the arm.
how can i be free
just wanna lie in the moonlight.
and see the light shine in, you in the outline
it never gets too dark to find anybody at
any time.

9

An Ocean in Between the Waves

THE WAR ON DRUGS

I've found a sweet heaven of sunshine at last
Jesus abiding above / His warm arms
around me are lovingly cast
and sweetly he sings his love

The tempest is o're
The danger the tempest forever is o're
I'm safe evermore
my anchor is holding I'm safe evermore
What gladness what rapture is mine
what gladness what rature is mine
The danger is past
The waters are peaceful the danger is past
I'm anchored at last
I'm feeling so happy I'm anchored at last
I'm anchored in love
I'm anchored in love devine
devine

He saw me in danger and lovingly came
to pilot my storm beaten soul //
Sweet peace he has spoken and
bless his dear name / The billows no longer
roll

chorus

His love shall control me in life + in death
compleatly I'll trust 'till the end //
I'll praise him each hour + with my last
breath I'll sing of my soul's best friend.

chorus

ANCHORED IN LOVE DEVINE

THE CARTER FAMILY

10

Anchored in Love (the Carter Family)

PRUNO TRUMAN AND FRIENDS

$\frac{3}{4}$ V: I | I | IV | I | I | I | V | V

Chor.: I | I | IV | I | I | I | V | I

I | I | VI | VI | IV | I | I | I | V | V | I | I

| I | I | V | I

I | I | VI | VI | I | I | I | I :)

Maja Solveig Kjelstrup Ratkje 2012:

"And Sing While Thou On Pressed Flowers Dost Sleep"

NOTES

- General rule: *non vibrato* through the entire piece.
- Accidents last through the bar.
- All trills are half-tone trills if not specified.
- Ties are sometimes unrealistically long, marking ideal phrases. Split up when needed, and use circular breathing and inaudible bow changes when possible.
- Strings: Dynamics above staff are always valid for top voice only. Dynamics below staff are valid for both when no special dynamics for top staff.
  In the *pizzicato* section in letter J, the movements of *glissandi* is notated, but all pizz. sustains should be natural.
  Crush tones are indicated with a slashed note head. The grade of crush is written above and is valid for the following crush tones.
- The sampler loads audio files provided by the composer. A keyboard is suggested with individual keys for each sample. The sampler has to play samples at exact start point.
  The keyboard used must have locked dynamics for the samples, and it should not be necessary to hold the key through the sample. The sample should play out even though a tight overlapping with the next sample occurs.

The piece is commissioned by Cikada with support from Arts Council Norway.

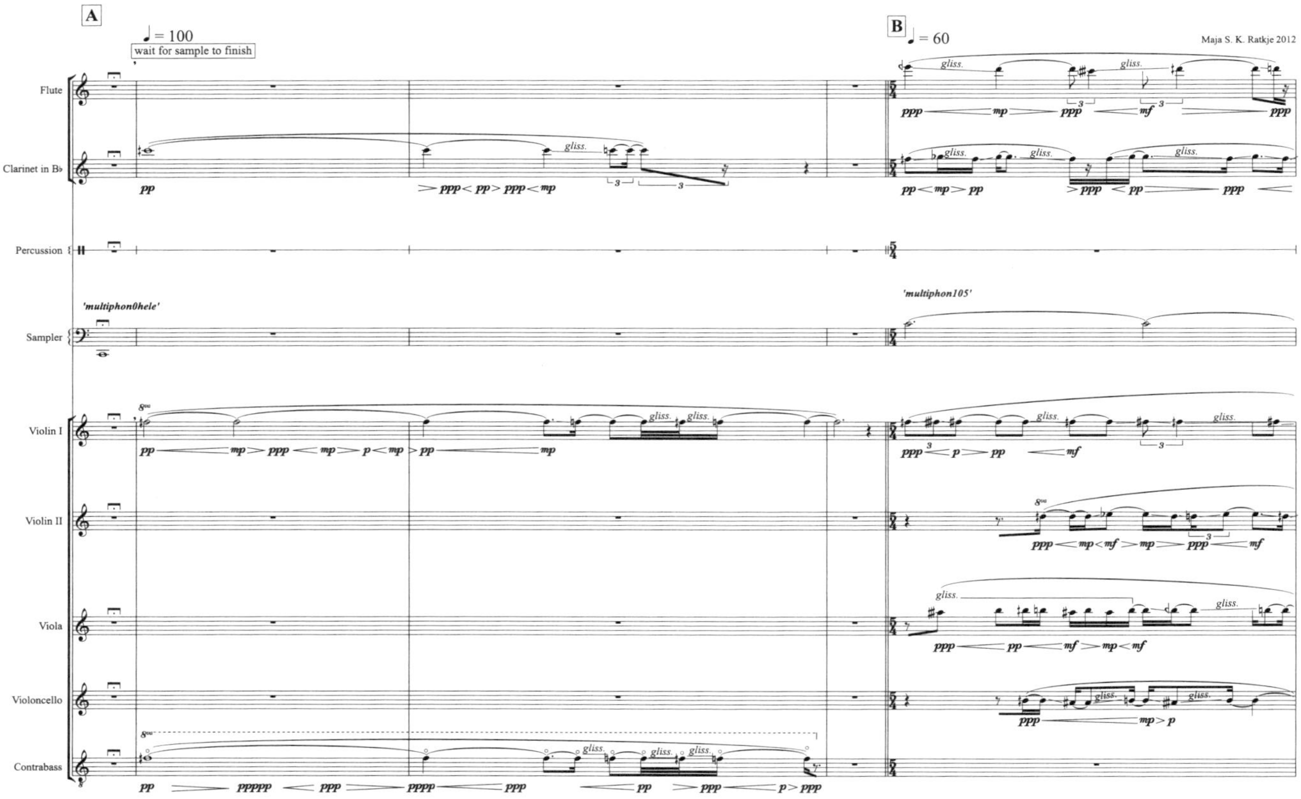

A
♩ = 100
wait for sample to finish
B
♩ = 60
Maja S. K. Ratkje 2012
Flute
Clarinet in B♭
Percussion I
'multiphon0hele'
Sampler
'multiphon105'
Violin I
Violin II
Viola
Violoncello
Contrabass
gliss.

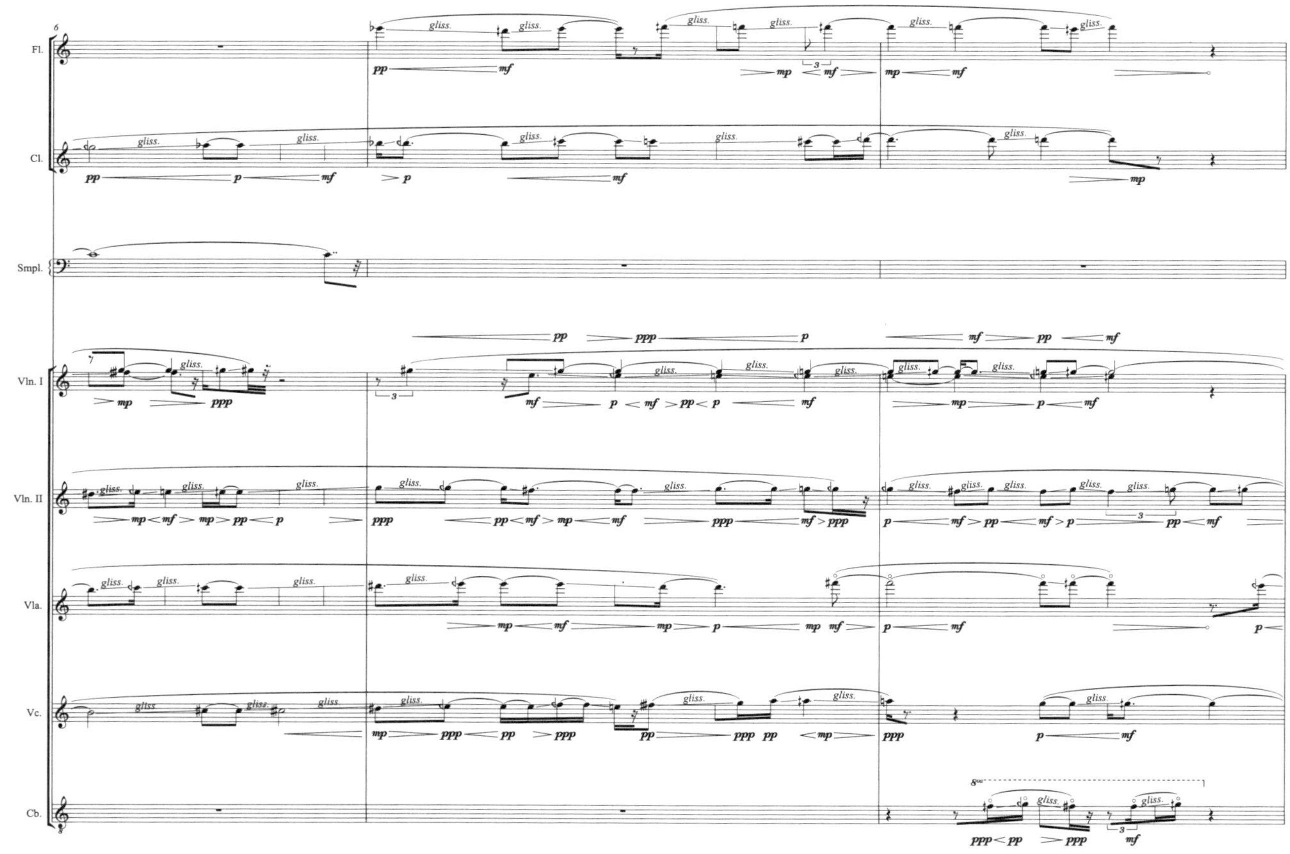

6
Fl.
Cl.
Smpl.
Vln. I
Vln. II
Vla.
Vc.
Cb.
gliss.

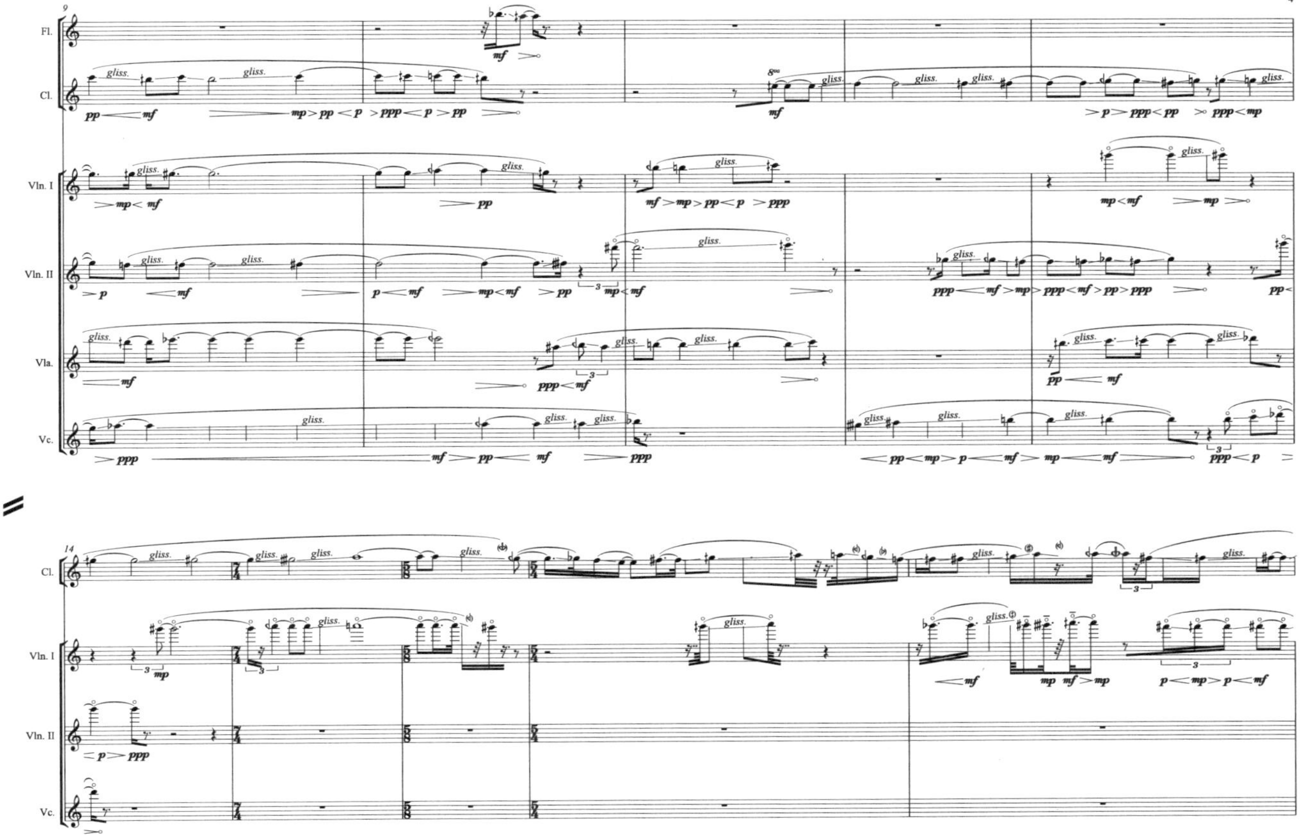
Fl.
Cl.
Vln. I
Vln. II
Vla.
Vc.
gliss.

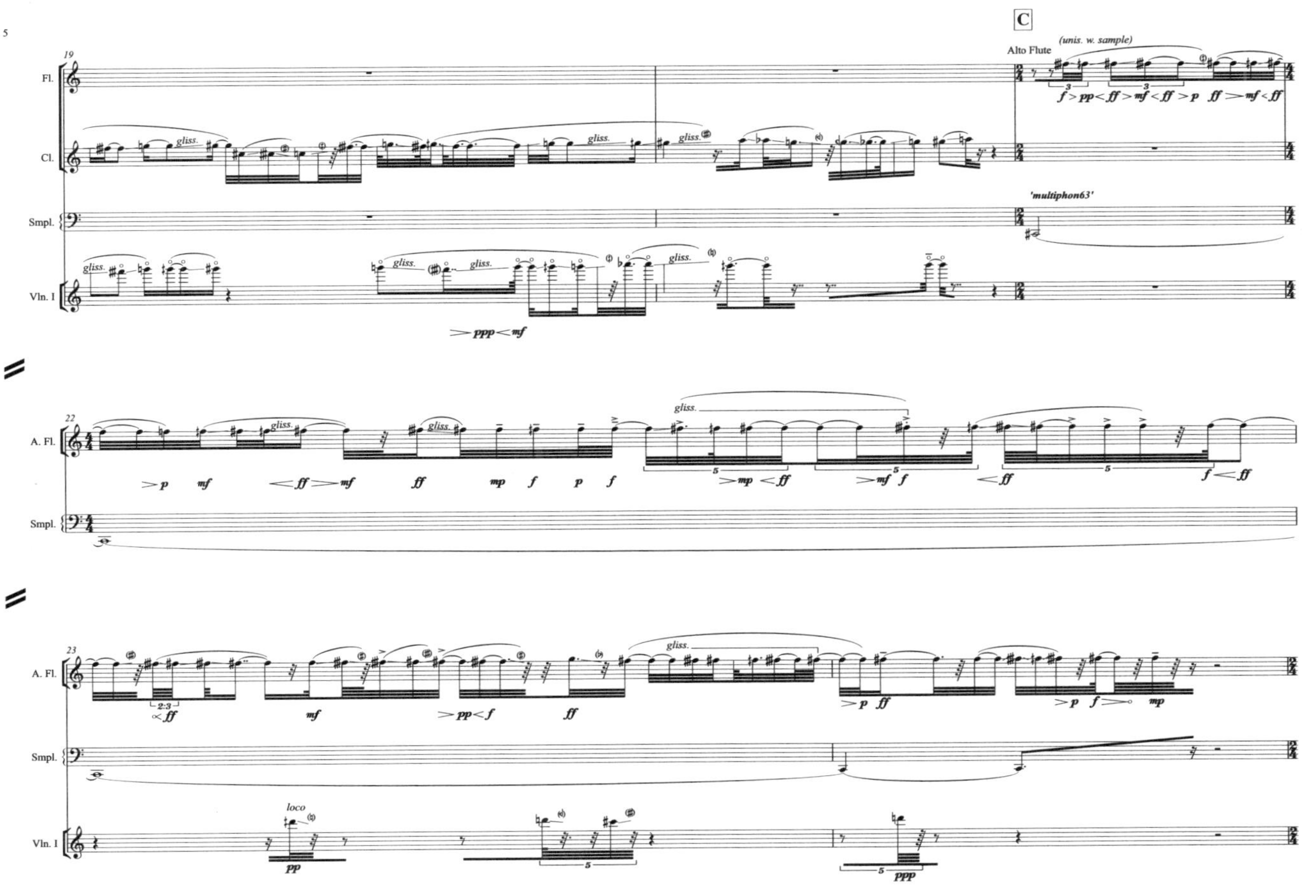
C
Alto Flute
(unis. w. sample)
'multiphon63'
Fl.
Cl.
Smpl.
Vln. I
A. Fl.
gliss.
loco

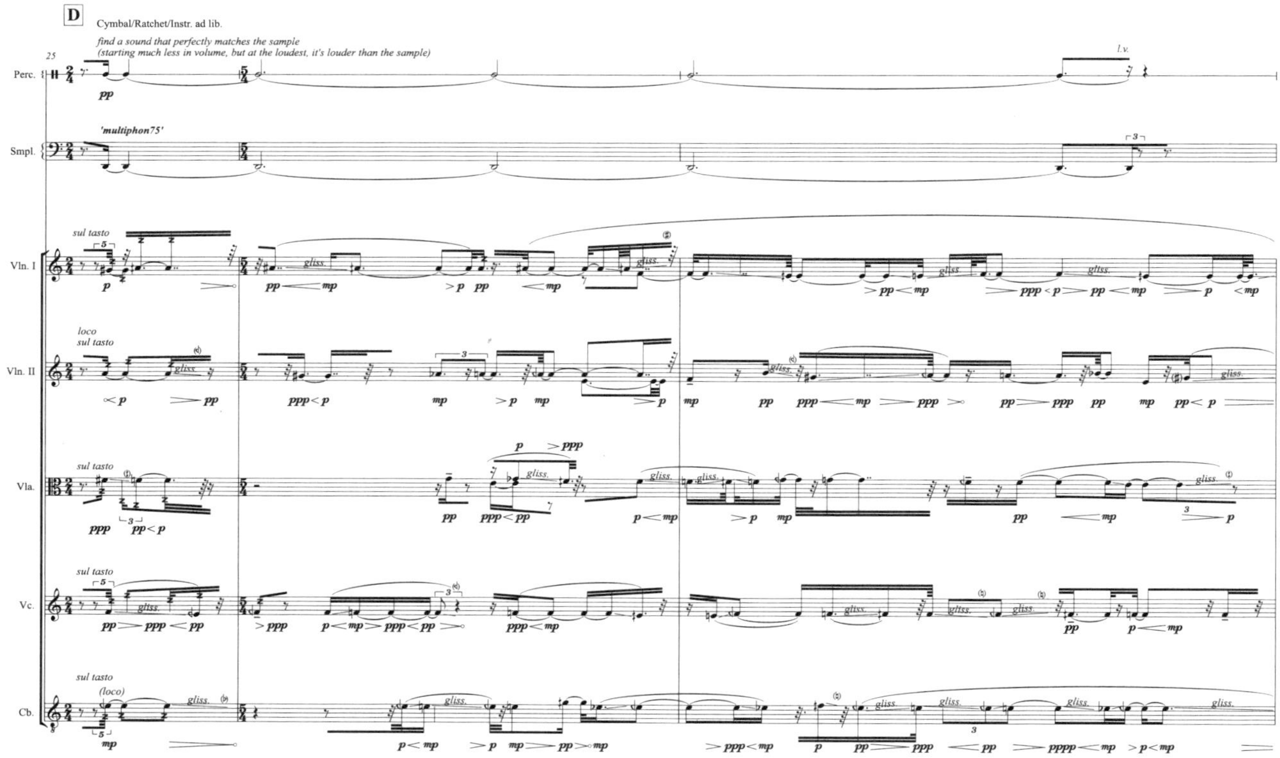
D
Cymbal/Ratchet/Instr. ad lib.
find a sound that perfectly matches the sample
(starting much less in volume, but at the loudest, it's louder than the sample)
25
l.v.
'multiphon75'
sul tasto
loco
sul tasto
(loco)
gliss.
Perc. 1
Smpl.
Vln. I
Vln. II
Vla.
Vc.
Cb.

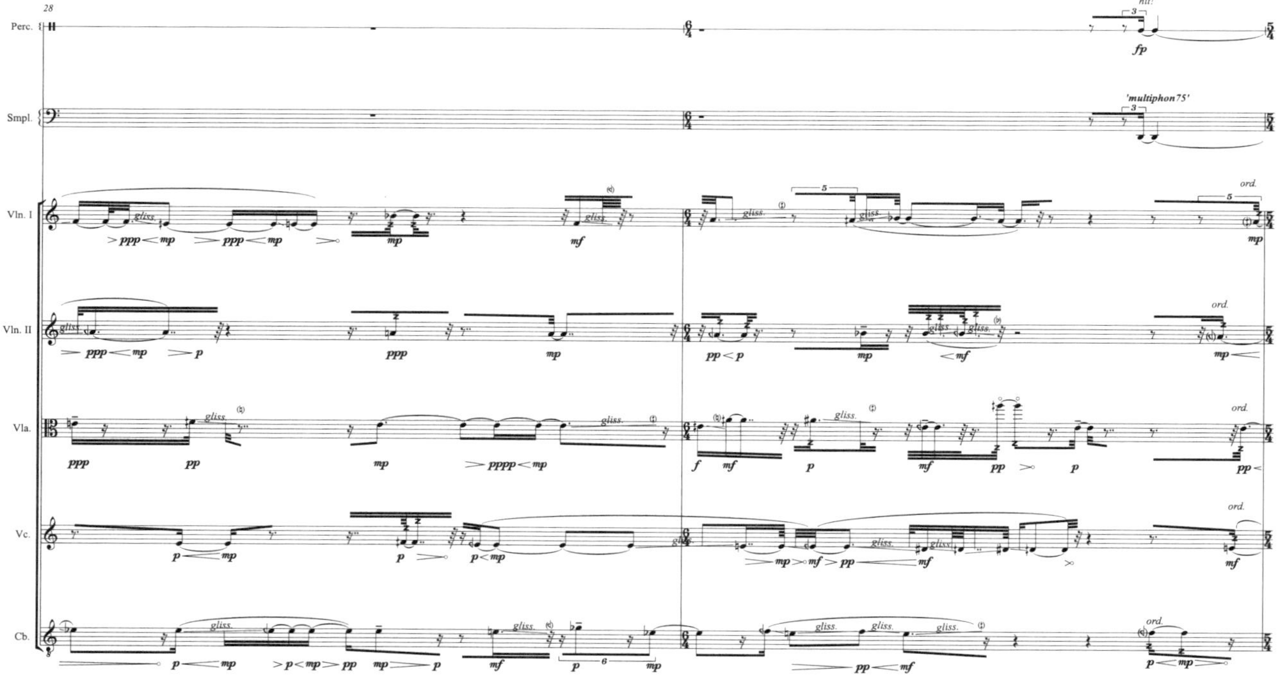
28
hit!
'multiphon75'
ord.
gliss.
Perc. 1
Smpl.
Vln. I
Vln. II
Vla.
Vc.
Cb.

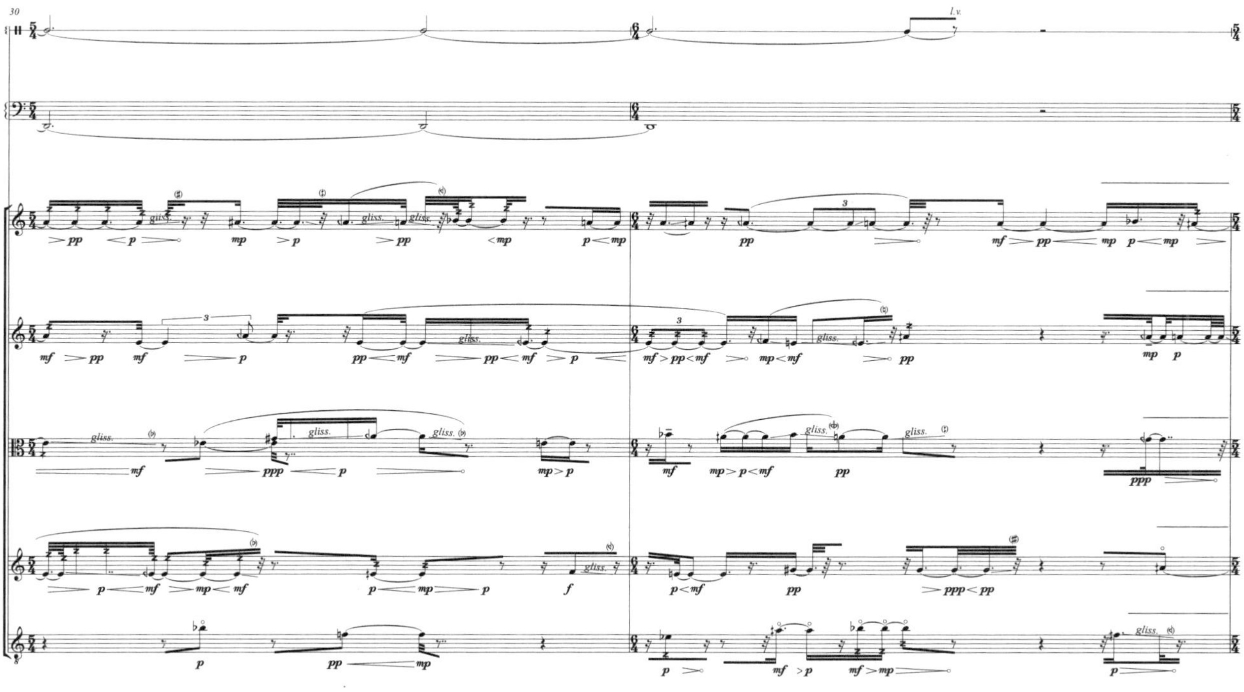
30
Perc. I
Smpl.
Vln. I
Vln. II
Vla.
Vc.
Cb.
l.v.
gliss.

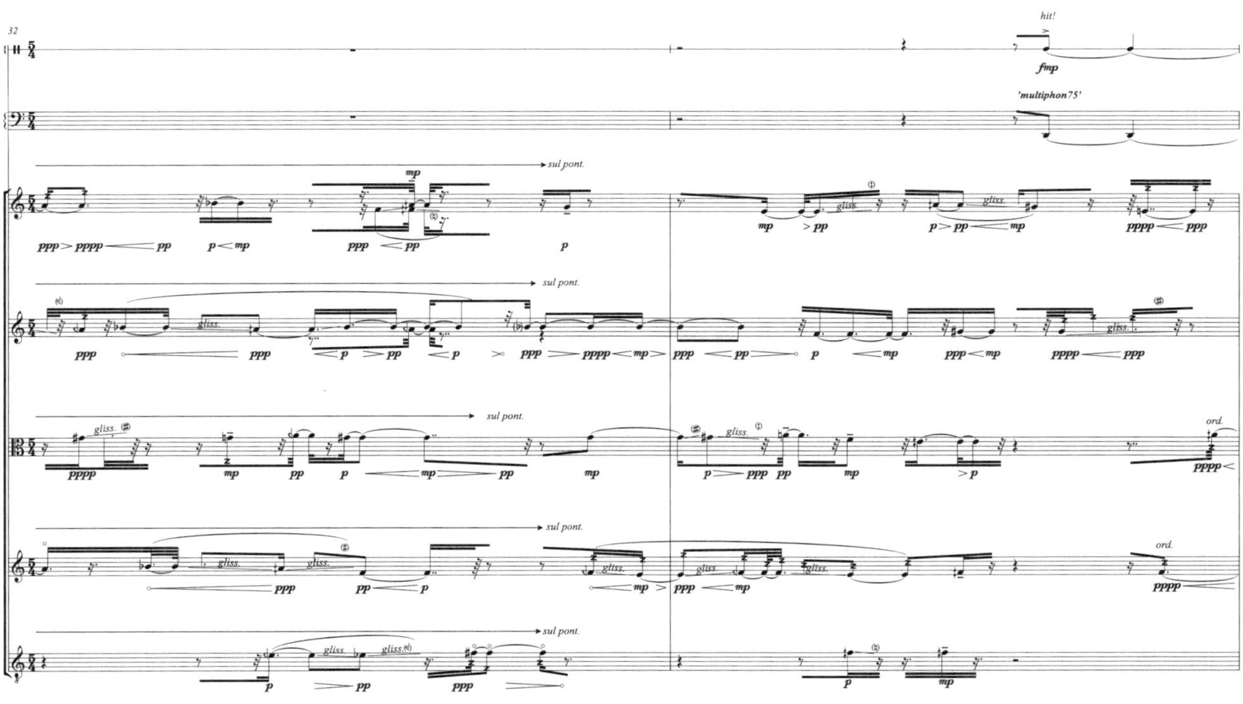
32
Perc. I
Smpl.
Vln. I
Vln. II
Vla.
Vc.
Cb.
hit!
'multiphon75'
sul pont.
gliss.
ord.

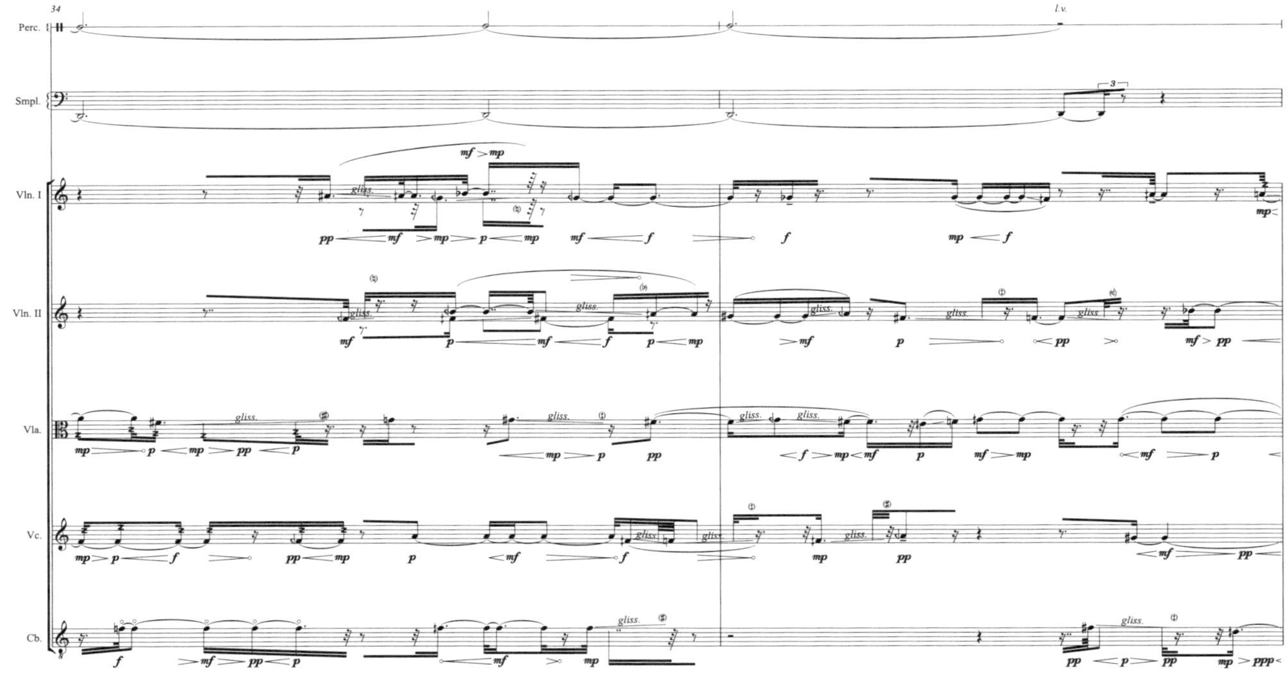
34
Perc.
Smpl.
Vln. I
Vln. II
Vla.
Vc.
Cb.
l.v.
gliss.

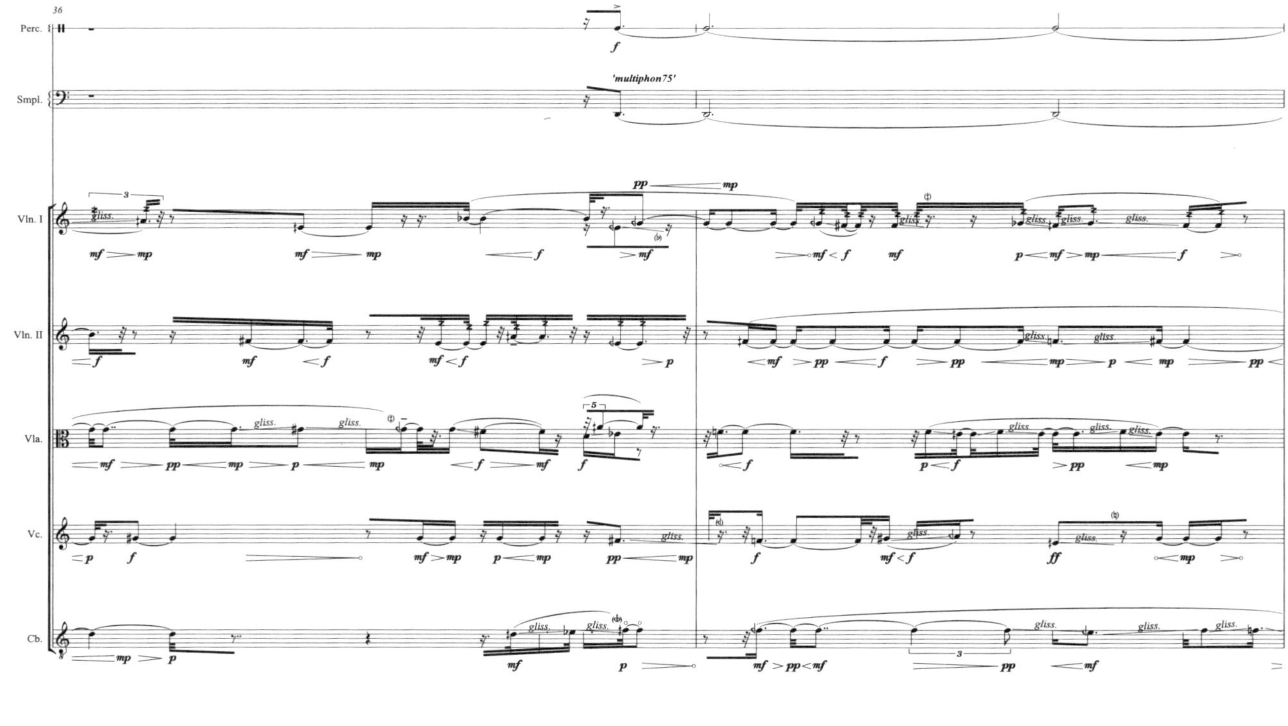
36
Perc.
Smpl.
'multiphon75'
Vln. I
Vln. II
Vla.
Vc.
Cb.
gliss.

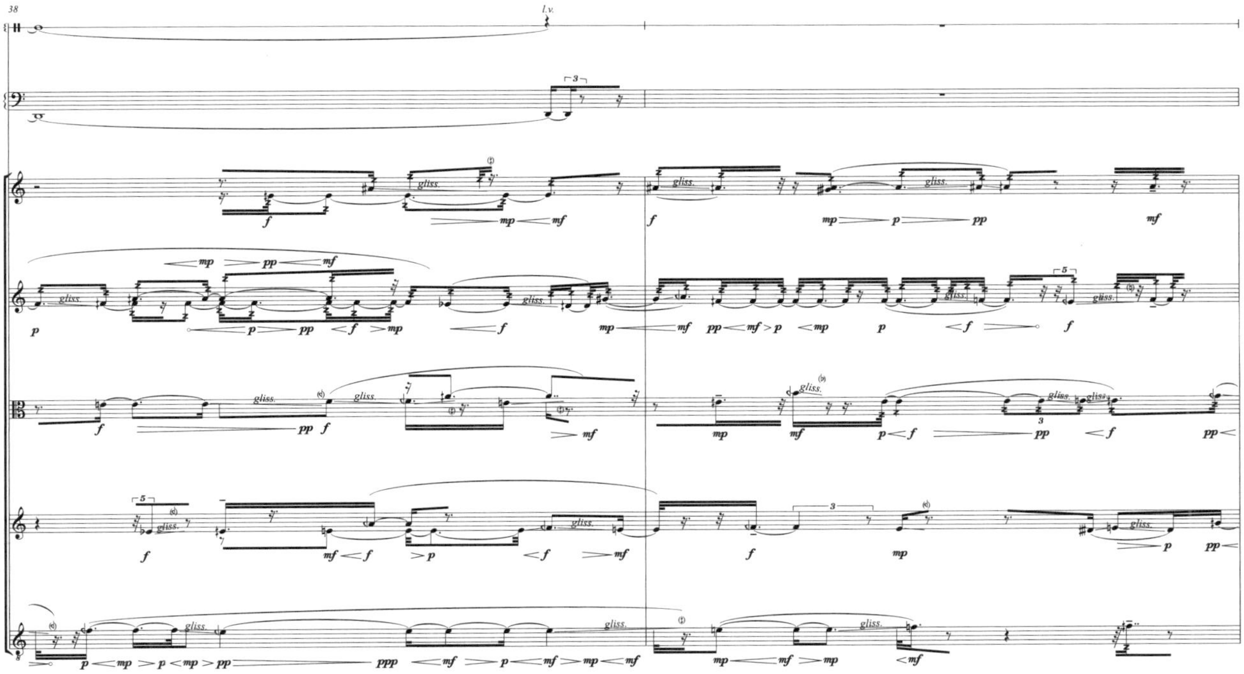
38
l.v.
Perc. 1
Smpl.
Vln. I
Vln. II
Vla.
Vc.
Cb.
gliss.

11

And Sing While Thou on Pressed Flowers Dost Sleep

MAJA RATKJE

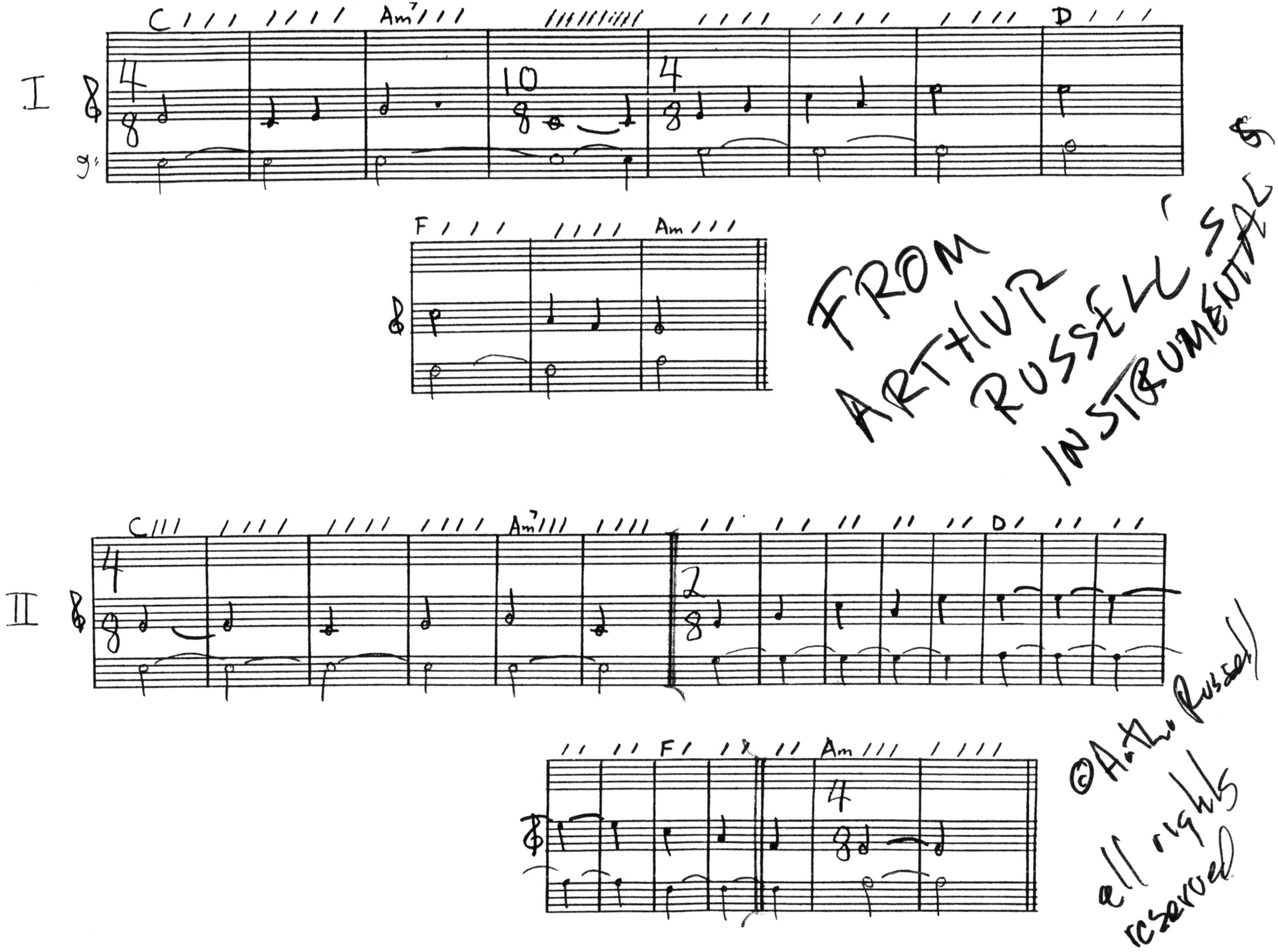
FROM ARTHUR RUSSELL'S INSTRUMENTAL
I
II
C
Am7
D
F
Am
©Arthur Russell
all rights reserved

A - 10.11

12

Arthur Russell's Instrumentals

PETER GORDON, PETER ZUMMO, ERNIE BROOKS, RHYS CHATHAM, BILL RUYLE, GAVIN RUSSOM, MAX GORDON, GERRY O'BEIRNE

HELL

JESSICA93

ASYLUM

DR-880

STEP I → 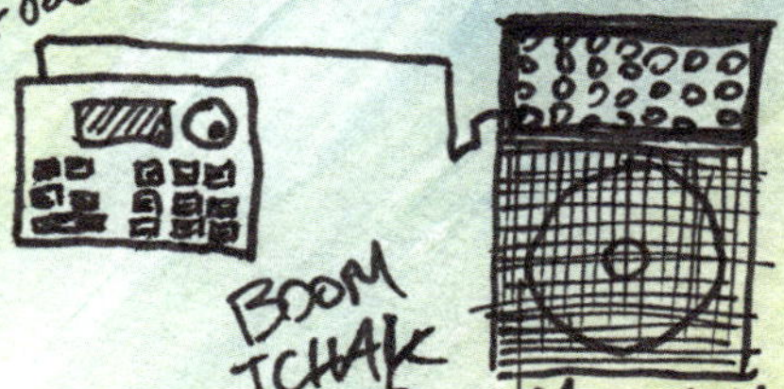 PRESS THE FOOTSWITCH TO START DRUMACHINE ON ASYLUM PATTERN

BOOM TCHAK BOOM TCHAK

STEP II → GUITAR 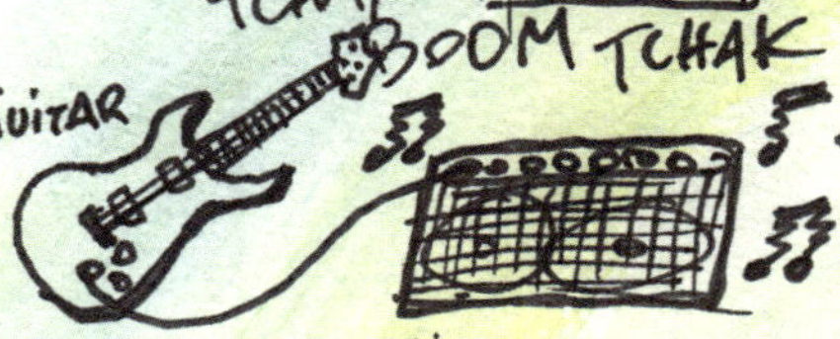 PLAY THE FIRST RIFF AND LOOP IT

STEP III → BASS 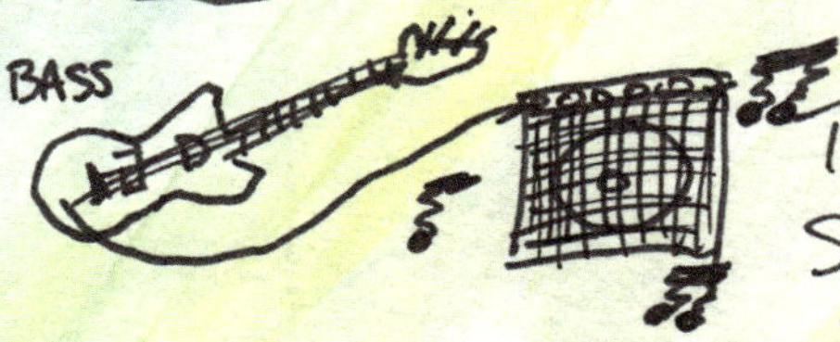 TAKE THE BASS AND START PROPERLY THE SONG WITH THE PROPER KEYS (YOU CAN FIND THEM YOURSELF STOP BEING LAZY!)

STEP IV → SING (WITH FRENCH ACCENT):

VERSE ↓

AMONG THE SECULAR TREES
TWO CIRCULAR GEMS ARE STARING AT ME
IT COULD CRAWL AT MY FEET
THERE'S NO GUILT TO FEEL SINCE I FED THEM WELL
ON THE SAME PATH EVERYDAY
AN INDIAN WIZZARD TURNS ME AWAY
I COULD STAB HIM EASILY
THE MORE I WANT THE LESS I CAN HIT

CHORUS → LOOK AROUND, YOU'RE THE ONE OUT OF TOWN
IT LOOKS LIKE A DREAM, DREAMS ARE MADE TO MAKE THEM REAL
TOO LATE TO TURN AROUND

VERSE → I CROSS FEARLESSLY THE PHLEGETHON
COMPARE TO YOUR FIRE IT SEEMS SO COLD
AND I COULD DIE AT YOUR FEET
THERE'S NO GUILT TO FEEL SINCE YOU FED ME WELL

CHORUS → LOOK AROUND, I'M THE ONE OUT OF TOWN
IT LOOKS LIKE A DREAM, DREAMS ARE MADE TO MAKE THEM REAL
TOO LATE TO TURN AROUND

STEP V → LOOP THE BASS

STEP VI → THEN TAKE BACK THE GUITAR AND DO THE WORSE SOLO EVER UNTIL AUDIENCE LEAVE THE PLACE

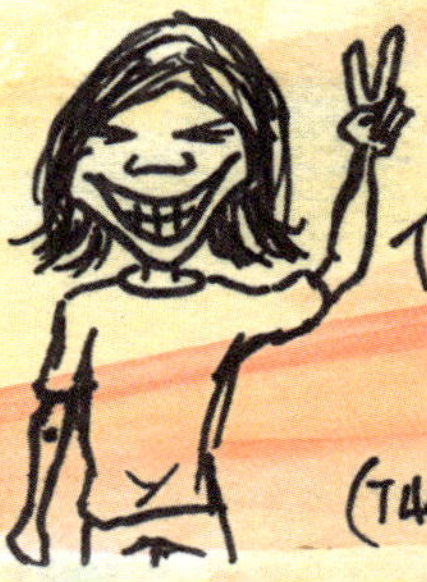

THAT'S ALL FOLKS!!

(THANKS FOR YOUR ATTENTION)

HEAVEN

13

Asylum

JESSICA 93

1. Left hands hold the leashes
and the right hands hold the torches
2. and the grandpas holding shotguns
swing on porch swings hung on porches
3. and the grandmas in the gardens
plant more seeds to cut their losses
4. while the poachers with the pooches
and the nooses preheat crosses

1. Then the pooches see the grandpas
and they bare their teeth and growl
2. While their owners turn their noses up
like they smell something foul
3. And they fumble with their crosses
and they start to mumble curses
4. and they plot ways to get grandpas
off of porches into hearses

1. But the grandpas on the porches
are just scarecrows holding toys
2. And the grandmas in the gardens
are paper machier decoys
3. Because the real grandmas and grandpas
are with all the girls and boys
4. Marching downtown to the city hall
to make a lot of noise

HANDS UP

14
At the Seams
KIMYA DAWSON

& HANDS UP

1. Sometimes it seems like we've reached
the end of the road
2. we've seen cops and judges sleep together
wearing long white robes
3. They put the white hoods on
try to take the black hoods down
4. And they don't plan on stopping
til we're all in the ground

1. Til we're dead in the ground
or we're incarcerated
2. Cuz prison's a big business
form of enslavement
3. Plantations that profit on
black folks in cages
4. They'll break our backs
and keep the wages

1. It's outrageous that's there's no place
we can feel safe in this nation
2. not in our cars not at the park
not in the subway station
3. not at church the pool the store
not asking for help
4. not walking down the street
so we've gotta scream and yell

1. people tweet me my own lyrics
and tell me to stop
2. letting a few bad apples
ruin the bunch
3. dont minimize the fight
comparing apples to cops
4. This is about the orchards poisoned roots
not loose fruits in a box

1. Once the soil's been spoiled
the whole crop's corrupt
2 thats why we need the grassroots working
from the ground up
3. And we look to black twitter
to stay woke & get some truth
4. Instead of smiling cops and black mugshots
from biased corporate news

1. Because if you steal cigarellos
or you sell loose cigarettes
2. Or you forget your turn signal
will they see your skin as a threat?
3. will they kill you and then smear you
and cover it up and lie
4. will they call it self defense
will they call it suicide

1. Decades of cultivation starts
from tiny seeds that were once planted
2. and we mustnt take the gardens
that our elders grew for granted
3. Though it is up to our youth how
new rows sown are organized
4. Because movements cant keep moving
if old and unsharpened eyes

1. Don't see the need to hear
what those on the ground have to say
2. In Ferguson and Cleveland
Staten Island, The East Bay
3. Charleston, Phoenix, Detroit, Waller
4, Seattle, Los Angeles, Chicago, Baltimore

1. Climbing flagpoles, taking bridges
locked together to the Bart
2. Speaking up about injustice
in our music and our art
3. Storming Stages to ask candidates
when they're gonna start
4. Really addressing these issues
That are breaking our hearts

1. If the altars are torn down
we'll just keep on placing flowers
2. for the boy whose body was in
the road for more than four hours
3. we will honor the dead of
every age and every gender
4. because we can't just have it be
the brother's names that we remember

1. Black boys with skateboards
and black boys and hoodies
2. and little black girls who are
on the couch sleeping
3. and all of the black
trans women massacred
4 And the black people brutalized
where there's no justice served

1. after the lynchings of our people
by the murderous police
2. who stand like hunters 'round their prey
gasping helpless in the street
3. feet from the teen sister they tackled and locked
handcuffed in the car 4. right by her 12 year old brother dying
while no one did cpr

3. We will keep on planting flowers
and we'll fight until the day
4. That we dont have to pick them all
to put onto graves x2

B

BACK IN THE TALL GRASS (1st Verse): FUTURE ISLANDS

by: SAMUEL T. HERRING w/ GERRIT WELMERS + WILLIAM CASHION

Home isn't open, its like when you get here...

Drums: Bum bitta pop bitta bum bitta pop (repeat) bitta

Bass: Bumbum Bumbum Bumbum Bumbum Bumbum Bumbum Bumbum bitta bitta (repeat) note: C (everything is sed)

Keys: (sound like rising tide [then ship lights blinking in the distance])
note: C (DE) ↓ (A) C (C) B (G)

the tracks by the creek bed

the minnow's the body

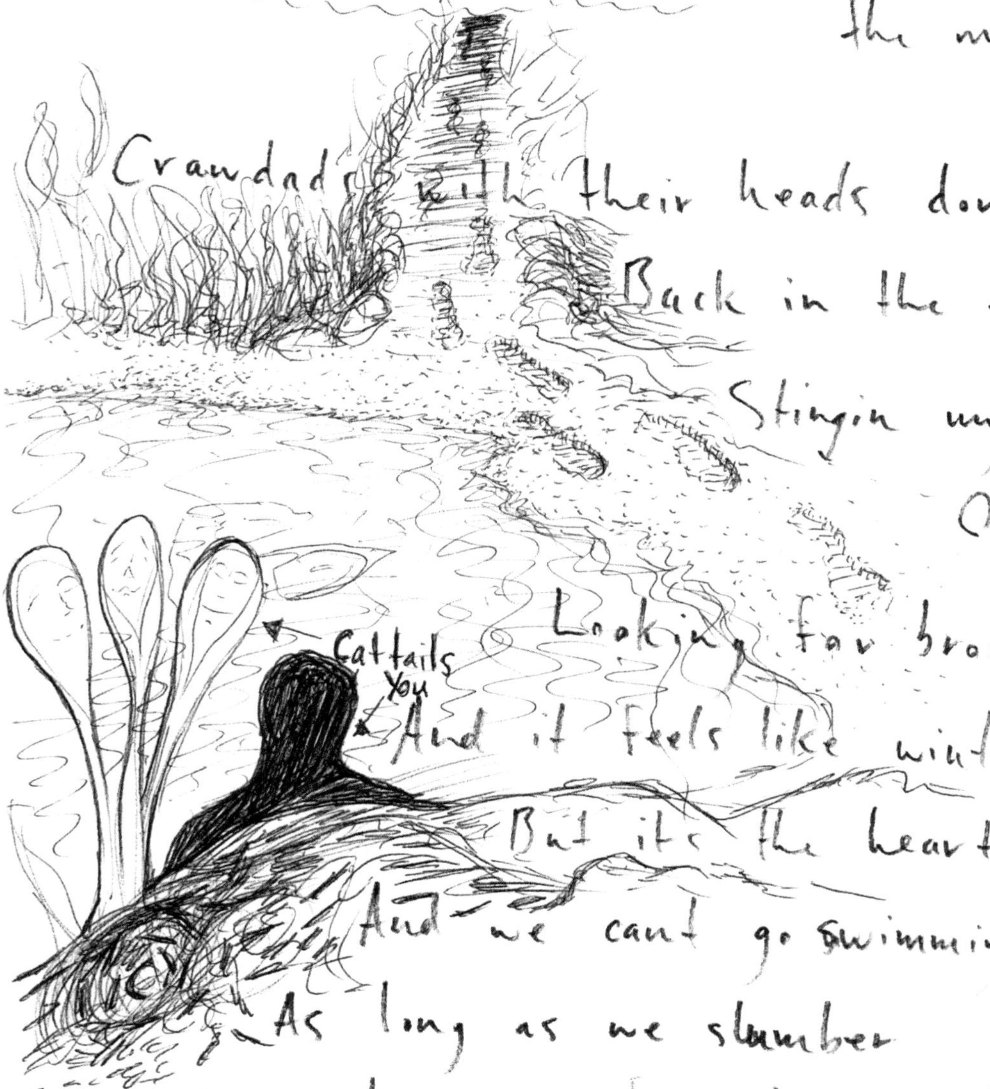

Crawdads with their heads down low

Back in the tall grass

Stingin my cattails

Oh oh oh oh

Looking for brother

And it feels like winter

But it's the heart of the summer

And we cant go swimming

As long as we slumber

Cuz we're a long way from home, a long way from home

A long way from home...

...and how did we get here...

{(*) Don't worry about the chorus! You can write your own! Then write a 2nd verse too!}

15
Back in the Tall Grass
FUTURE ISLANDS

SAPTASUR

SOLFA LETTERS

No.	NAME OF SWARAM	INDIAN SOUTH			INDIAN NORTH	WESTERN			SOUNDS FROM
1	SHADJAMAM	S	1	shadjamam	shadjamam	doh		C	PEACOCK
2	RISHABHAM	R	2/3	sudhah (r)/ chatusruti (r)	komal (r)/ tivra (r)	ray	FLAT/ SHARP	D/D	BULL
3	GANDHARAM	G	4/5	sudhah (g)/ antara (g)	komal (g)/ tivra (g)	me	FLAT/ SHARP	E/E	GOAT
4	MADHYAMAM	M	6/7	sudhah (m)/ prati (m)	komal (m)/ tivra (m)	fa	FLAT/ SHARP	F/F	CRANE
5	PANCHAMAM	P	8	panchamam	pancham	soh		G	CUCKOO
6	DHAIVATAM	D	9/10	sudhah (d)/ chatusruti (d)	komal (d)/ tivra (d)	lah	FLAT/ SHARP	A/A	HORSE
7	NISHADHAM	N	11/12	kaisiki (n)/ kakali (n)	komal (n)/ tivra (n)	te	FLAT/ SHARP	B/B	ELEPHANT
8		$\dot{S}$				to			

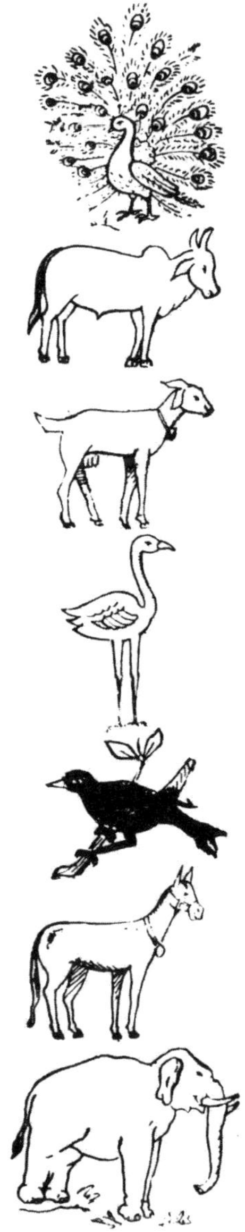

OCTAVE

16

Bad Bonn Raag

AL COMET

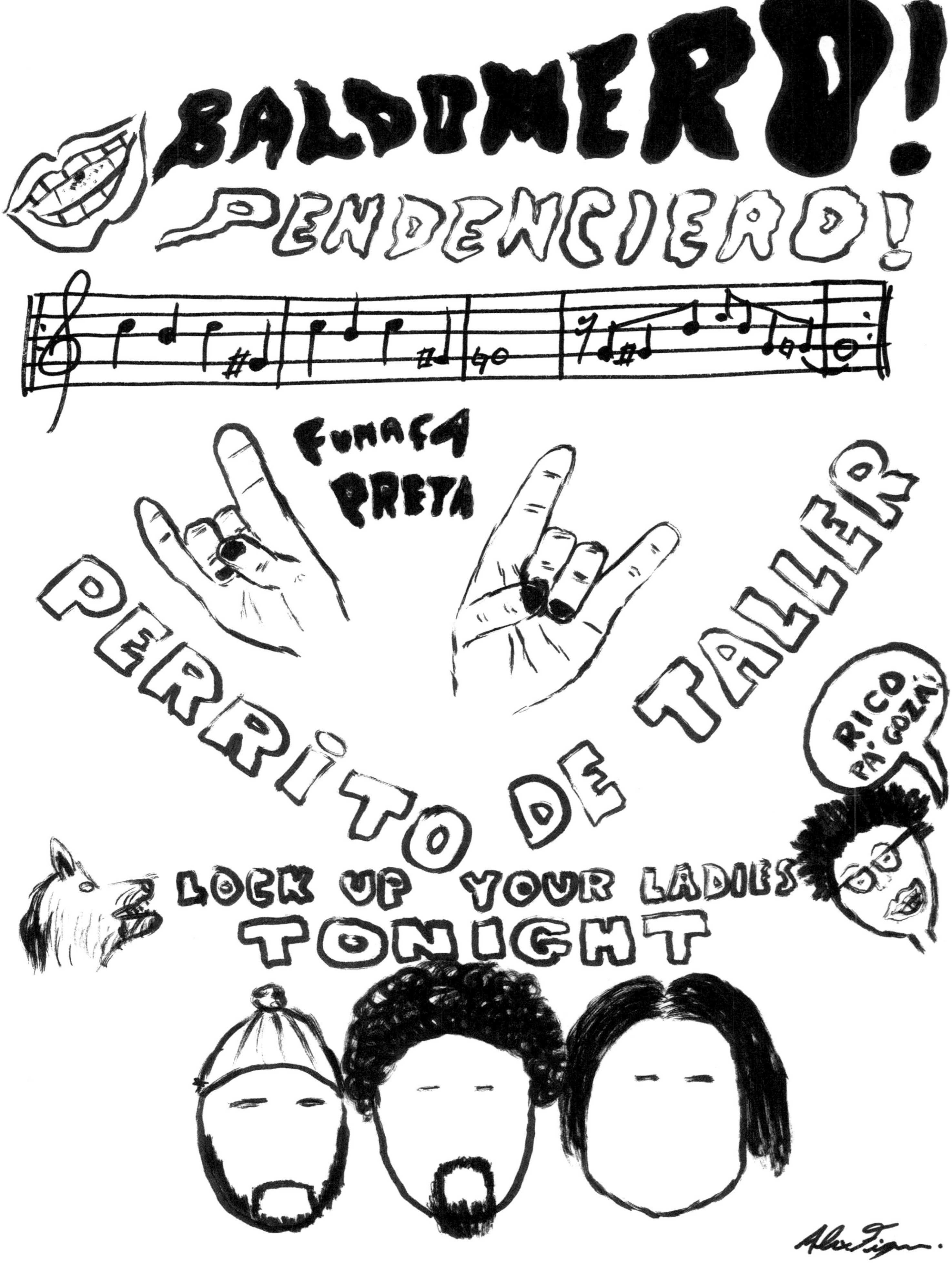
BALDOMERO!
PENDENCIERO!
Fumaça
PRETA
PERRITO DE TALLER
RICO PA' GOZA!
LOCK UP YOUR LADIES
TONIGHT

17

Baldomero

FUMAÇA PRETA

"BERBERIAN WEDDING"

THE BEAT:

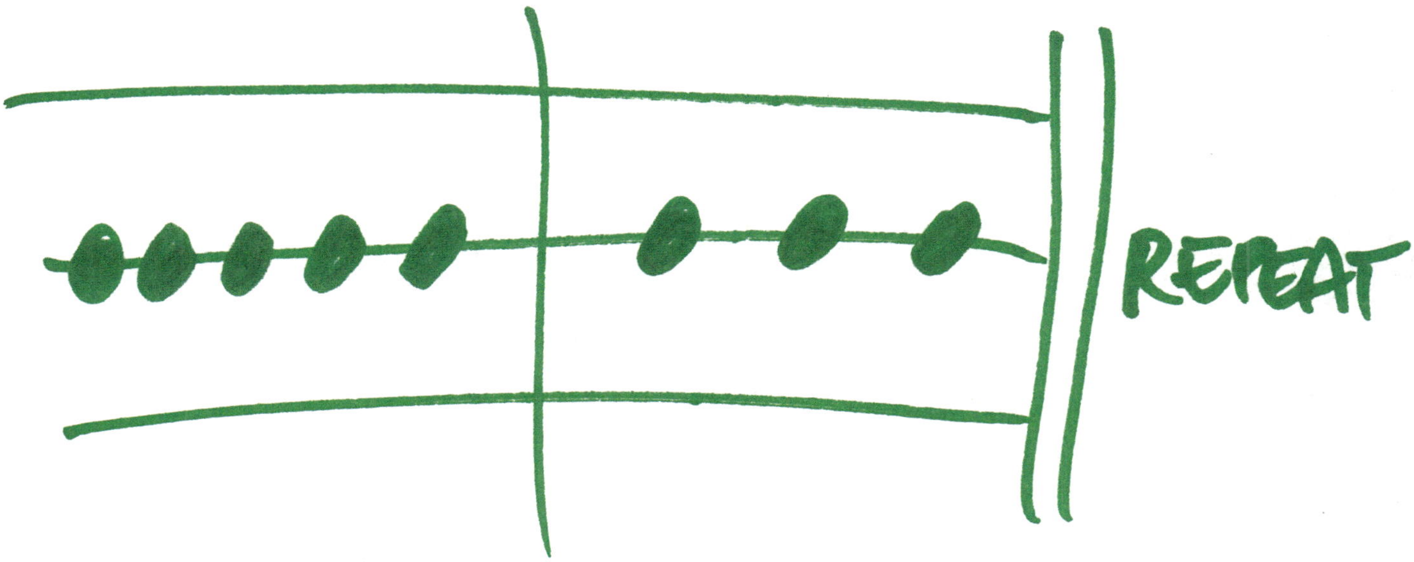

ACID
ARAB

18
Berberian Wedding
ACID ARAB

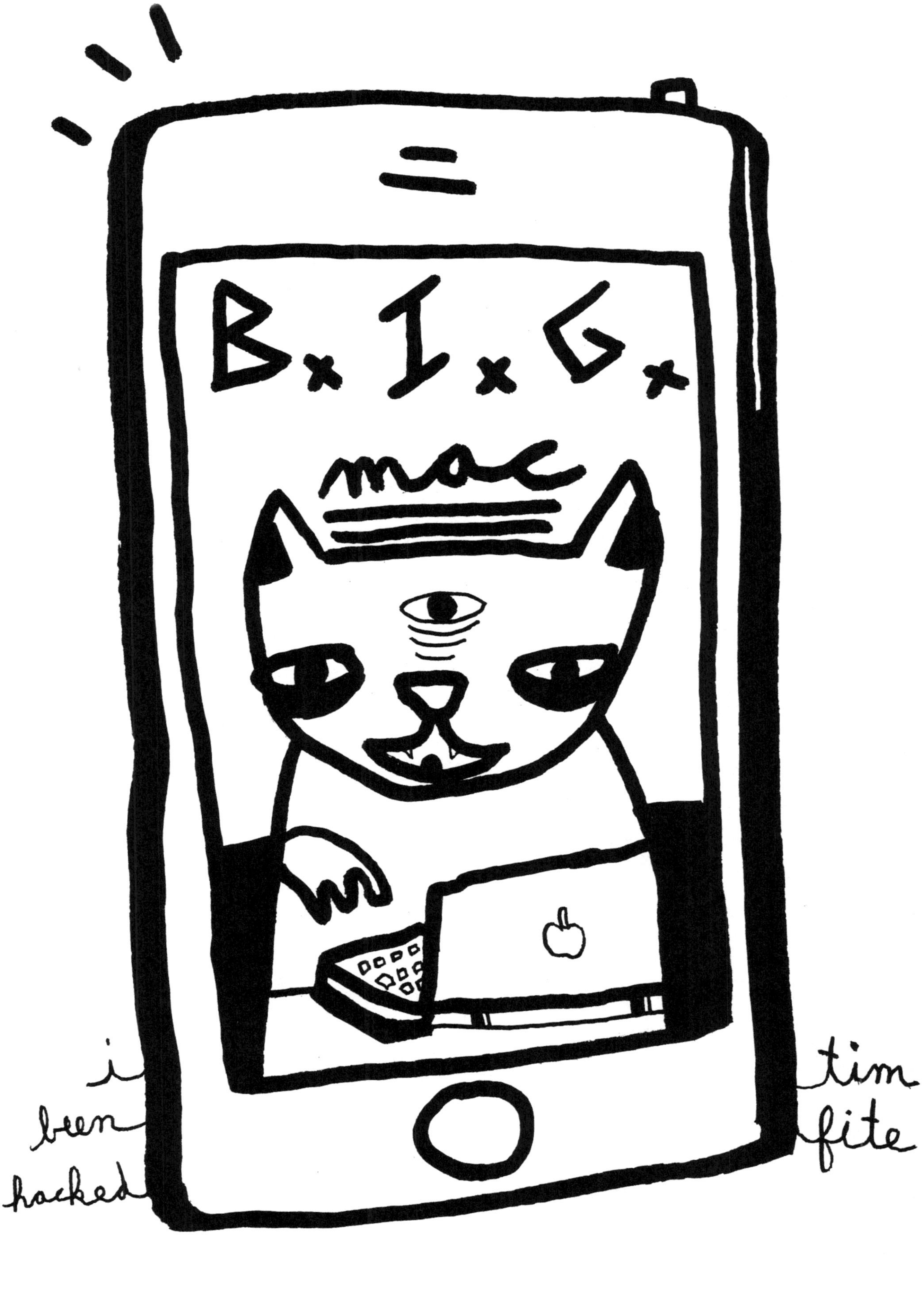
B. I. G.
mac
i
been
hacked
tim
fite

19

Big MAC

TIM FITE

HOW TO PLAY BLACK GREASE

by THE BLACK ANGELS

FIRST:

RUSSIAN BIG MUFF

SECOND:

FENDER TWIN REVERB ('65 REISSUE)

THIRD:

RICKENBACKER 345

FOURTH:

PLAY IN G

20

Black Grease

THE BLACK ANGELS

MAIN
RIFF:

INSPECTED BY #33

```
E --3336----3336--3336---------------3-
A ---------------------------543-------
D ----------------------53-------------
G -------------------------------------
B -------------------------------------
E -------------------------------------
```

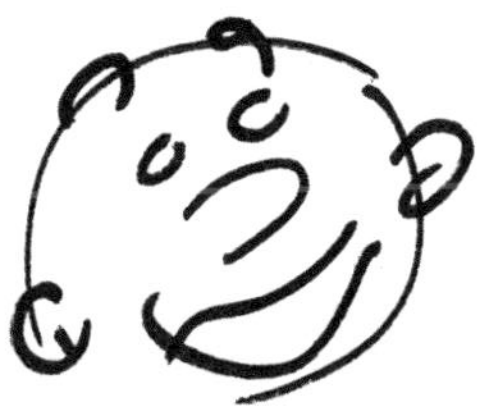

DON'T FORGET TO TURN
THE REVERB UP TO 10.

LOVE,
CHRISTIAN

2

BLOODSUCKER

BY MOZES AND THE FIRSTBORN

CHORUS: Em | G

"DO YOU REALLY THINK, ETC."

BRIDGE 1: C|B|A (UP AND DOWN A COUPLE O'TIMES)

VERSE: Em|G|C|A

(THIRD TIME: E instead of Em)

(FOURTH TIME: D instead of A)

"HEY, YOU SAY I'M, ETC."

BRIDGE 2: G | C

"BLOODSUCKER, ETC"

SOLO: Em|G|C|A|Em|G|C|D

"CONCRETE-JUNGLE-HAND-TO-HAND-COMBAT-ELECTRIC-GUITAR-PLAYING!!!"

CHORUS 4X - BRIDGE 1 - VERSE 4X - CHORUS 4X - BRIDGE 1 - VERSE 4X - BRIDGE 2 6X - CHORUS 2X - BRIDGE 1 - SOLO 2X - BRIDGE 2 4X

21

Bloodsucker

MOZES AND THE FIRSTBORN

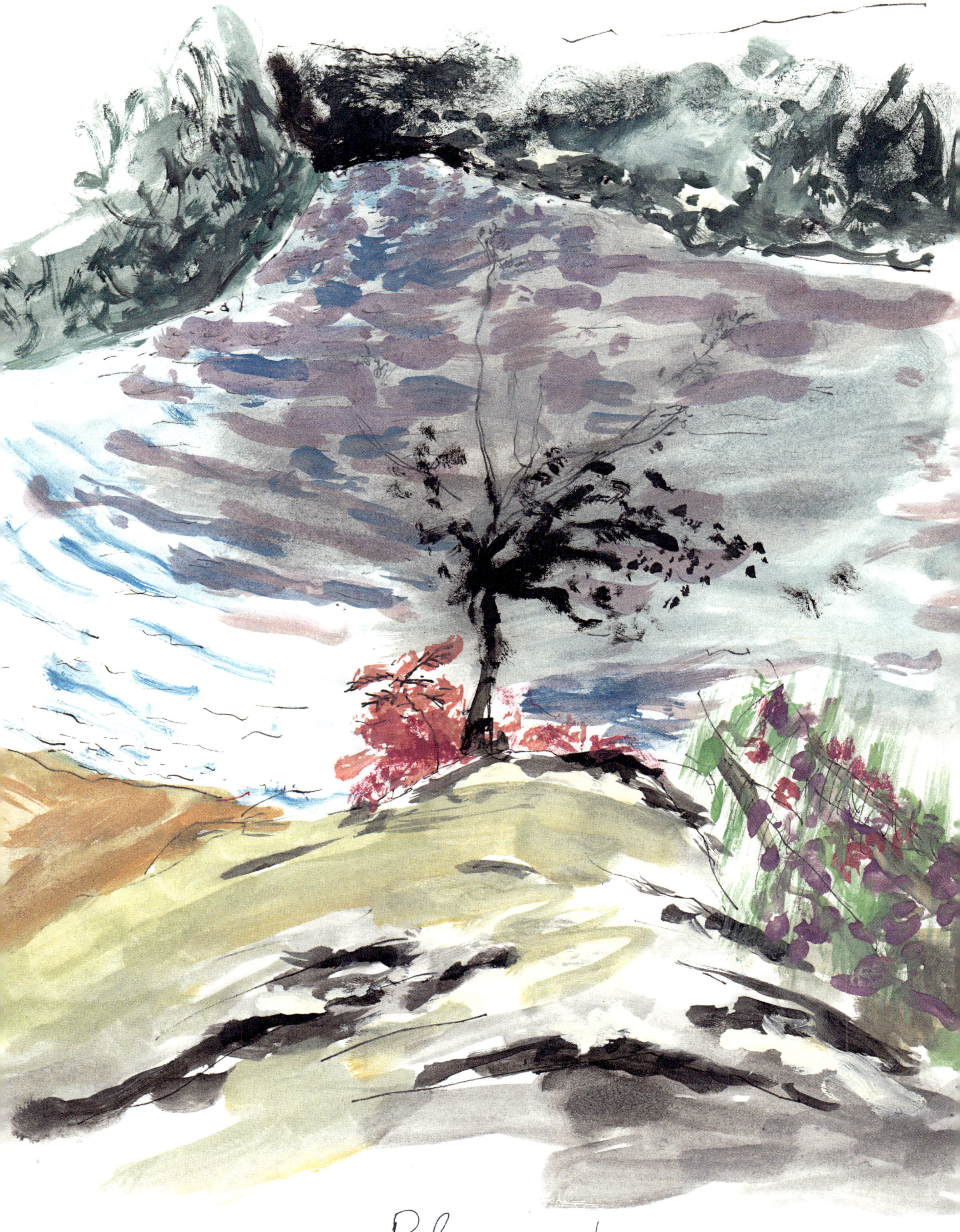

Bloom by Oscar & The Wolf.

22

Bloom

OSCAR AND THE WOLF

RÖKKURRÓ

BLUE SKIES

YOUR HANDS

HOLDING SO TIGHT

YOUR LUNGS

BREATHING SO LOUD

This is where it ends
watching blue turn into black
This isn't you
This isn't you

All you ever learned
but you wanted to forget
Keep throwing stones
Keep throwing stones

Disappearing dreams
all is lost when you're awake
It's so long since you felt fear
fear that made you take the first step

Blue skies all your dreams are dying
Blue skies come and bring them back to life
Blue skies the day after the storm is brighter
Blue skies this is all you wanted, bright lights guide your way
Blue skies the feeling that you get is golden

All your secret fears
that are hiding in your head
Now let them go
Now let them go

Just a fragile thought
is enough to turn the world
All your hopes are holding on
for a chance to see a new life

23

Blue Skies

RÖKKURRÓ

ΛΑΡΥΓΓΑΣ
"ΟΓΚΟΛΙΘΟΣ"

στο μπαλκόνι ήμασταν /
και ήρθε η πέτρα /
το σπίτι στα δύο άνοιξε /
από μέσα πέρασε

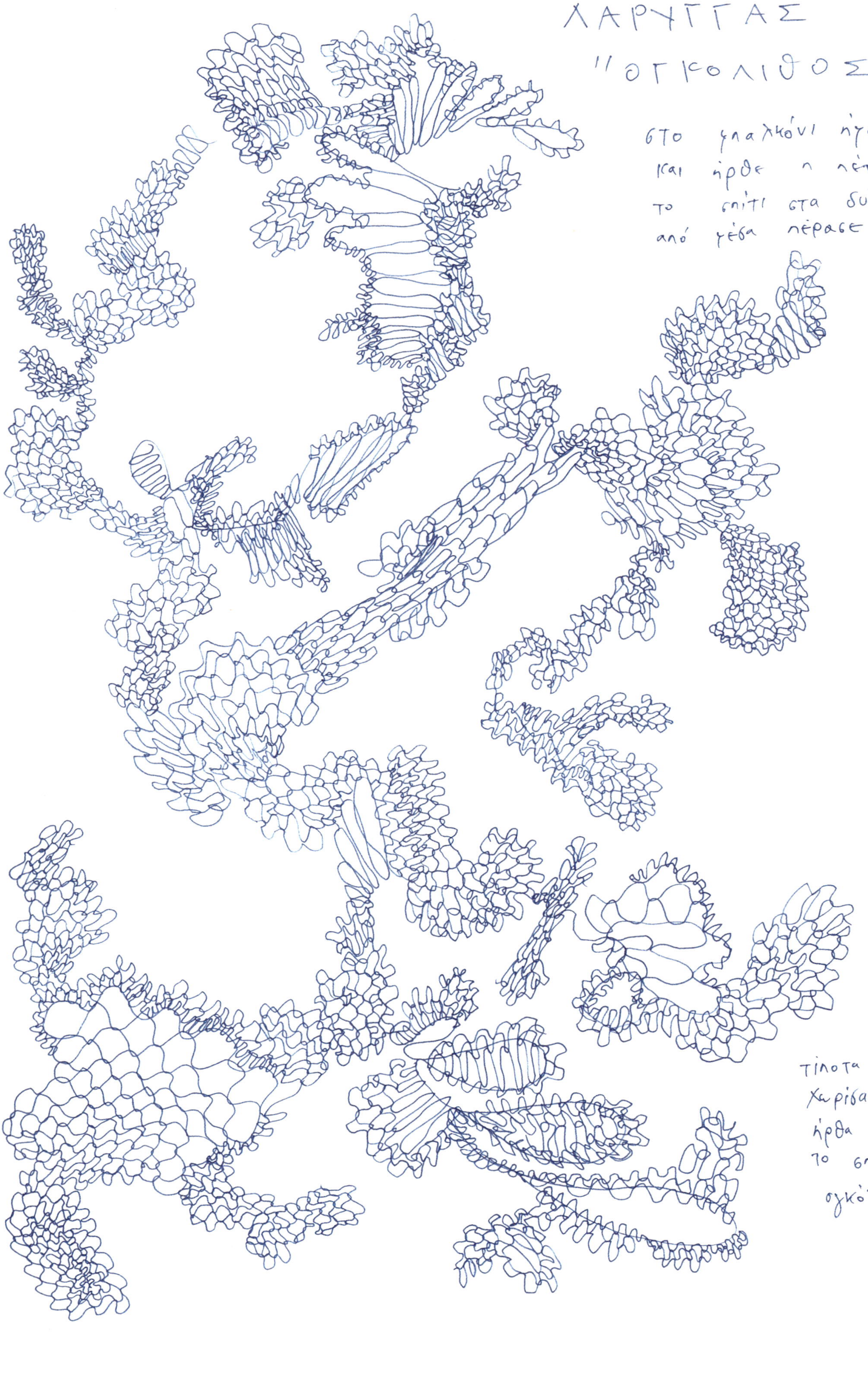

τίποτα δεν άλλαξε /
χωρίσατε /
ήρθα κι έφυγα /
το σπίτι έφτιαξα /
ογκόλιθος

24
Boulder (Ογκόλιθος)
LARRY GUS

BRONX IN A SIX

SLEAFORD MODS.

HE NEVER GAVE ANY REFUNDS TO HIS MATES
NOW HE WONDERS WHY HE SITS IN HIS BIG HOUSE
WITH ALL HIS PLASTIC AND NICE PAINTED PLATES
BRONX IN A SIX LETS DO A ONE SKINNER YOU TEN
BOB, LAUGHING ME HEAD OFF AT THE COWS THAT
GRAZED ON GRASS FROM THE BOOM, IT SOON TURNED
ITS JETS ON YA FACE AND BOOM! BURST YA
PUFF DADDY, MACED YA BASTARDS GOOD! I LAUGH
LIKE FUCK AT YA WANNABE LABELS SHOOTS ON
LOCATIONS GOT BLOKES IN STABLES RA RA RA!
ALL YA CHINNY WINE TASTERS DIE IN BOXS LIKE
THE REST OF US WASTERS ~~GOOD I LAUG~~ BASTARD
I FUCKIN TIE YA VEINS ROOKS YA VEINS LTD
EDITION, STITCH TOURIES BOND ST, LIKE THE VON
BONDIES HE GOT SLAPPED UP RIGHT I WOULDNT
FUCK ABOUT WI JACK WHITE! YA JAMMY SLUG
MISSED THE SALT A TWAT WI NINE LIVES YA
A LUCKY LITTLE TIT CAKE DIE! DIE! DIE!

BRONX IN A 6
A SINGLE SKINNER, HOW TRICKS x 2.

25
Bronx in a Six
SLEAFORD MODS

I COULDN'T GIVE A FUCKIN SHIT WHAT, YA THINK ABOUT ME CUNT,, WHAT YA SAYIN NOW WHERES YA WIFE YA KIDS YA HOUSE, YOU AINT GOT NONE YA SILLY BILLY, ALL GONE QUIET ON THE WANKER FRONT, EARY COOPERS ON THE GLUE COS HE STUCK TO HIS GUNS JUST LIKE YOU WITH YA MAHARISHI SNOW PANTS, WALKING THE LIKE YA FUCKIN OWN THE PAD, YA WONDER WHY YA GOT NO MATES YOU PRETEND TO BE PROUD OF YA OWN CULTURE WHILST SIMULTANEOUSLY NOT GIVIN TO FUCKS ABOOT YA OWN CULTURE WHAT CULTURE! FUCK CULTURE! THE BLUE PRINT FOR ALL CONTROL, ON THE DOLE, THE MONEY MONKS FAINT FUCKS OF REFERENCE PAINT A VAGUE IDEA - FUCK COLLY ON THAT SCALE YOU CUNT YA MUGGES - THE MONEY MONKS SAYIN ITS PRAYERS ON BANK BOOKS.

BRONX IN A 6
A SINGLE SKINNER, HOWS TRICKS x2.

BURRED BONN

By: Absolutely Free 2015

INSTRUMENT — HOW TO PLAY

- A low pulse
- A Cave
- 2 thin planks
- A Chain
- A bone wrapped in human hair
- A Car alarm
- A moog mg1

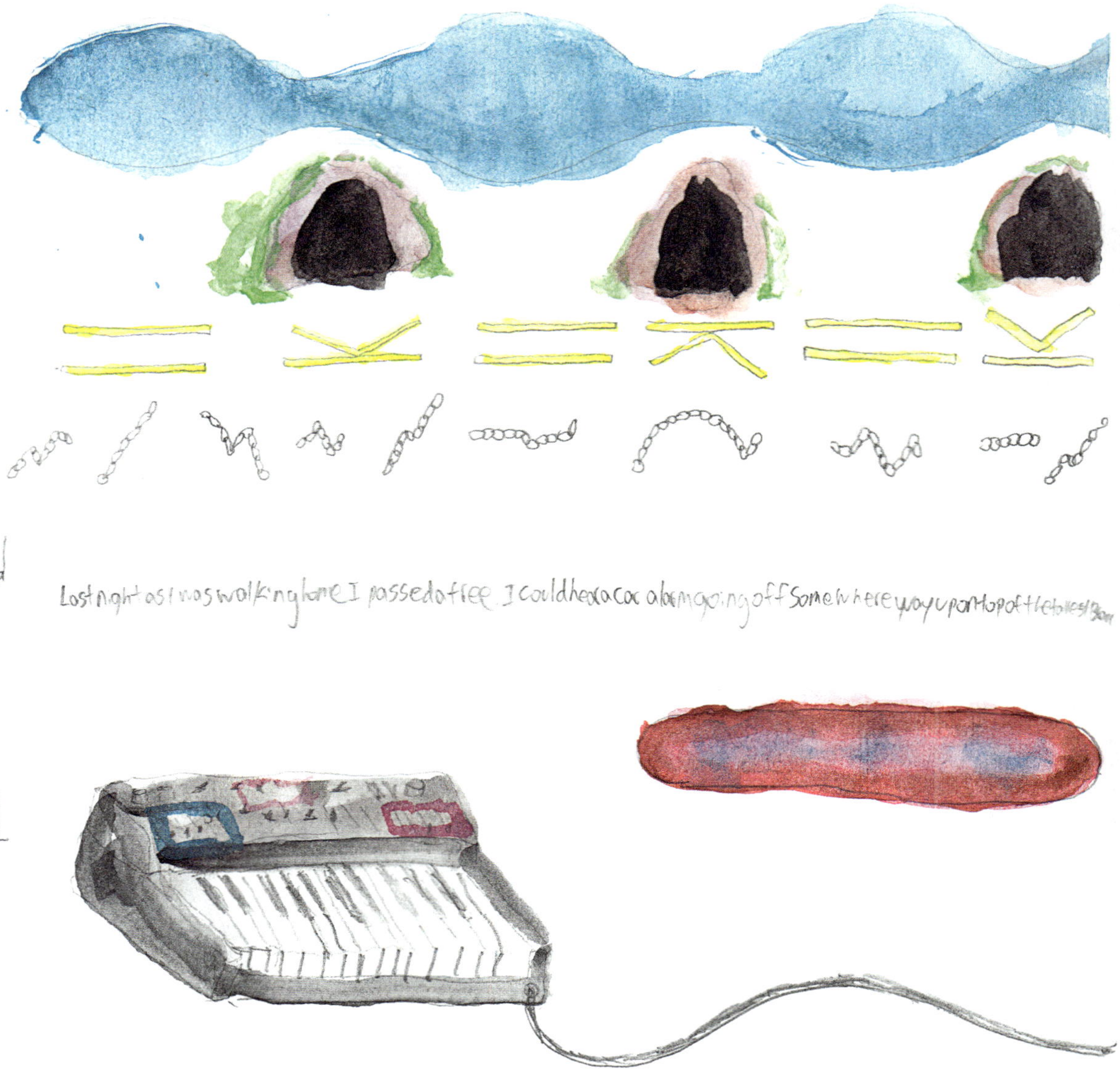

26
Burred Lens
ABSOLUTELY FREE

C

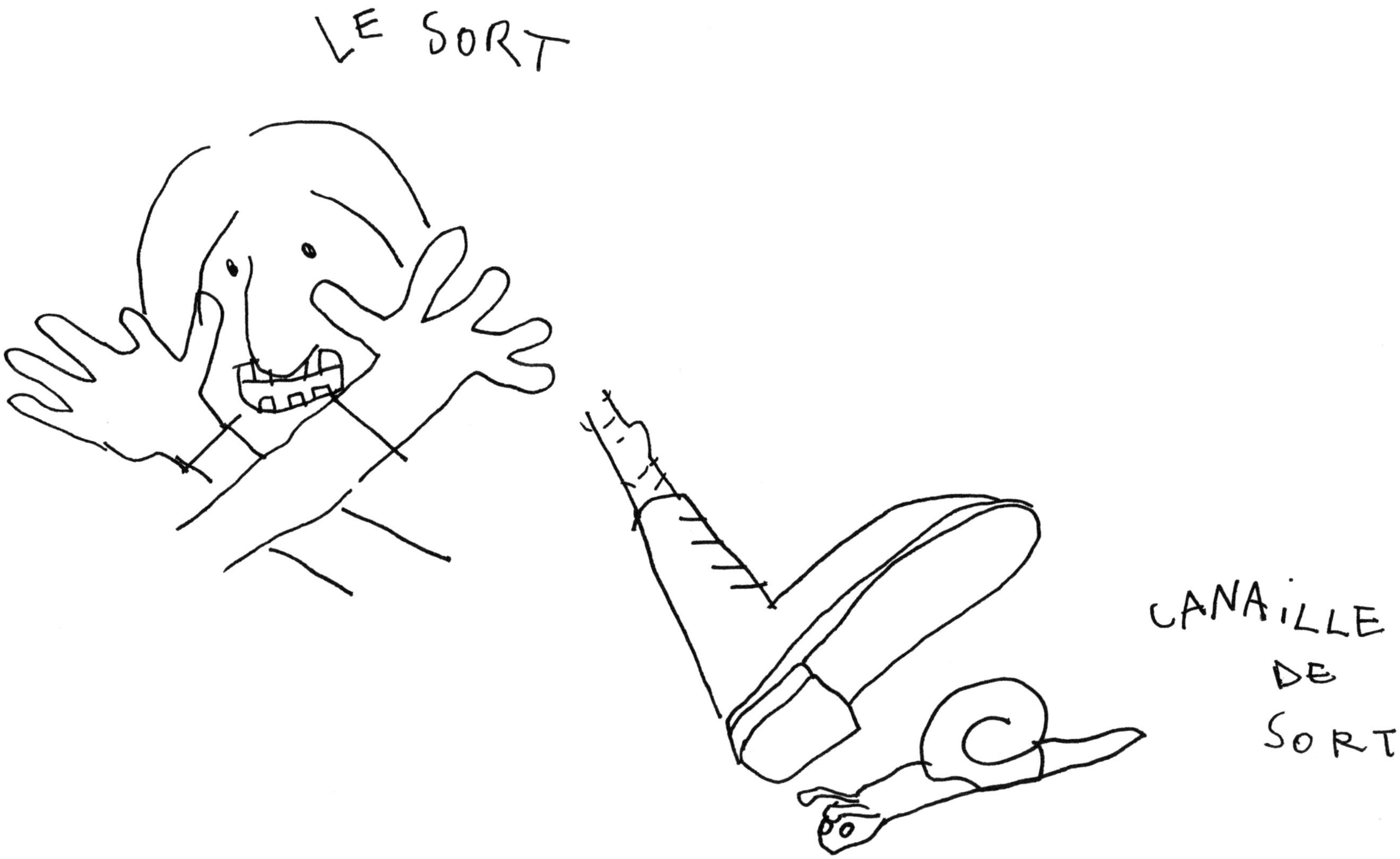
LE SORT
CANAILLE
DE
SORT

27

Canaille de sort

SALUT C'EST COOL

CANAILLE DE SORT
CANAILLE DE SORT
CANAILLE DE SORT
RE DOUTABLE.

TRÈS RIGIDE
PLUS FORT QUE MOI
PLUS INVENTIF
MAIS MOINS SOUPLE
QUE MOI.

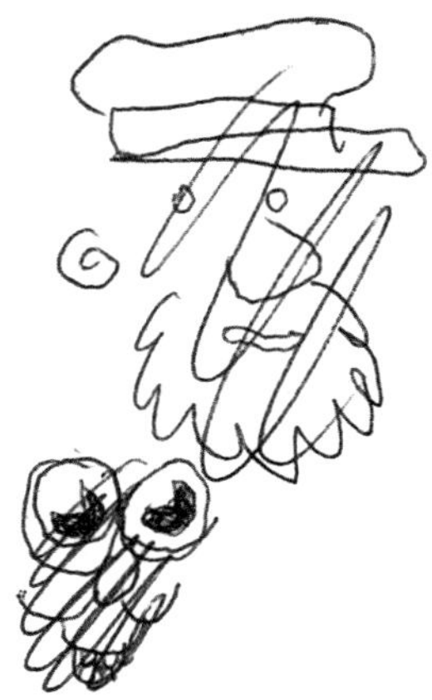

MOI JE FAIS
DE LA GYM
JE ME PLIE
AU SORT.

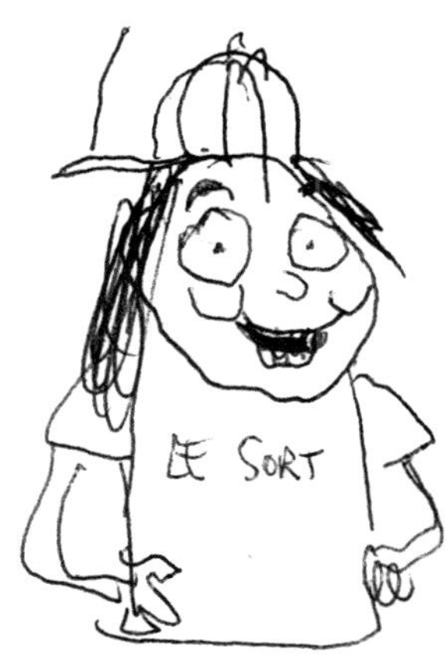

27

"CHERRY LANE"

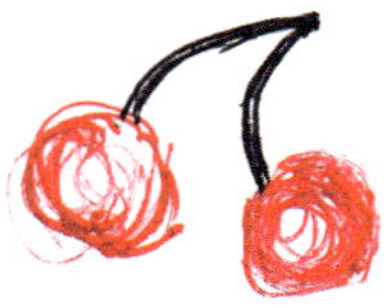

A little ditty by Ezra FURMAN

FROM THE PLATINUM-SELLING RECORD "DAY OF THE DOG"

Use a Capo on the 4th FRET OF a Guitar in ~~standing~~ Standard tuning

Then Play these chords: | C | F | G | E | Am

Repeat this pattern for all of the couplets

```
F                G          C          E      F              G       C
  Past    the    wounded    cars    reflecting    all  their  dirty  light
F                G           E          Am            F              G            C
  Past    the    unnamed   bars,  the   unnamed    prisoners   of   the   night
```

Past the ~~good~~ Winnebago dreaming all its iron dreams
Past the haunted drugstore where the fortune teller leans
Past the gravel parking lot where blood is always blood
Past the storefront church where they say God made man from mud
There you'll find the broken toys who chased their love in vain
If you wander over yonder down my Cherry Lane

Past the dimming county line where all turns black and red
Past the winners' trash bags where the losers lay their head
Listen for the freight trains rumbling, talking in their sleep
Hear the lonesome drifter ask the Lord her soul to keep
Walk beneath the signpost where the purple neon hums
See the ugly cardboard world where Someday never comes
And you may see my old man Gideon walking with a cane
If you wander over yonder down my Cherry Lane

I got sick, then I got sicker, and then I lost my way → let chords ring dramatically out on this line
Heard a song without a singer at the close of day
I went driving, I went walking, I went far away
Went somewhere you can't come back from, ~~a~~ somewhere you can't stay
If you see me on your journey, try and say my name
You can turn and trace your footsteps back the way you came } Same deal for these two lines
Or you can take the highway running wild through joy and pain
If you wander over yonder down my Cherry Lane

28

Cherry Lane

EZRA FURMAN

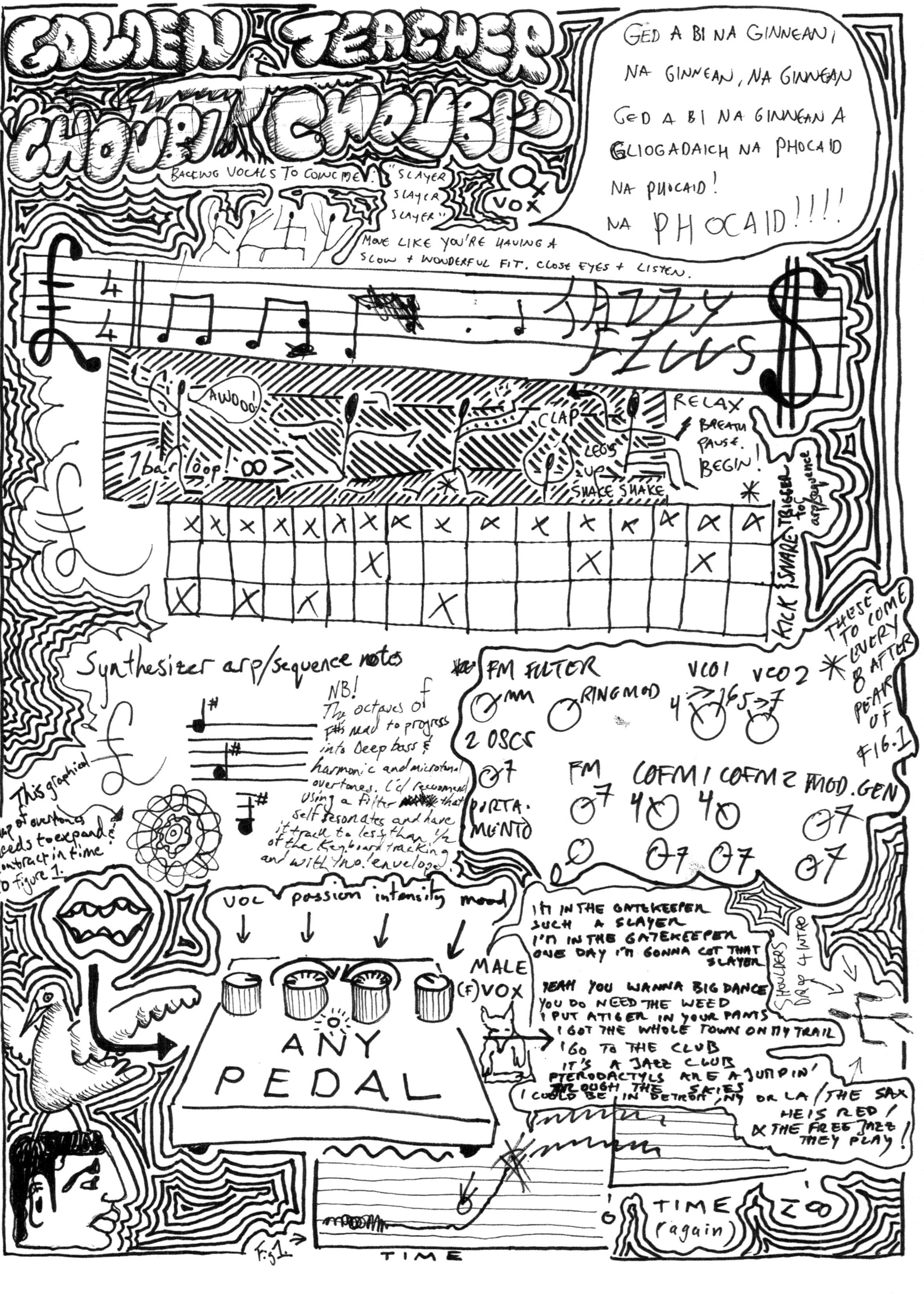
GOLDEN TEACHER
CHOOPY CHERUBS
GED A BI NA GINNEAN, NA GINNEAN, NA GINNEAN
GED A BI NA GINNEAN A GLIOGADAICH NA PHOCAID
NA PHOCAID!
NA PHOCAID!!!!
BACKING VOCALS TO COINCIDE: "SLAYER SLAYER SLAYER"
♀ VOX
MOVE LIKE YOU'RE HAVING A SLOW + WONDERFUL FIT. CLOSE EYES + LISTEN.
4/4
JAZZY FIZZUS
AWOOO!
1 bar loop! ∞ >
CLAP
LEGS UP
SHAKE SHAKE
RELAX
BREATH
PAUSE.
BEGIN!
TRIGGER arp/sequence
SNARE
KICK
Synthesizer arp/sequence notes
NB! The octaves of F#s need to progress into Deep bass & harmonic and microtonal overtones. I'd recommend using a filter that self resonates and have it track to less than 1/2 of the keyboard tracking and with no envelope!
This graphical map of overtones needs to expand + contract in time to figure 1.
FM FILTER
RINGMOD
VCO1
VCO2
2 OSCS
FM
COFM1
COFM2
MOD. GEN
PORTA-MENTO
THESE TO COME IN EVERY 8 AFTER PEAK OF FIG.1
VOL
passion
intensity
mood
MALE (F) VOX
ANY PEDAL
I'M IN THE GATEKEEPER
SUCH A SLAYER
I'M IN THE GATEKEEPER
ONE DAY I'M GONNA CUT THAT SLAYER
YEAH YOU WANNA BIG DANCE
YOU DO NEED THE WEED
I PUT A TIGER IN YOUR PANTS
I GOT THE WHOLE TOWN ON MY TRAIL
I GO TO THE CLUB
IT'S A JAZZ CLUB
PTERODACTYLS ARE A JUMPIN' THROUGH THE SKIES
I COULD BE IN DETROIT, NY OR LA / THE SAX HE IS RED! & THE FREE JAZZ THEY PLAY!
SHOULDERS DROP 4 INTRO
Fig 1.
TIME
TIME (again)

29
Choubi Choubi
GOLDEN TEACHER

CIRCLES

by MOON DUO

Yeah, I wanna circle right round again, and I don't ever want the ride to end, it seems you please won't you give a little back now—hey, I'll get with it maybe later, oh, wherever the time is! we'll, nevermind I'm staying here now. Circle back my love, look out here we come, strange to the sun of everything now. Two back to one we'll never die, no. It's so strange at the slipping in the slipstream. Hey, there are seasons here comes another, way on the all circling. The end is beginning

30
Circles
MOON DUO

CIRCULAR FFCGCC

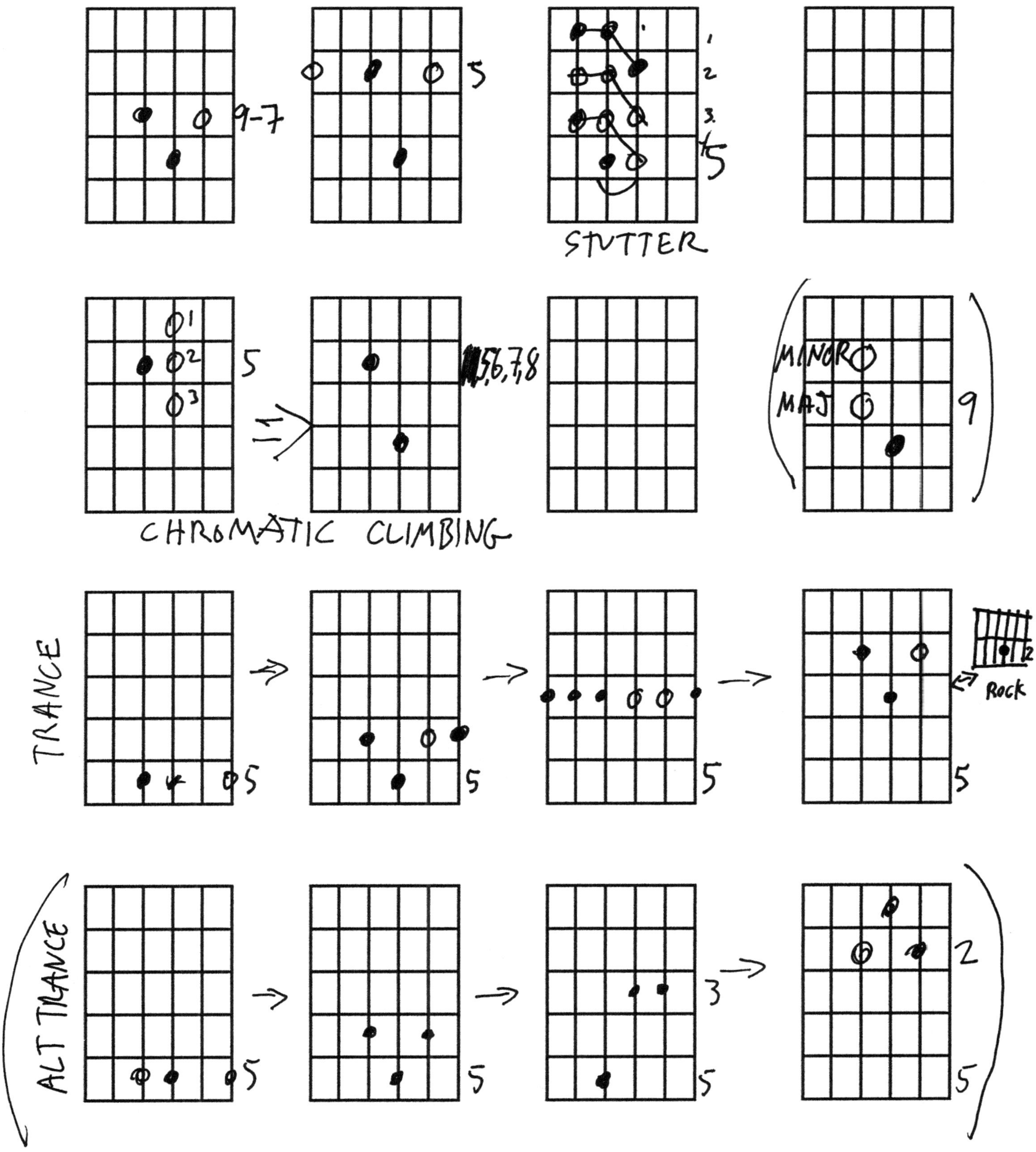

31
Circular
LEE RANALDO

LATEST DESCENT #1 FFD#FA#C S+P
LATE "Blackout tuning" 111012

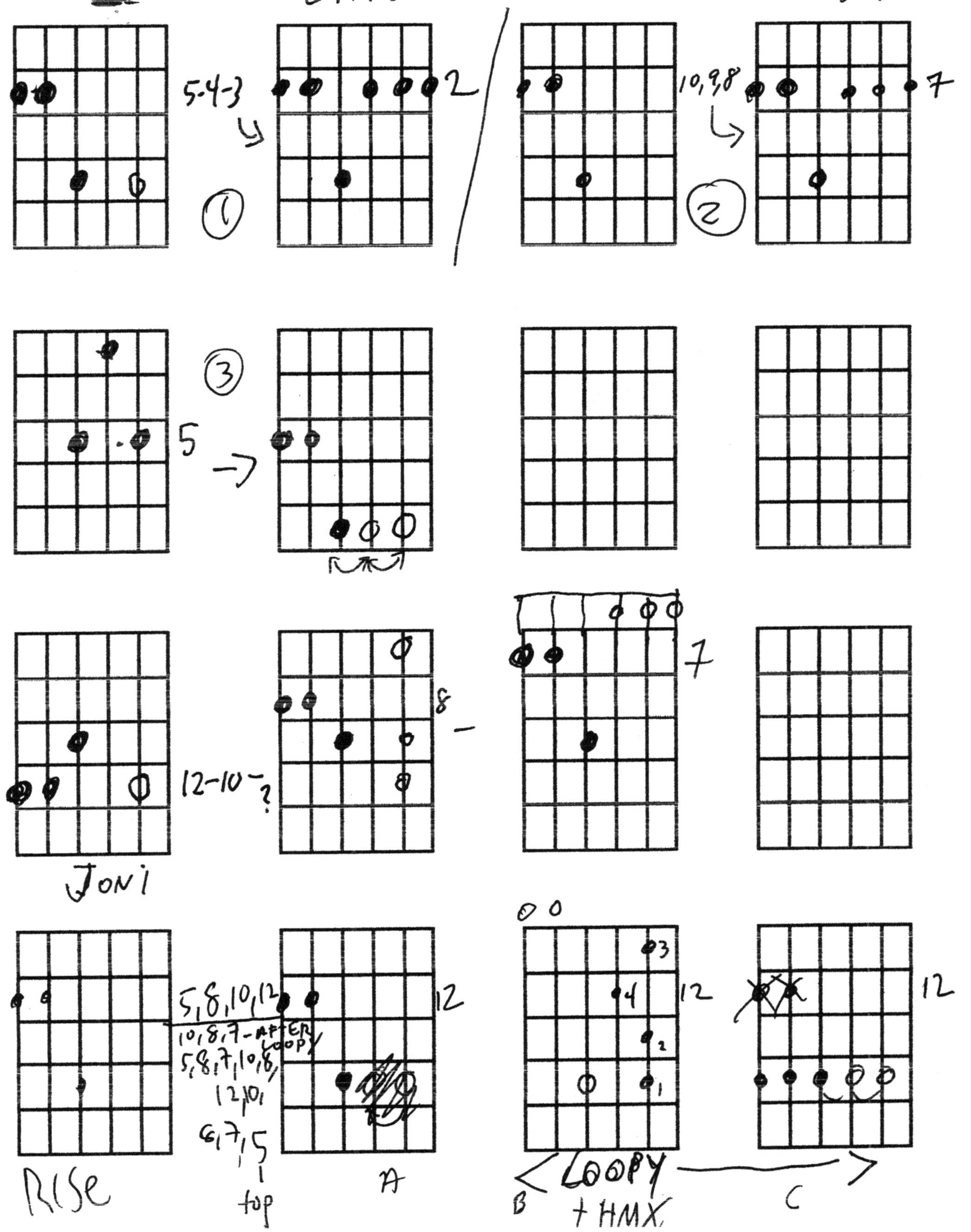

31

Late Descent #1

LEE RANALDO

GGC GCC   080811/ Lecce SONG

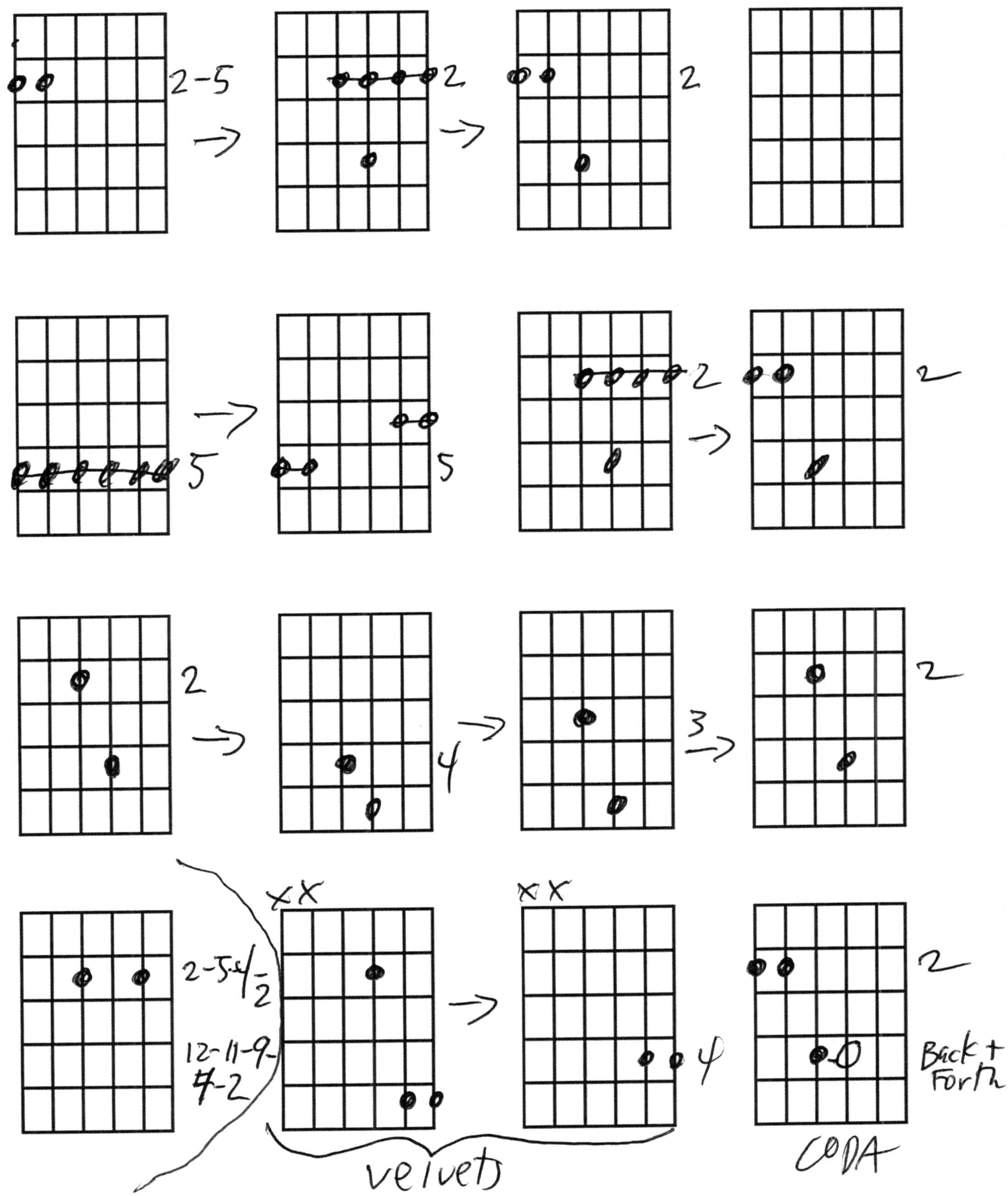

31

Lecce

LEE RANALDO

DA#DFCA# NEW XTINA SECTION S

042714
030714
081715

(1)

BPM
174
?

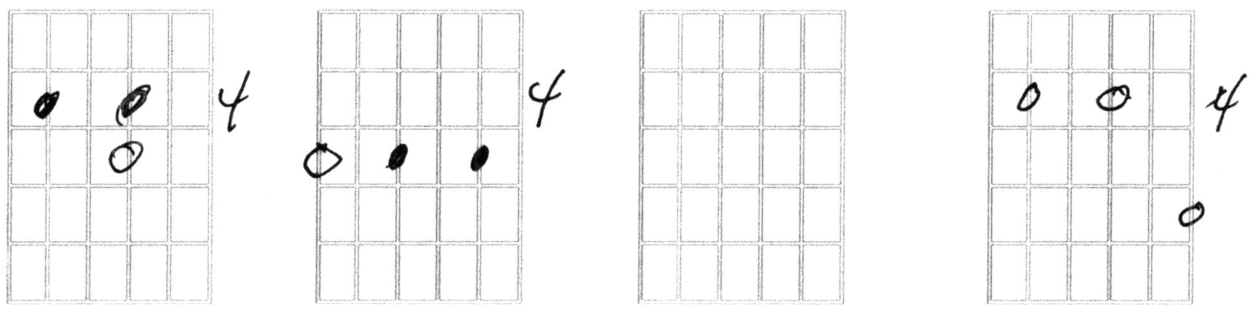

I A/B

II ~~9ff~~

RIDE CHORD
strummy / Motorik

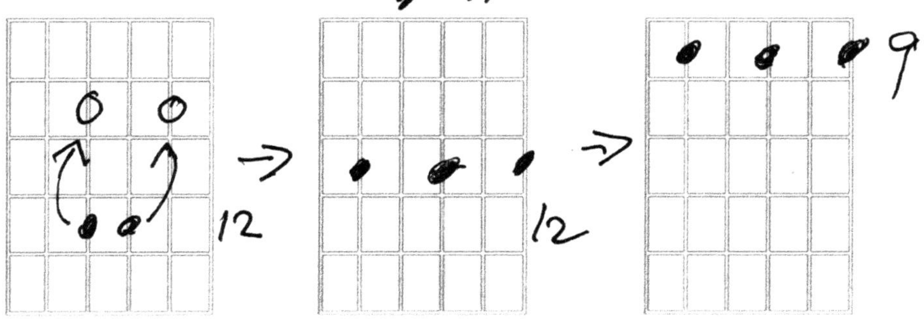

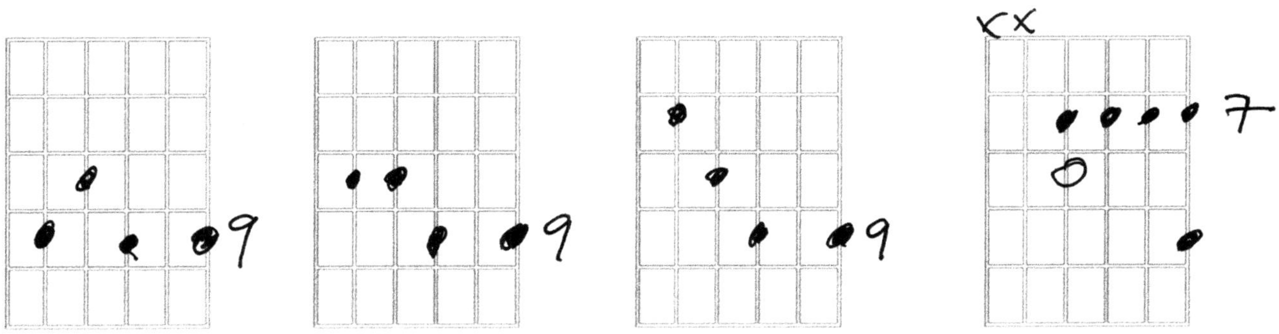

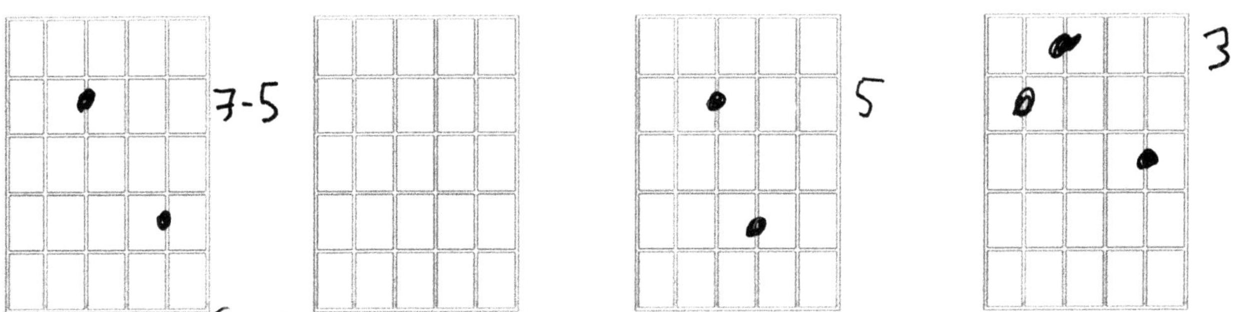

9-7-12-14
?

(10-12)
CHORDAL
CHROMATIC

Cumiunt

BEFORE RTN
to
TOP

31

New Thing

LEE RANALDO

NEW XTINA SECTIONS p 2

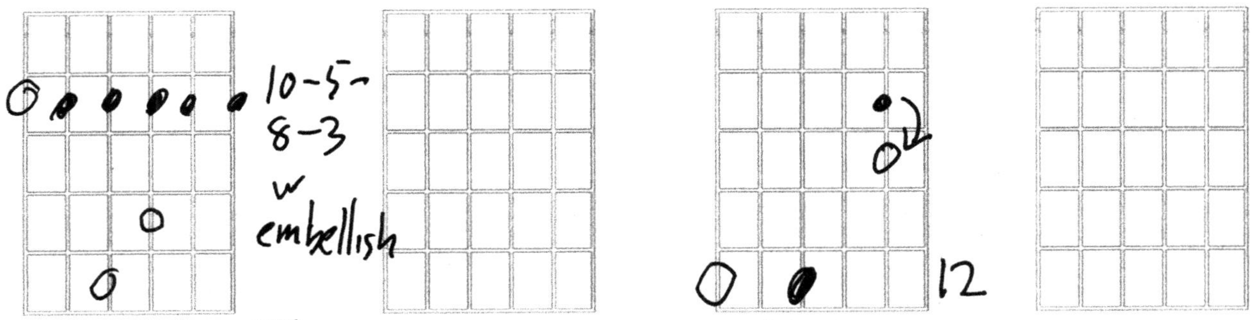

LOST PART FOUND

BIRDS

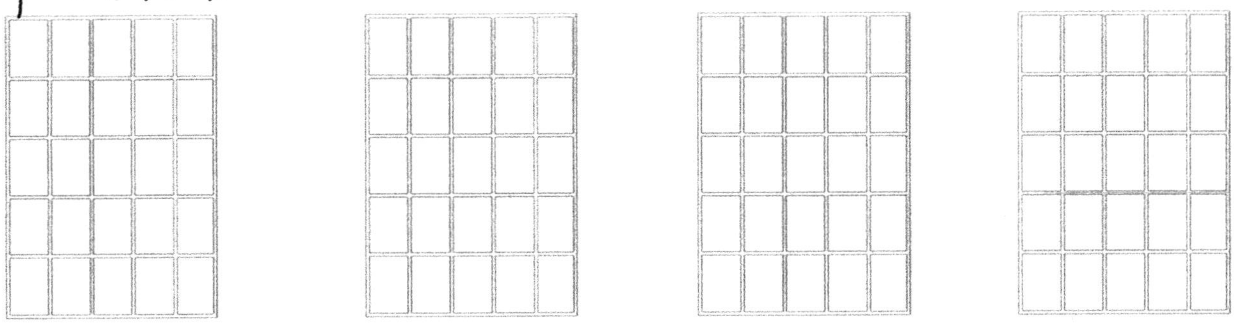

INVERSION (?)

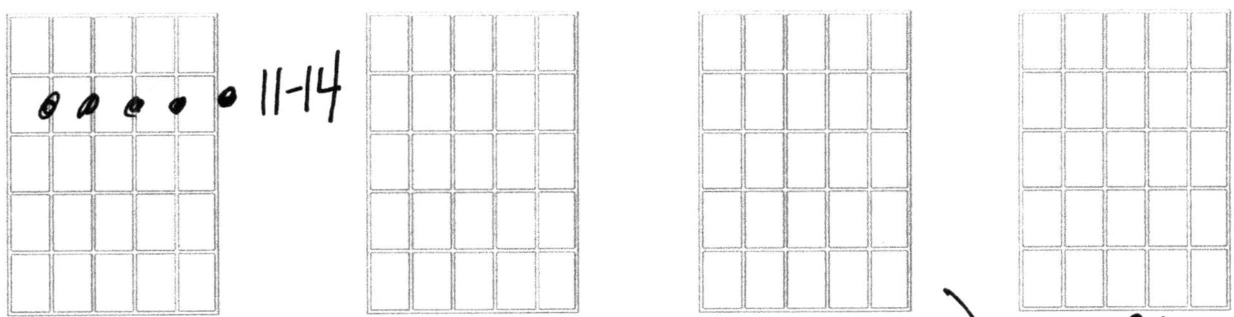

FOCUS ON NFF
COMBO STRINGS

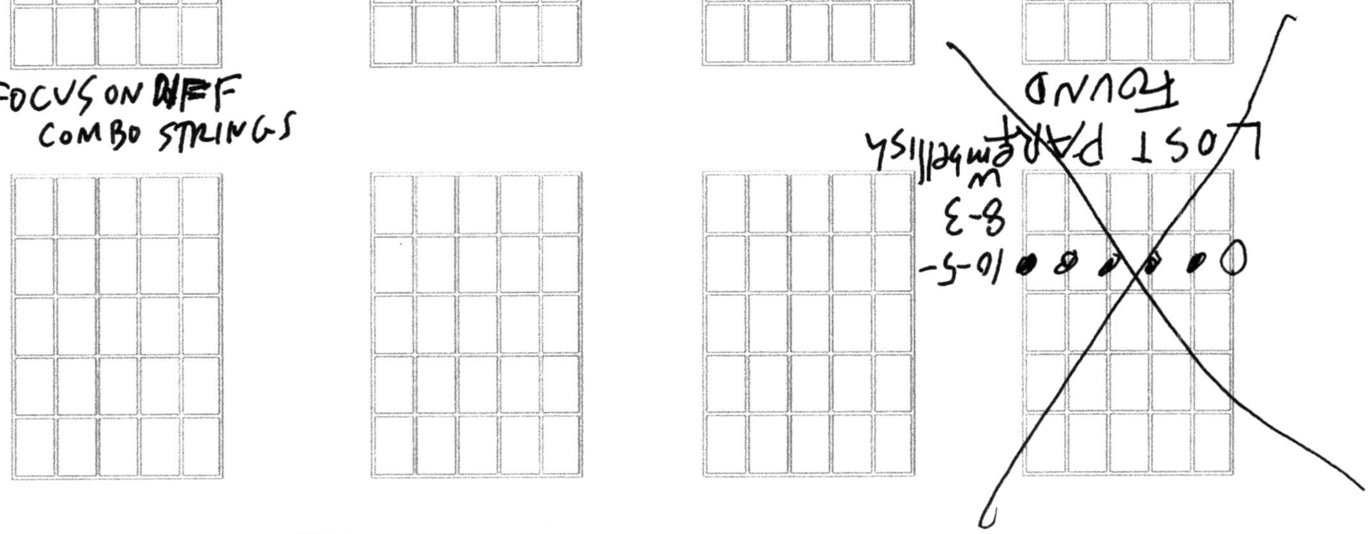

31

New Thing

LEE RANALDO

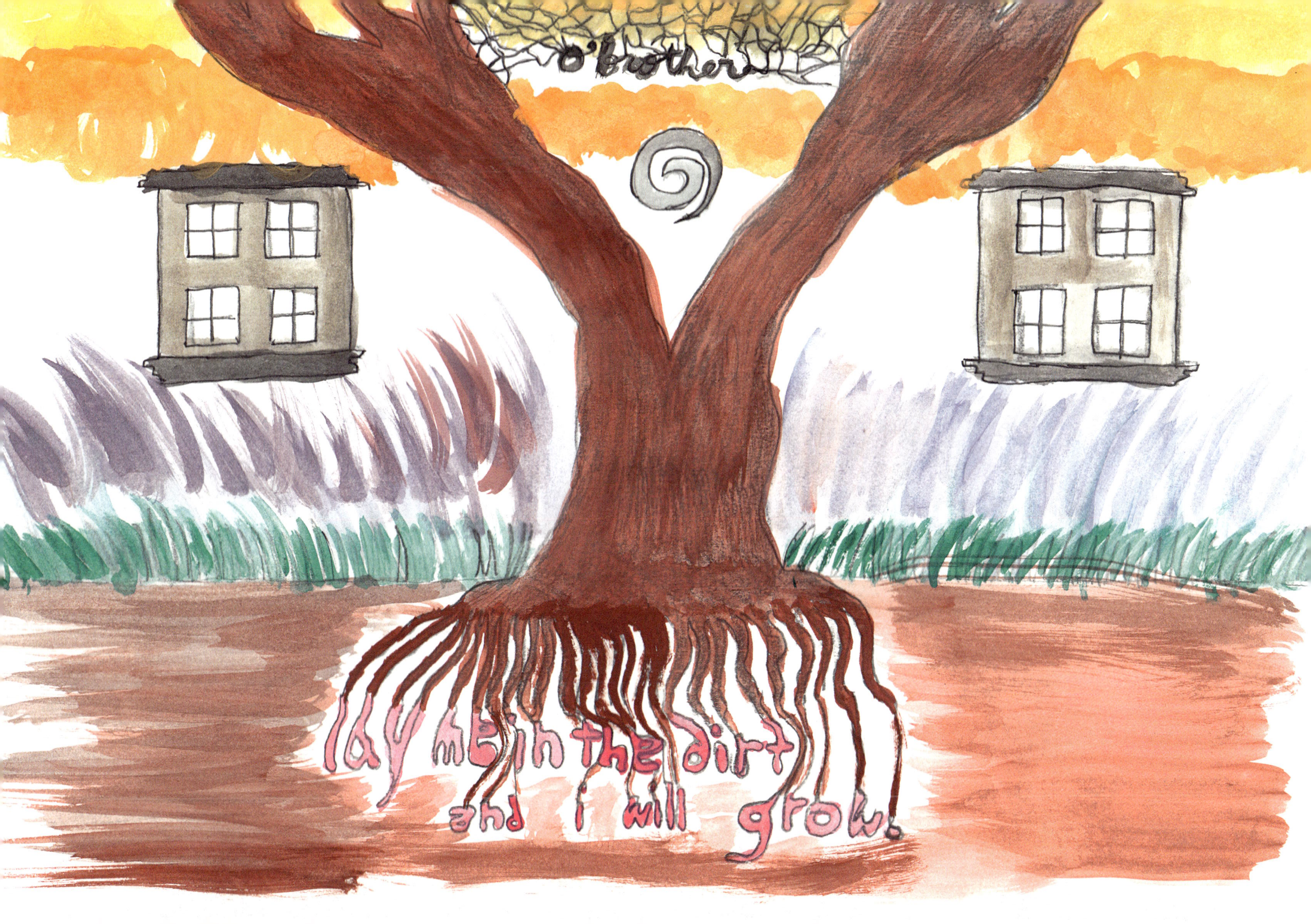
o'brothers
lay me in the dirt
and i will grow!

32

Cleanse Me

O'BROTHER

SUN GLITTERS
6 MAY 2015
GALAXY TOUR!
ALEXANDER OGG
MARV RUDNICK
M/R
CLOUDS IN YOUR EYES
featuring SARAH P.

33
Clouds in Your Eyes
SUN GLITTERS

Toronaut - Colors
From the album "HISS" - 2013

Capo 3rd fret
Cmaj7 02201x
5/4

Intro
Dm A
Dm A

```
         Dm                    A
Are these nightmares cast in stone?
           Dm                 A
May the backyards drown in shades
        Cm                     G
Things that we thought defeated
           Cm              G
Are now turning against us


          Dm              A
In the morning, in the gray
         Dm             A
I was silent, without defense
      Cm                   G
Things that we thought defeated
      Cm                 G
Are now turning against us
          Em7
      against us
          Em6
      against us
        Cmaj7
      against us
          Em
      against us
          Em7
      against us
          Em6
      against us
        Cmaj7
      against us
          Em
      against us

        Dm  A
        Dm  A


           Dm           A
As the colors diversified
          Dm             A
It was silent beyond compare
         Cm              G
I thought I was defeated
        Cm                  G
Although there'd been no fighting
          Em7
      no fighting
          Em6
      no fighting
         Cmaj7
      no fighting
          Em
      no fighting
```

Repeat

34
Colors
TORONAUT

(Core Trance Hero) 001

Bass Line

by Grand Atlas Mondial

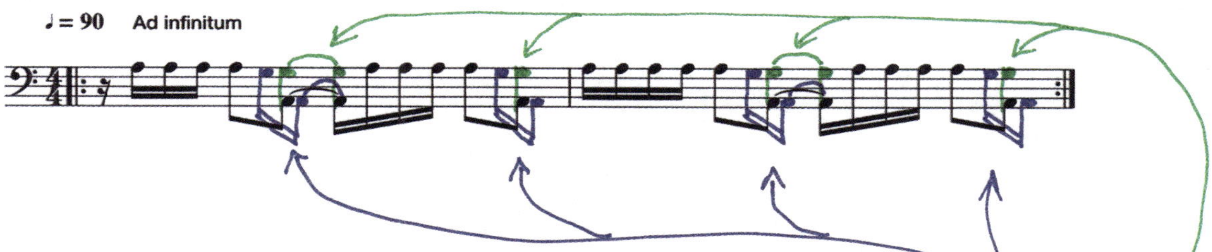

Bored playing this all the time?
Here's a variant:
(we use this in what is kind of the chorus)

And here's another variant:
(we use it in the final part of the live version)

For those not familiar with scores (like us):
Play note A on the 12th fret on the A string a few times rapidly, then play once the open A string a little longer. Repeat.
The first variant is to play instead of open A note G on the 10th fret. The second variant is with both G and open A, but at half length of course. To get the rhythm, listen to the record.

35
(Core Trance Hero) 001
GRAND ATLAS MONDIAL

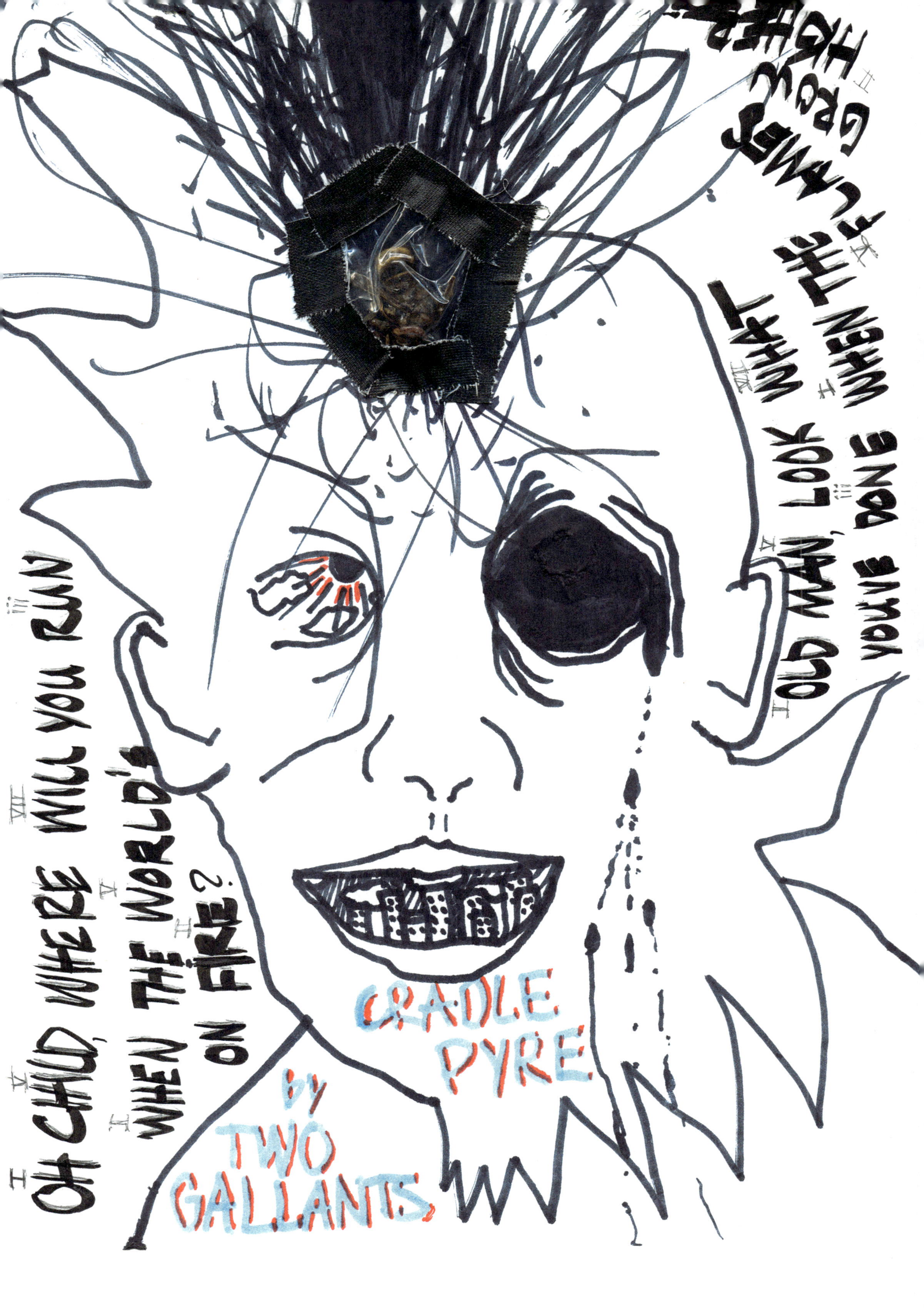

OH CHILD, WHERE WILL YOU RUN
WHEN THE WORLD'S
ON FIRE?
OLD MAN, LOOK WHAT THE FLAMES
YOU'VE DONE WHEN GROW HOTTER
CRADLE PYRE
by
TWO GALLANTS

36
Cradle Pyre
TWO GALLANTS

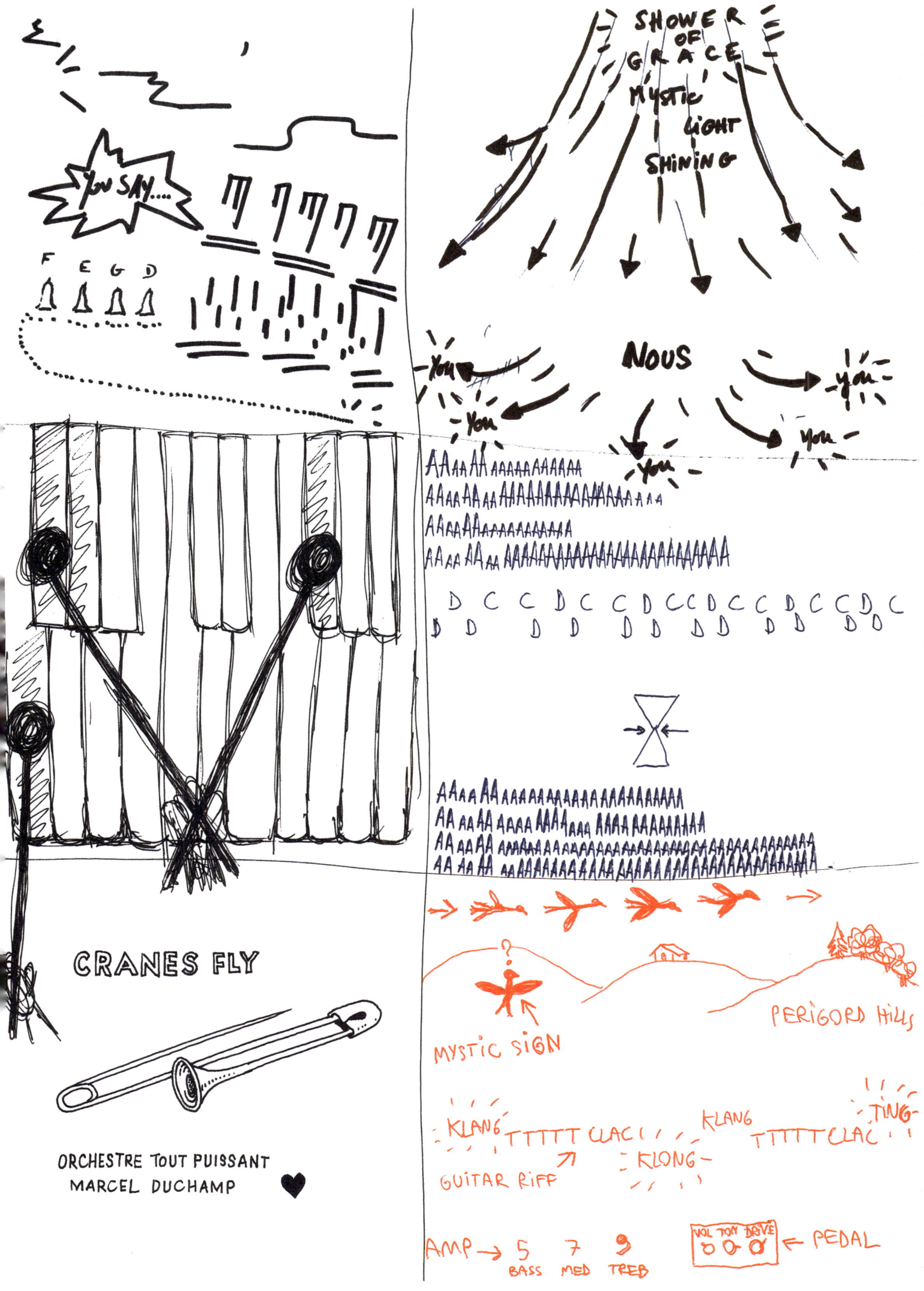
YOU SAY....
F E G D
SHOWER OF GRACE
MYSTIC LIGHT SHINING
NOUS
YOU
YOU
YOU
YOU
YOU
CRANES FLY
ORCHESTRE TOUT PUISSANT
MARCEL DUCHAMP
MYSTIC SIGN
PERIGORD HILLS
KLANG TTTTT CLAC
KLANG TTTTT CLAC
TING
KLONG
GUITAR RIFF
AMP → 5 7 9
BASS MED TREB
VOL TON DRIVE
← PEDAL

37

Cranes Fly

ORCHESTRE TOUT PUISSANT MARCEL DUCHAMP

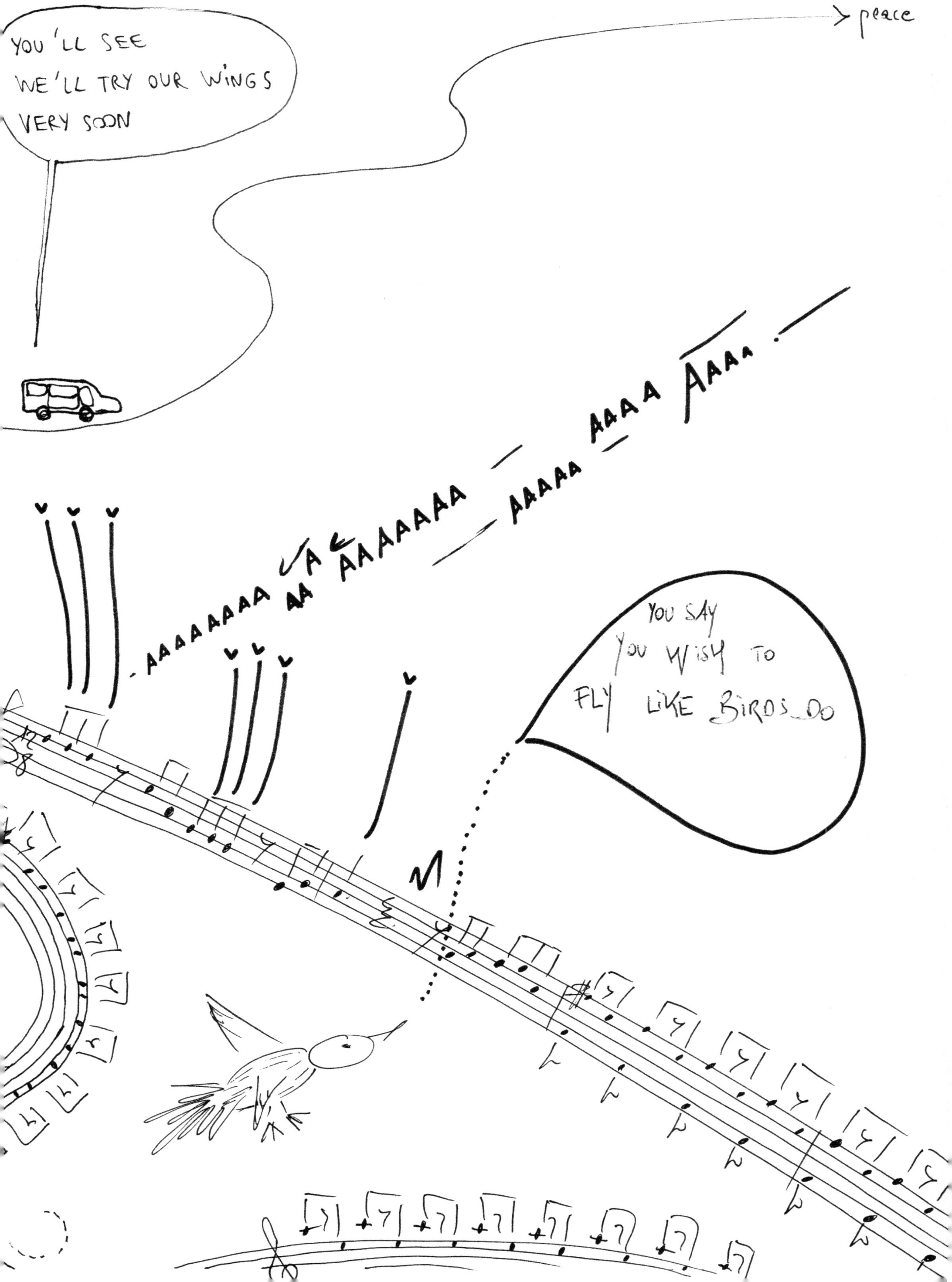
YOU'LL SEE
WE'LL TRY OUR WINGS
VERY SOON
peace
AAAAAAAA
AA A AAAAAAA
AAAAA
AAAA AAAA
YOU SAY
YOU WISH TO
FLY LIKE BIRDS DO

D

ΔΑΦΝΗ

Μεσ' την καρδιά ειν' η ρίζες σου
και στο μυαλό μου ανθίζεις
και κολυμπώ στσι μυρωδιές
γιατί μοσχομυρίζεις.

Δεν είδα σαν τη σκέψη σου
πιο πεισματάρα σκέψη
μαλώνω και ποβγάνω τη
μ' αυτή που να μισέψει

Μήτσος Σταυρακάκης

Μουσική Γιώργης Ξυλούρης

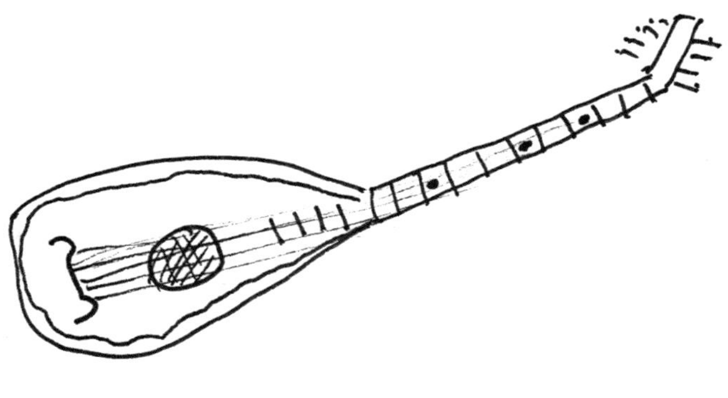

38
Dafni (Δάφνη)
GEORGE XYLOURIS

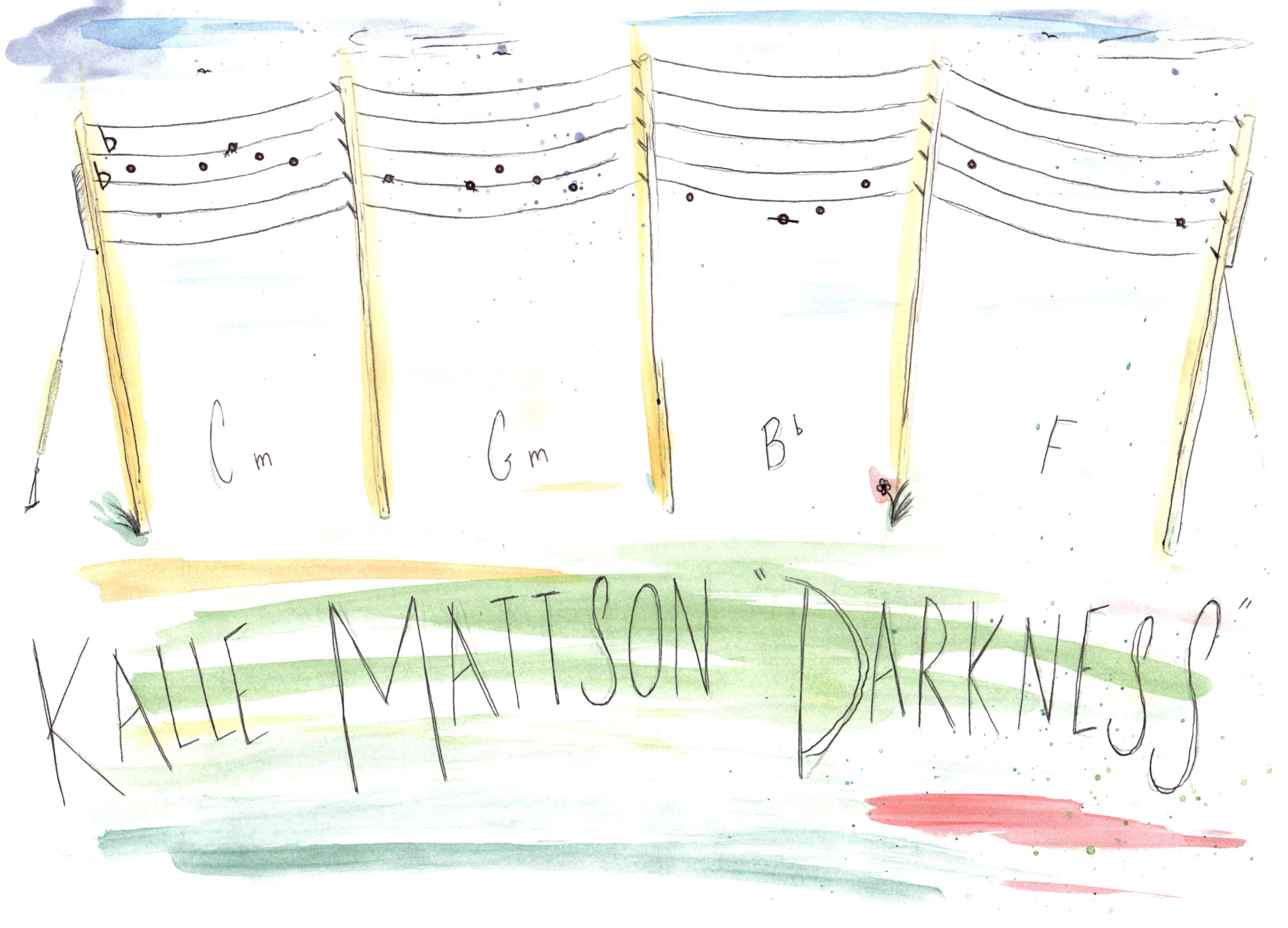
Cm
Gm
B♭
F
KALLE MATTSON "DARKNESS"

39

Darkness

KALLE MATTSON

DAYDREAMING

NONA MARIE INVIE

Swing ♩ = 140
Guitar capo 3

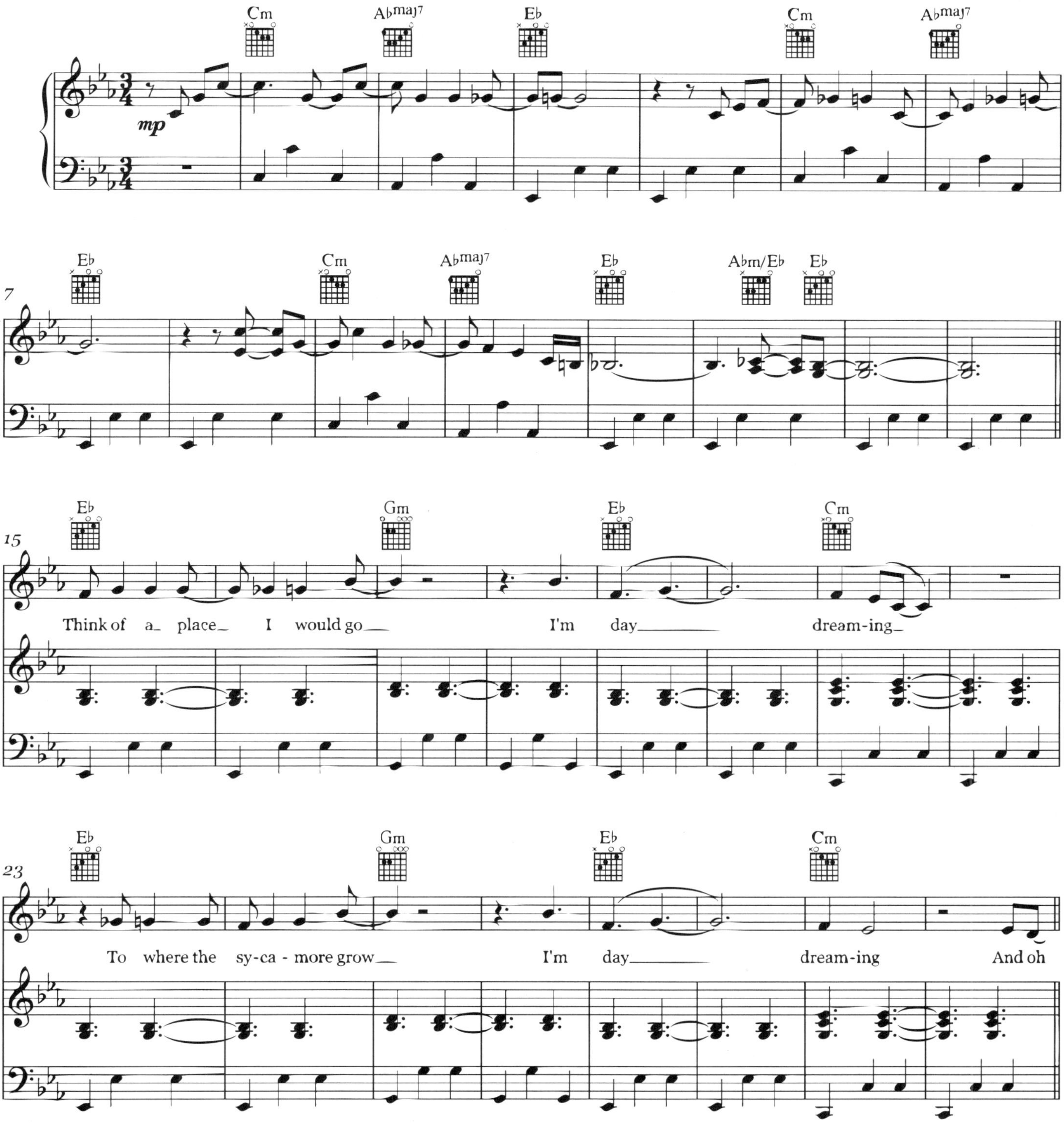

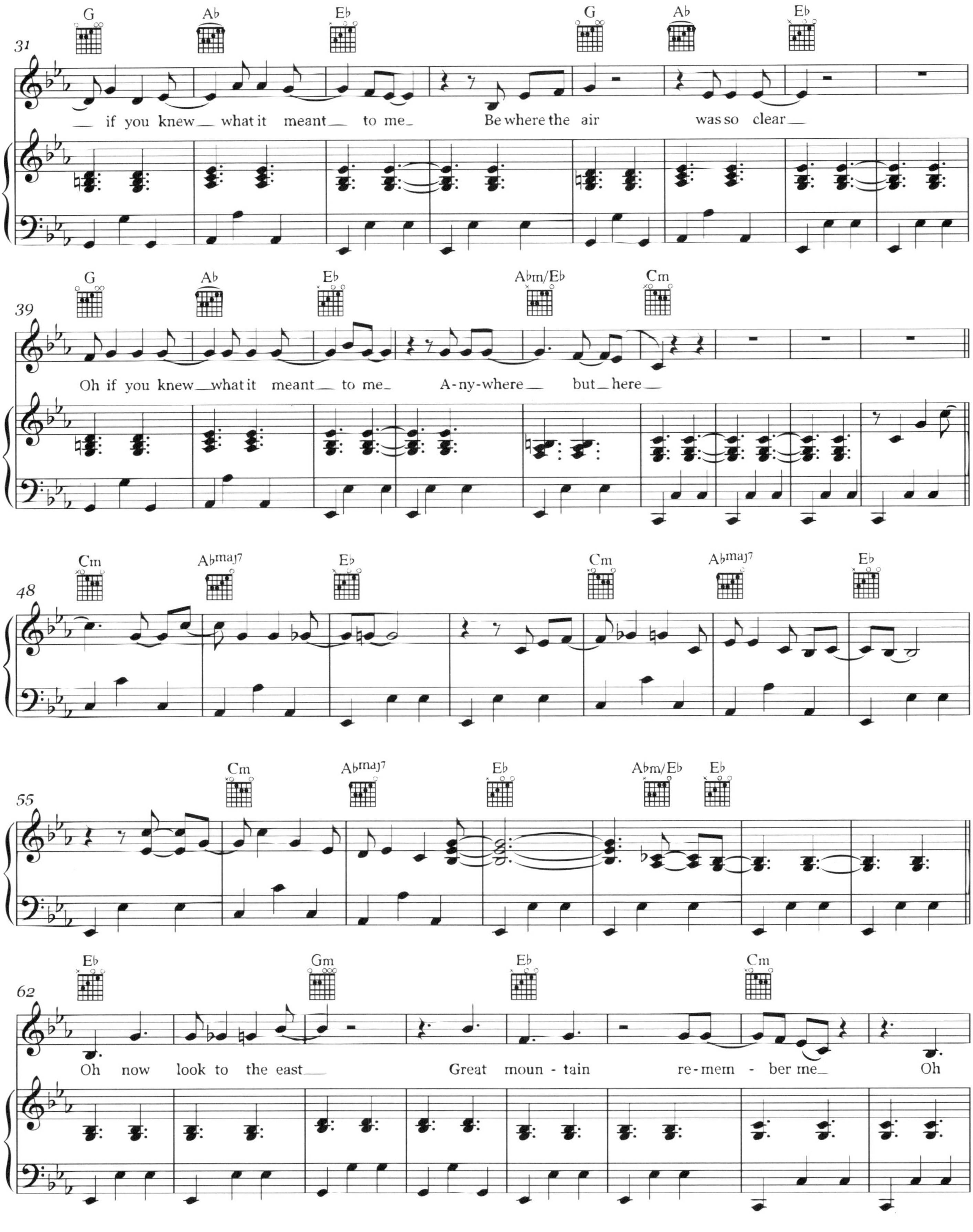
G Ab Eb G Ab Eb
if you knew what it meant to me
Be where the air was so clear
G Ab Eb Abm/Eb Cm
Oh if you knew what it meant to me
A-ny-where but here
Cm Abmaj7 Eb Cm Abmaj7 Eb
Cm Abmaj7 Eb Abm/Eb Eb
Eb Gm Eb Cm
Oh now look to the east
Great moun-tain
re-mem-ber me
Oh

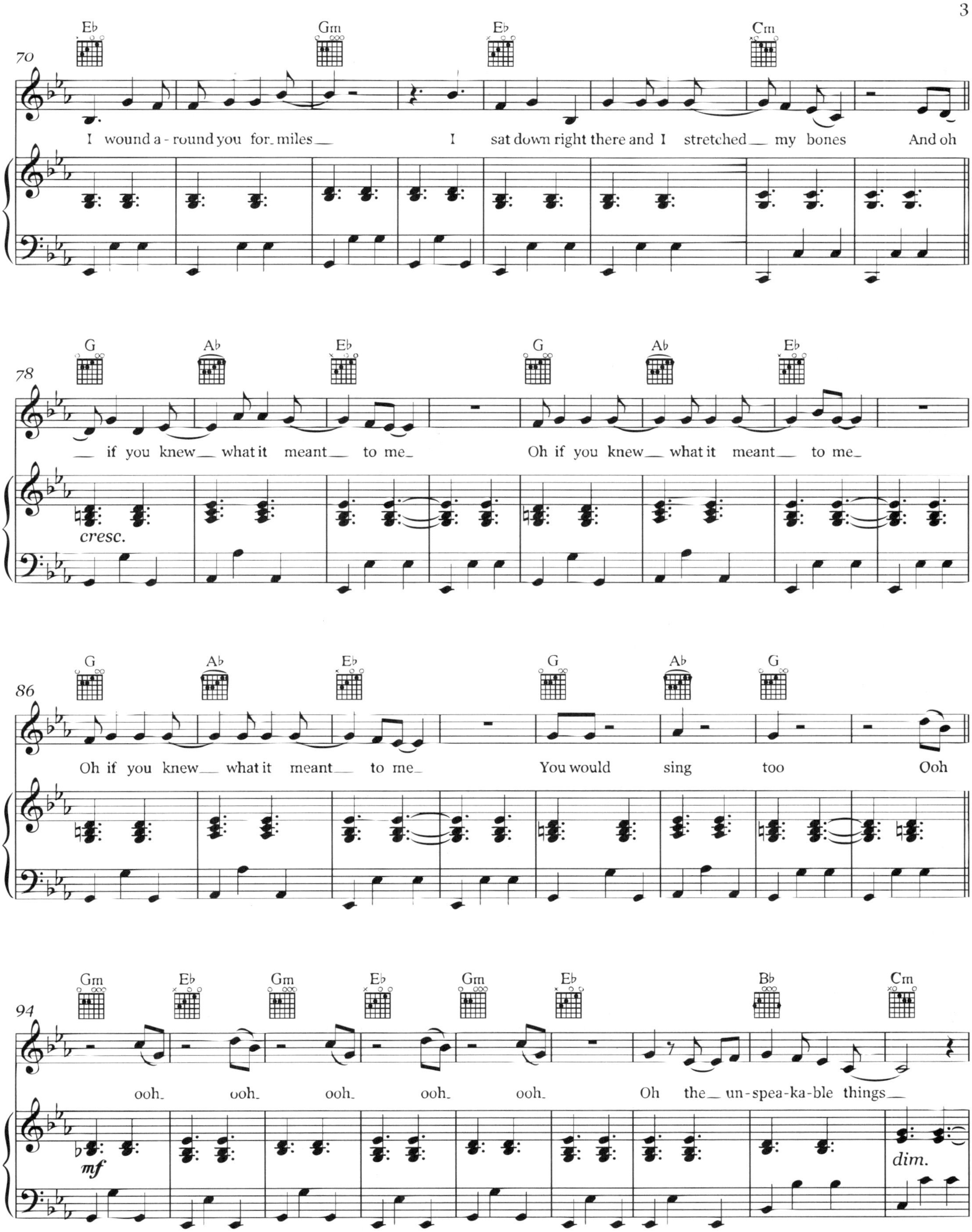
70
Eb Gm Eb Cm
I wound a - round you for miles I sat down right there and I stretched my bones And oh
78
G Ab Eb G Ab Eb
if you knew what it meant to me Oh if you knew what it meant to me
cresc.
86
G Ab Eb G Ab G
Oh if you knew what it meant to me You would sing too Ooh
94
Gm Eb Gm Eb Gm Eb Bb Cm
ooh ooh ooh ooh ooh Oh the un-spea-ka-ble things
mf
dim.

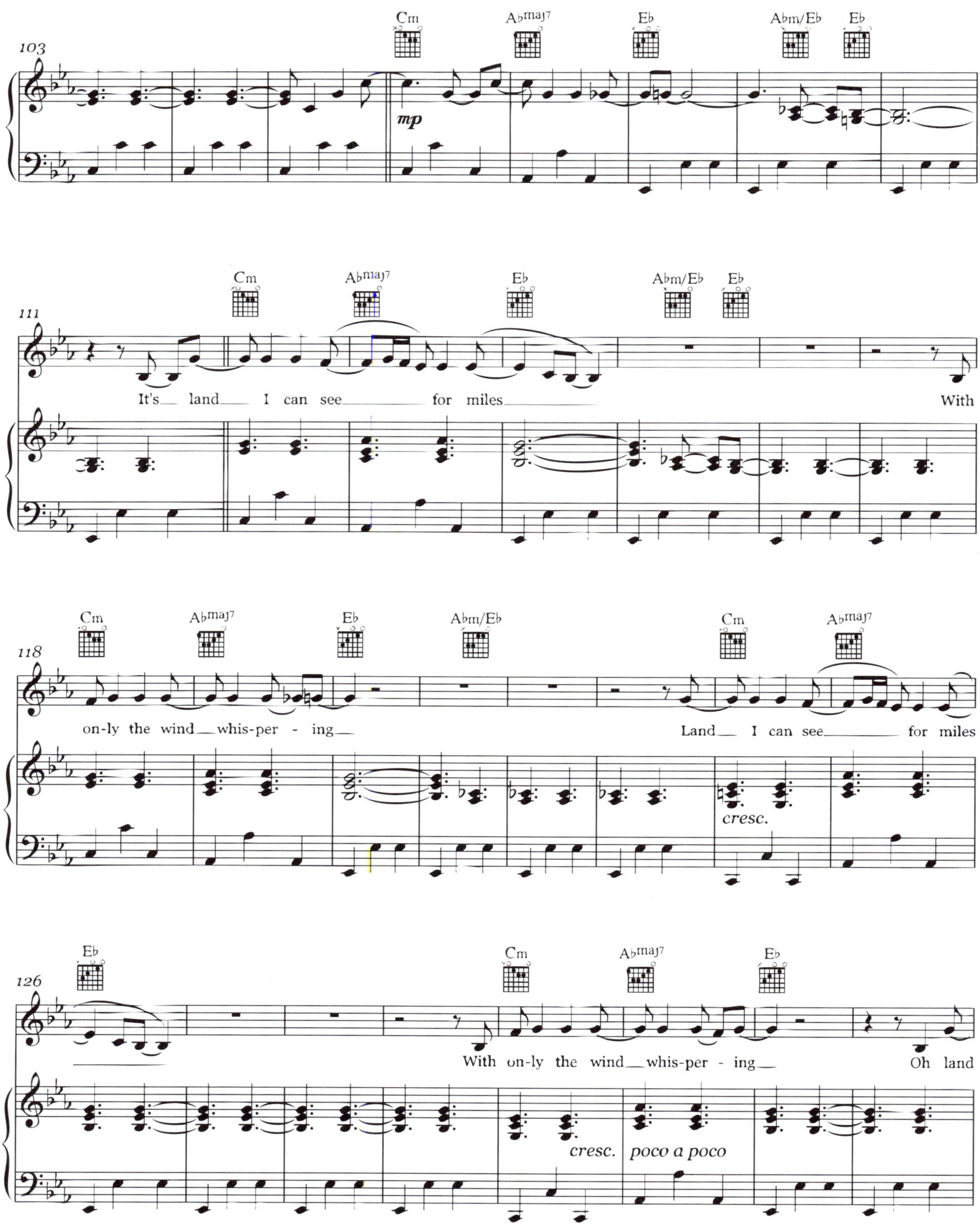
103
Cm
A♭maj7
E♭
A♭m/E♭
E♭
mp
111
Cm
A♭maj7
E♭
A♭m/E♭
E♭
It's land I can see for miles
With
118
Cm
A♭maj7
E♭
A♭m/E♭
Cm
A♭maj7
on-ly the wind whis-per - ing
Land I can see for miles
cresc.
126
E♭
Cm
A♭maj7
E♭
With on-ly the wind whis-per - ing
Oh land
cresc.
poco a poco

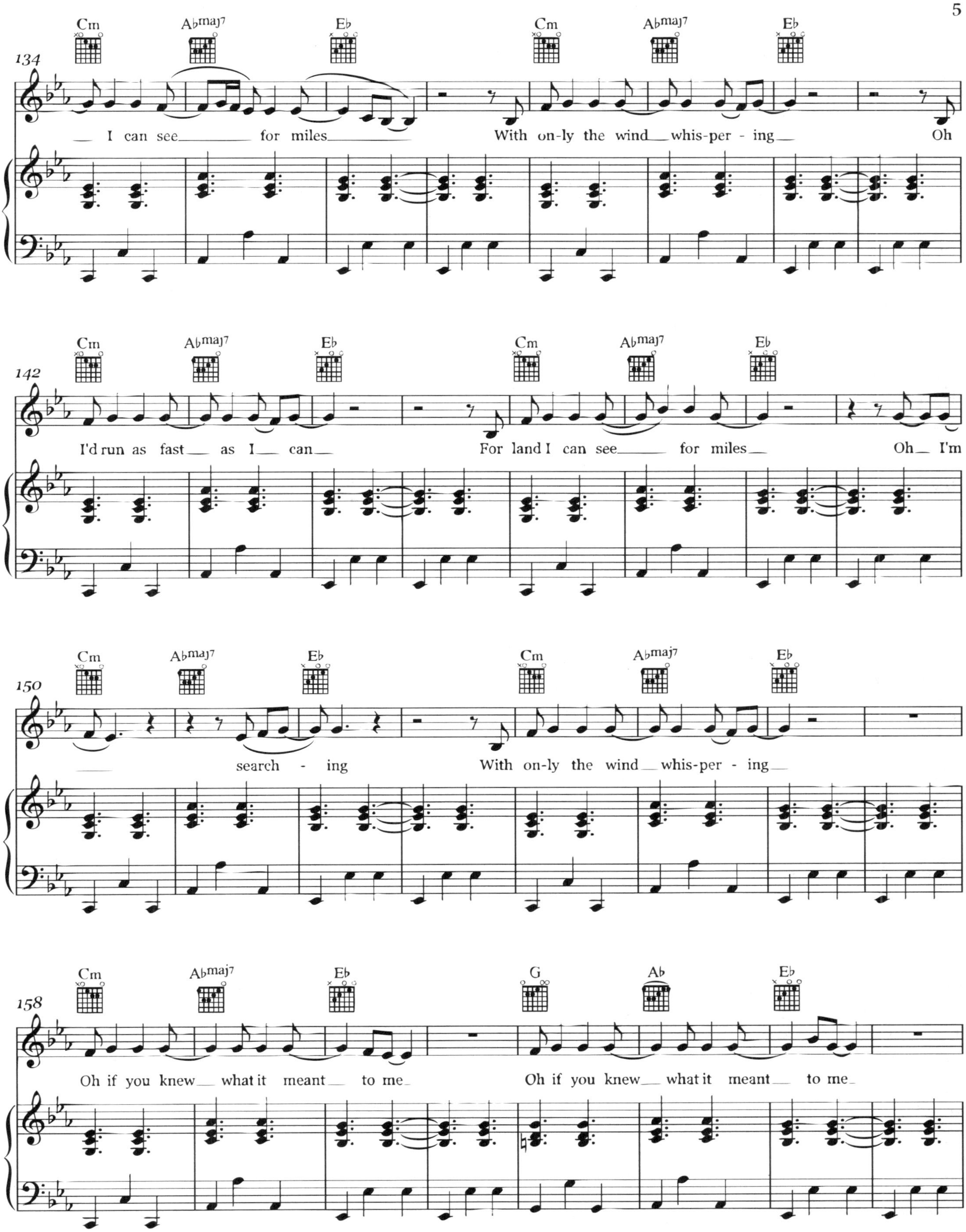
Cm Abmaj7 Eb Cm Abmaj7 Eb
134
I can see for miles With on-ly the wind whis-per-ing Oh
Cm Abmaj7 Eb Cm Abmaj7 Eb
142
I'd run as fast as I can For land I can see for miles Oh I'm
Cm Abmaj7 Eb Cm Abmaj7 Eb
150
search - ing With on-ly the wind whis-per - ing
Cm Abmaj7 Eb G Ab Eb
158
Oh if you knew what it meant to me Oh if you knew what it meant to me

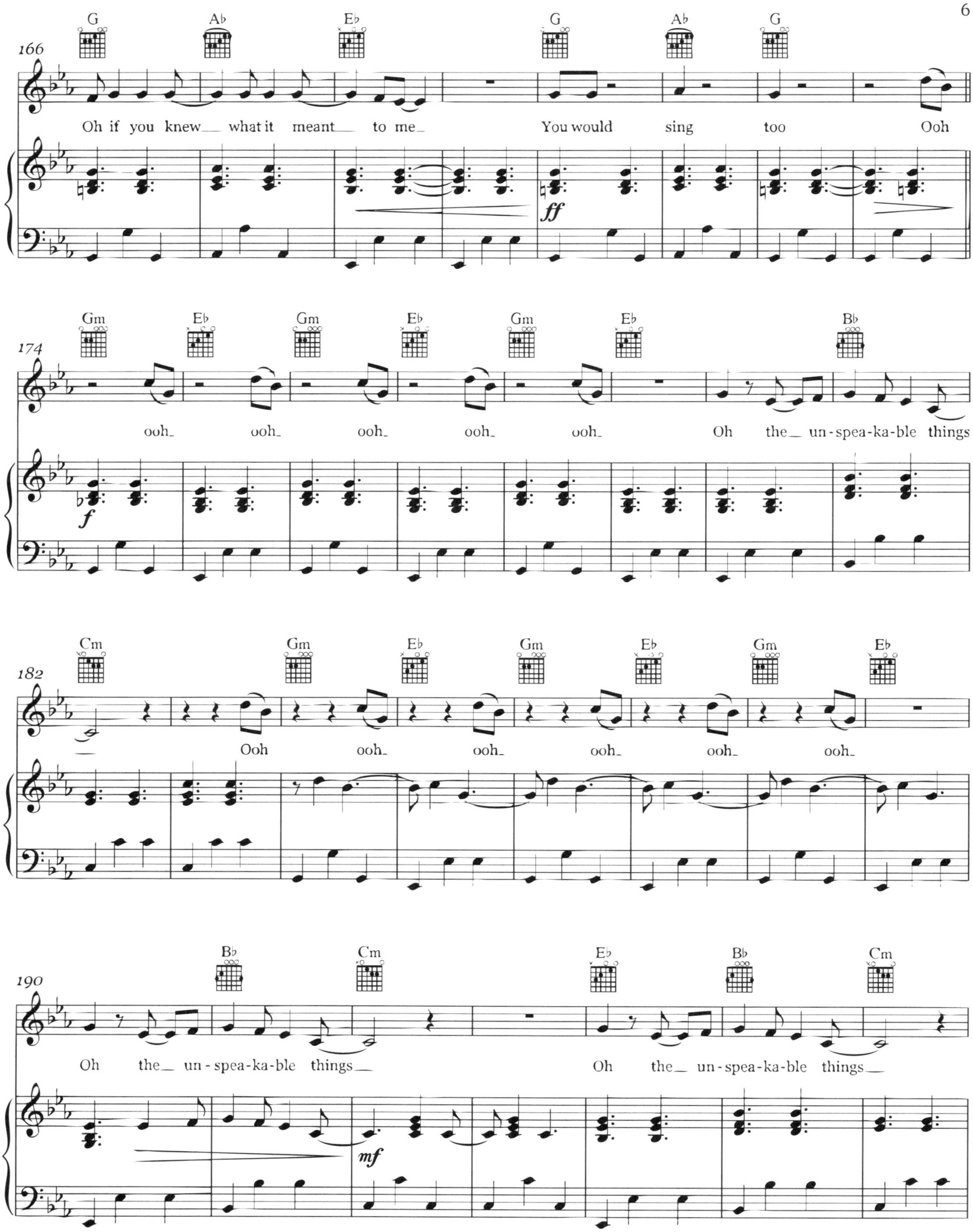
166
G Ab Eb G Ab G
Oh if you knew what it meant to me You would sing too Ooh
ff
174
Gm Eb Gm Eb Gm Eb Bb
ooh ooh ooh ooh ooh Oh the un-spea-ka-ble things
f
182
Cm Gm Eb Gm Eb Gm Eb
Ooh ooh ooh ooh ooh ooh
190
Bb Cm Eb Bb Cm
Oh the un-spea-ka-ble things Oh the un-spea-ka-ble things
mf

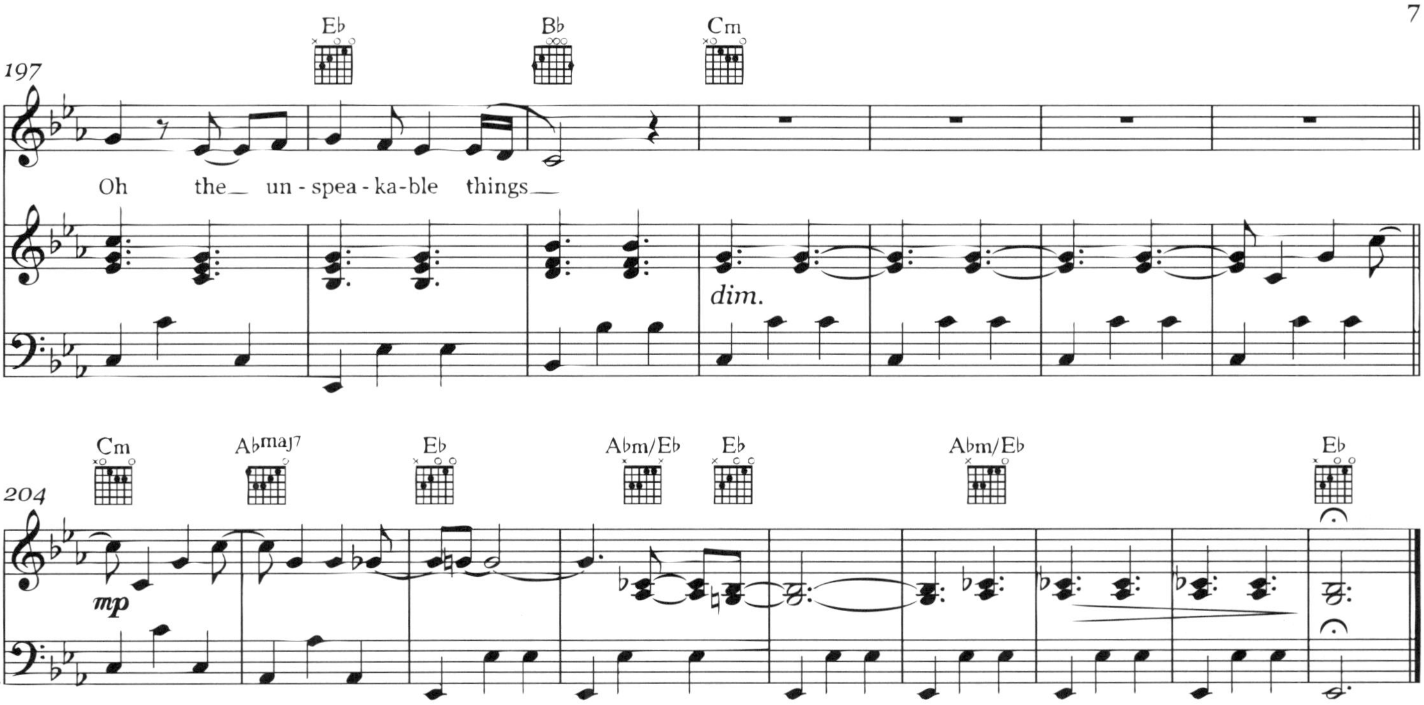
197
Eb
Bb
Cm
Oh the un-spea-ka-ble things
dim.
204
Cm
Abmaj7
Eb
Abm/Eb
Eb
Abm/Eb
Eb
mp

40
Daydreaming
DARK DARK DARK

ENDING LEAD TO DREAM HOUSE

BY DEAFHEAVEN

w/ delay

```
e
b 15
g     14 12 11   | x2
d
a
D
```

```
e
b 15
g     14 12 11 9 11 12 11   | x3
d
a
D
```

```
e
b 15          17          19               20        19                20        19
g     14 12 11    14 12 11    14 12 11 9 11     11       14 12 11 9 11     11       14 12 11 9 11 12 11
d
a
D
```

w/ delay,

```
e
b 15 / 15 / 14 / 15 / 15 / 15 / 15 / 15 / 15 / 15 / 15 / 15 / 14
g 12 / 11 / 11 / 12 / 14 / 16 / 18 / 19 / 18 / 16 / 14 / 12 / 12
d
a
D
```

November 2, 2013

Kerry McCoy

41
Dream House
DEAFHEAVEN

Drive

by Marissa Nadler

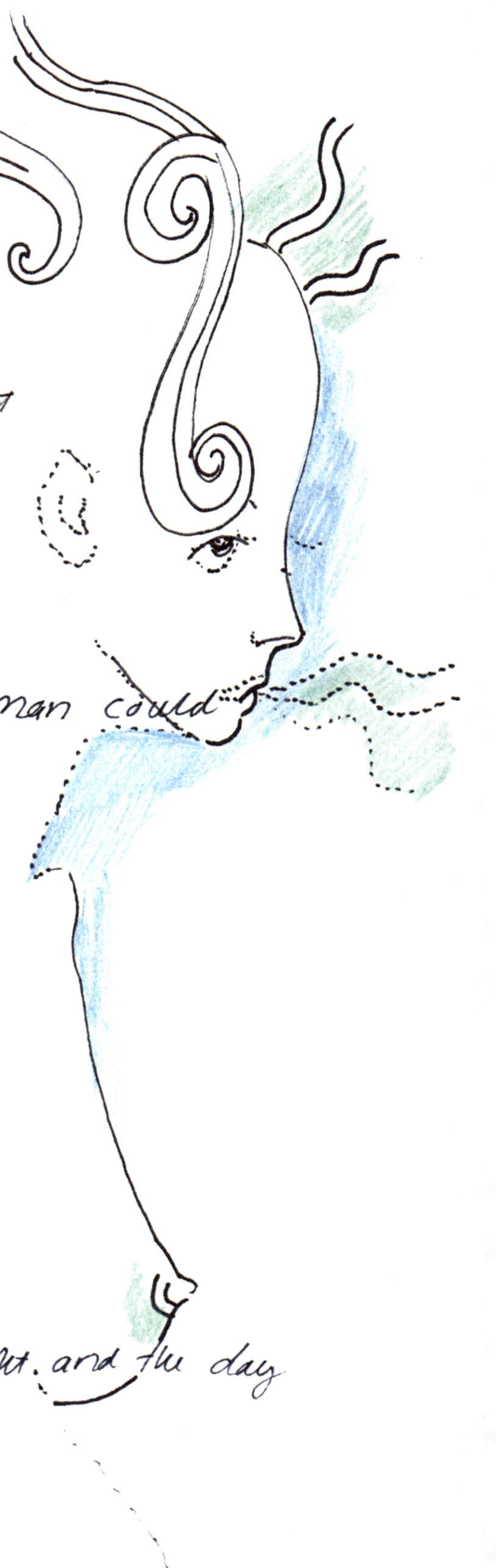

V1 If you ain't made it now
you're never gonna make it
seventeen people in the dark tonight
you see some familiar faces
behind the cellular lights

V1 Chi-town in the winter
then we saw the Hollywood sign
you used to drink more than your man could
Waiting for the light
Waiting for the light
Waiting for the light

ch. Nothing like the way it feels
Nothing like the way it feels
to DRIVE
Still remember all the words
to every song you ever heard
DRIVE.

V3 all the things are still in the car
let it freeze let it crack
you slept through the day and the night and the day
your never coming back
never coming back
never coming back

ch. Nothing like the way it feels
nothing like the way it feels
to drive
Still remember all the words
to every song you ever heard
DRIVE

42

Drive

MARISSA NADLER

FOR INSTRUMENT: HUMAN VOICE

DURATION: ∞

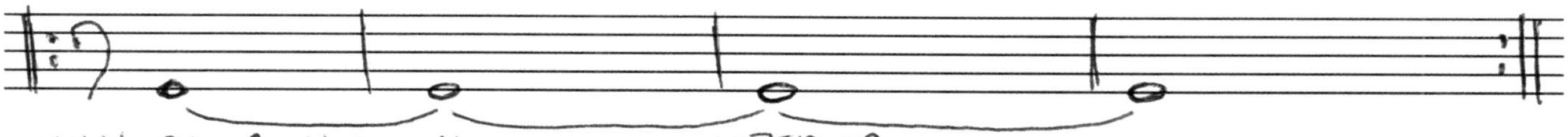

ONLY BREATHE WHEN TRULY NEEDED

TO BE PERFORMED UNAMPLIFIED

[FOREST SWORDS — 'DRONE FOR B·B·K']

TEMPO: 3 BPM

THINK OF NICE THINGS

ONLY POSITIVE VIBRATIONS

CAN BE PERFORMED ASLEEP

NOT TO BE SHARED BETWEEN FRIENDS

EATING AND DRINKING PERMITTED

ENJOY YOURSELF

43
Drone for B.B.K.
FOREST SWORDS

E

echoed arpeggios to bonn beach

feldermelder

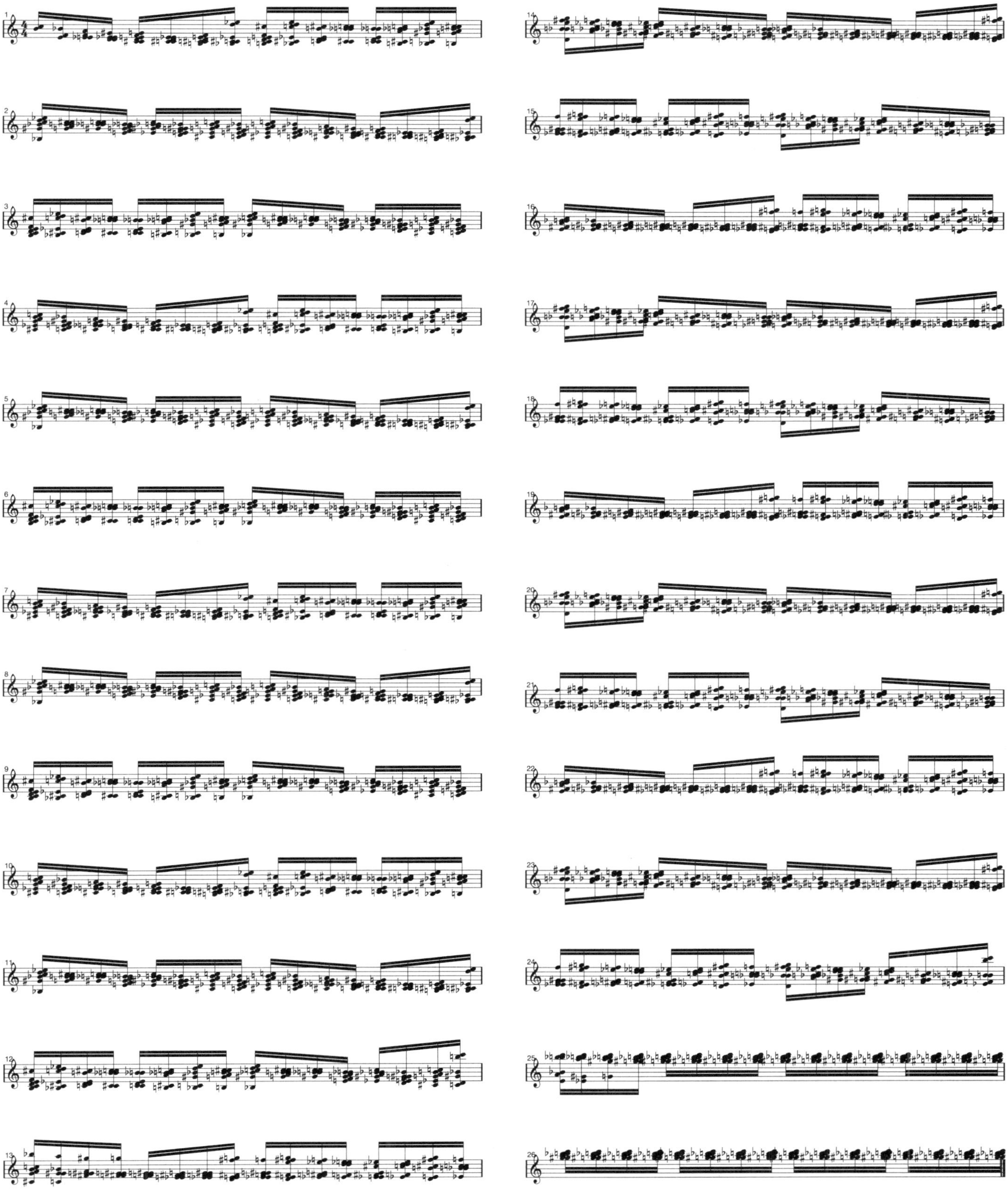

44
Echoed Arpeggios to Bonn Beach
FELDERMELDER

3-12-08 EYES FOR EARS (mini) ---entitled Emma

Dear Suzanne, Thank you so much for asking me to create a
special Eyes for Ears production for the Issue Project. I will
finally be able to do it! I will bring my group Evangelista into
the project. Evangelista has a revolving cast of characters. In
this case Tara Barnes, Dominic Cramp, Lisa Gamble, Shahzad Ismaily, Andrea
Serrapiglio and maybe more. Eyes for Ears is a project that takes place
among the audience. It is dependent on unique architectural characteristics
and I think your unusual sound system will be amazing. We'd like to
incorporate more live MAX patch interaction. I hope your engineer who
I've heard is a wizard, can work with us closely on that. I'm a little
opinionated to work with and yet highly interested in incorporating
things you love about the space into the "story". I hope that gets well
with your invitation. Here is our plan preceded by some questions
for you:

We really want to understand about the lights--- various questions---
for instance can there be a period of complete darkness? Can we get
platforms that move? What kind of outboard gear is available to the
sound engineer? I've lost his contact. Can I have it? We can rehearse
around noon on the 13, 14, and maybe 15? Are you available for these times
and to rehearse with us? How many mics do you have? How much money are
we making? We would like to spend a little on toys for the audience.
If you are interested in the process, here's my basic ever-changing plan:

1: We will make a print out---beautiful art with instructions for the
audience. One part of these instructions will be for people with cell
phones to call a friend who would be willing to talk on and off and hung
up on without being spoken to during the next hour. Set phone so
that the backlit stays on. Do not hold phone up, et cetera.

2. Andrea Serrapiglio's cello soundscape already in progress.

3: Audience comes in/Dominic introduces low low frequency loop loop

4: Pass out some egg shakers and small whistles

5: Do the egg thing ending til someone collects them

6: Dominic starts to cross fade back into Frozen Dress

7: Carla does Frozen dress (lamp goes on) lights will go off/ends
with slow deathing

8: Dominic field recordings. Shahzad, Gambletron, Tara
haunt the room sit or move chairs, talk quietly, talking to
yourself... scraping things, breaking empty easter eggs slowly
in their paws... it's still dark except for cell phone lights
going on and off

9: Shahzad starts to play a melodic tune on guitar/keyboards/both a
very lazy melody... sort of happy sad slowly getting weird,
walking, moving slowly from place to place in the room\
Tara stands on platform, stays straight plays a riff to the
little song \ Dominic and Gamble stand on platforms,
play keyboards and percussion--- Someone (Steve) manipulates
this in MAX\ Car sings on the little song, Emma walking
around the room

Song ends. Room goes almost black for a solid minute. We are
silent. Since the song itself is ridiculous I expect something strange...
After that the audience is cued to call someone on their cell
phone... on SPEAKERPHONE and ask them to tell something---we
haven't decided what yet but something specific. Pass a few
mics around. We drone very quietly, humming. Lights go completely
off. Glow from cell phones--- people on speaker phone are
humming the note they hear coming from my casio ---the
pitch of Emma. Mic these phones. MAX patch ~~for phone~~
the phone thing? Transitioning into us carrying mics
around the room recording breathing and whispers from the
audience as live samples being manipulated in MAX into an odd din
We perform Frozen Dress-- it's a seething dark layering
of terror and harmony improv. Tara's bass super dark and also
a lot of low end/crackle. Darkness adds so much reverb
using the Issue project speakers to make a seasick
feeling single note drone of end that finally. We do
something small and pretty with audience singing... the
simple words of Emma prominently displayed... revisit
Shahzad's theme/melody/song at the end here really like very
not New York. Really simple, happy song. The whole
thing... Eyes for Ears--- ends with just morphing into a
different, more delicate form and the lights dimming
while we continue all singing as dissonance sets innnnnn

45

Emma

EVANGELISTA

That's it. I'm really happy with this. The song was super fun to write in Shahzad's cement floor and evry thing else fell around it.

She could crawl under the table and shake
I could crawl inside of there into her hair
I'd just breathe and breathe and breathe
Shivering in thunder she won't go out in the rain
and barks all day
She takes me under with the neverending sounds
of sadness scared of loud sounds scared of sky
cracking in a monkey eye
Oh, Emma, why you gotta be this way
why can't you come out and play?
It's only rainrair
rainrain rain

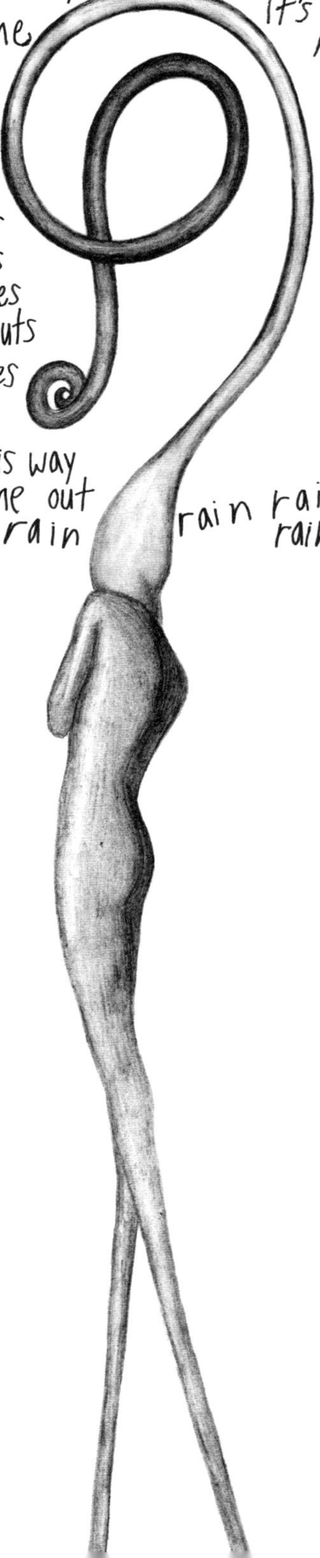

Banging in the
belfry. furry ear
that can't quite
hear no more
but somehow it
Smells like ginger
snaps thunder claps
she cries and cries
the lightning shuts
her half blind eyes
Oh, Emma, why
you gotta be this way
Why can't you come out
and play it's only rain
rain rainrain rain
rain x2

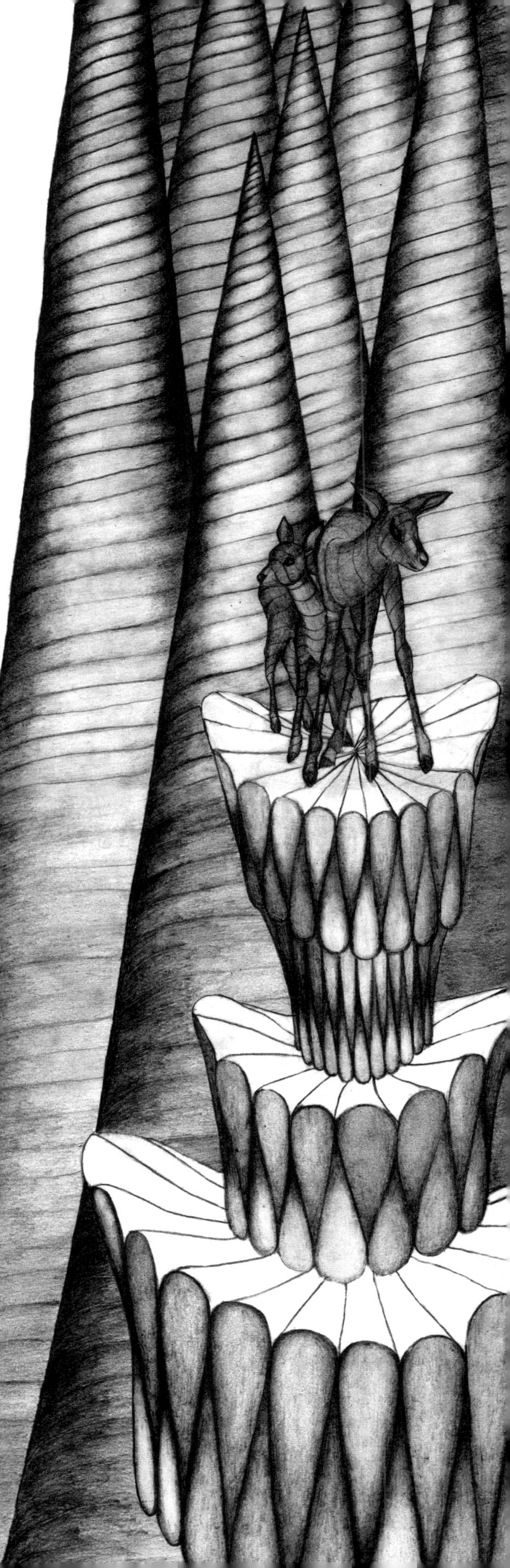

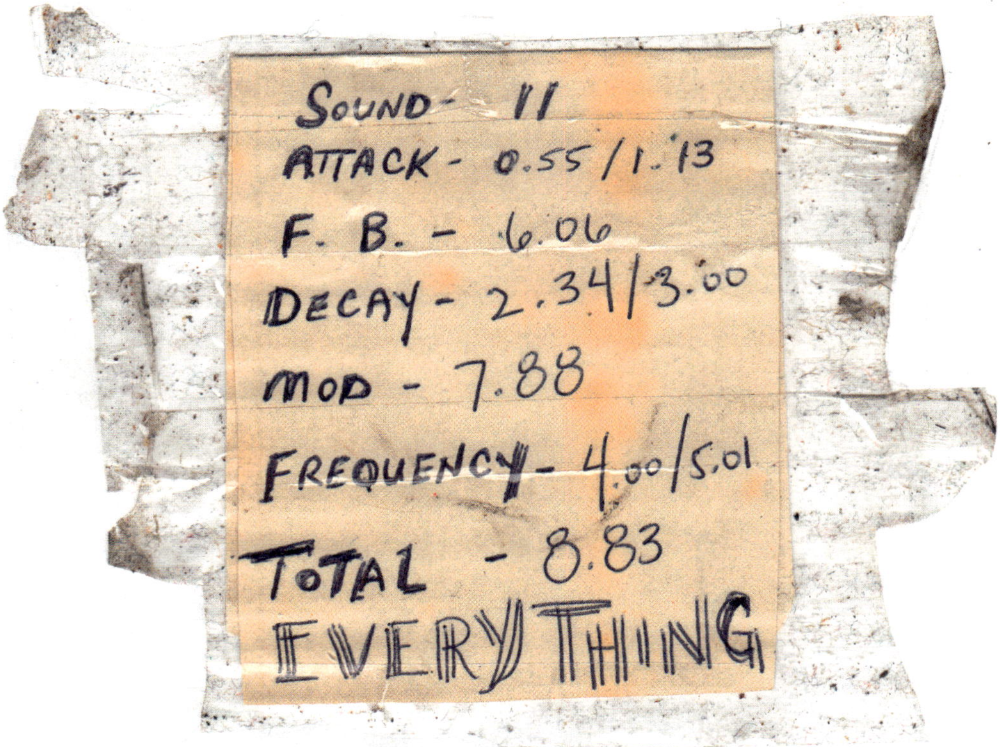

SOUND - 11
ATTACK - 0.55/1.13
F. B. - 6.06
DECAY - 2.34/3.00
MOD - 7.88
FREQUENCY - 4.00/5.01
TOTAL - 8.83
EVERYTHING

When we first discovered
This sound, We took note
on a little page and taped
it to the keyboard
in order to get
the sound again.
This (above),
is that page.

The song is: EVERYTHING CHANGES
The band is: WE ARE THE CITY.

46

Everything Changes

WE ARE THE CITY

F

Far too Witchy

Diane Cluck

People say she's far too witchy
Growin' a bean vine, stringin' a clothesline
I wonder who's she? Go have a look-see
Sunnin' her behind out in the sunshine

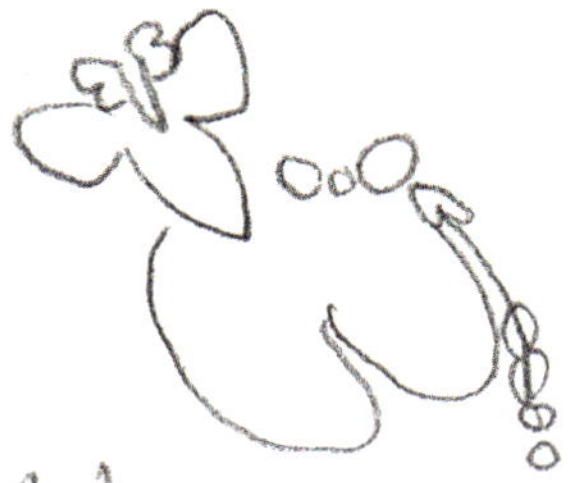

She grows MAD HAIR; no man goes there—
Well, I saw one go; he didn't come back though!
Oh, she don't need them? Maybe she eat them?
What's with these folks' gossip & mean jokes...

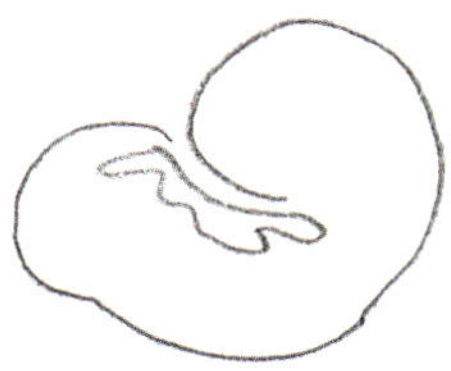

She gonna getcha, better run right by
Her kind are no good and at night they fly
I seen her dancin' under big dark sky
When there's a bright moon, she wails her tune
I seen her sweepin' with her riding broom

People say she's far too witchy
Knobby knees and hanky sneezes
I wonder who's she? Go have a look-see
Talkin' to trees & sniffin' at breezes

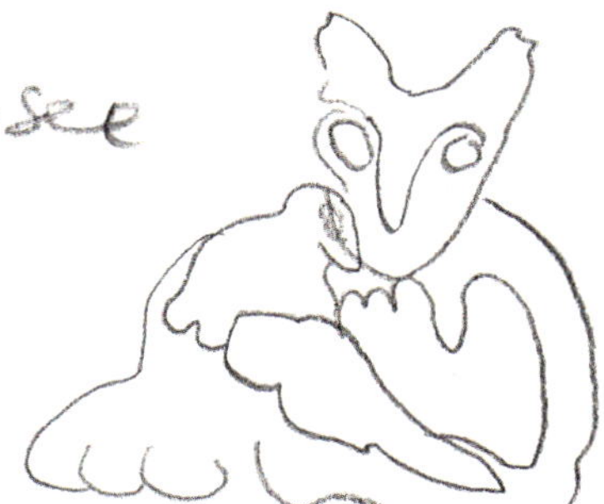

She got no phone; she lives alone—
Rich & crazy or poor & lazy?
She's kickin' a stone; she's pickin' a bone—
What's with her, y'all? Sticks in my craw!
She got no car: that witch fly far—
She takes the bus, don't make a fuss
She's a renter; I wonder who sent her?
Wasn't me, no, she's doin' no harm, tho

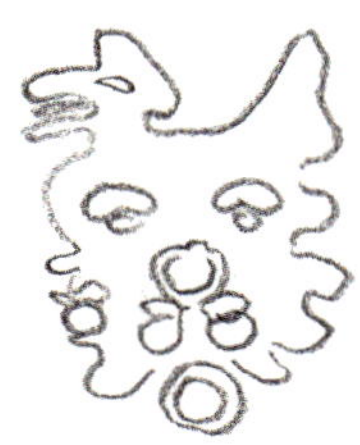

People say she's far too witchy
I wonder who's she? Go have a look-see
People say she's far too witchy
I wonder who's she? I wonder, who's she?

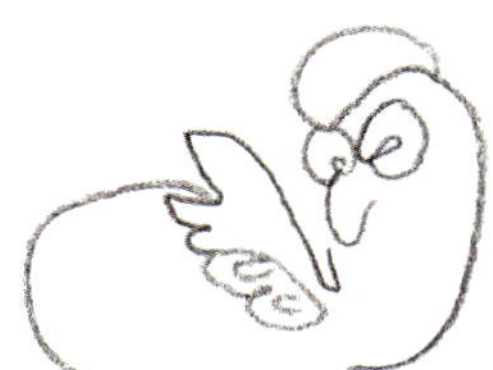

47
Far Too Witchy
DIANE CLUCK

FLOATING

DO YOU RECALL TIME BETTER SPENT
ARE YOU CONVINCED THAT YOU'RE CONTENT
I ONLY SEE YOU FLOATING

AND WHEN THE LONG WHITE COATS ARE SENT
DO YOU PRESCRIBE
DO' YOU REPENT
I ONLY SEE YOU FLOATING

GET BACK TO YOUR LOVER
GET BACK TO YOUR ART
SHOW ME YOUR DECISIVE
MAKE A START
OH I ONLY SEE YOU FLOATING

THEY NAME YOU DUMB
THEY NAME YOU MAD
THEY NAME TO NAME
ITS ALL THEY HAVE

I ONLY SEE YOU FLOATING

48

Floating

NADINE SHAH

The FRENCH REVO-LUTION

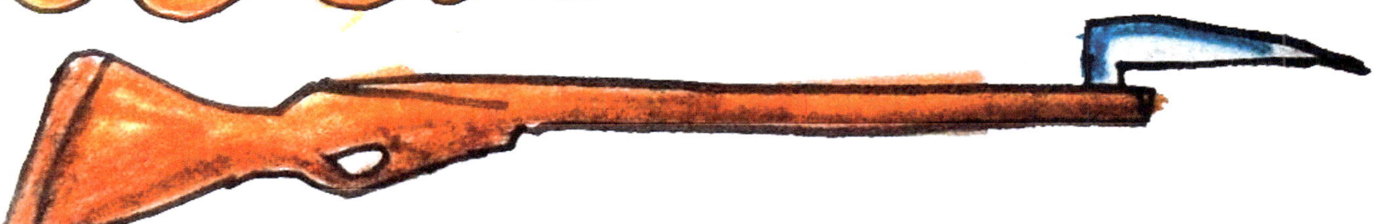

49

The French Revolution

JEFFREY LEWIS

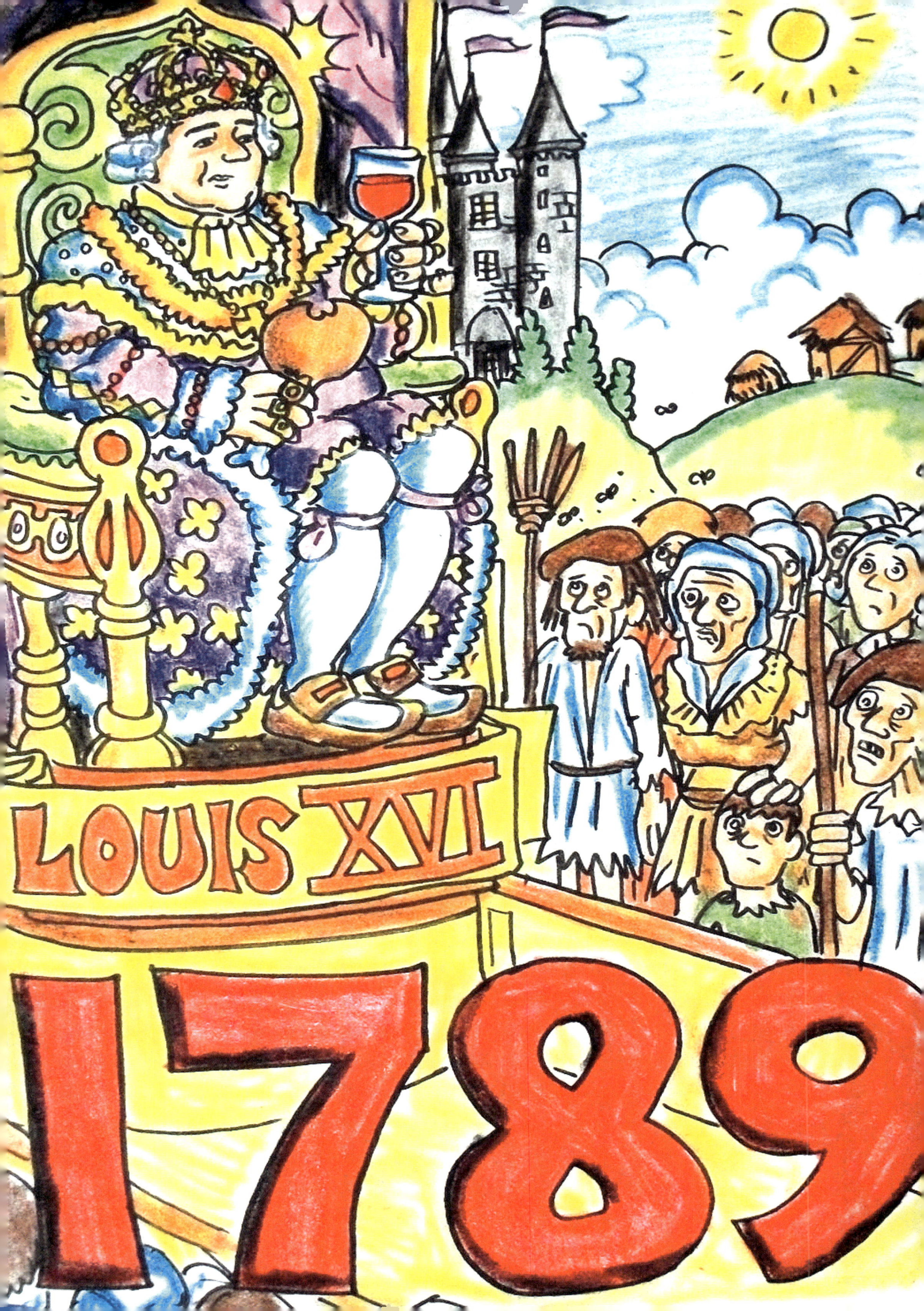
LOUIS XVI
1789

THE ENLIGHTENMENT
LIBERTÉ
ÉGALITÉ
FRATERNITE
VOLTAIRE
LOCKE
LOCKE
KANT
ROUSSEAU

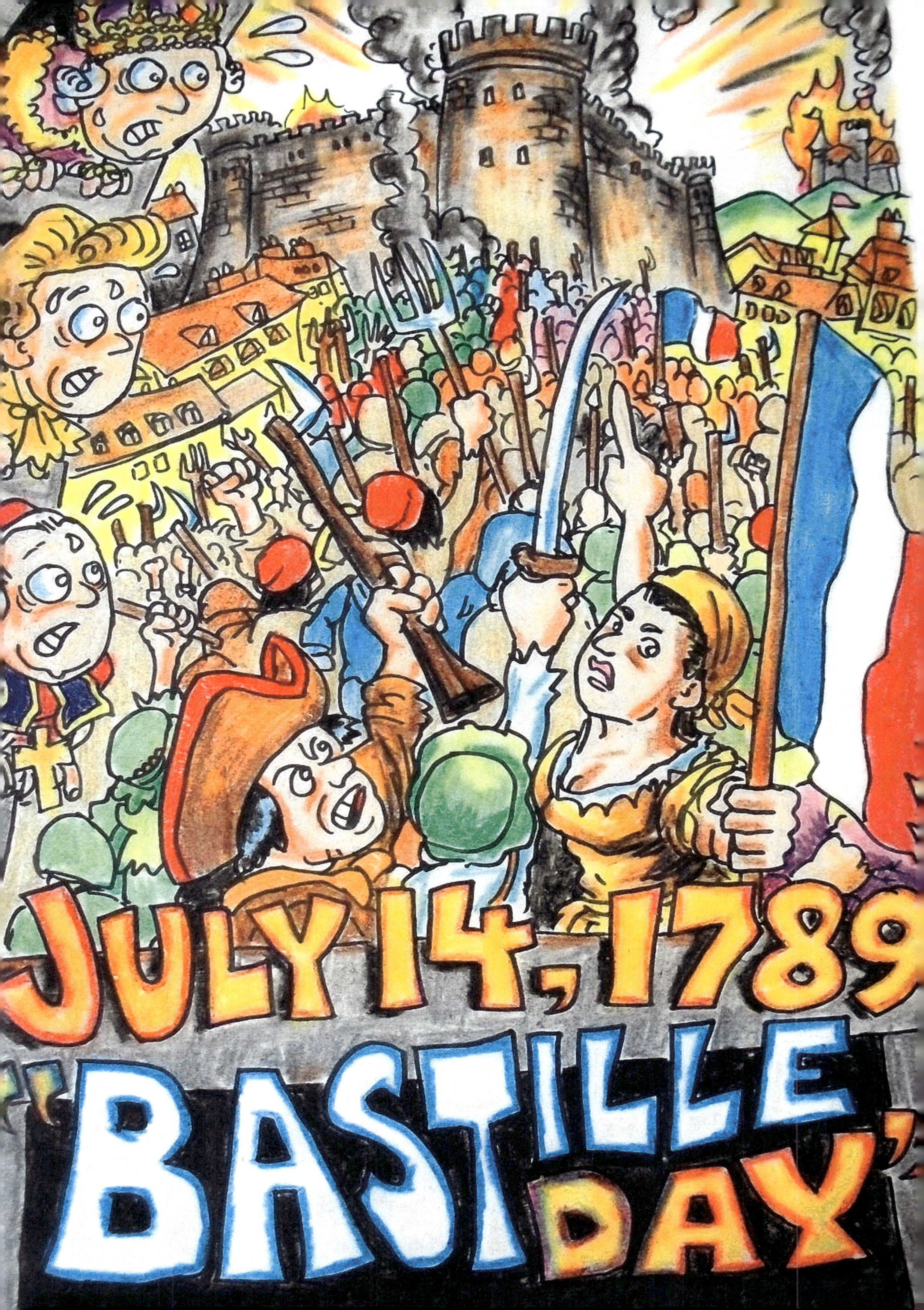
JULY 14, 1789
"BASTILLE DAY"

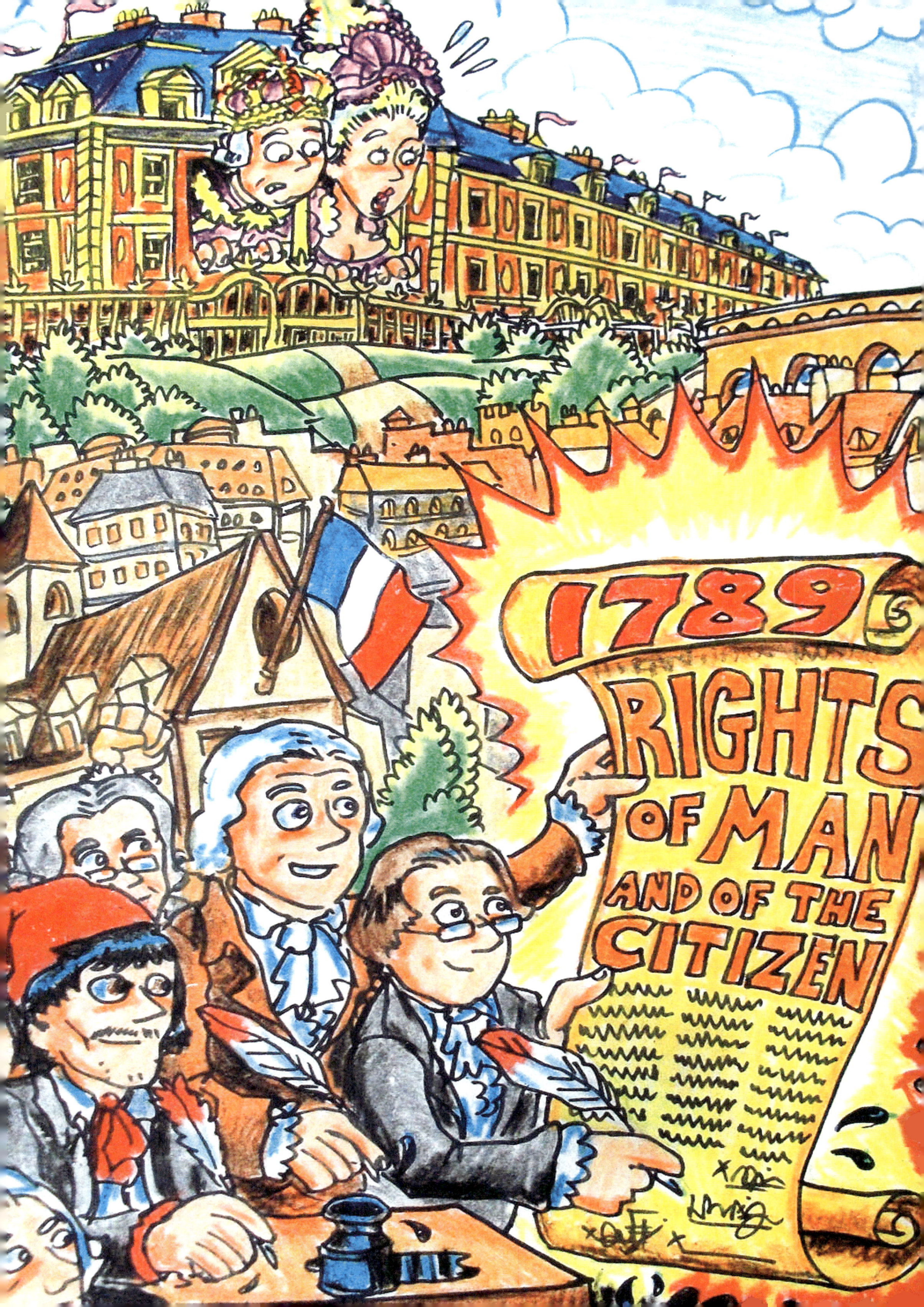
1789
RIGHTS OF MAN AND OF THE CITIZEN

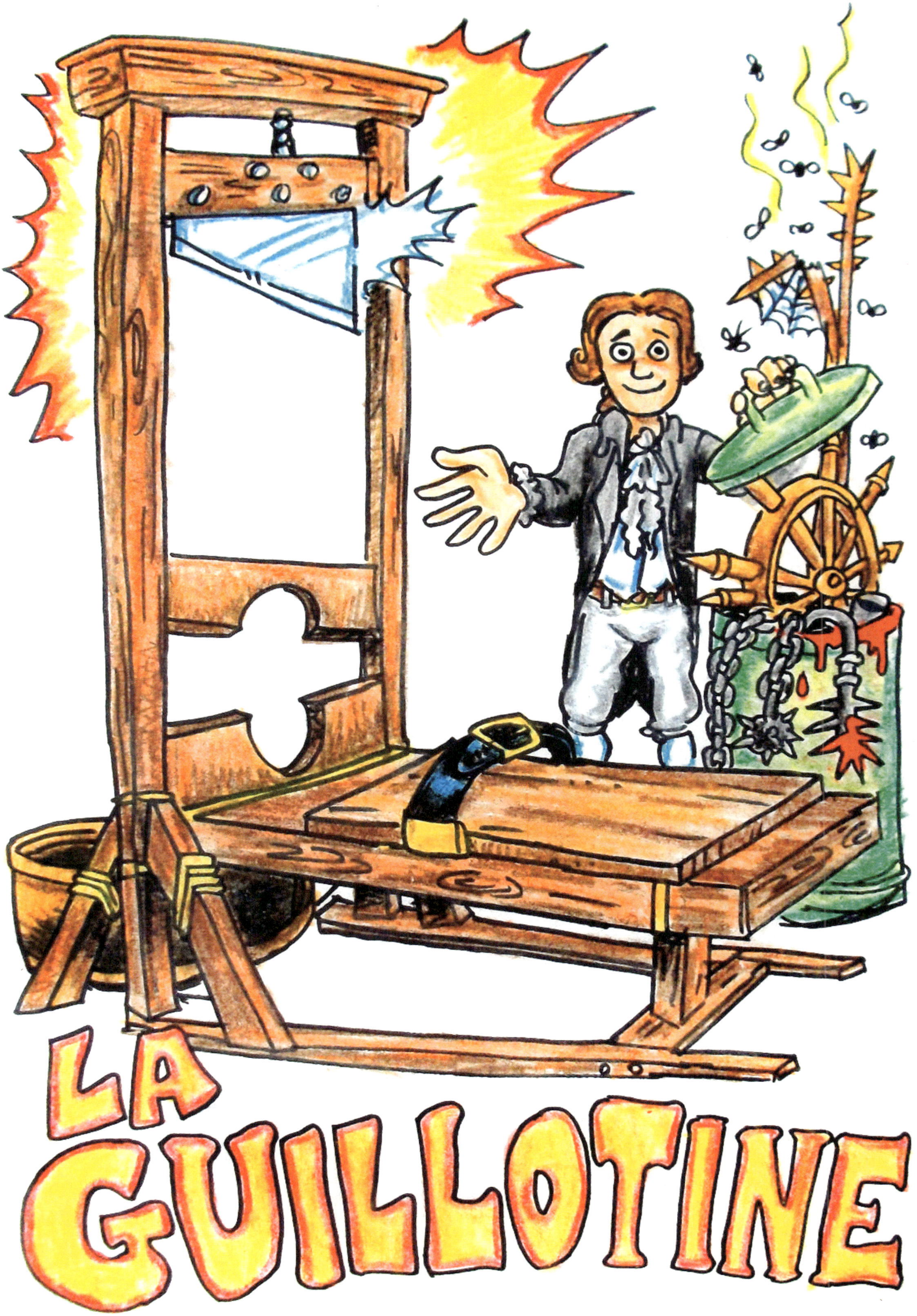
LA
GUILLOTINE

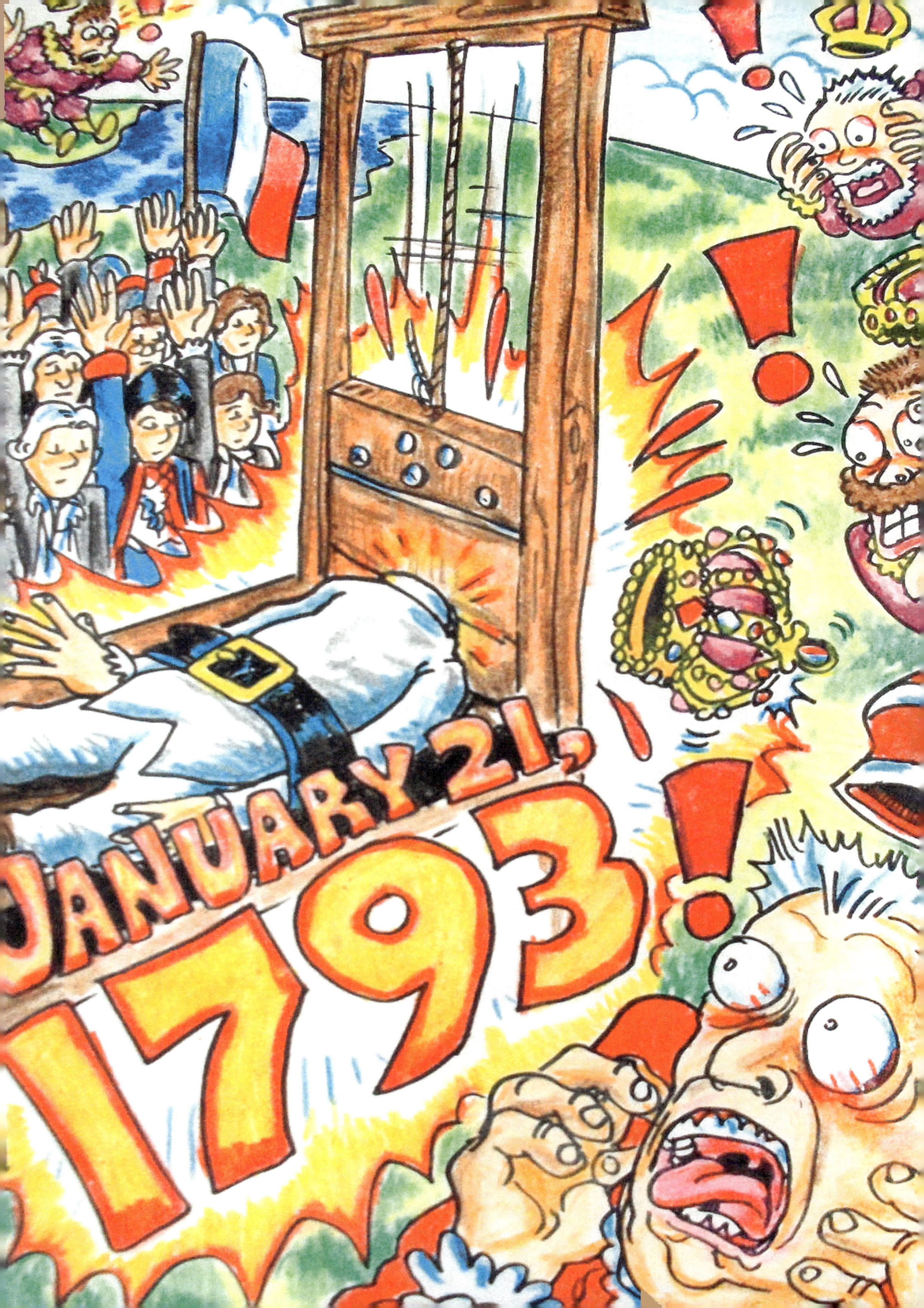
JANUARY 21, 1793!

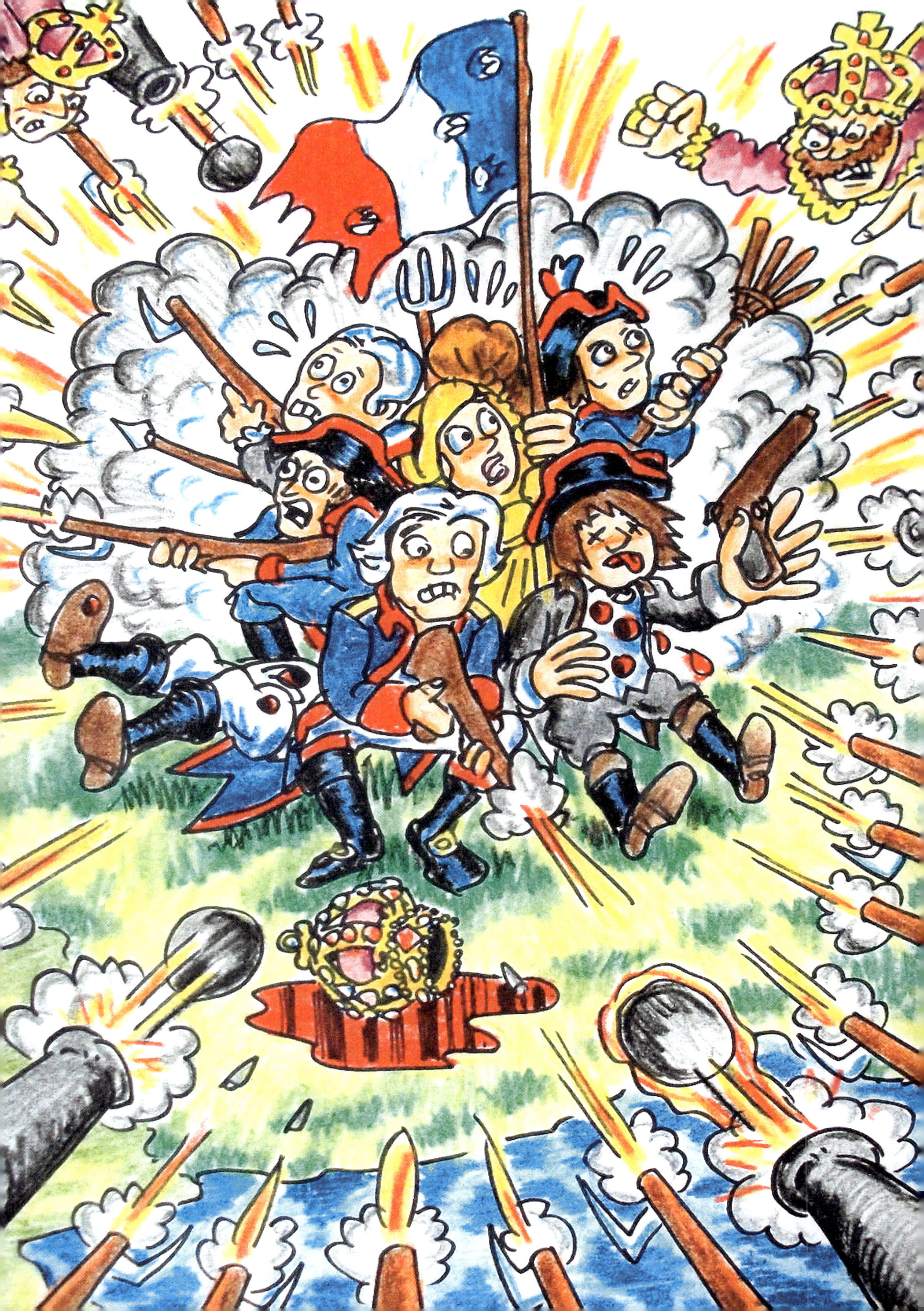

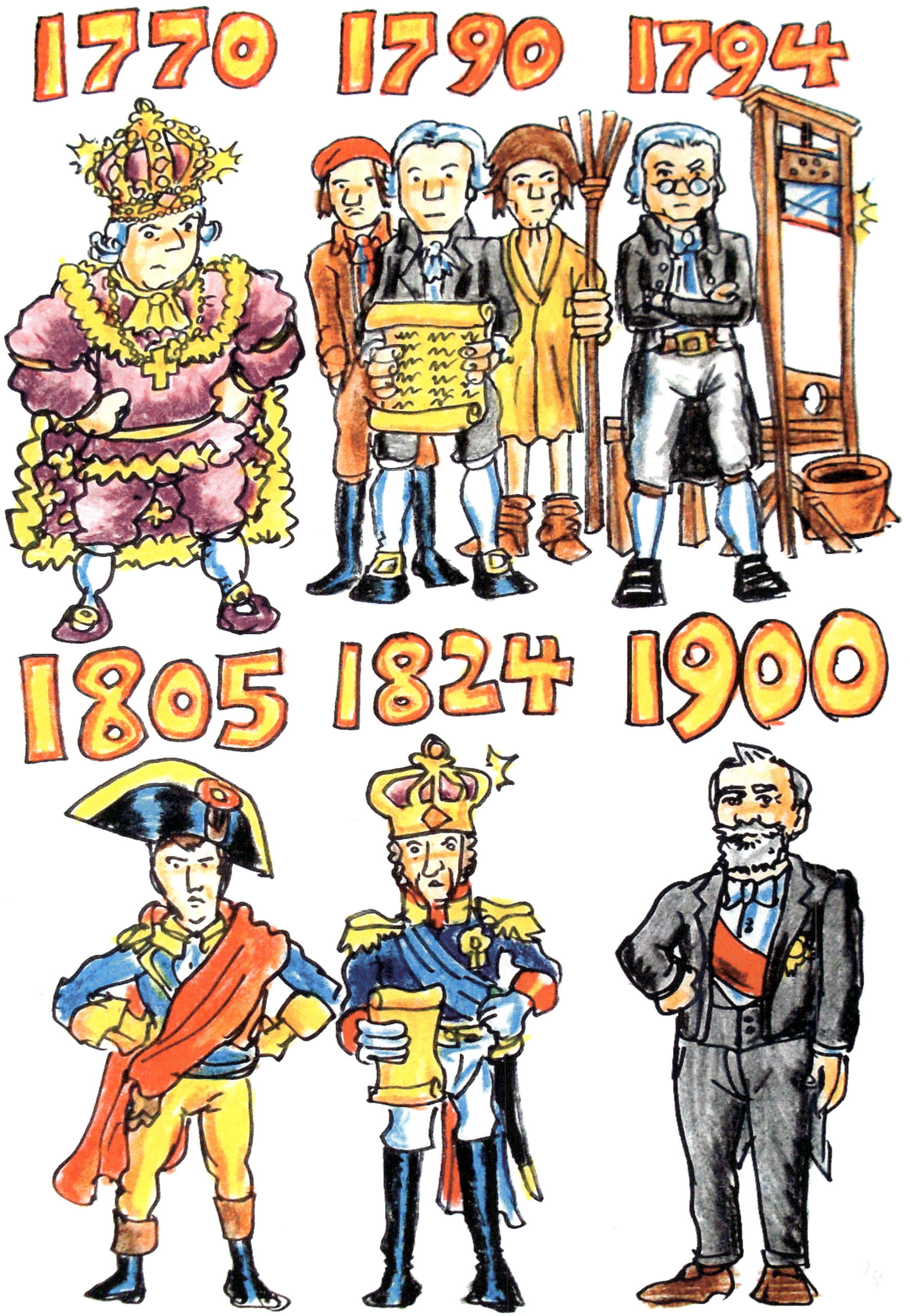
1770
1790
1794
1805
1824
1900

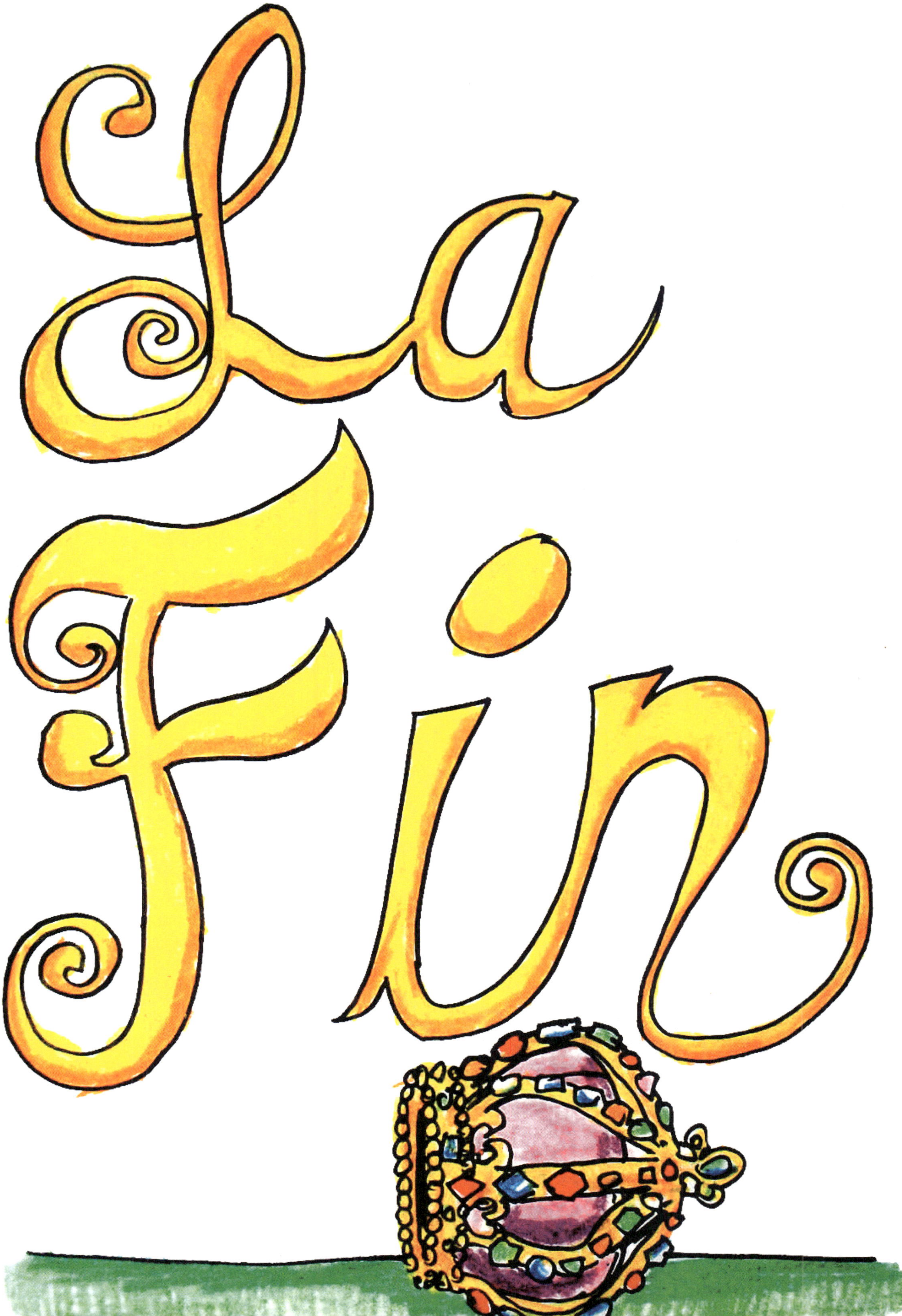
La Fin

Friends and Foes

G C
There's a family that prays
G Bmin
'Cause we've turned out this way

G C
and a sickly sect condones
G Bmin
they say that I've turned out wrong

G C
and they twist and they turn
G Bmin
The truth that we have learned
G D G
in the darkest of oceans there's light

La La La La
La La La La.

G C
And to all my friends and foes
G Bmin
Simply all we need to know
G C
To LOVE is to Live
G Bmin
To Receive is to give
G C
So saddle beside me
G Bmin
We'll sing and celebrate changing
G D G
from the darkest of moments to LIGHT

50

Friends and Foes

SCOTT MATTHEW

G

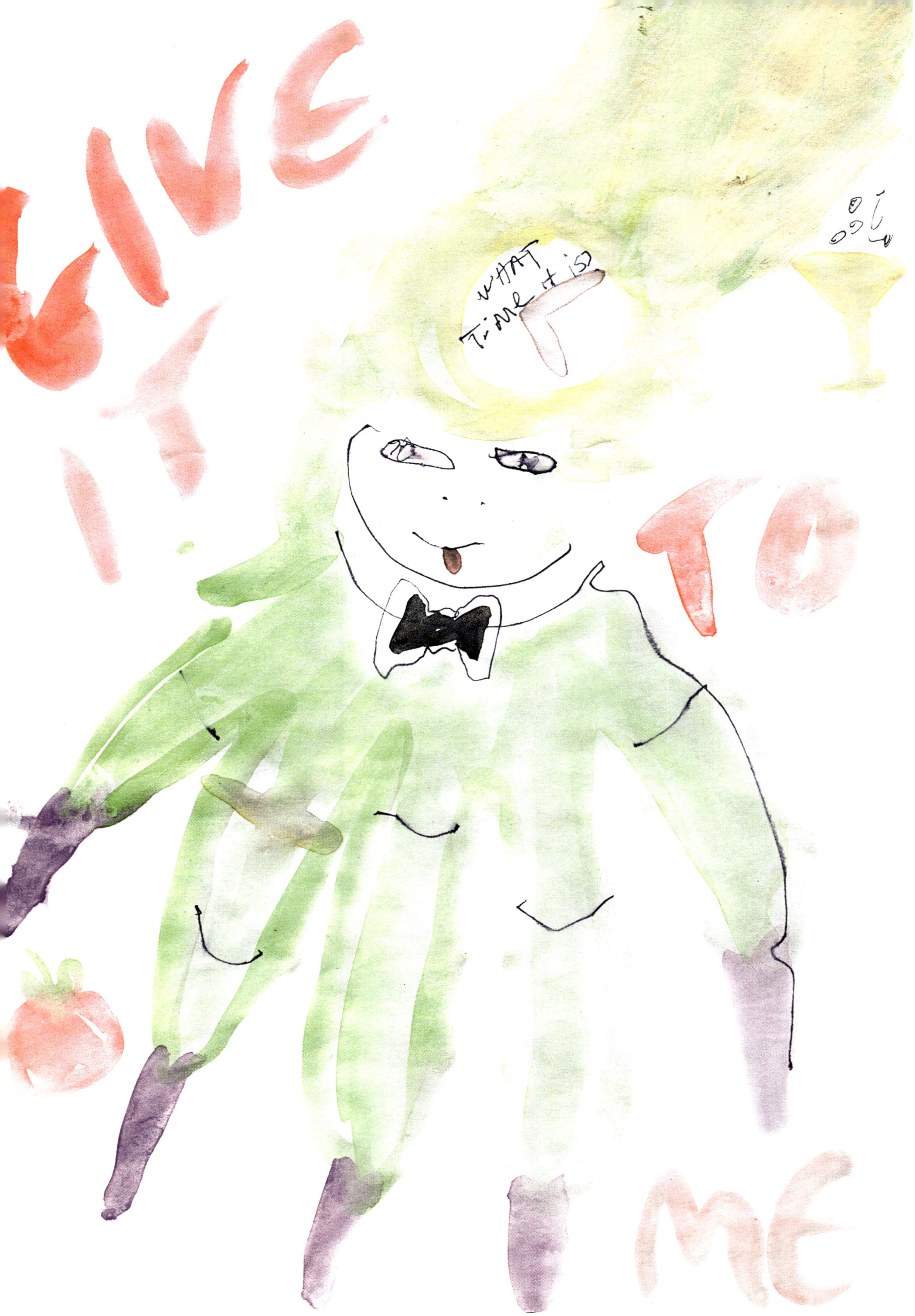
GIVE
IT
TO
ME
WHAT
TiME it is?

51

Give It to Me

BLACK BANANAS

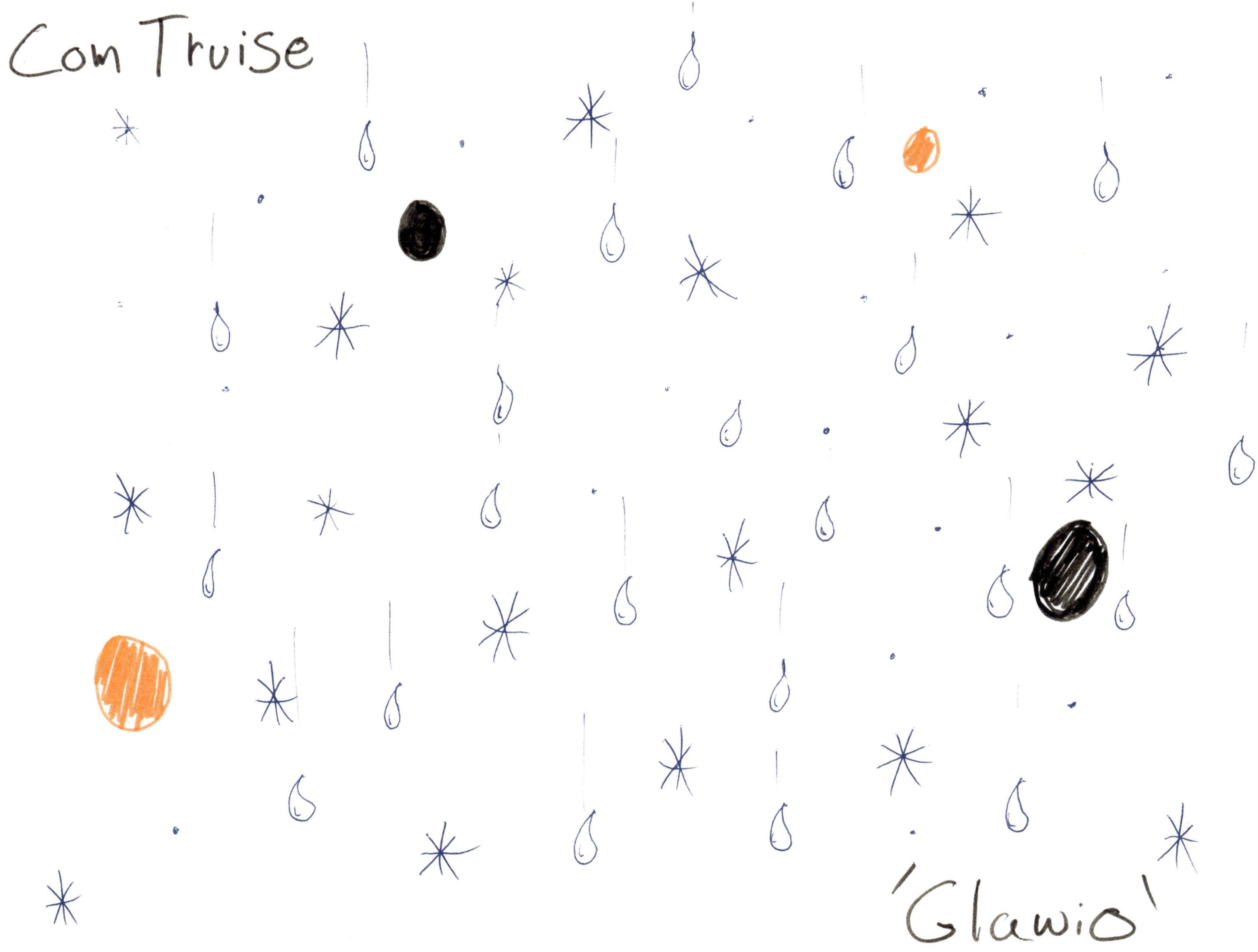
Com Truise
'Glawio'

52

Glawio

COM TRUISE

Speedy Ortiz
"The graduates"

Verse: E F C

We were the French club dropouts
But we never got excused from class
The secretary must have been high
To turn a blind eye on us sneakin' out back

Then we were pregnant on the balcony
You caught me with a cigarette
I never put the thing to my lips
Just crushed it & spit on where I laid it to rest

Chorus: B C G
D D# A#
G# F# E F A A# F

I was the best at being second place
But now I'm just the runner up
At being the second one you think of every day
Before you go back to one.

Bridge: D C A# G
Am A# G
D C F G
Am A# G

Verse:

We were the law school rejects / so we quarrelled at the bar instead / shot out in 4 words or less / you want a jail, you want a mess / you have the right to drink less // Then we were floating on a balcony / I fell into a trampoline / I never should've looked for a hand from an invisible push me pull you pushin' on me

Chorus:

I was the best at bein' second place but now I'm just the silver you dread / and only in the shape of a bullet am I ever the shape you see when you wake up dead

Bridge:

So will U cauterize the bleeding or bastardize the meaning. I'm the one worth seeing. As a waif, a friend. I guess that's the extent, more than assisted when U cut inside the paper

best at bein' second place. I was the best at bein'

I was the lighthouse's eject it out into the void!

To pressure the room

second place but now I'm just the runner up. And only the second one you think of

53

The Graduates

SPEEDY ORTIZ

GRAND CANYON

21/12/13

:: C - G - F ::

FROM THE PHEONIX LIFT OFF SOMEWHERE NEAR BLACKFOOT RESERVE
HIGH ABOVE DRUMHELLER THE SKY HOSTESS STARTS TO SERVE
CLOUD SHADOWS ON THE MOUNTAINS
AND OUR SHADOW ON THE MOUNTAINSIDE
AFTER SALT LAKE CITY I HAVE TIME TO CLOSE MY EYES
BEFORE THE GRAND CANYON SWALLOWS US AS WE MOVE SOUTH
I PRAYED THE GRAND CANYON TAKE OUR PLANE INSIDE IT'S MOUTH

:: MORRICONE LINE ::

WE KNOW THE MATERIAL IN THE PSALMS OF SERIOUS LINES
UNDER PALMS ETHEREAL IN HOLYWOOD'S MYSTERIOUS WILD
THESE ARE COARSE IMAGININGS WHERE CANNIBAL INSPECTORS LIE
ON DELIRIOUS RAMBLINGS NOW IN REAL AND TROUBLING TIMES
IN THE WARM CONFUSION OF THE LOOMING FOLIAGE OUTSIDE
THE MOTEL ROOM OBSCURA
A DIVINING BY ~~VENETIAN~~ PHOENICIAN BLINDS

:: SAXOPHONE XUAZZ ::

– BLACKSMITH –

:: MORE C - G - F ::

FOR L.F.

(HAPPY HOLIDAY BAD BONN)
XO TAYLOR

54
Grand Canyon
TIMBER TIMBRE

GREEN EYES

I don't know what to say
So I'll say nothing that's ok
Don't know what to do
So I'll stand green eyes black skin in front of you
Chariot will take me down
To the curious part of town
In the ocean I'm in motion
My eyes full of devotion

What were you like in Norway
Not you but the first one down the hallway
Open blue-eyed dull mind
Golden graceful constantly
Northern light upon my bed
From the window I descend

In the ocean it was spoken
My eyes full of devotion

55

Green Eyes

AMEN DUNES

I think about you now + then
But it's just a moment and I forget again
In fact the last time I thought of you
I was three-fourths the way into a friend
On the roof I can see you now
Still don't know what you're on about
In the ocean no emotion
That's the sound of devotion.

A.D.
10/11/14

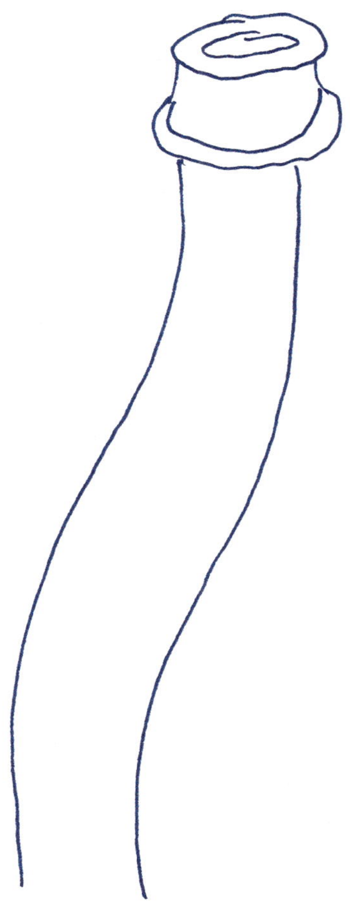

55

Guaracha U.F.O (Meridian Brothers)

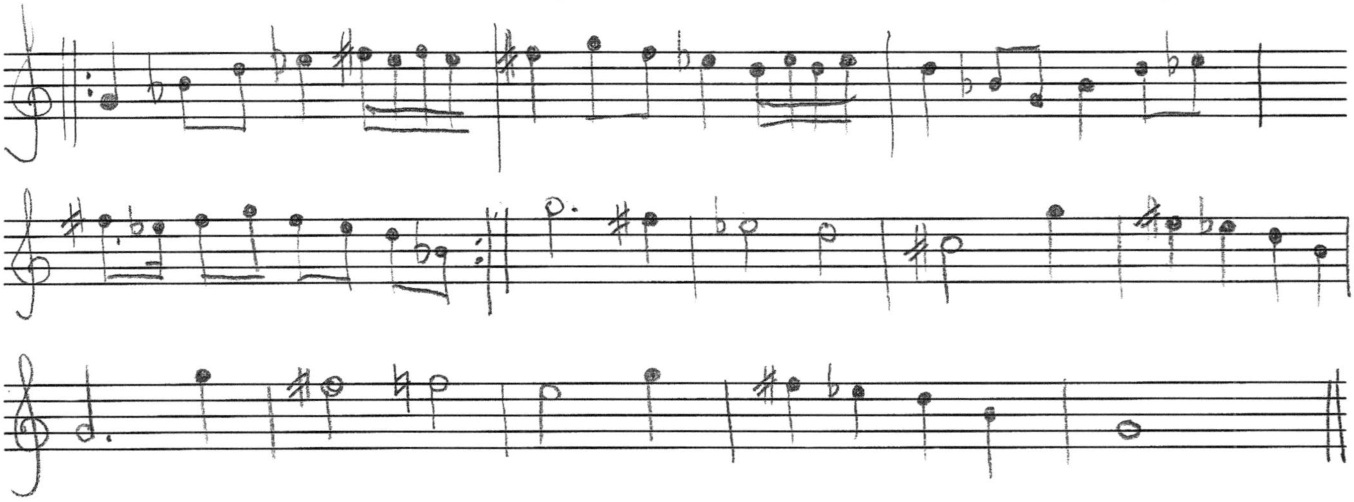

56
Guaracha U.F.O.
MERIDIAN BROTHERS

H

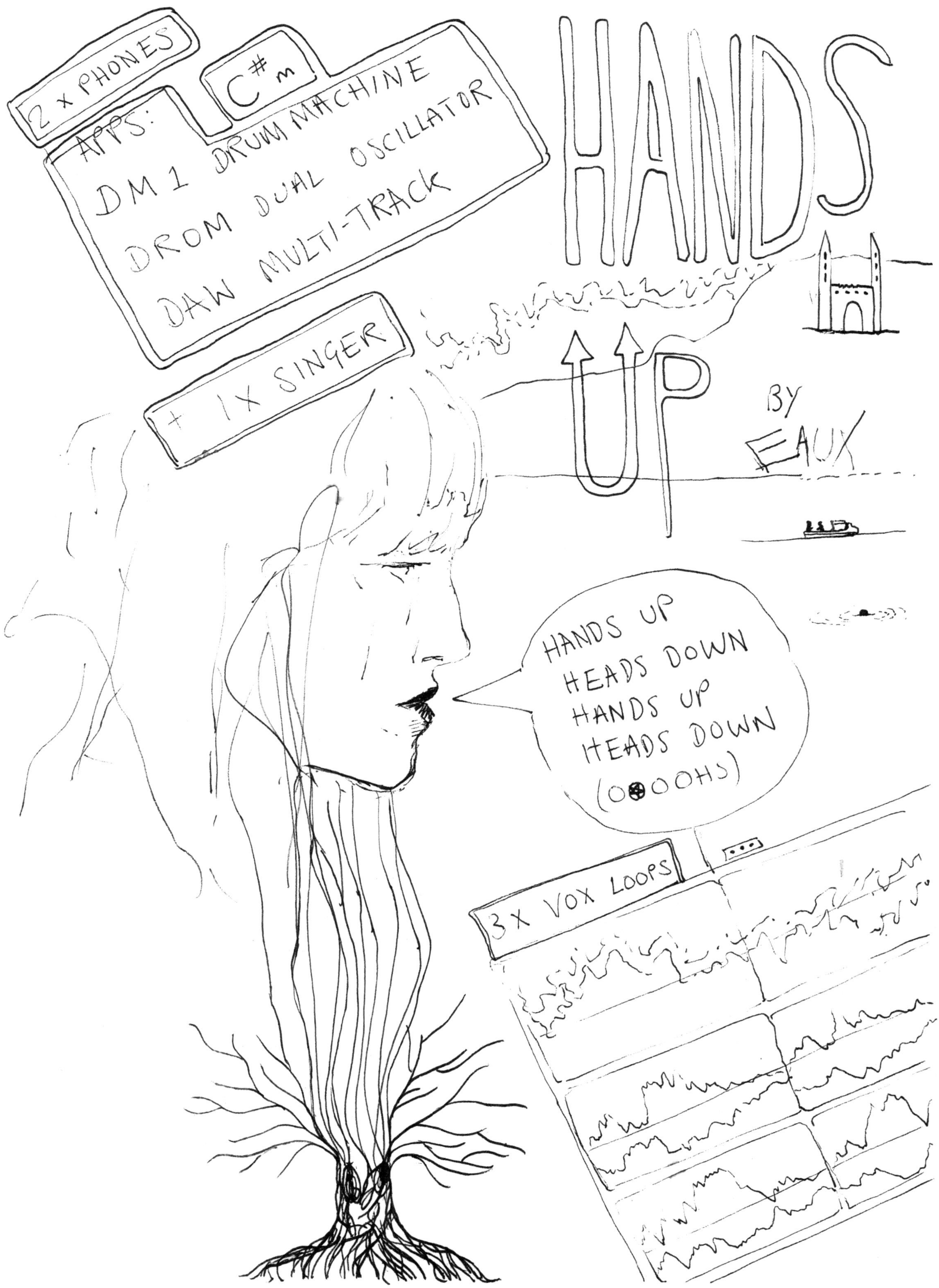
2 x PHONES
C#m
APPS:
DM1 DRUM MACHINE
DROM DUAL OSCILLATOR
DAW MULTI-TRACK
+ 1X SINGER
HANDS UP
BY FAUX
HANDS UP
HEADS DOWN
HANDS UP
HEADS DOWN
(OOOOHS)
3 X VOX LOOPS

57
Hands Up
EAUX

HANG OF SUMMER

3C 5A^b OPEN 2a^b

D2^E 3E5B4G 5a^b 3c^b

D2^E E35B4G 4a^b 9a^b 5c^b 7a^b 5c^b

9A^b 5c^b 7a^b 5c^b 4A

9A^b ~~[illegible]~~ 8EDB11G 5E7B7G D4E/ 7D2 5A^b

DID YOU GET IT ON? DID YOU TURN it all ON?
Did you play your game right? CAN you roll with it?

CH- THIS IS NOT WHAT IT SEEMS, OVER my HEAD 2X
HEARD THE RUMOR, it's the future. NOW THEY're calling, NOW THEY'RE telling - ABSENT TO THE purified. AT THE BANKS THE crystal EYES, blossom Heavy got the NEW WORD.

Sweet thing GOT HIGH AND WIDE TONES, PACIFIC BLUE HOME. LIFER CHAOS Summer. STAY WITH THE RANDOM STRIP.

CH- THIS IS NOT WHAT IT SEEMS.

ex - LOOK INTO THE LIGHT. GOT THE FEELING, GOT THE HEIGHT. LOOK INTO THE LIGHT, THE LOOK OF LIGHT

Samara Lubelski
Hang of Summer / WAVELENGTH 2012

58
Hang of Summer
SAMARA LUBELSKI

Hang of Summer - WAVELENGTH 2012

This started with a friend, she had come from Europe to N.Y.C., and The States, to find her "Adventure", or Something bigger. But it's really about a chick who's very open and looking, and falling for a cult and cult think – the confusion of the mind set - Reality and Vision crashing into each other...

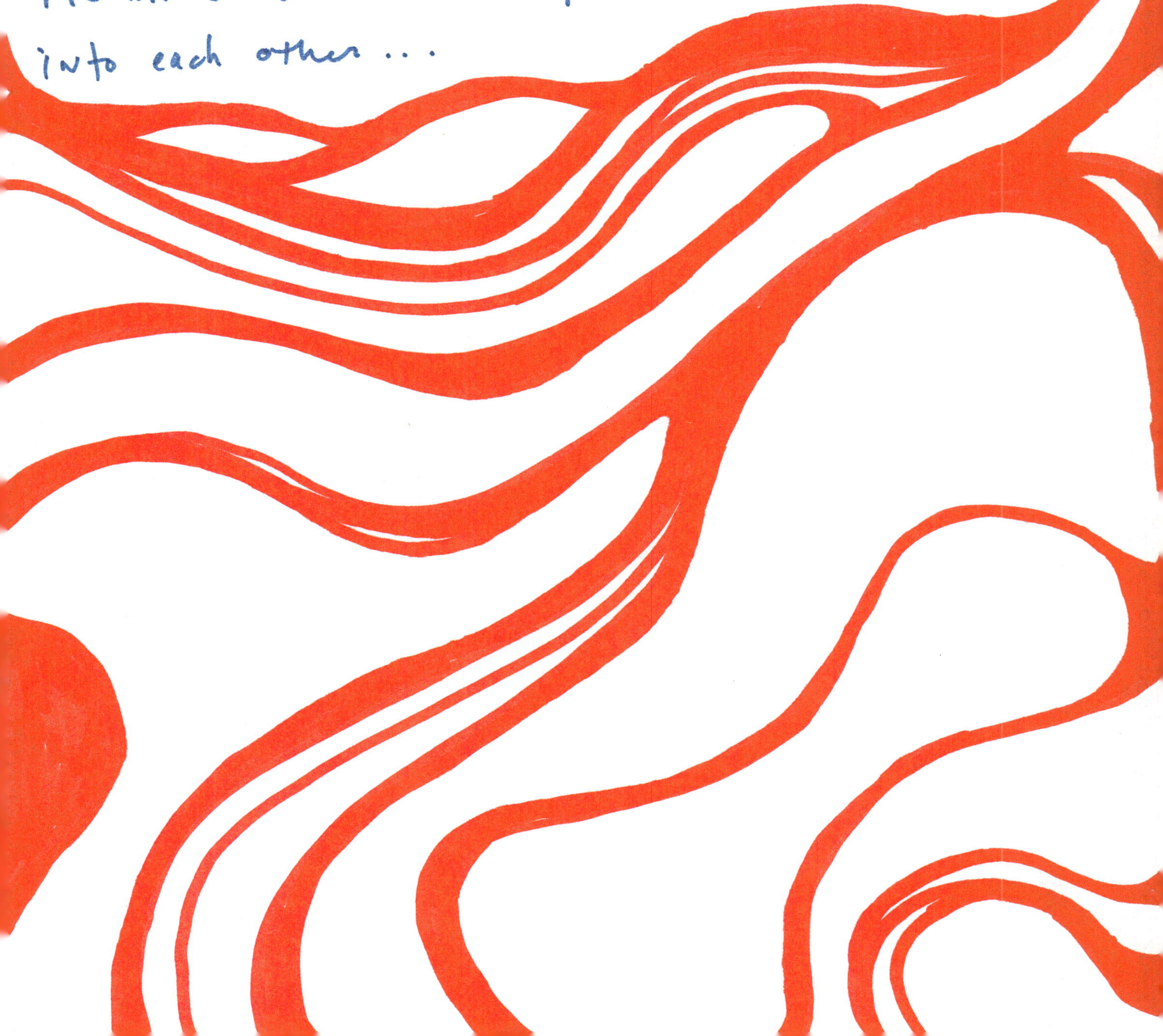

WARM GRAVES

3/4 HEADLINES:

↳ Intro: F Am B♭ F Am B♭ (keep in mind, it comes back)

When,

We couldn't wake up
from the horrible F
sound that our heads caused
They put it in the headlines
they were yelling it Dm loud
it is C happening it's F real
in the moment we Dm found
the C place where we belong F
Bb F Am with the C whole world in F front of you
Bb F Am won't you C go and tear it F down.

F Am Bb (here it comes back)

Bb They say this time it is really Dm over
let us hope they're not Gm wrong
Bb And they say none of us will grow Dm old
but colder we might Gm become
Bb They say this time it is really Dm over
to the altars they F call

4X

F Am Bb (again ... repeat all over ...)

F Am and over and going down and Bb over and going down
and F over and going down and Am over and going down and Bb over and
going down and F over and going down A it is going down with Am you Bb F

INSTRUCTION:

3/4 BAR just count to 3 and change chords as suggested ... and add as many effects as you like plus sing as loud as you can!

59
Headlines
WARM GRAVES

TENERE |A| (DESERT)

|A|·|AB|·|C|·|FECD|·|E|
|HBC|·|CBG|·|H| → Chorus

A: |G.A||E||·|G|C|·|D|·|E|·|C.D||A|

B: |G.A|E||·|G|C|·||D||
|E||·|C.D||A|

TENERE
Hegh Ténéré
usuf yigane
Dagh Ténéré
Warhene ammane
~~Tak~~ ikhimadas, samad, ranagh
Tikmawene, tin Ténéré

Bombino

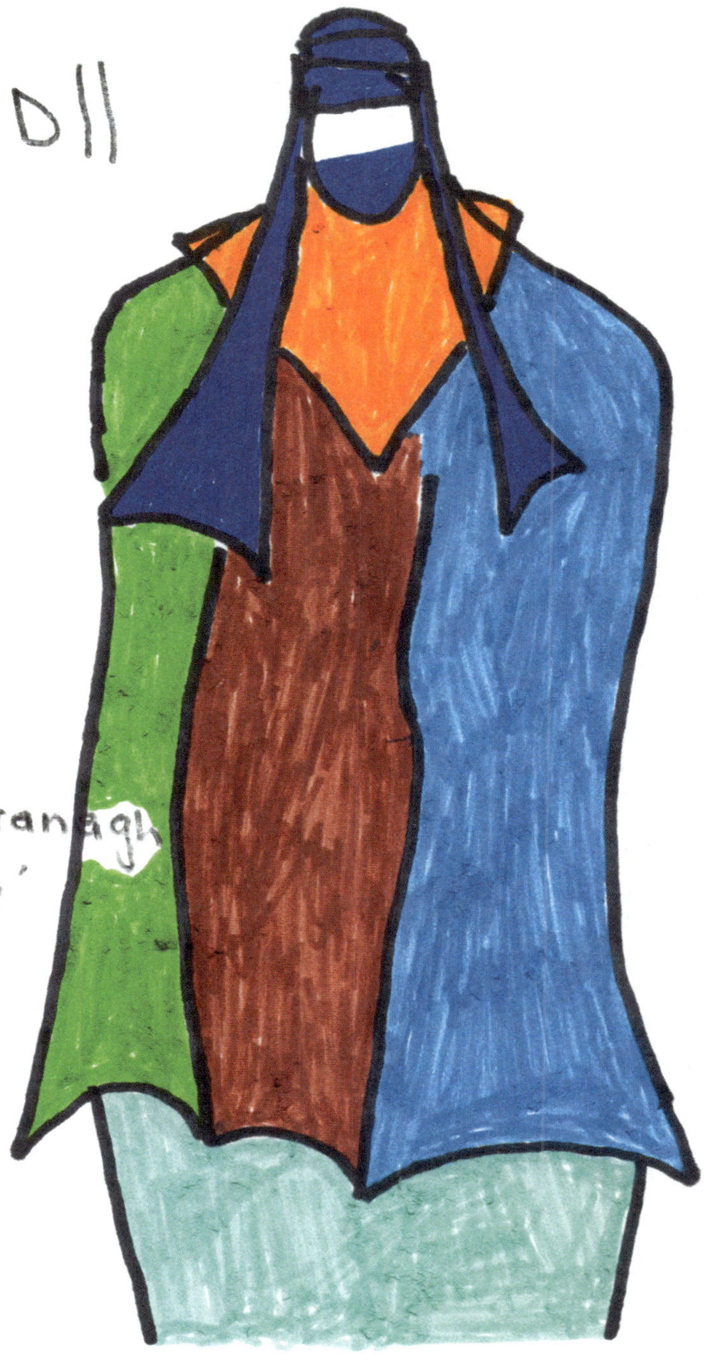

60
Her Tenere
BOMBINO

I

WAS BACKSTAGE IN MOSCOW LATE ONE NIGHT
WE SHARED A CIGARETTE & A KISS GOODBYE
HER NAME WAS OKSANA YOU A SOFT HER
HANDS TREMBLED BACK [illegible] EVERYTHING
OFF TO BOTTLES & OBJECTS AROUND THE
ROOM MY BALL UP [illegible] & [illegible] THAT
OF [illegible] [illegible] [illegible] HAVE VERY
MUCH TO SAY SHE SAID THAT SHE
COME & [illegible] [illegible] OTHER PLACES A
TOWN CALLED [illegible] OR [illegible] JAROMSK
WAS PRETTY DISMAL PACKED MY STUFF
BUT I DID MAKE A [illegible] TO [illegible] HER
& STATE [illegible] SHE SAID SHE
HAD FRIENDS SHE HAD TO GO SEE
LATER THAT SUMMER I WAS PICKED
UP MY MAIL SHE SENT ME A LETTER
WITH A TOUCHING DETAIL SHE USED
UP HER MINUTES CALLING HOME
TO [illegible] ME THAT NIGHT BUT IN
NO [illegible] I KNOW ITS PATHETIC
SHE CONTINUES TO WRITE BUT
THAT WAS THE GREATEST NIGHT OF MY LIFE

61

I Know It's Pathetic but That Was the Greatest Night of My Life

SUN KIL MOON

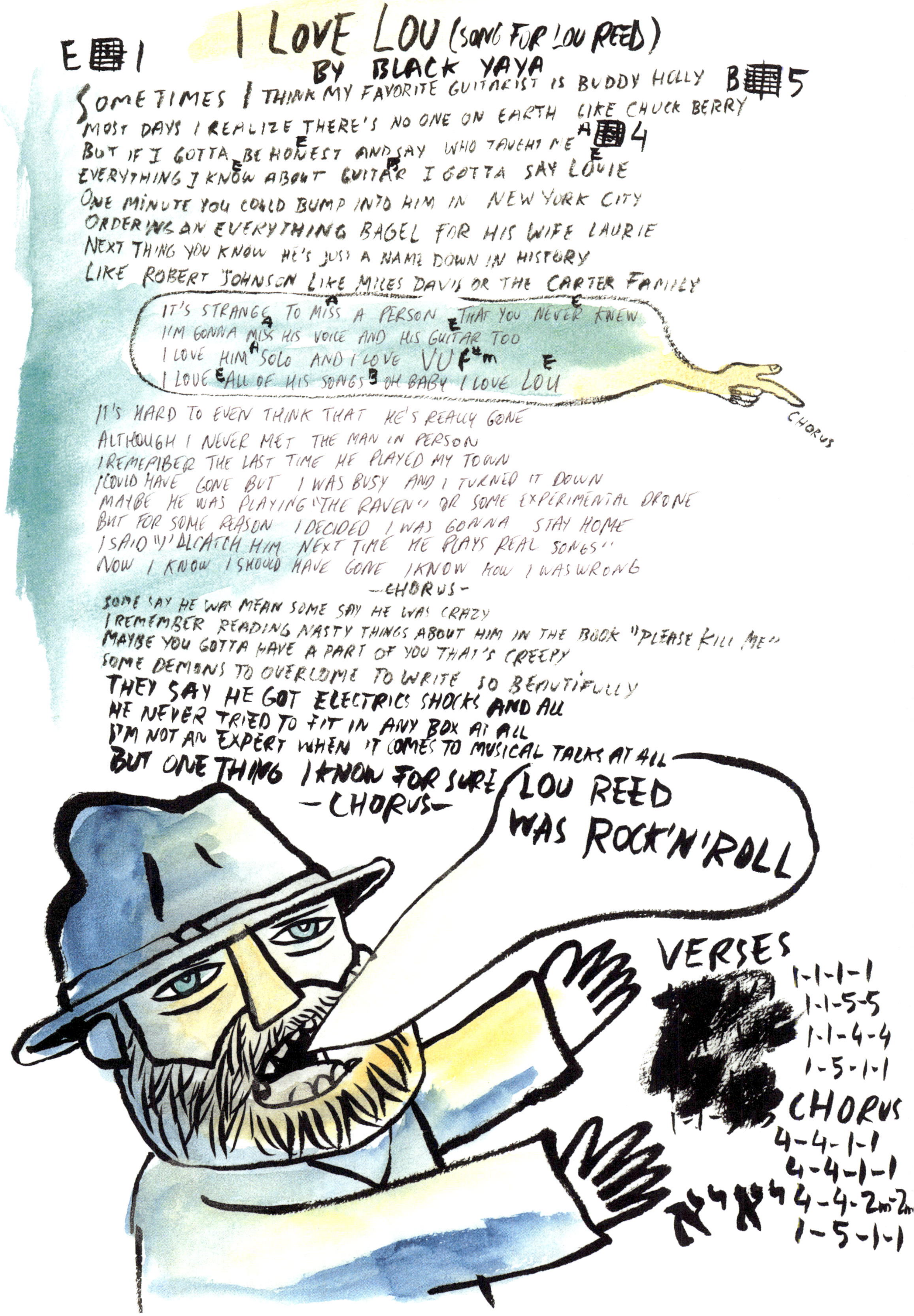
I LOVE LOU (SONG FOR LOU REED)
BY BLACK YAYA
E 1
B 5
A 4
SOMETIMES I THINK MY FAVORITE GUITARIST IS BUDDY HOLLY
MOST DAYS I REALIZE THERE'S NO ONE ON EARTH LIKE CHUCK BERRY
BUT IF I GOTTA BE HONEST AND SAY WHO TAUGHT ME
EVERYTHING I KNOW ABOUT GUITAR I GOTTA SAY LOUIE
ONE MINUTE YOU COULD BUMP INTO HIM IN NEW YORK CITY
ORDERING AN EVERYTHING BAGEL FOR HIS WIFE LAURIE
NEXT THING YOU KNOW HE'S JUST A NAME DOWN IN HISTORY
LIKE ROBERT JOHNSON LIKE MILES DAVIS OR THE CARTER FAMILY
IT'S STRANGE TO MISS A PERSON THAT YOU NEVER KNEW
I'M GONNA MISS HIS VOICE AND HIS GUITAR TOO
I LOVE HIM SOLO AND I LOVE VU F#m
I LOVE ALL OF HIS SONGS OH BABY I LOVE LOU
CHORUS
IT'S HARD TO EVEN THINK THAT HE'S REALLY GONE
ALTHOUGH I NEVER MET THE MAN IN PERSON
I REMEMBER THE LAST TIME HE PLAYED MY TOWN
I COULD HAVE GONE BUT I WAS BUSY AND I TURNED IT DOWN
MAYBE HE WAS PLAYING "THE RAVEN" OR SOME EXPERIMENTAL DRONE
BUT FOR SOME REASON I DECIDED I WAS GONNA STAY HOME
I SAID "I'LL CATCH HIM NEXT TIME HE PLAYS REAL SONGS"
NOW I KNOW I SHOULD HAVE GONE I KNOW HOW I WAS WRONG
—CHORUS—
SOME SAY HE WAS MEAN SOME SAY HE WAS CRAZY
I REMEMBER READING NASTY THINGS ABOUT HIM IN THE BOOK "PLEASE KILL ME"
MAYBE YOU GOTTA HAVE A PART OF YOU THAT'S CREEPY
SOME DEMONS TO OVERCOME TO WRITE SO BEAUTIFULLY
THEY SAY HE GOT ELECTRICS SHOCKS AND ALL
HE NEVER TRIED TO FIT IN ANY BOX AT ALL
I'M NOT AN EXPERT WHEN IT COMES TO MUSICAL TALKS AT ALL
BUT ONE THING I KNOW FOR SURE
—CHORUS—
LOU REED WAS ROCK'N'ROLL
VERSES
1-1-1-1
1-1-5-5
1-1-4-4
1-5-1-1
CHORUS
4-4-1-1
4-4-1-1
4-4-2m-2m
1-5-1-1

62

I Love Lou (Song for Lou Reed)

BLACK YAYA

"I Miss Your Bones" by Hospitality

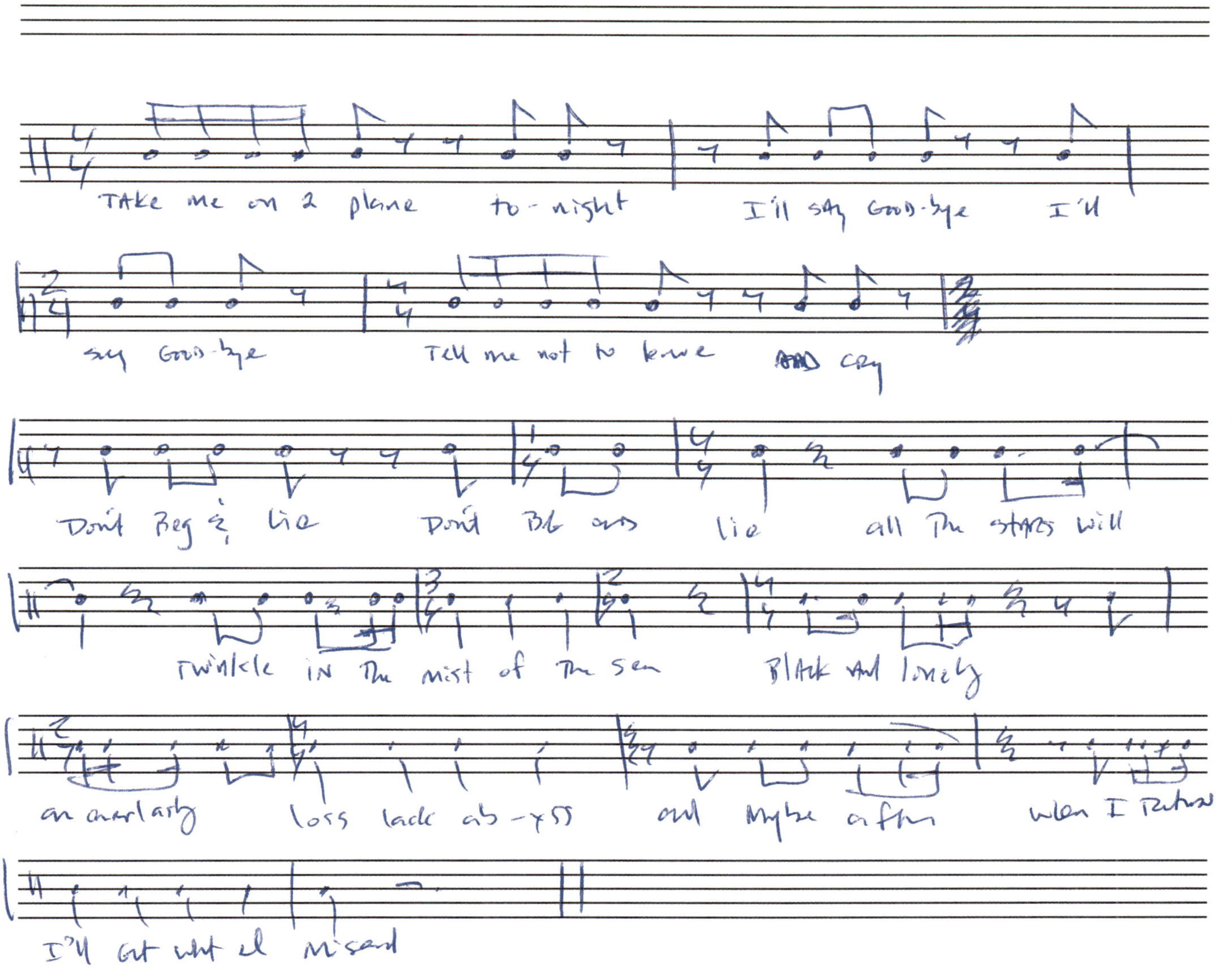

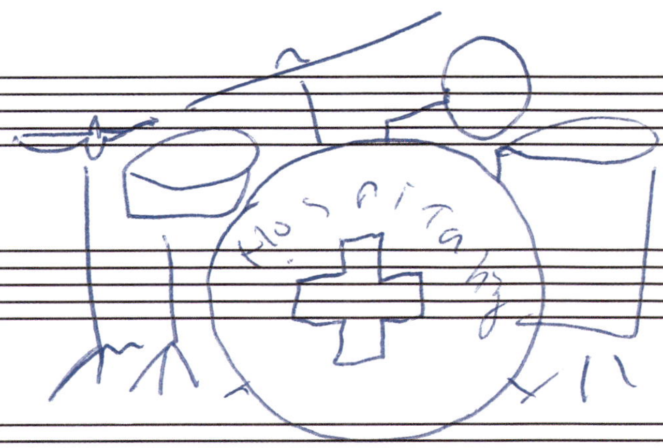

63
I Miss Your Bones
HOSPITALITY

CGCD 4-String Tuning

0 I ↓ 4th Fret

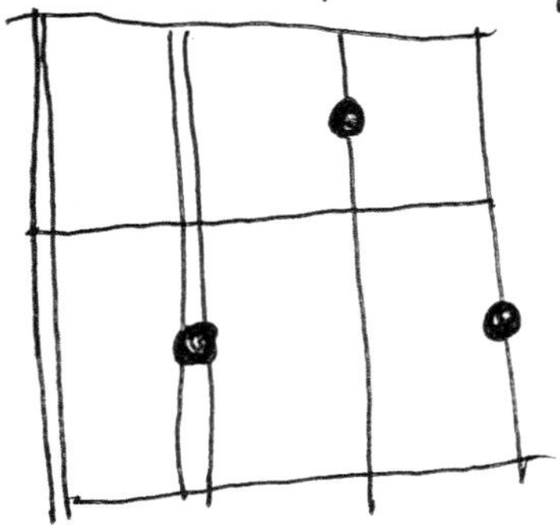

II ↓ 8th Fret

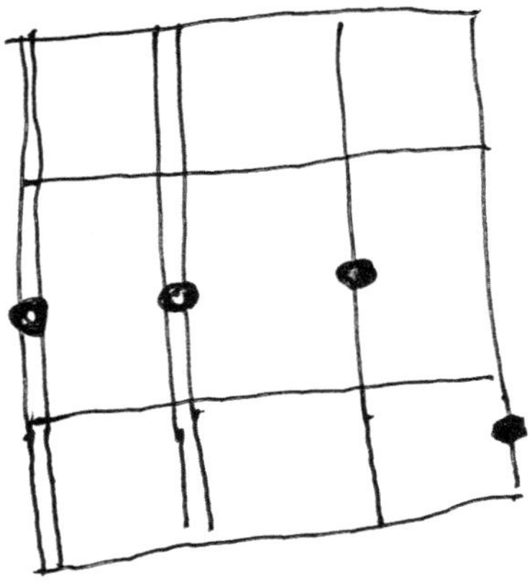

III ↓ 4th Fret

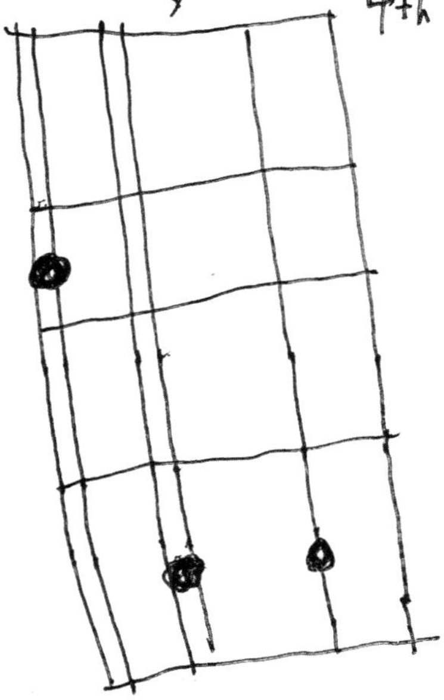

IV 6th Fret

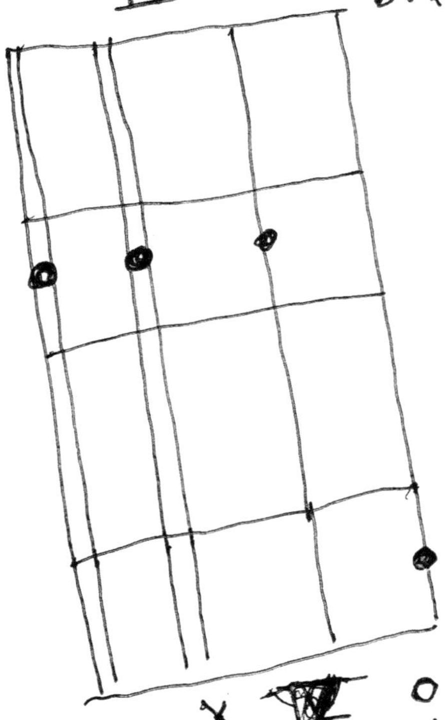

V ↓ 4th Fret

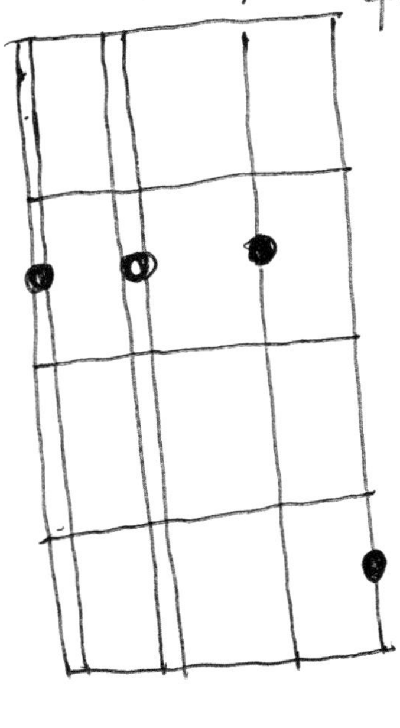

x VI 0 1st Fret

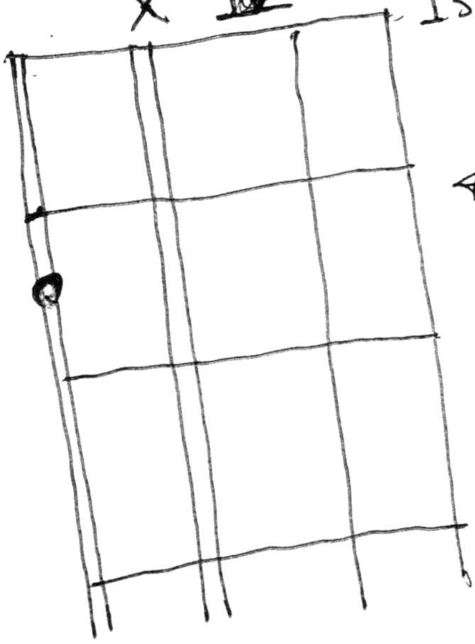

VI

64
I Will
SEBADOH

VII

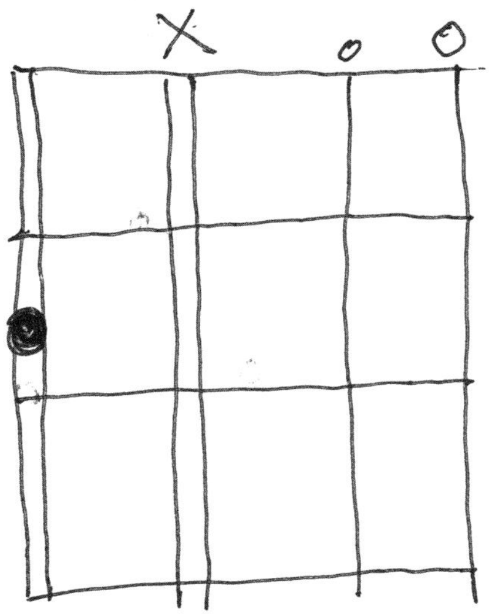

6th Fret

VIII (open chord)

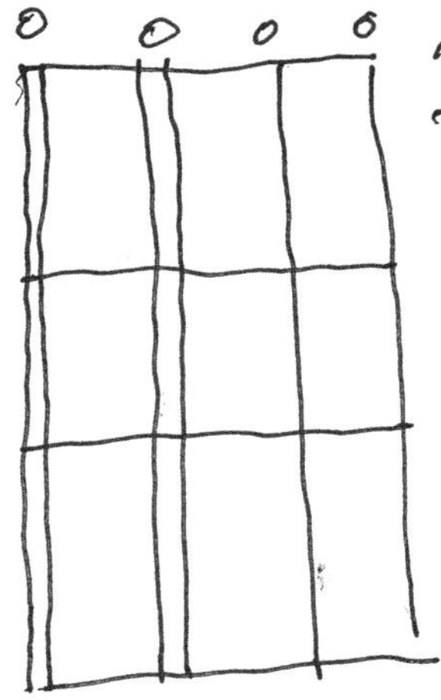

1st Fret

Twelve String Guitar modified to a 4-string tuning C G C D top (heavy) tuned to C (Doubled), bottom (thin) tuned to D (single) etc....

VERSES

Chord → I II

words → Can you tell that I'm about to lose control

III IV

I II

Someone else has found a way into my soul

III IV

I II

things have changed no longer need to be with you

III IV

I

I'm still the same but if it's leaving I must ~~[illegible]~~e II

III

do ... to be true ... IV VIII I WILL

VERSE 2 (the same)

CHORUS

I

who am I and what did I begin II

all to feel a nail drag my skin II

IV

to draw this blood from me V VI

I

In the end there never is an end II

nothing we protect will let us in II

IV

so find your way, I will ..... V VI VII VII

2nd verse (words)

So I make a plan and start to move

and I follow as she follows me away

and this will be the hardest thing we've ever done

getting more than we were hoping for is not fun

but it's done, and I will

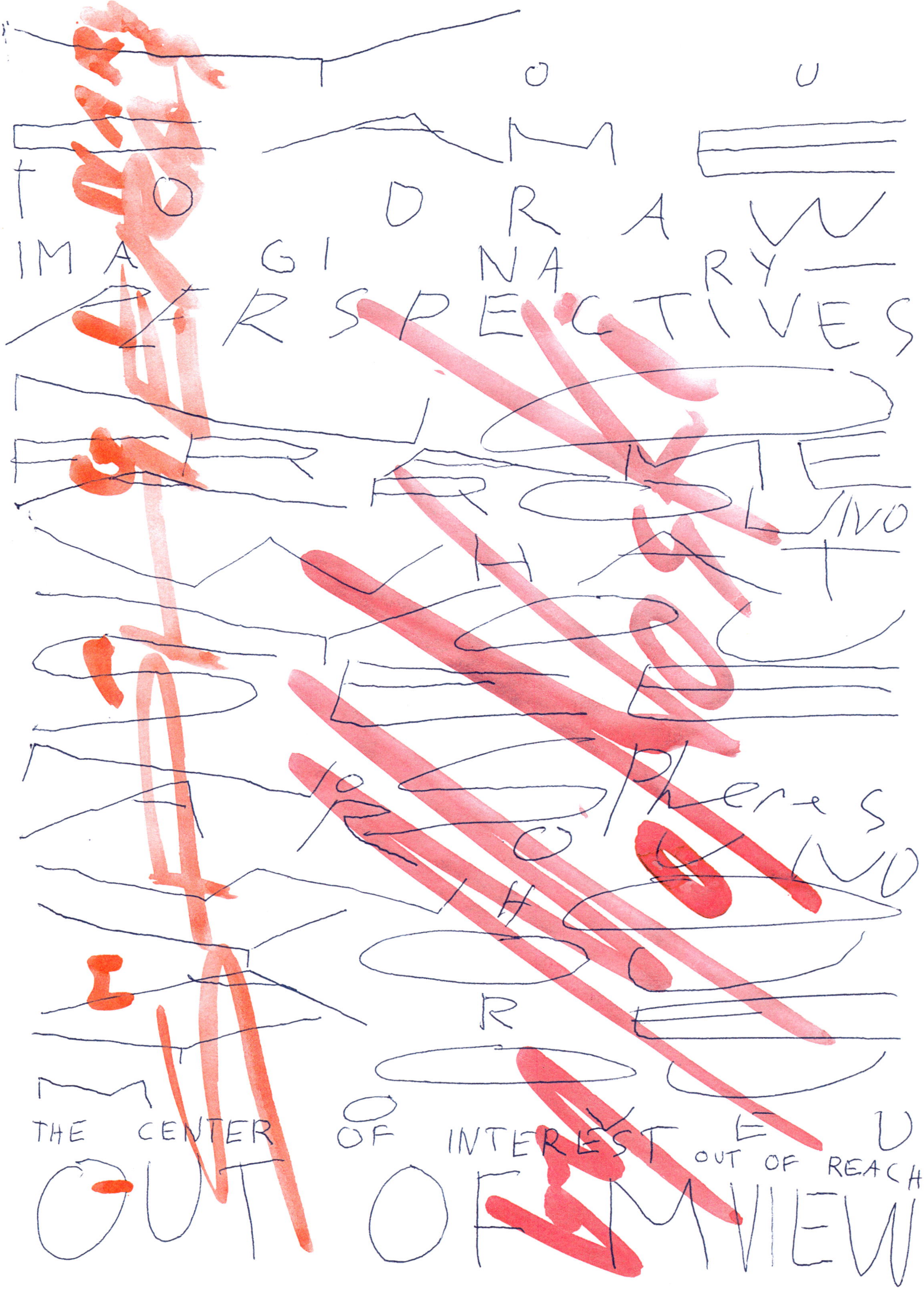
TO DRAW
IMAGINARY
PERSPECTIVES
THE CENTER OF INTEREST
OUT OF REACH
OUT OF VIEW

65
Imaginary Spheres
MONOSKI

In Conflict

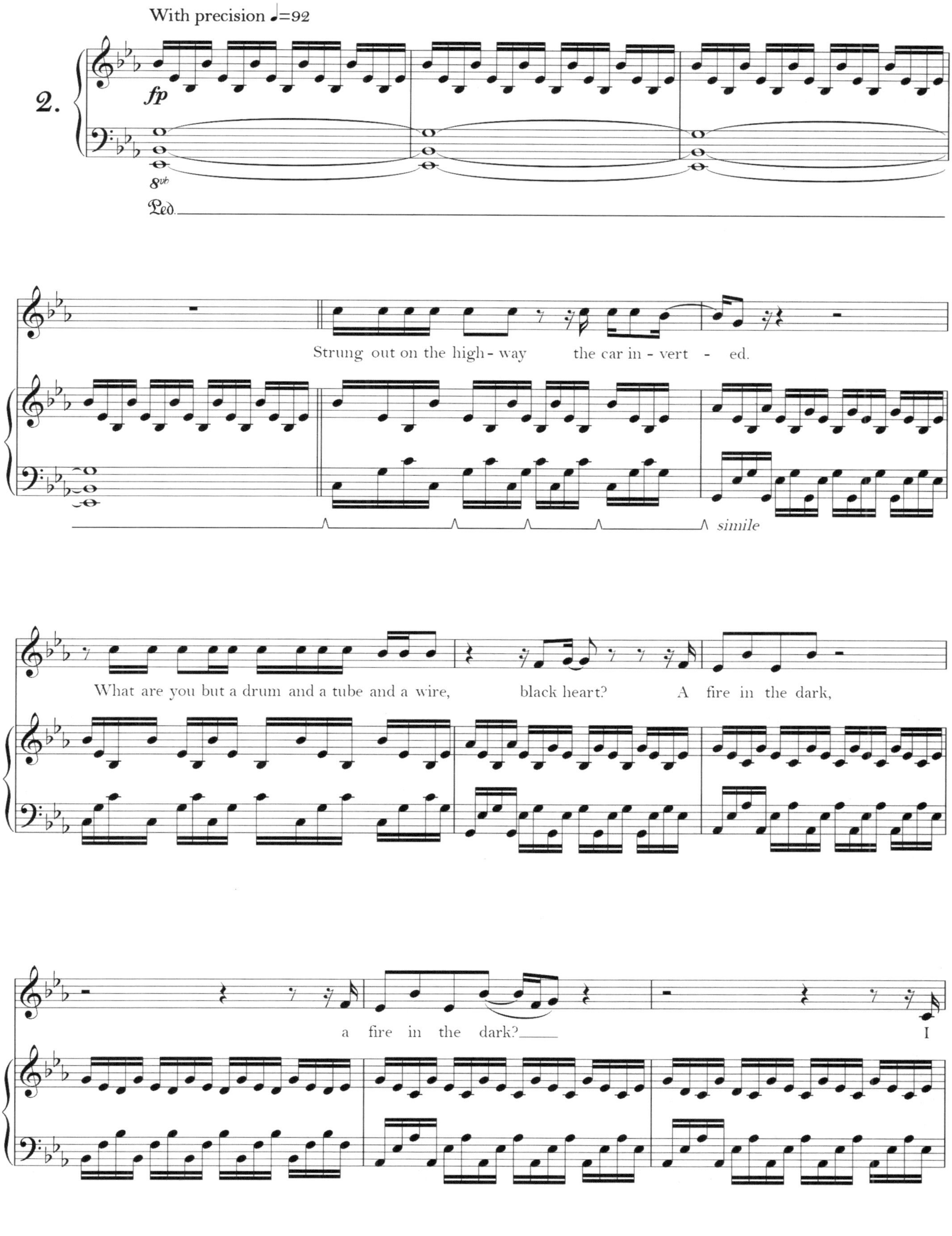
With precision ♩=92
2.
fp
8vb
Ped.
Strung out on the high - way the car in - vert - ed.
simile
What are you but a drum and a tube and a wire, black heart? A fire in the dark,
a fire in the dark? I

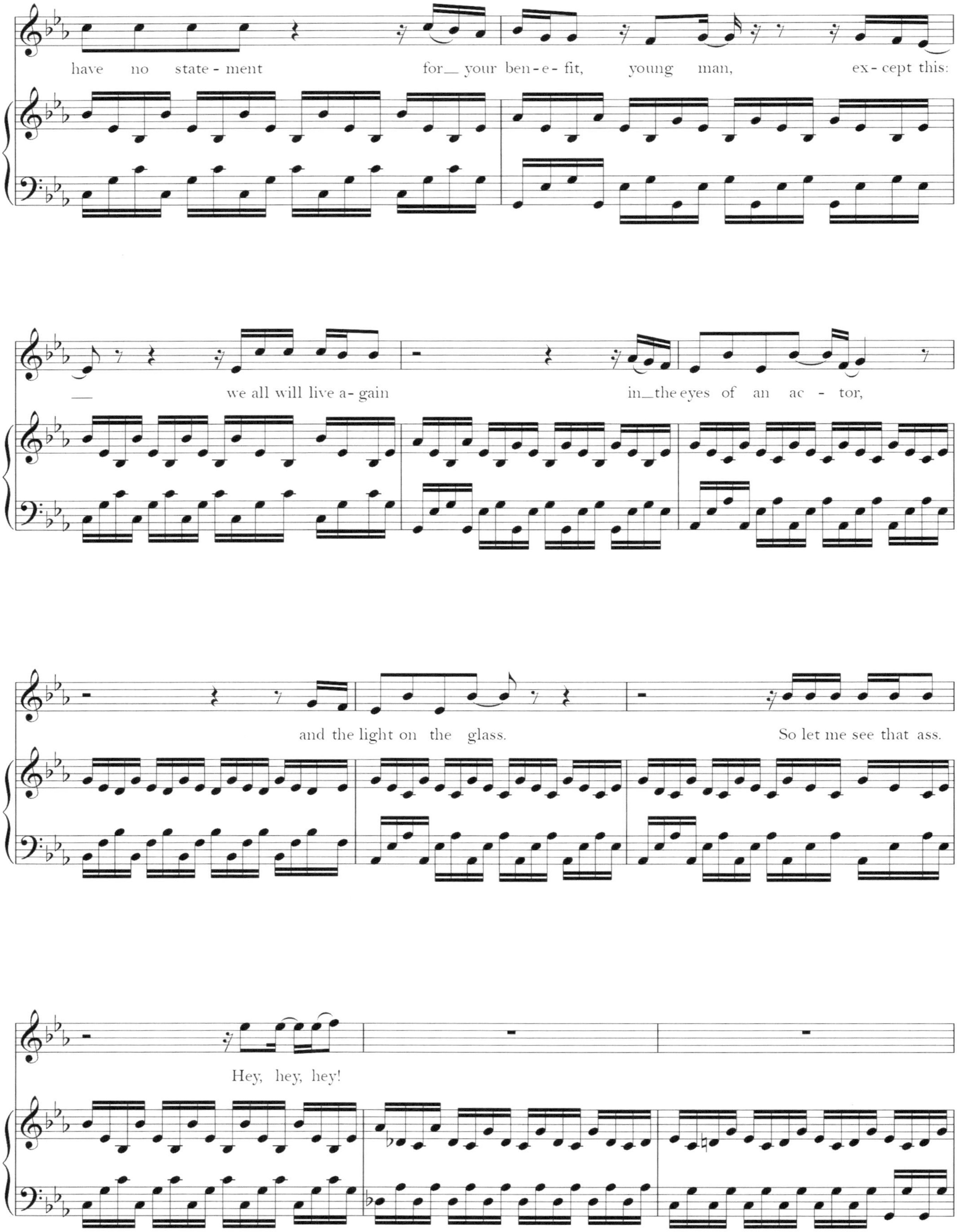
have no state - ment for__ your ben - e - fit, young man, ex - cept this:
__ we all will live a - gain in__the eyes of an ac - tor,
and the light on the glass. So let me see that ass.
Hey, hey, hey!

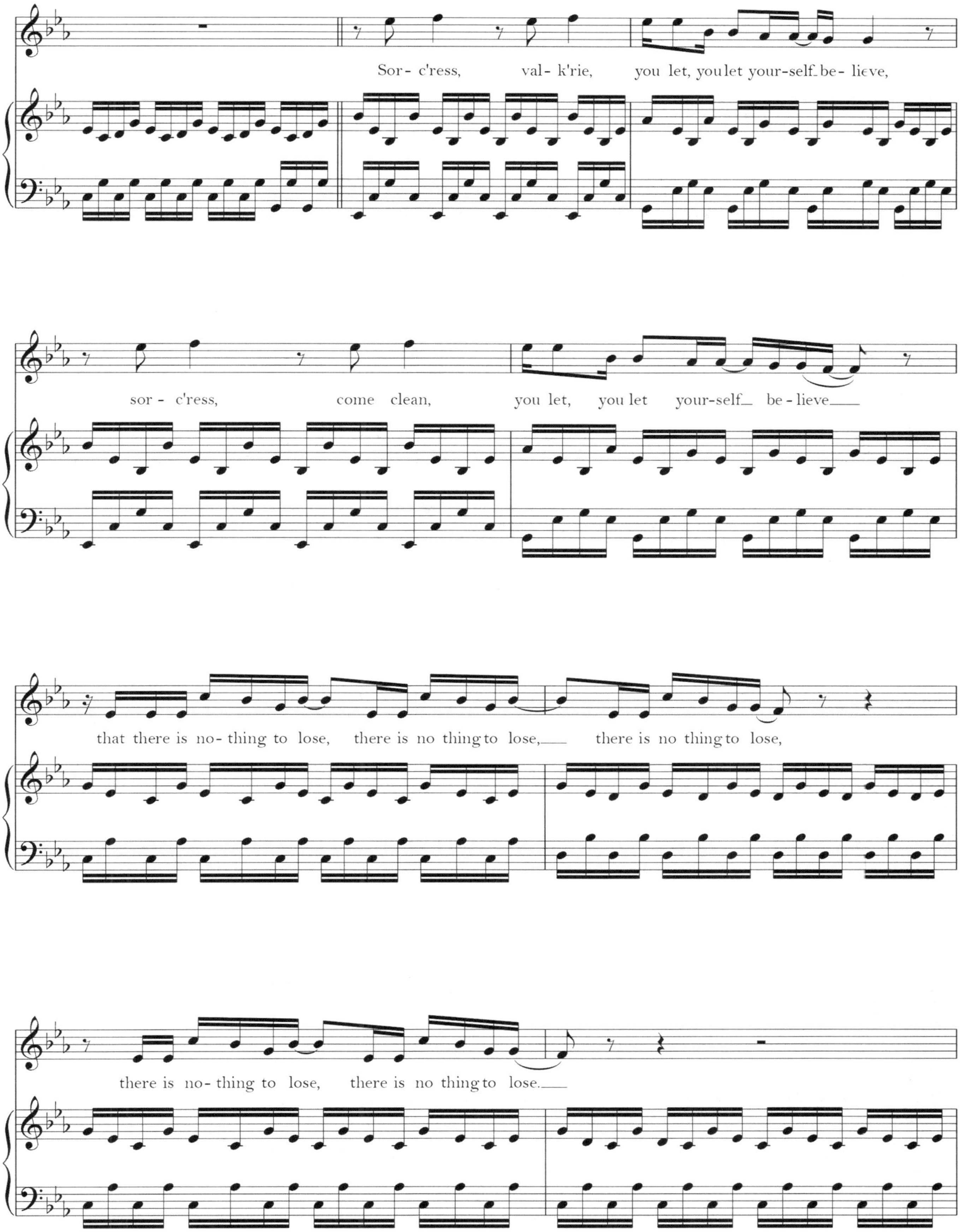
Sor- c'ress, val- k'rie, you let, you let your-self be- lie-ve,
sor - c'ress, come clean, you let, you let your-self be - lieve
that there is no- thing to lose, there is no thing to lose, there is no thing to lose,
there is no- thing to lose, there is no thing to lose.

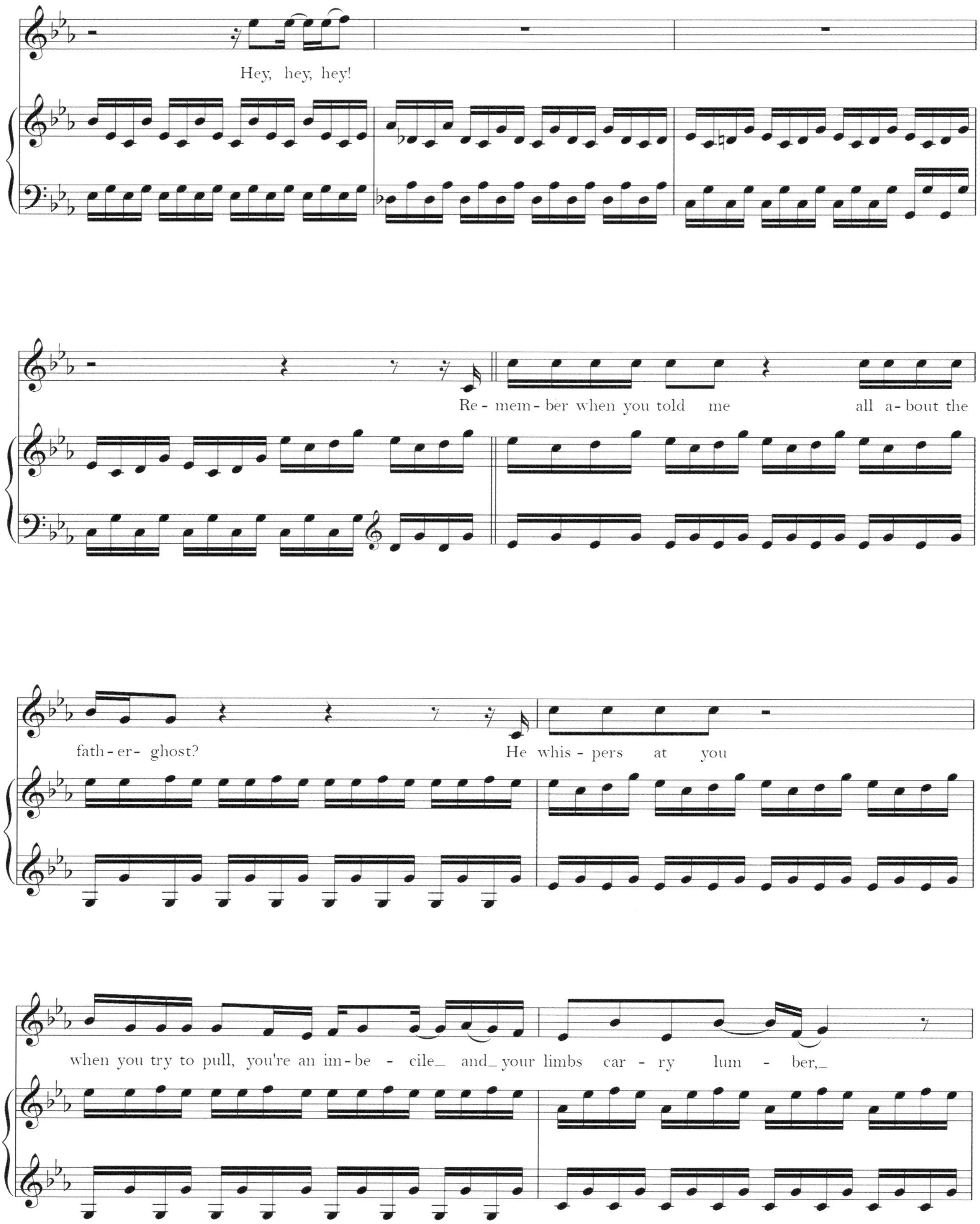
Hey, hey, hey!
Re- mem- ber when you told me all a- bout the
fath- er- ghost? He whis - pers at you
when you try to pull, you're an im- be - cile_ and_ your limbs car - ry lum - ber,_

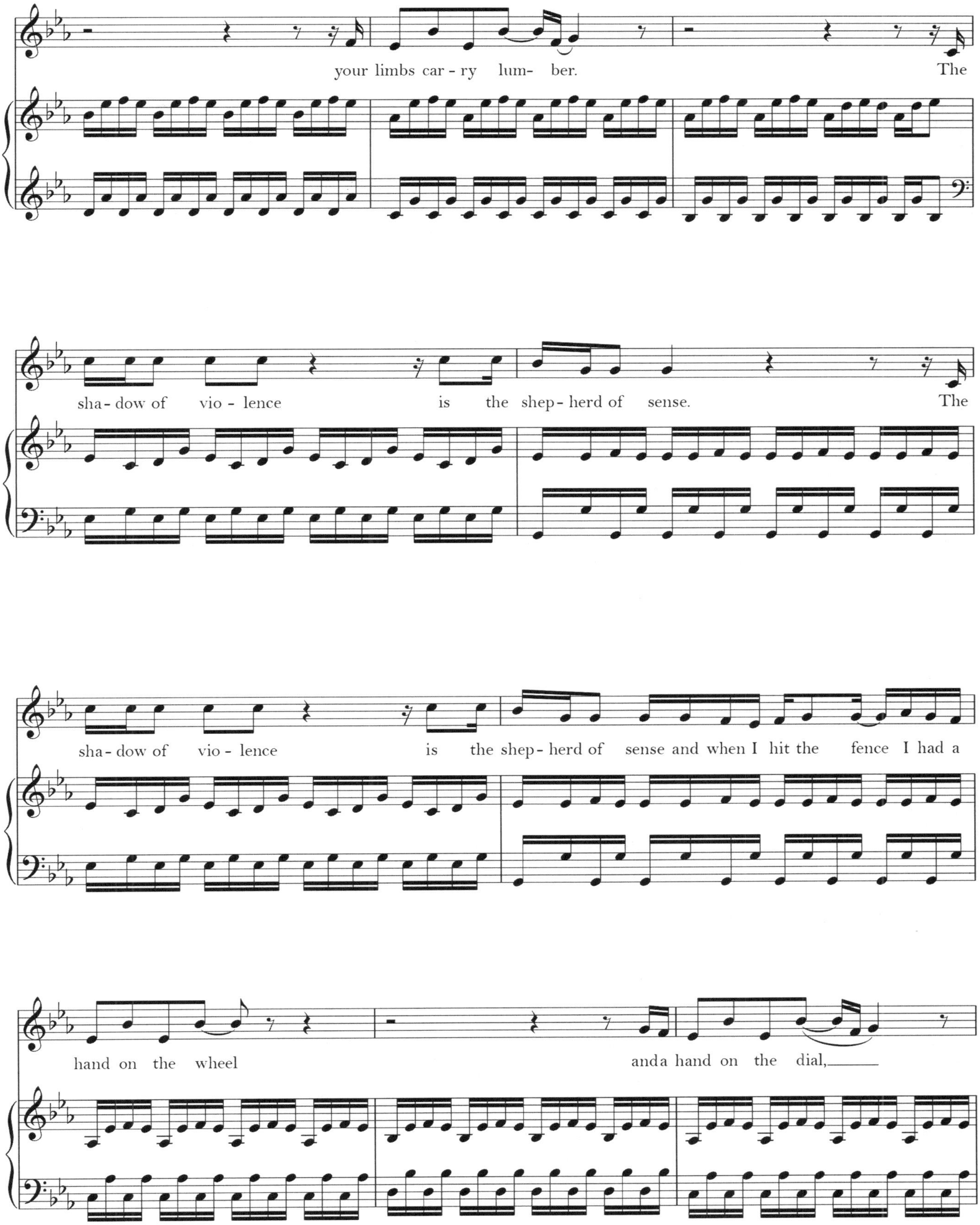
your limbs car - ry lum- ber. The
sha - dow of vio - lence is the shep - herd of sense. The
sha - dow of vio - lence is the shep - herd of sense and when I hit the fence I had a
hand on the wheel and a hand on the dial,

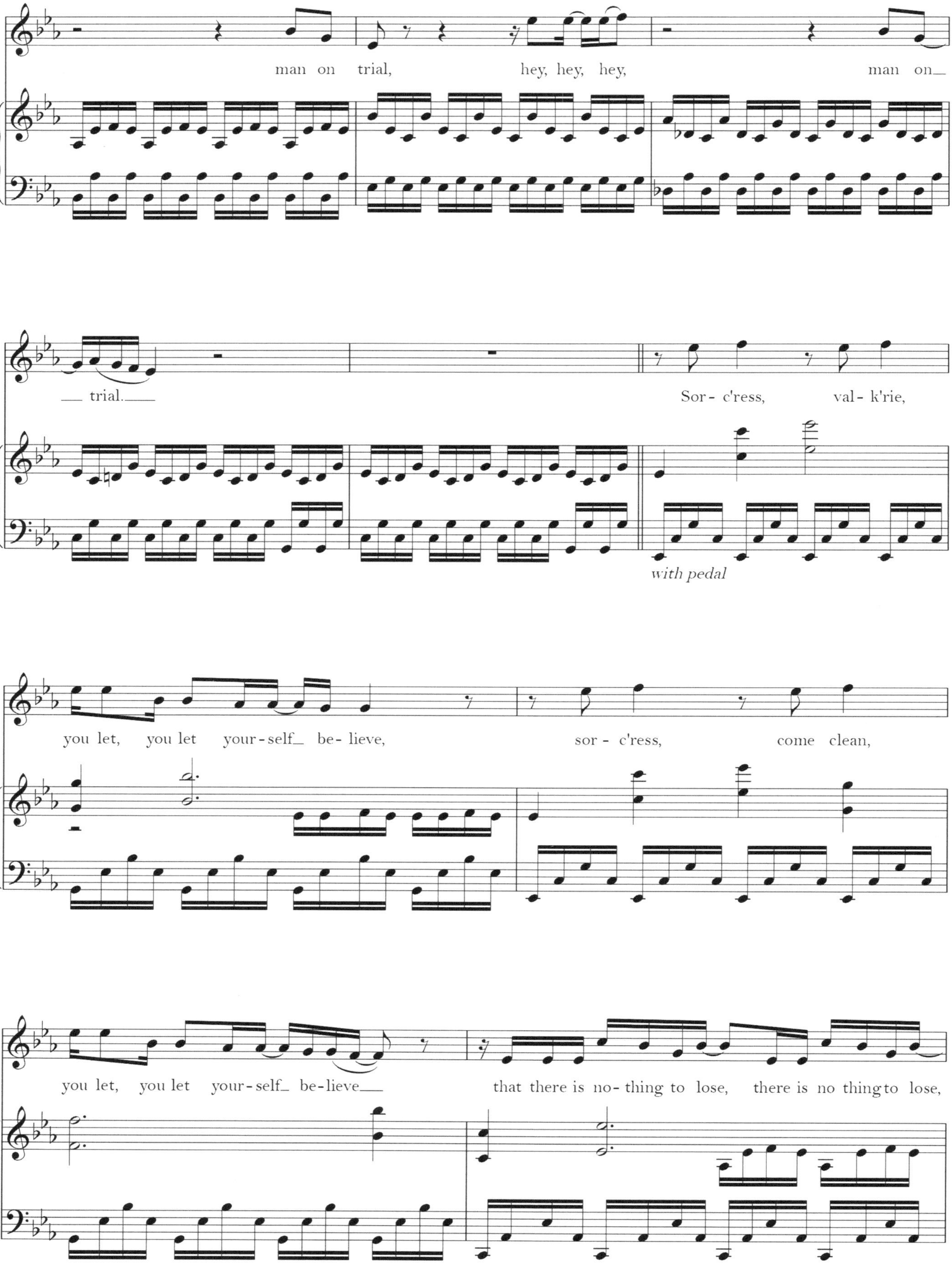
man on trial, hey, hey, hey, man on
trial.
Sor- c'ress, val- k'rie,
with pedal
you let, you let your-self be- lieve, sor - c'ress, come clean,
you let, you let your-self be-lieve
that there is no- thing to lose, there is no thing to lose,

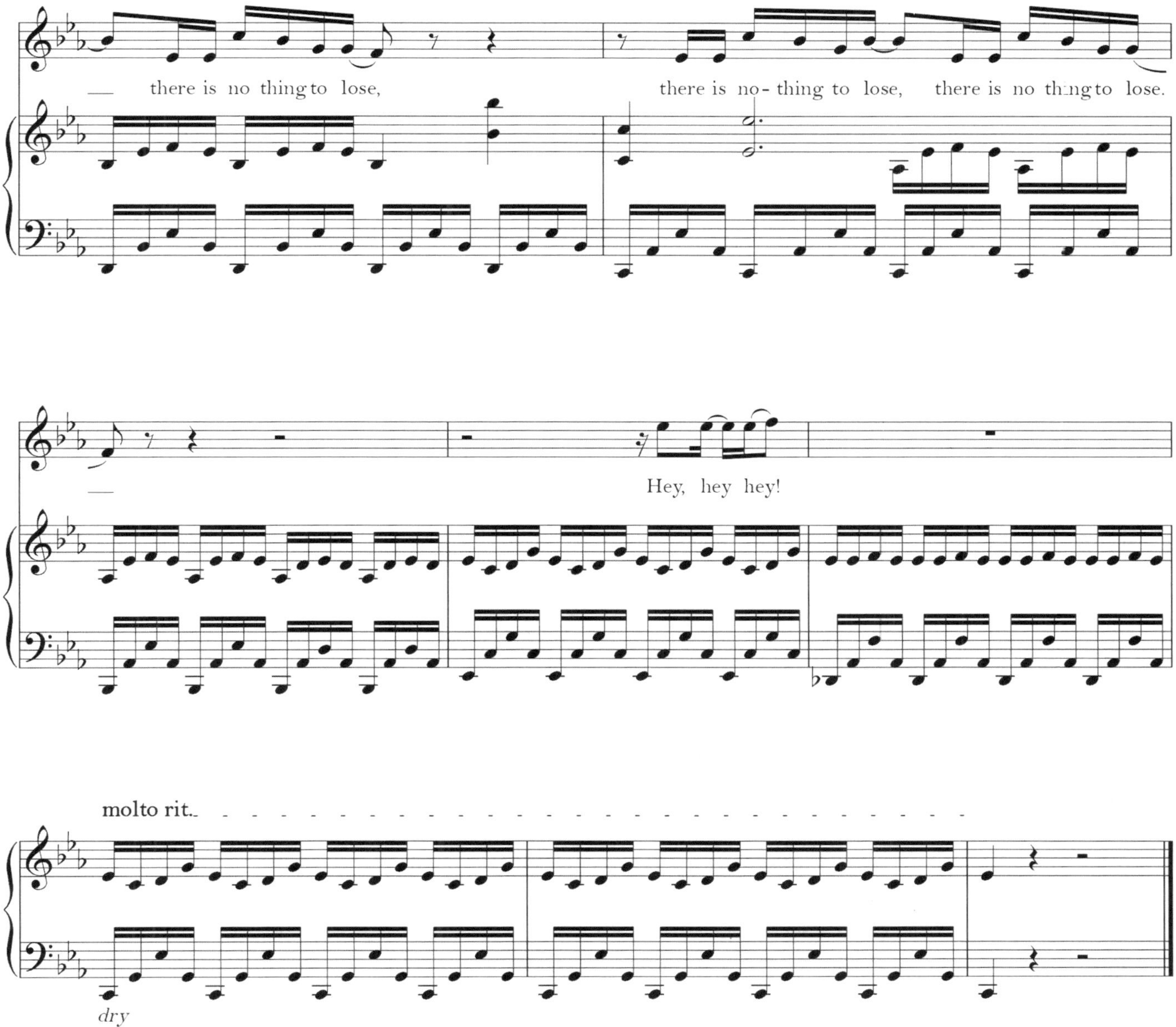
there is no thing to lose,
there is no- thing to lose,
there is no thing to lose.
Hey, hey hey!
molto rit.
dry

66

In Conflict

OWEN PALLETT

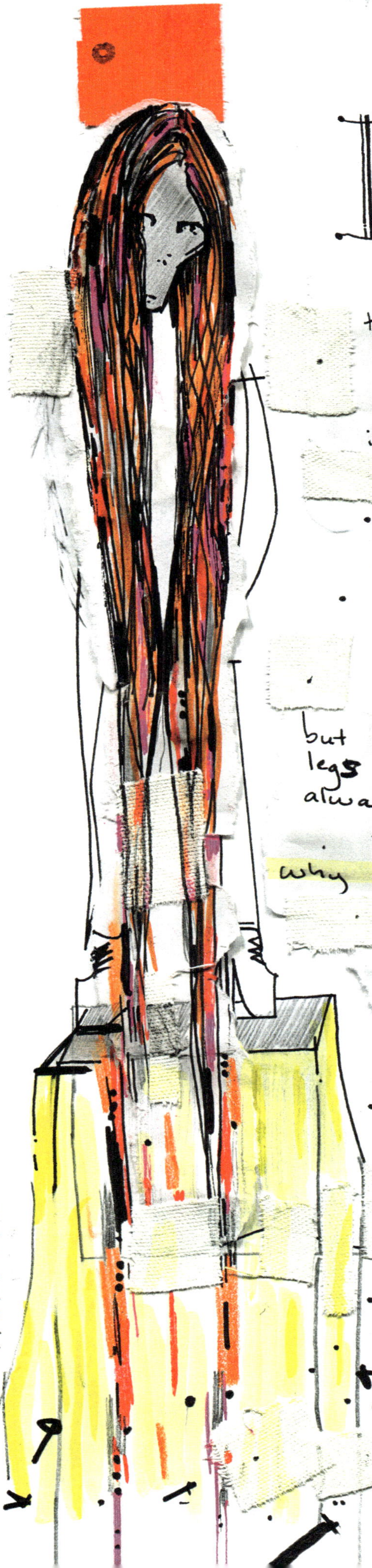

HUNDRED WATERS

Innocent...

there was a light on, a light on inside
I saw it. crawling
looming, low ringing sigh.
it's smooth skin sliding
where the line of illusion
is so very loose.
(ain't it darlin)
come ~~lie here~~ say
it's okay
there's nothin
no one
no real reason...

...

but every other word is a war inside
legs are no good when they're paralyzed.
always wondering, always worrying.
innocent innocent
why do I worry if you're I'm innocent?

....

but the roaring.. the crash!
it's all very cruel (ain't it darlin)
come lie here, say
it's okay
there's nothing

no one...

no real reason

67

Innocent

HUNDRED WATERS

- IOTA - written by Angel Olsen

"if only all our memories were one
we only had to blink and it was done
if all the world could see it with one eye
in perfect color to the perfect sky

if only we could turn ourselves around
and all the things we're looking for were found
if only we grew wiser with each breathe
if only we could dance our way to death -

if only all our dreams were coming true
maybe there'd be some time for me & you
if only all the world could sing along
in perfect rhythm to ~~the~~ perfect song

we'd close and then we'd go to bed
we'd never have to do it all again
there wouldn't be one thing to fight about
and time would turn our bodies inside out

68

Iota

ANGEL OLSEN

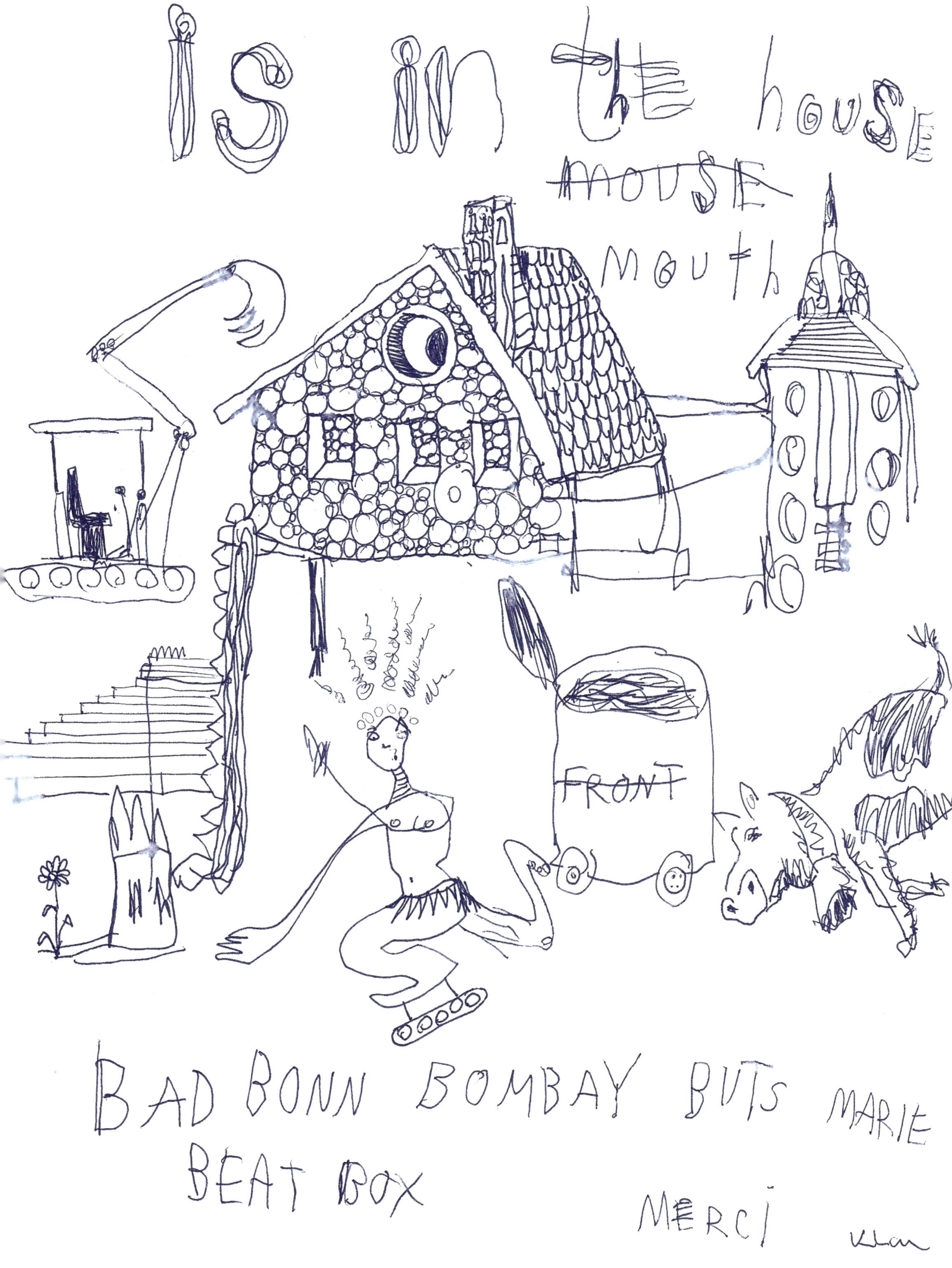
is in the house
mouse
mouth
FRONT
BAD BONN BOMBAY BUTS MARIE
BEAT BOX
MERCI

69

Is in the House Ya, Is in My Mouth Ya

PUTS MARIE

IT'S ALIVE

by La Luz

STOLEN, & then left in the car
We can always tell where you are
all alone in your secret
waiting somewhere to meet us

Walking alone past the park
someone calls out from the dark
look around, nothings moving
but I can tell that its human

ITS ALIVE!

Oh take me into the city,
Oh let me out in the crowd
If you see me lying on the ground
Walk around.

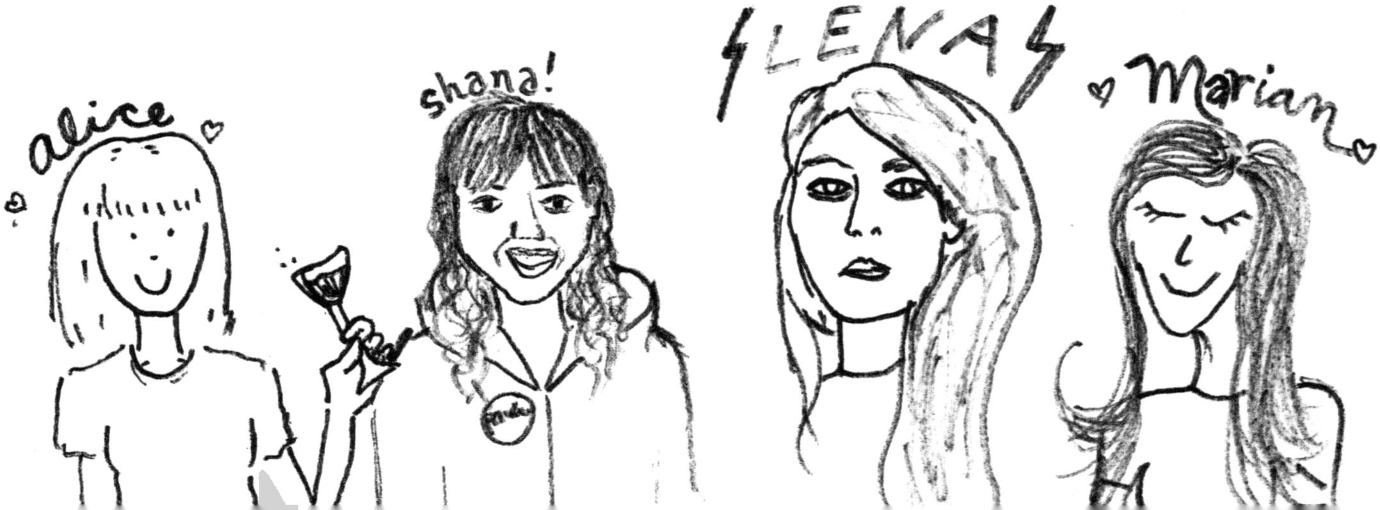

70
It's Alive
LA LUZ

J

When my son **Jude** was born, I was bewildered with the concept of how many trillions of chaotic entities and variables had to fall into place to make one perfect little human. But it could be no other way. If there was a plan, it could be deviated from, but all occurences just <u>are</u>, and cannot be deviated from. Thus, there is no plan.

<u>This is freedom.</u>

G	A	D	F#m
x	x	x	2
x	x	x	2
x	x	2	2
4 (5)	2 (4)	4	4
2	4	5	4
3	5	x	2

G A G A
So much for bones to pick. So much for fear.

G A D G
So much to fill you in on now that you're here.

G A G A
Timing is everything. Moments arrive.

G A D G
And it ain't no accident planets align.

D G F#m G A G
Forces combine. Chances collide. Agents decide.

F#m A G

71

Jude

DAN MANGAN

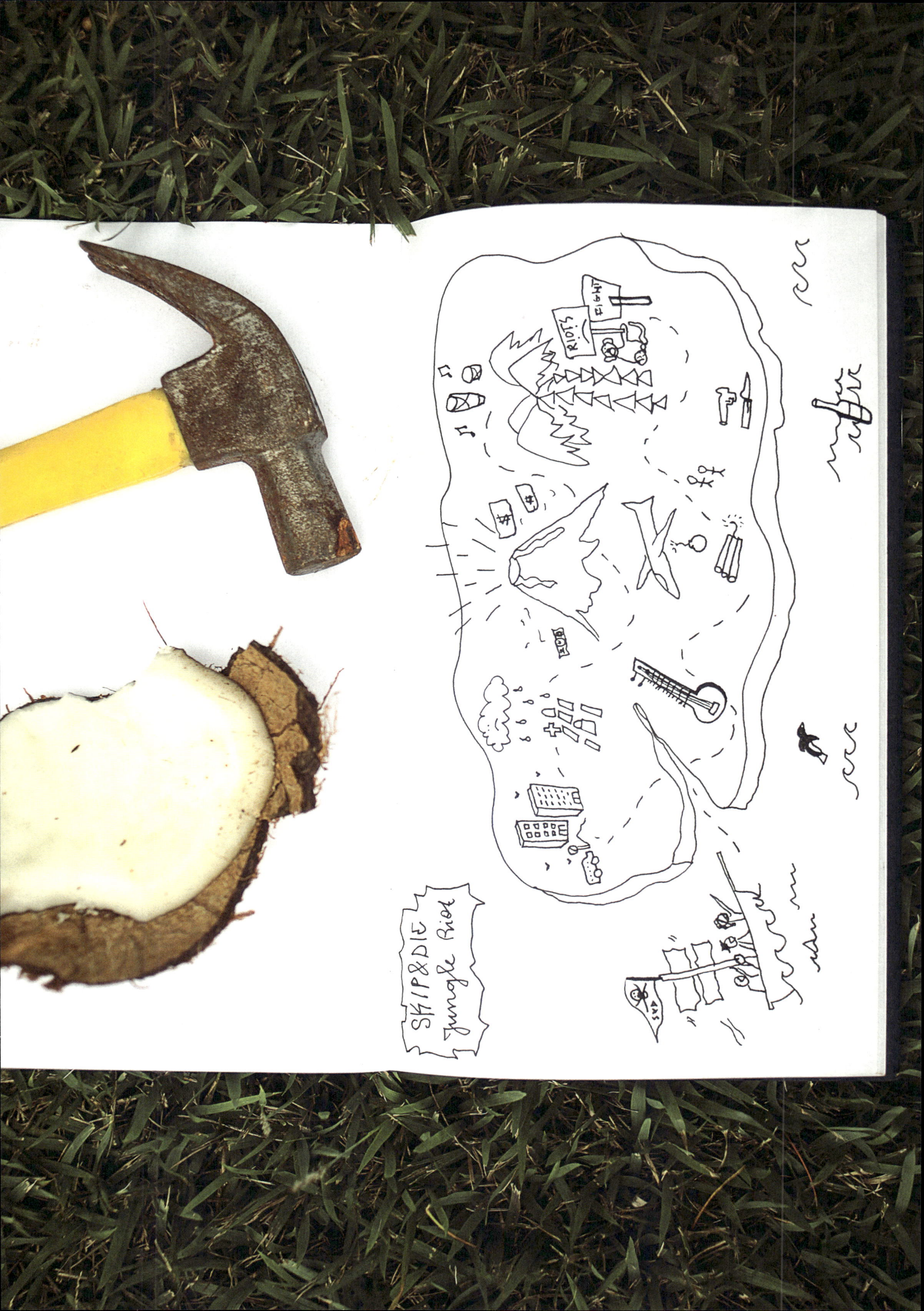
SKIP&DIE
Jungle Riot
RIOTS
FIGHT

72

Jungle Riot

SKIP&DIE

K

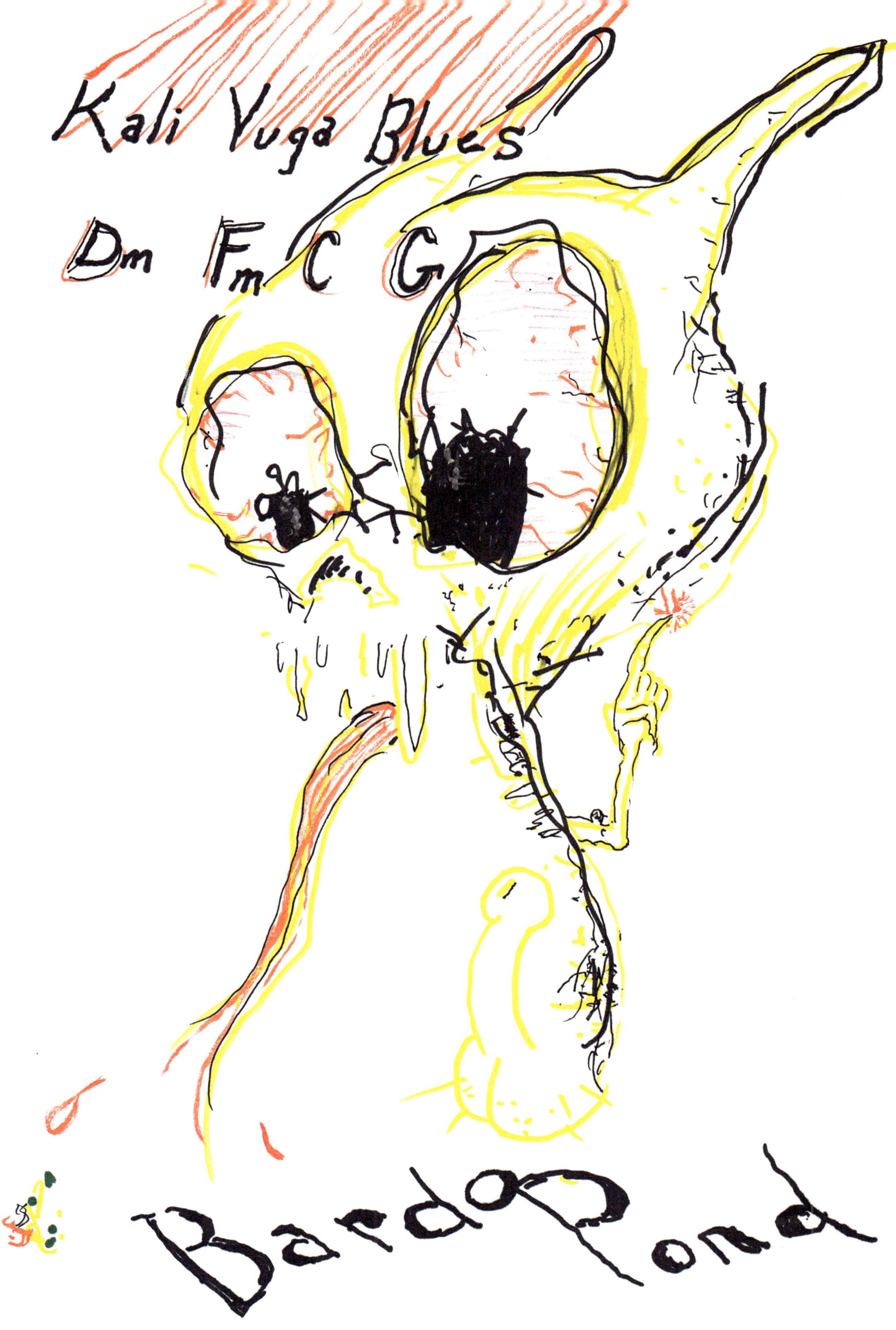
Kali Yuga Blues
Dm Fm C G
Bardo Pond

73
Kali Yuga Blues
BARDO POND

BRAHMA-LOKA

Key of It All 4/4

Gm (2 bars) D# (1 bar) Cm (1 bar)

Verse

Hold my hand lead the way
to a shallow grave where I lay
Painted nails dig the holes
And carry the stone
At the shrine the Devine separates the sea
What arose from Gold isn't make believe
I Believe I've got to find my

Chorus → Key of it all you have to find
Key of it, key of it
Key of it all you have to find
The Key of It All

Verse 2

Guiding light lead the way
From the shadow games that they play
All my words turn to grey
As I float away
At the shrine the Devine separates the sea
What arose from Gold isn't make believe
I Believe! I've got to find my
Key of it all you have to find. **THE KEY OF IT ALL!**

BENE HA EL OHIM

74
Key of It All
BRAHMA-LOKA

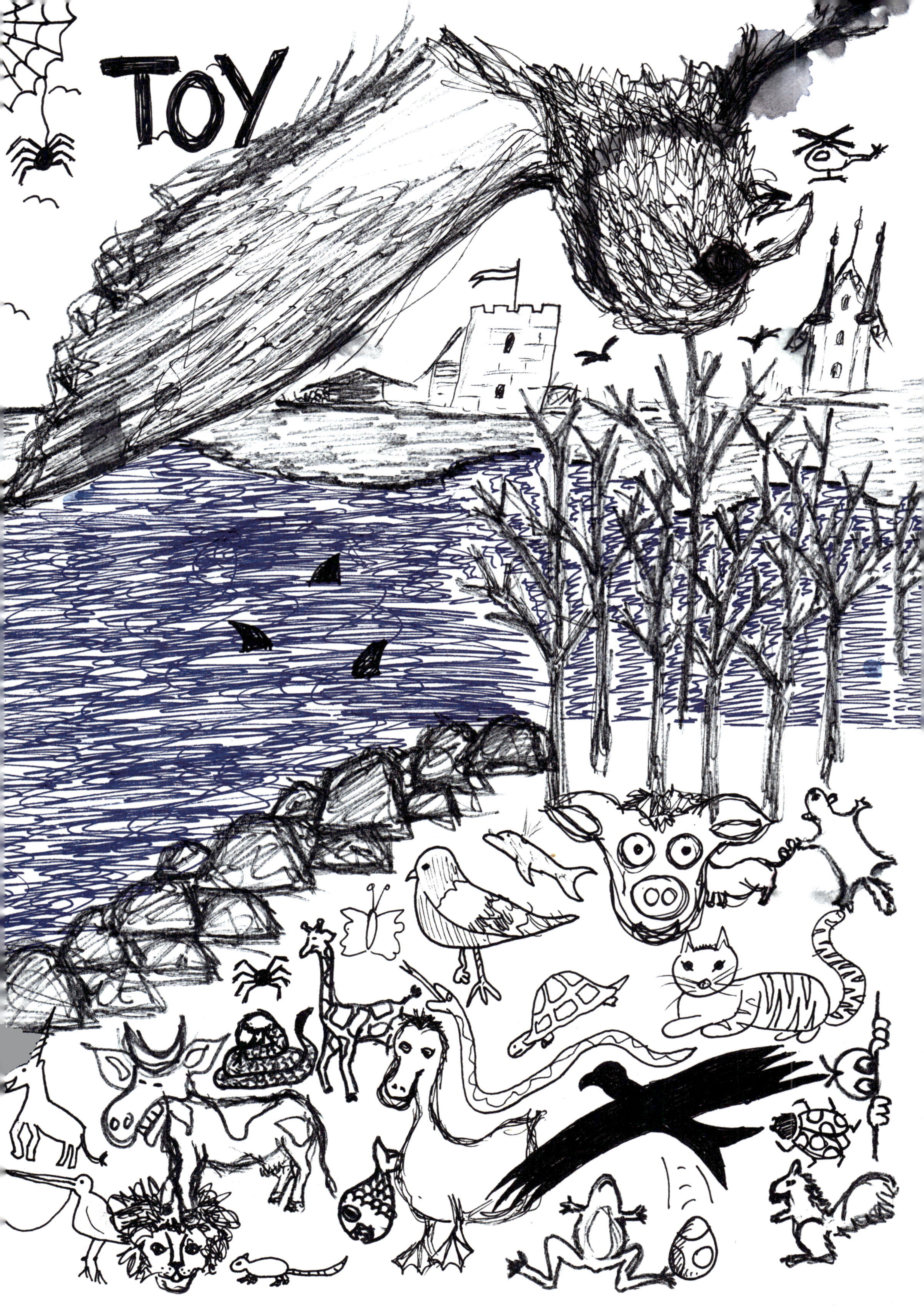
TOY

75
Kopter
TOY

L

open maybe lower? (to C on my guitar)

from what I've seen
you are magnificent
you fight evil
with all you do
your every act
is spectacular
it makes me lay here
and love you

9/28 verses D ending in F#mD

bar of D →
from what I ~~know~~ hear
you are wonderful ← change (generous)
you make sunshine
and glory too
when you walk in
things go luminous
it makes me lay here
and love you

C#m A +3
inst. ~~verse~~

from what I ~~hear~~ know
you're terrified
you have mistrust
running you through
your smile is hiding
something hurtful
it makes me lay here and love you A ~~(to Bm on walk to end part?)~~

it makes me lay here
and love you
I'm filled with ~~purple,~~ violet
and red and blue
I have a feeling
from what I do
that you might lay there
and love me too

half-length verse?

A APME (body)

last verse E

end C#m A; D A

76

Lay and Love

BONNIE "PRINCE" BILLY

Petit

de déthé

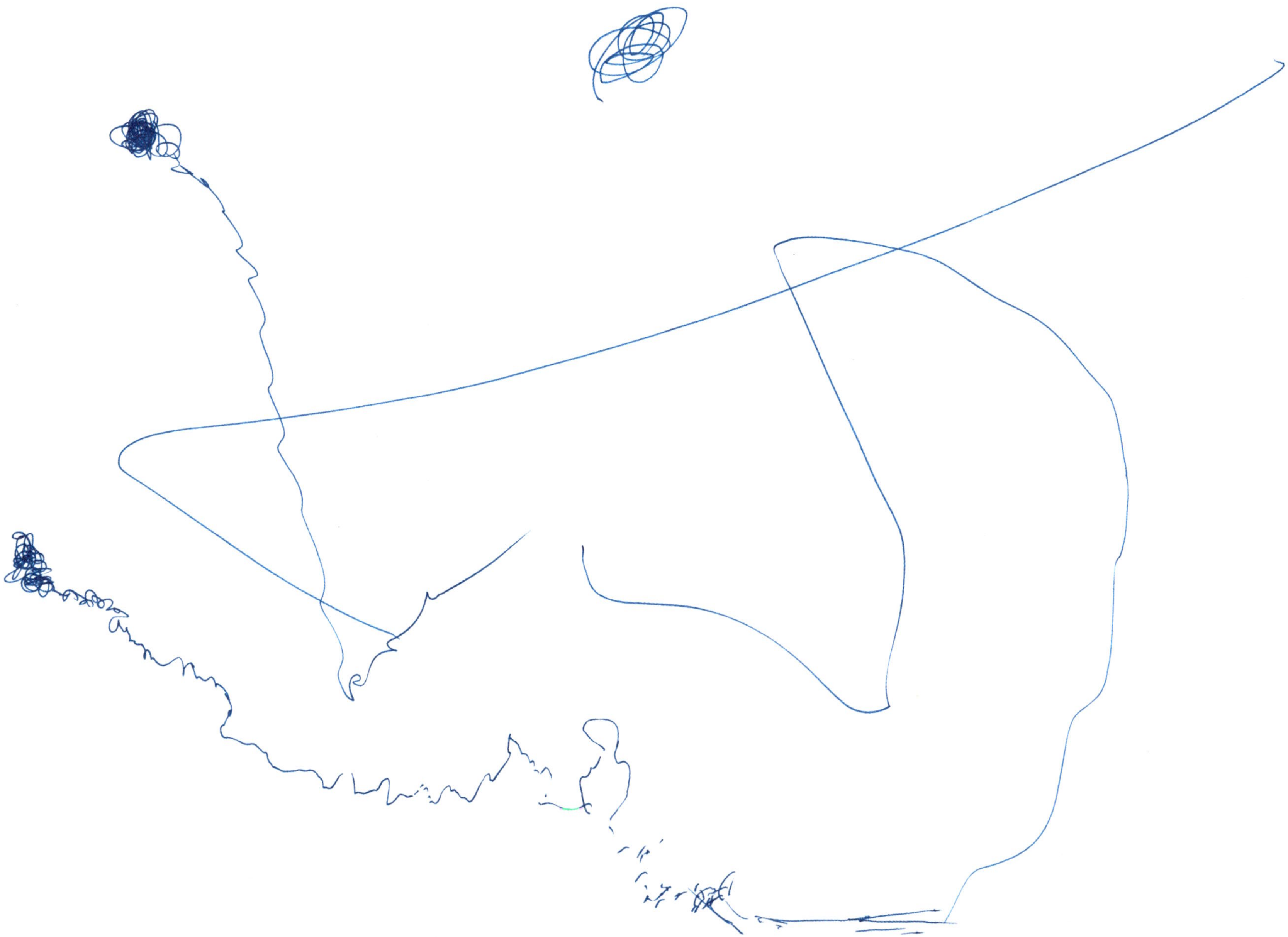

77

Le Léthé

PHILIPPE PETIT

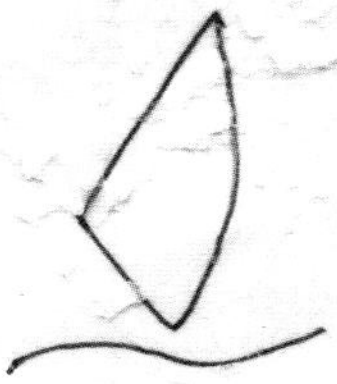

~ MOT LABYRINTHE ~

/D'AILLEURS/VIENS/JE/VOIR/N'AI/
/LES PLANCHES/
/ONI À VOILE/JAMAIS/RÉALISE/
/UN/LÀ-BAS/FAIS/ROCK DOC!/
/SUR LA MER/DE/SUR/
/PLANCHE/ACQUARELLE DE/ÀILA/
/TOURNÉE/MARS_/VOILE/J'ESPÈRE/
/QU'IL /BUVETTE/COLLÈGUE/AMI/VAI
/ÊTRE /M'EMMÈNE EN VOYAGE/BIEN/
WELCOME TO THE BAD BONN
NOS COPINES FONT LES IMAGES
MENTALES POÉTIQUES PENDANT LES
L*I*V*E*S

~

09.07.15
*B*B*B*B*

~

78

Les Véliplanchistes

FLAVIEN BERGER

LET IT BLEED

MANCHEGO ALL DRESSED IN BLACK
C Am D Am
MACHINE-MUM SCOOTER LOVE (SCHOOL OF LÖÖVE)
C Am D Am
THE WALKING DEAD THEY MUST READ
C Am D Am
GOT TO GO LET IT REEK
C Am D Am

FORGOTTEN SOAP, INDEED IT'S FRESH
C Am D → Am
LEATHER-FUR FOR TOURIST
C Am D C
KILL! FORE! PEAS! KILL! FORE! BREAST!
C Am D Am
DANCING BEES A BLOODY MESS
C Am D Am

79
Let It Bleed
GOAT

LILAC GARDEN

5-25-13

DOESN'T MATTER WHAT YOU DO
IN THE GARDEN OF LILACS

CORWOOD

80
Lilac Garden
JANDEK

(little pony)

i'm so afraid of myself
my skin is red to the touch
i'm so ashamed of myself
the little pony will touch

prepare the ice cubes
so prepare the glue
stand up and cry there (be opposed to everything there)
help me change my luck

i've lost the will to read or write
bend me over your knee
turn away from the light
while i giggle and squeal

so prepare the mop
and prepare the den
i'm so ashamed (i'm very much ashamed)
i'm ashamed of you and me

81

Little Pony

ARTO LINDSAY

"LOOKIN' TO GET RIGHT"

BY

MASTERS OF REALITY

OPEN D TUNING 4|4

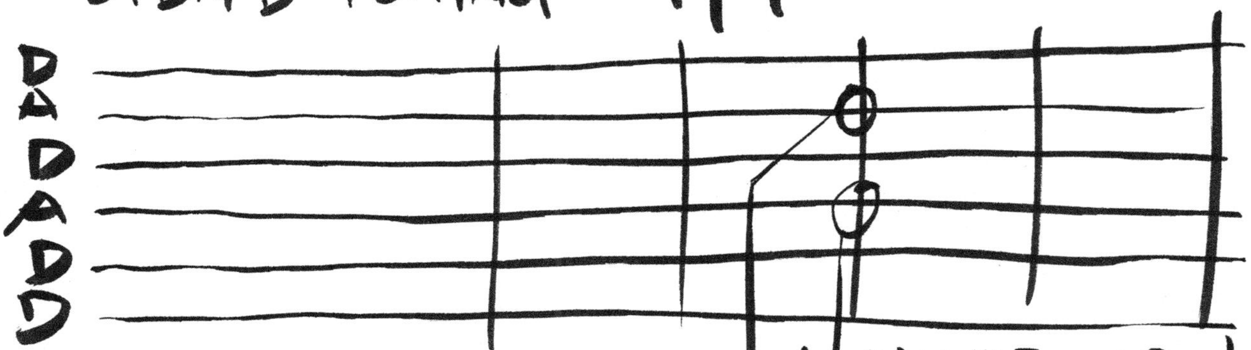

PHRASE 1

1 HAMMER ON (OFF|ON|OFF)

2 HAMMER ON 2X

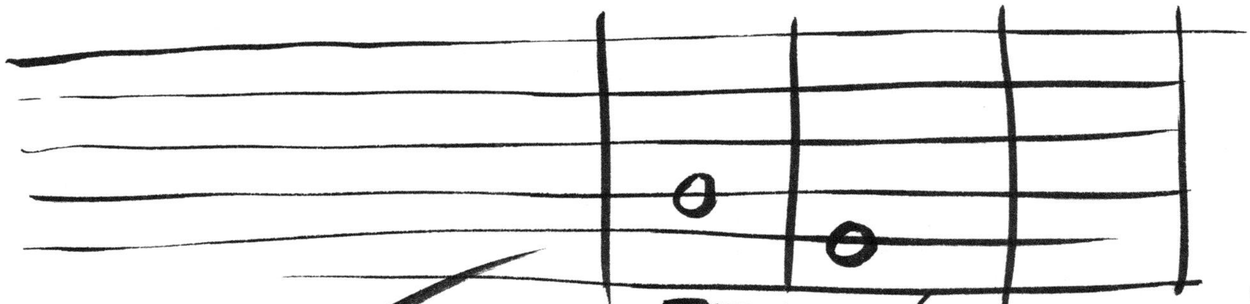

BRIDE (WITH SPIRIT)

3 OVER 4

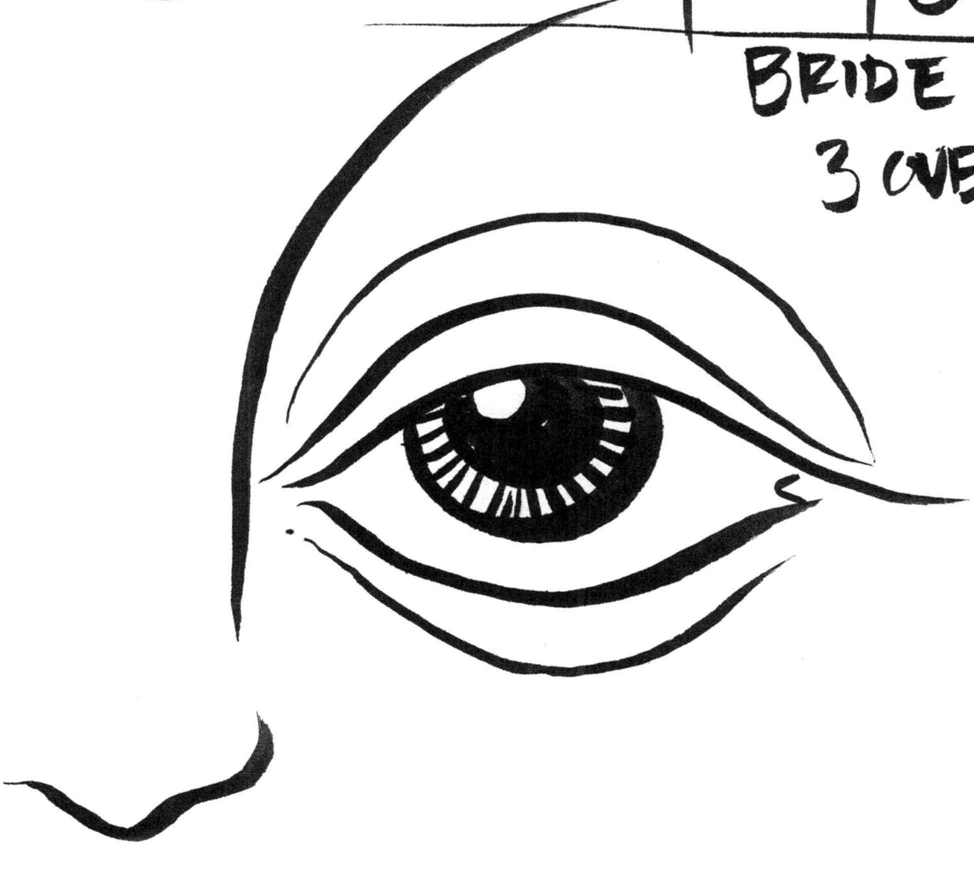

82
Lookin' to Get Right
MASTERS OF REALITY

}

```
void looperdata_write_sample(looper_data_t* data,float* L, float* R){
	if (!data->buf) return;
	if (!buffer_get_size(data->buf))  return;

	if (buffer_get_channels(data->buf) > 1){
		if (data->inmaxL < fabs(*L)){data->inmaxL = fabs(*L);}
		if (data->inmaxR < fabs(*R)){data->inmaxR = fabs(*R);}

		buffer_lock(data->buf);
		*L = *L * data->recmixnew +
			buffer_readsample_interpolated(data->buf, 1,data->recpos, data->buffer_group) *
			data->recmixorig;
		*R = *R * data->recmixnew +
			buffer_readsample_interpolated(data->buf, 2,data->recpos, data->buffer_group) *
			data->recmixorig;
		if (data->limiter){
			if (*L > data->limknee) *L = data->limit - data->limconst / *L;
			else if (*L < -data->limknee) *L = -data->limit - data->limconst / *L;
			if (*R > data->limknee) *R = data->limit - data->limconst / *R;
			else if (*R < -data->limknee) *R = -data->limit - data->limconst / *R;
		}
		buffer_writesample(data->buf, 1, data->recpos, 0, *L);
		buffer_writesample(data->buf, 2, data->recpos, 0, *R);
		buffer_unlock(data->buf);
	}else{
		if (data->inmaxL < fabs(*L)){data->inmaxL = fabs(*L);}

		buffer_lock(data->buf);
		*L = *L * data->recmixnew +
			buffer_readsample_interpolated(data->buf, 1,data->recpos, data->buffer_group) *
			data->recmixorig;
		if (data->limiter){
			if (*L > data->limknee) *L = data->limit - data->limconst / *L;
			else if (*L < -data->limknee) *L = -data->limit - data->limconst / *L;
		}
		buffer_writesample(data->buf, 1, data->recpos, 0, *L);
		buffer_unlock(data->buf);
	}
	if (++data->recpos > data->recend){
		data->recpos = data->recstart;
		if (data->recmode == LOOP_RECMODE_ONCE)
			data->isrecording = 0;
	}
	if (data->recpos < data->recstart){
		data->recpos = data->recstart;
	}
}
```

83
Looperdate_write_sample
DIEB13

We'll dance till we drop
and you'll sing to me,
Lucky you lucky me....

C F	C	Am F	C
Dm	G	Dm	G
F G	Am C

The Slow Show

Lucky you

Lucky Me

84
Lucky You, Lucky Me
THE SLOW SHOW

STEVE GUNN – LURKER

[signature] DADF# AD CAPO (3) FRET [signature]

CIRCULAR MELODY THROUGH THE WHOLE SONG – EASY!

/ AS THE STEADY HEADS RUSH, FROM THE PORCH HE FOLLOWS US
AND YOU THINK THAT HIS HANDLE IS SO WRONG
BUT YOU KNOW ITS NOT THE CASE, CAUSE HE WENT & SHOWED HIS FACE
FOUND A SPOT TO KILL SOME TIME AND LOOK AROUND.

/ AND YOU KNOW HIS RHYMES BY HEART, AND YOU DUCK HIS CHANCE
TO START, WALK ON BY WITH A SMILE AND NOT AN EAR. 2XS

/ AND HIS DEEDS ARE MET WITH SHOUTS, AS HE TURNS TO GO
BACK OUT, AND ITS DRIPPIN TO THE BOTTOM OF THE WELL 2XS

(BREAK – FUZZ WAH, ANYTHING, NOODLE FEST –
BRING BACK CIRCULAR MELODY FOR A BIT)

POOR THING VANISHED IN THE PARK, YOUR HOME WAS
EMPTIED IN THE DARK SHE TRIED TO LOOK YOU UP AND KEEP
YOU FAR AWAY.

BUT YOU WALKED A HUNDRED MILES, PUT THE HAG
ON TRIAL, GOT THE KEYS AND GAVE THEM TO HIS CHOSEN
SON – GOT THE KEYS AND GAVE THEM TO THE WRONG ONE.

FOUND A SPOT TO KILL TIME
GIVE A SMILE AND NOT AN EAR
AND ITS DRIPPING TO THE BOTTOM OF THE WELL 2XS

THEN PLAY WHATEVER YOU LIKE FOR AS LONG AS YOU LIKE

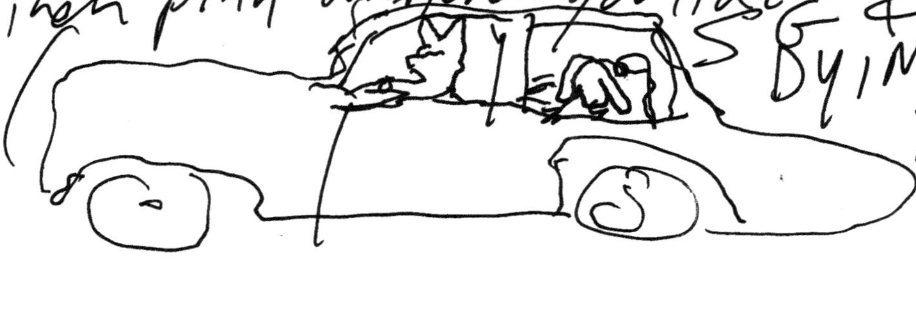

SG & THE DYING DOGS
TOMMY & ERIK

85

Lurker

STEVE GUNN

M

M

neuner-notenschreib-pa

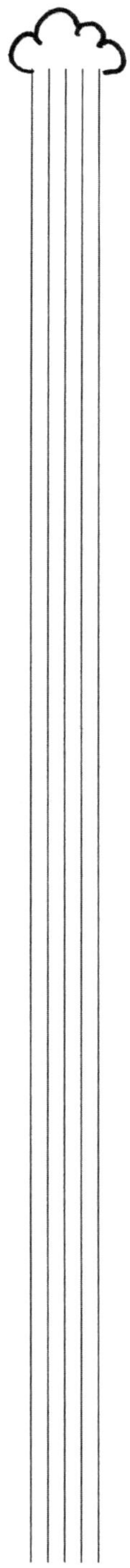

86
Many Weathers Apart
MERZ

March of Progress by Viet Cong.

Lately, there's a wound that needs
some healing soon,
before the infection can set in.
Slowly, this repulsion leads to Nausea
and fear for these old forgotten halls.
Maybe, you just need someone to
keep you warm,
with fire coming from a different sun.
Your reputation is preceding you,
we're all sufficiently impressed,
and this incessant march of progress
can guarantee our sure success...
We play the life secure with give and take
We build the buildings and they're built to
break.
tell me, tell it to me, tell it straight.
What is the difference between love + hate?

87
March of Progress
VIET CONG

ME & YOU &

intro & verse E - B - A - E x4

E - B - A - F#mi

A - B E - B - E

BRIDGE: C#mi - A - E

C#mi - A - B

C#mi - A - E

C#mi _ B

Breakdown / Chorus: 4x A - G# - F# - E

"me & you & Jackie mittoo: A - E B - E x4

4x A - G# - F# - E

OUTRO: 3x E - B - A - E

E - C#mi - B

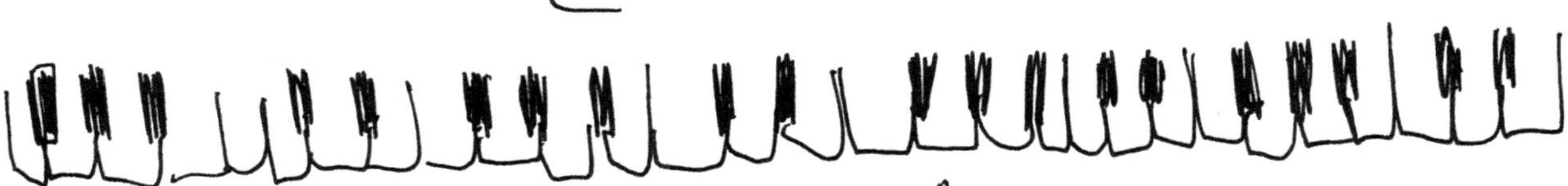

JACKIE MITTOO

88
Me & You & Jackie Mittoo
SUPERCHUNK

MIR SCHADED DE WIRTSCHAFT.

Text: Erdbebe schadet de Wirtschaft
Überschwemmig schadet de Wirtschaft
Ozonloch schadet de Wirtschaft
Atomusstieg schadet de Wirtschaft
Hoor wachse loh schadet de Wirtschaft
Inere Höhli wohne schadet de Wirtschaft
Gratis schadet de Wirtschaft
Und langsam schadet de Wirtschaft

Mir hend eigeti Tomate
Mir hend eigeti Idee
Mir schaded de Wirtschaft

Mir gönd inen Lade
Und gond wieder use
Zum de Wirtschaft schade
Mir schaded de Wirtschaft

Und d Wirtschaft seit:
D Welt isch en Drive-in
Jo, d Wirtschaft seit:
D Welt isch en Drive-in
Sie hät e Websiite
Und sie hät Öffnigsziite
Und mir hend eigeti Tomate
Mir hend eigeti Idee
Mir schaded de Wirtschaft
Mir schaded de Wirtschaft

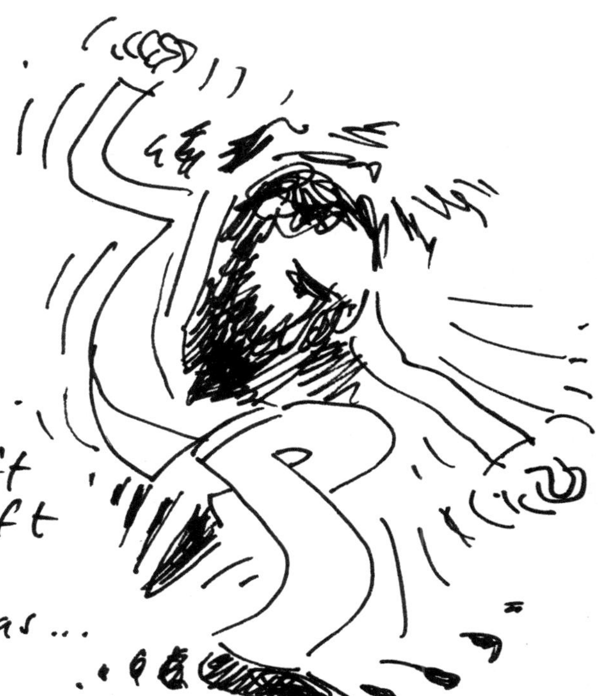

Musik: Rhythmus, Blues, irgendwas ...

89

Mir schaded de Wirtschaft

MANUEL STAHLBERGER

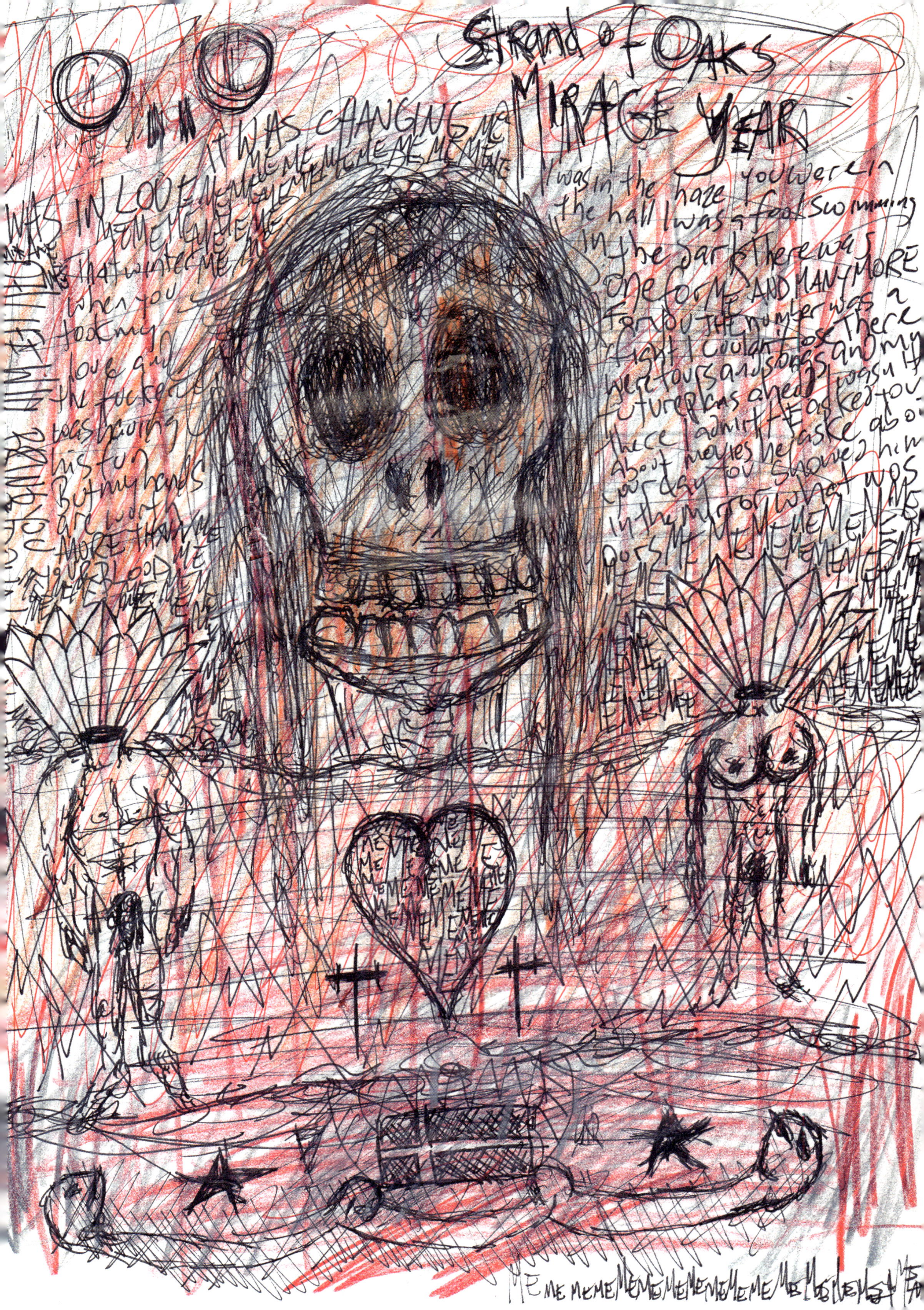

Strand of Oaks
MIRAGE YEAR
I WAS IN LOVE
IT WAS CHANGING ME
I was in the haze you were in the hall I was a fool swimming in the dark there was one for me AND MANY MORE for you the number was a fight I couldn't lose

90
Mirage Year
STRAND OF OAKS

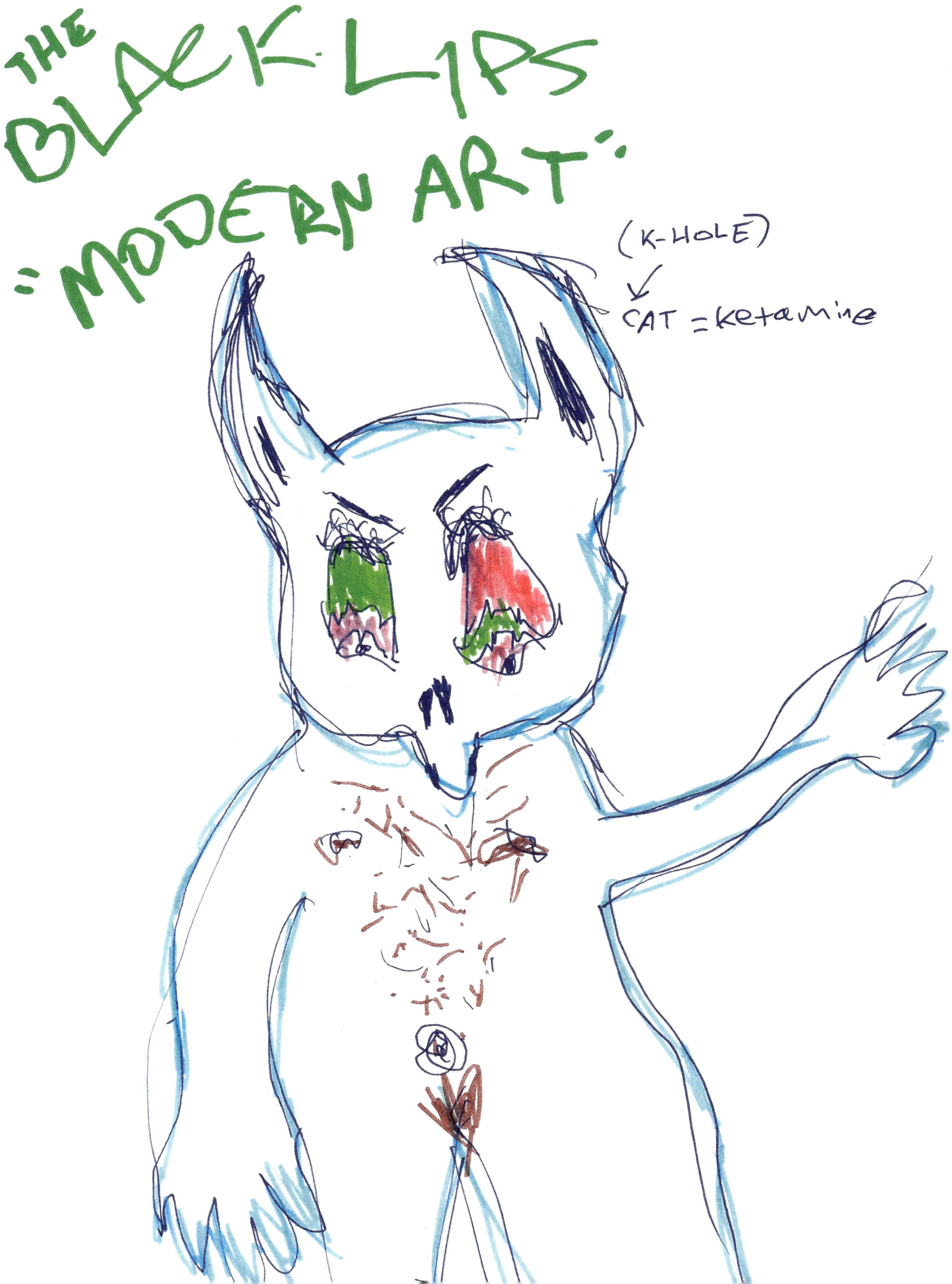
THE BLACK LIPS
"MODERN ART"
(K-HOLE)
CAT = ketamine

91
Modern Art
BLACK LIPS

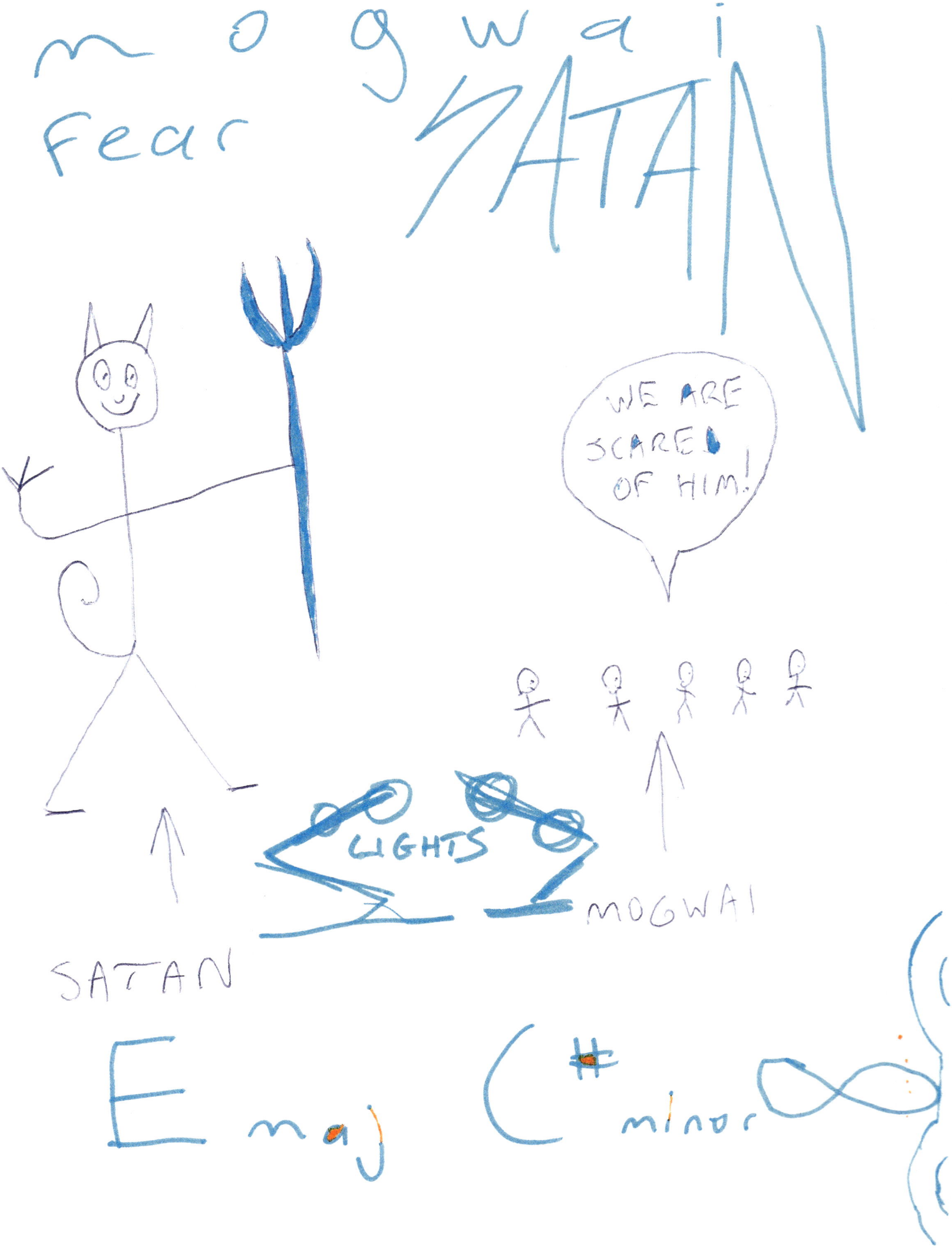
mogwai
Fear
SATAN
WE ARE SCARED OF HIM!
LIGHTS
MOGWAI
SATAN
E maj
C# minor

92

Mogwai Fear Satan

MOGWAI

Morning Sun

```
E ·                                                  ↑↑
B ·                  55                         55 5 5
G ·          666 44      44 66          666 44
D ·  444                          444
A ·
E ·
```

Oh honey,

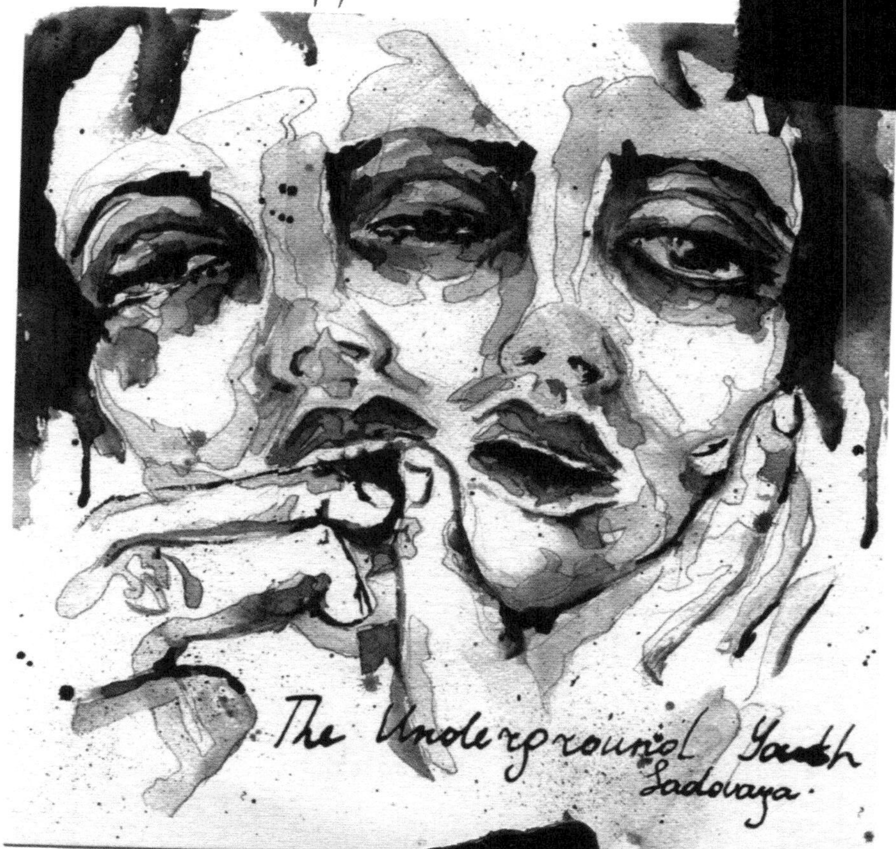

I don't believe
in a god.
But I believe in
your design as
one thing that's
divine, honey.

Your heart it
feels like a
loaded gun, let's run
honey run into the morning sun.

A – B F# E A B F# E

A B F# E A B F# E F# E F#

93

Morning Sun

THE UNDERGROUND YOUTH

Motel Money a Way - Birth of Joy

E G A

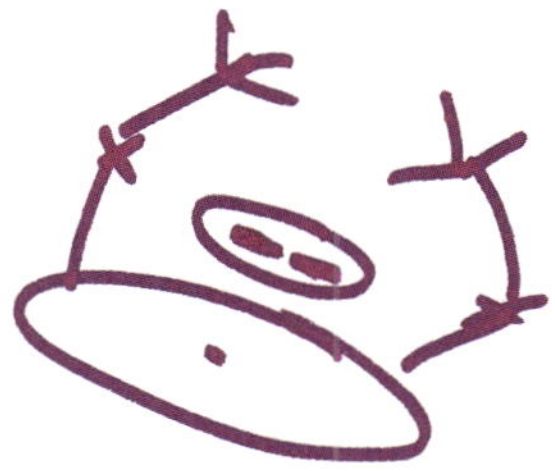

I'm tired of moaning
I'm doing that for years
It's time to get a home
It's time to get home

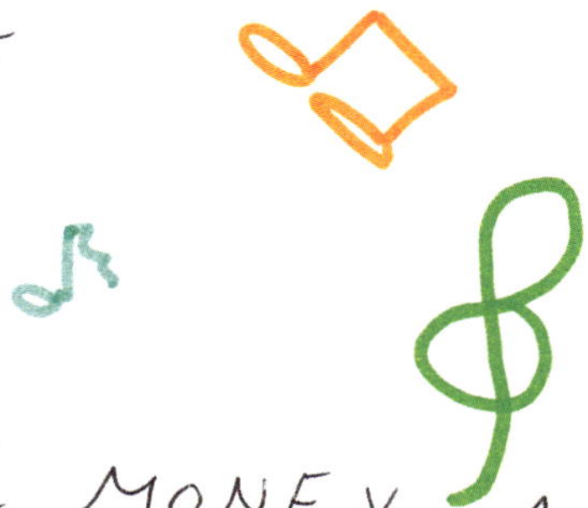

G B
E G A

But there is a motel money a way
~~there is a motel money a way~~

E G A

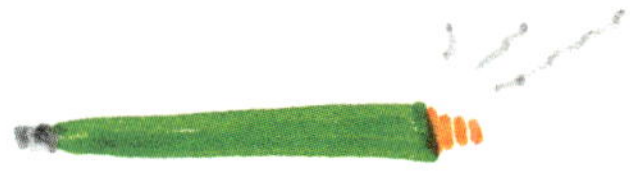

Driver keep on driving
Across the land
It's time to get a home
It's time to get home

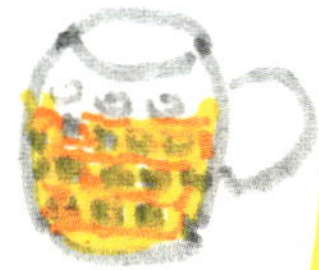

G B
E G A

But there is a motel money a way
There is a motel money a way
There is a motel money a way
There is a motel money a way

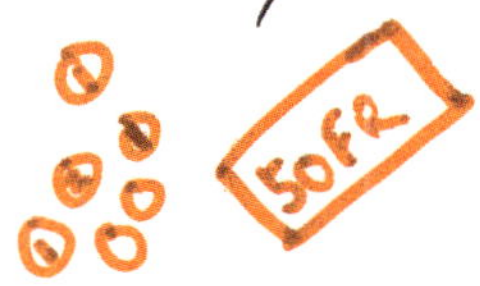

– SOLO!! –
REPÆAT TWICE with SCREAM!!

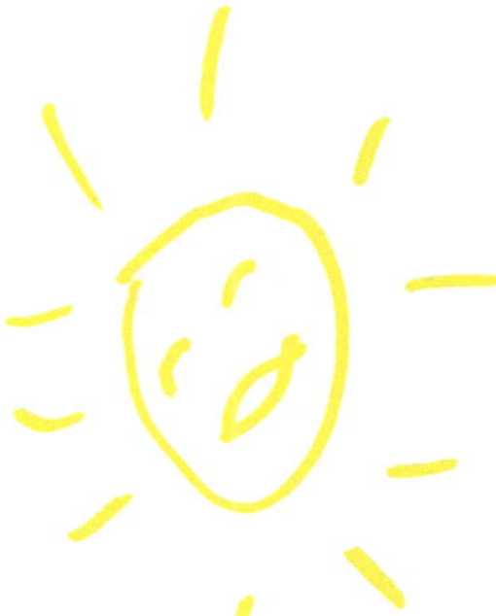

94
Motel Money a Way
BIRTH OF JOY

MOTHER

DOUX ET LENT
SON CLAIR

Ø capo

[4x 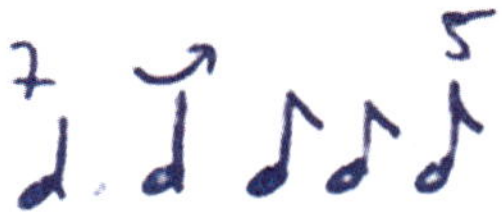]

MOTHER FATHER SISTER BROTHER
WE AIN'T GOT THE SAME FEATURES) 2x

FATHER BROTHER MOTHER SISTER
WE'RE TWO SIDES AND ALL OF US) 2x

8 7 6 5 0
AALL ALL OF US + [4x]
8 7 6 5 0
WEE SU...UU... FFER + [4x]

0 5
WE'RE / TWO SIDES
0
AND ALL OF US
) 2x

5
ALL OF US
0
WE SU FFER

V NOTE : 3e corde à vide

5 = 5 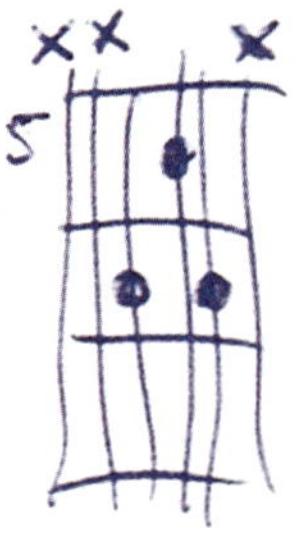

V NOTE : ACCORD

< TRUC CHRISTIAN

> APPRÈS AKU, AV.-DERNIER ACCORD AJOUTER

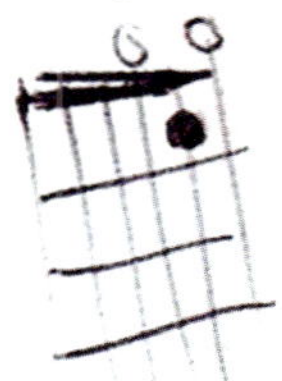

8 7 6 5 0
AALL ALL OF US [+4]
8 7 6 5 0
WEE SU UU FFER [+4] ← 2x

95

Mother

MERIL WUBSLIN

"Motorbike" Wooden Shjips

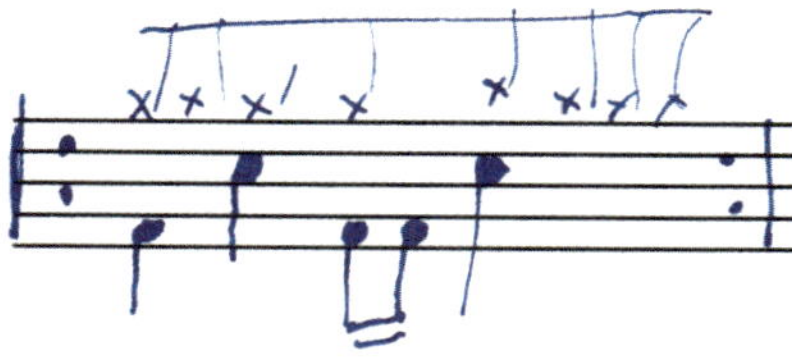

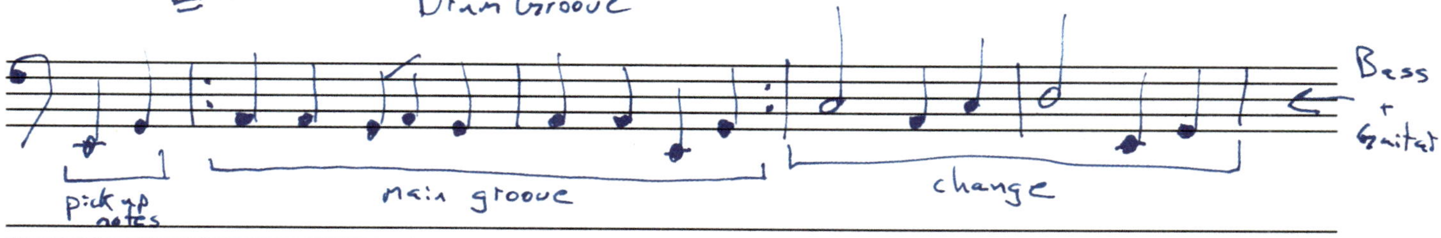

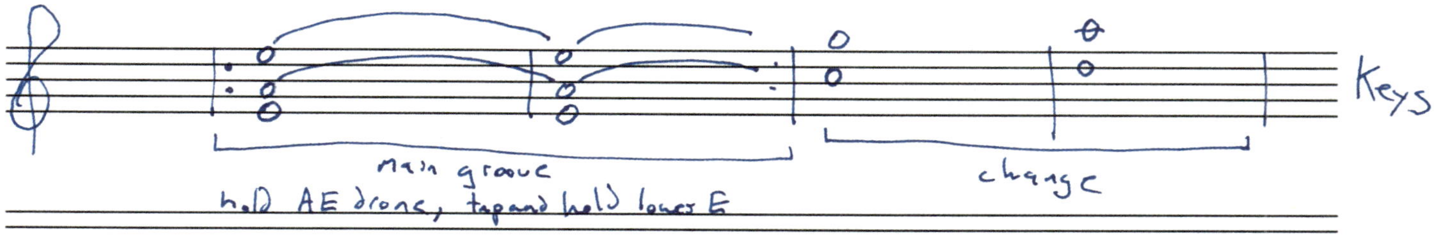

We're on the run, in the city at night
~~away from those not ... in chains~~
And not fearing a fight
We cut loose on our motorbikes, in the hills and streets
~~And take a load off too — for free~~

We came to be, in this city of light
~~We ... felt so good, we danced and f—d~~
we get off on our motorbikes, to the beat of the earth
~~It turns our way, and never hurts~~

We're leaving here, in a cloud of smoke
~~We run the town on a skid~~
And the streets are cold
~~We're now back on our motorbikes~~
~~The wind a cushion of air~~
We won't come back again, once we're there
~~Far from home~~

96
Motorbike
WOODEN SHJIPS

Mr. Carbon Copy

Call him Mr. Carbon Copy
King of all the double people
He's an echo
a reflection
nobody you'd want to be

Living among the body snatchers
making sets of matching people
piling up the body doubles
He has everything he needs

tired of turning blood into bourbon
Bones into ashes, mountains of glasses
shatter them all and start again

---

tired of turning slowly suburban
while memory passes from base to acid
erase the tapes & start again

Call him Mr. Carbon Copy
echoing his every order
We are only blurry copies . . .

97

Mr. Carbon Copy

MORGAN DELT

Muchacho's Tune

words + music
by
Matthew Houck
(aka PHOSPHORESCENT)
(PHOSPHORESCENT)

I Sang Roll away the Stone.
Set up a trembling in my bones
I sat there all alone
Just cried and cried
I saw the moonlight's mirrored glow
On that ol dirty city snow
I sat there feelin low
O my O my

— — — — — —

I found some fortune, I found some fame
I found they cauterized my veins —
I been fucked up. they
+ I been a fool
But like the shepherd to the lamb
Like the wave unto the Sand.
I'll Fix my self up.
To Come + Be With You

98
Muchacho's Tune
PHOSPHORESCENT

. . .

See, I was slow to understand
This River's ~~bigger~~ BIGGER than I am
It's runnin faster than I can
Tho Lord I Tried
Between the shadow & the storm
A little pup was bein born.
A little whelp without his horns

O my O my

Hey Mama meet me 'neath the moon
I will be hummin out that tune.
I been fucked up
And I been A fool

~~Hey Mama~~ AW NOW, Mama,
HERE I STAND
AW HONEY. I'm Reaching
FOR YOUR HAND
FIX MYSELF UP.
COME BE WITH YOU.

N

"NADA EM VÃO"

Rodrigo Amarante

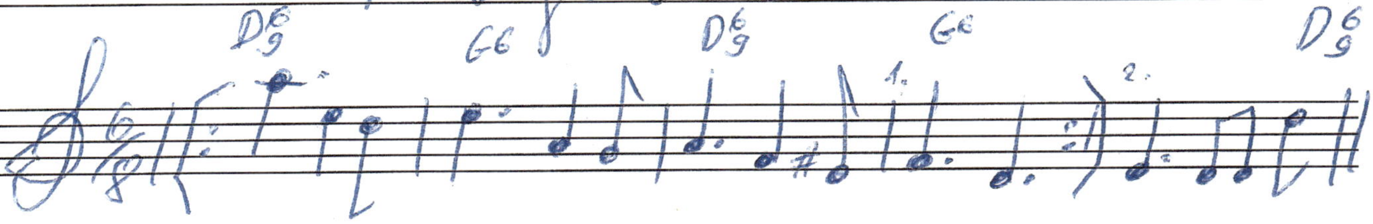

(main theme.)

D6/9 Gm6 D6/9 Gm6 D6/9
Nada Em Vão / no espaço entre eu

Gm6 D6/9 Gm6
e você / no silêncio um grito / o sim e o não

D6/9 Gm6 D6/9 Gm6 D6/9
eis então / que o pedaço de mim /

Gm6 D6/9 Gm6
que é só teu / é intento sem tanto intenção

Em7 A7/13 A7/A6 Em7 A7/13
Quando eu vejo você, oh, / me olhando assim

Em7 A7/13 Em7 A7/13 A7/B
vendo em mim / o que eu vejo em ti...

99
Nada Em Vão
RODRIGO AMARANTE

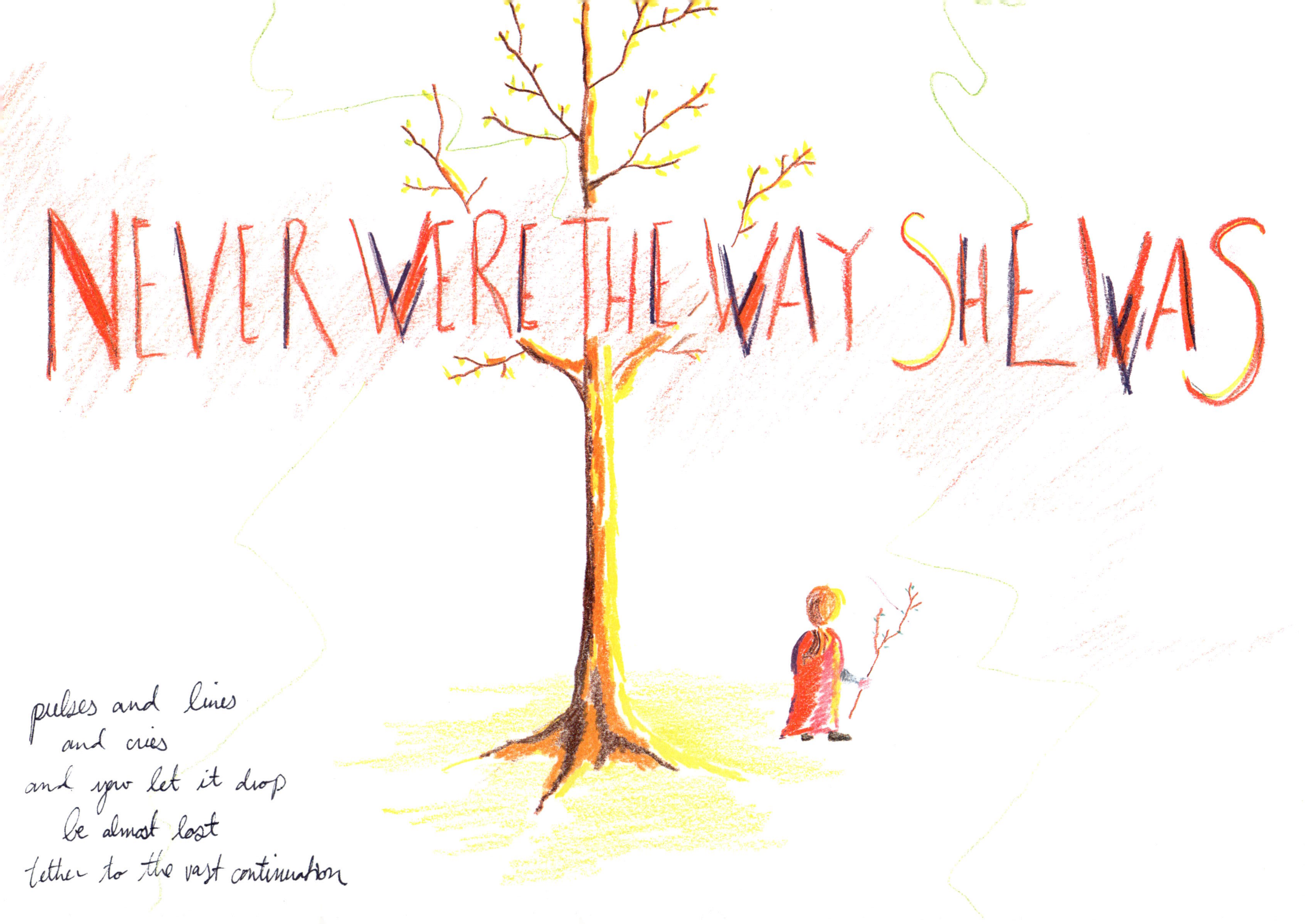
NEVER WERE THE WAY SHE WAS
pulses and lines
and cries
and you let it drop
be almost lost
tether to the vast continuation

100

Never Were the Way She Was

COLIN STETSON & SARAH NEUFELD

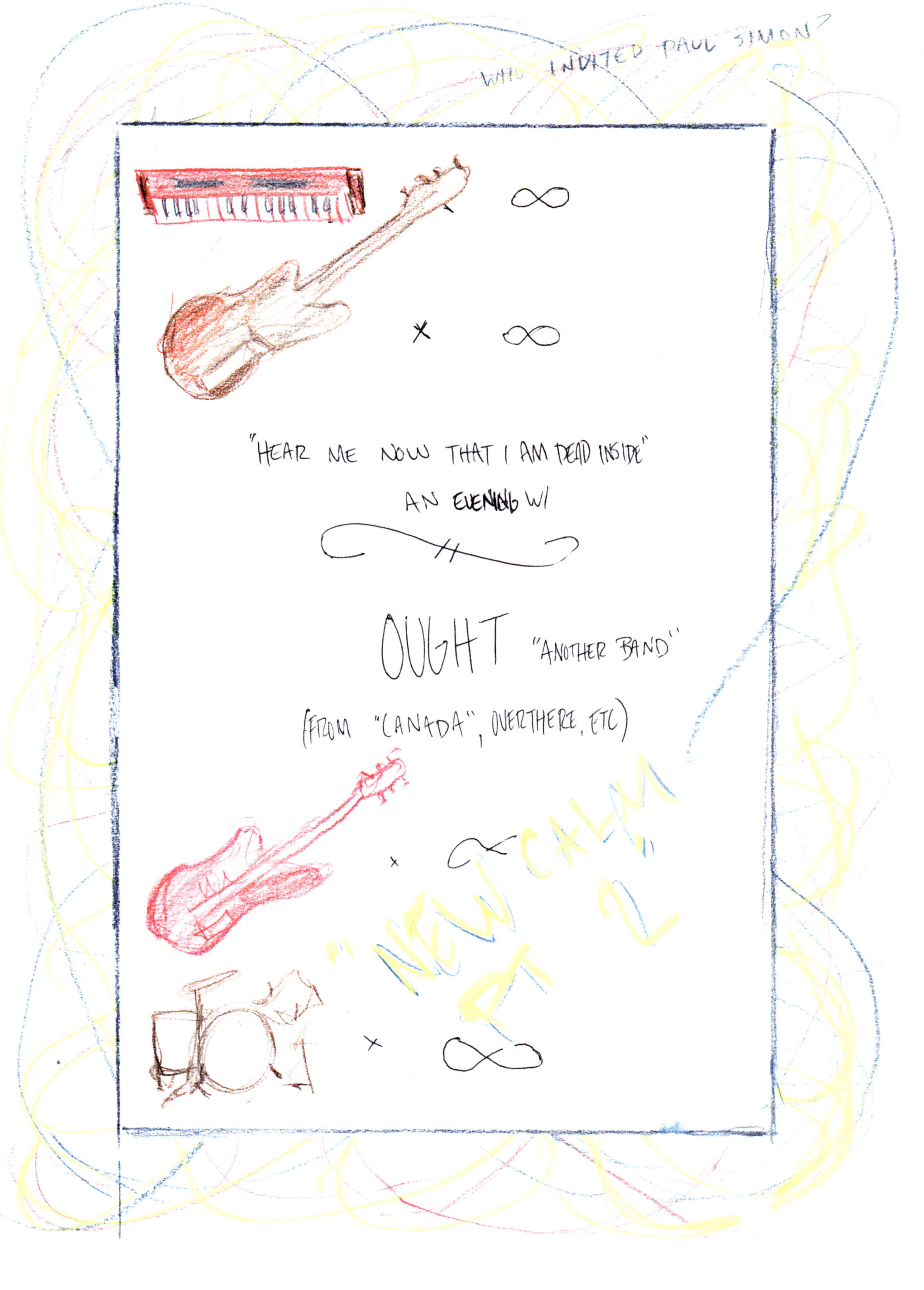
WHO INDITED PAUL SIMON?
"HEAR ME NOW THAT I AM DEAD INSIDE"
AN EVENING W/
OUGHT "ANOTHER BAND"
(FROM "CANADA", OVERTHERE, ETC)
"NEW CALM PT 2"

101
New Calm Pt. 2
OUGHT

5 6 7

≫NO!≪

≫NO GO!≪

4

Chelsea

No!

3

light

Thurston Moore

Thanx → Eva, Catherine, Daniel

No!

MMXiii

2

moving

No!

1

restes ou tu es

Disce que tu veux

Say what you will —

GO!

Vas-y

Stay where you are

NO!

102
No Go!
CHELSEA LIGHT MOVING

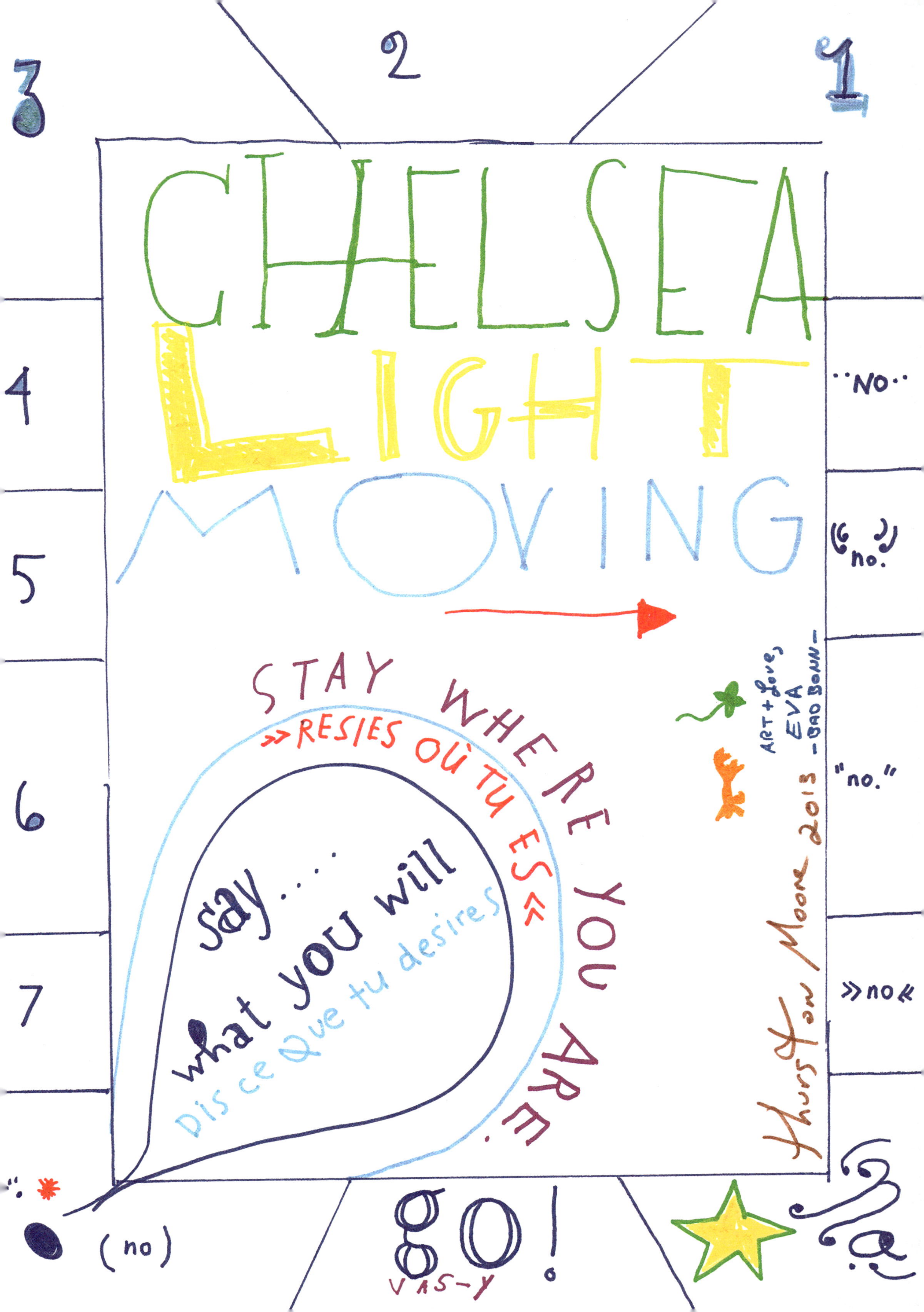

3
2
1
CHELSEA
LIGHT
MOVING
4
..NO..
5
no.
STAY WHERE YOU ARE.
→RESIES OÙ TU ES←
say.....
what you will
Dis ce Que tu desires
6
"no."
7
»no«
ART + Love, EVA -BAD BONN-
Thurston Moore 2013
(no)
go!
VAS-Y

0

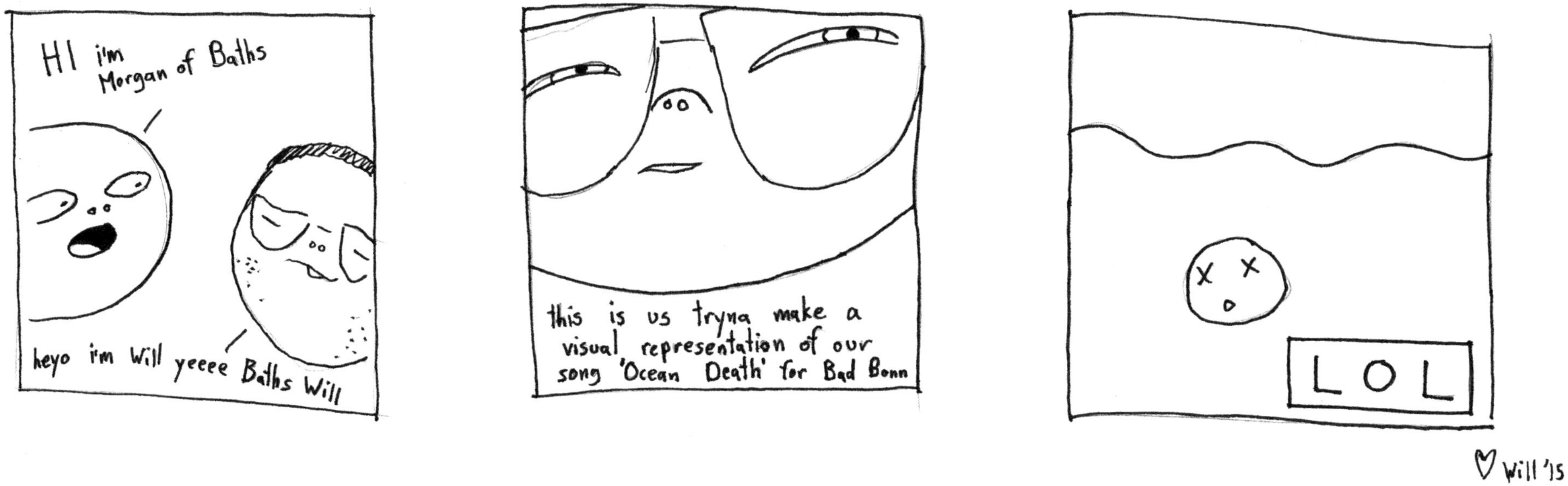
HI i'm Morgan of Baths
heyo i'm Will yeeee Baths Will
this is us tryna make a visual representation of our song 'Ocean Death' for Bad Bonn
LOL
♡ Will '15

103

Ocean Death

BATHS

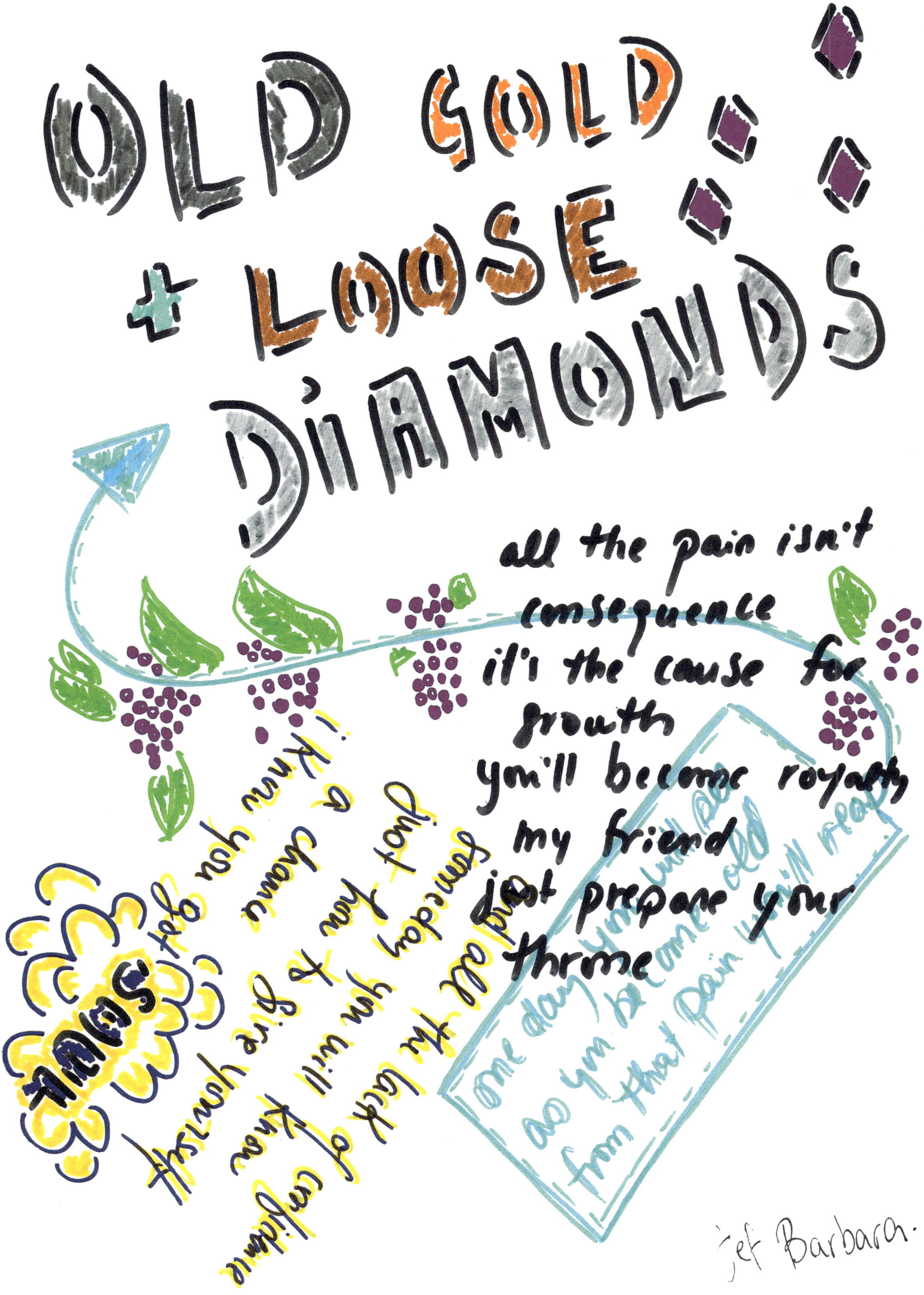
OLD GOLD
+ LOOSE
DIAMONDS
all the pain isn't
consequence
it's the cause for
growth
you'll become royalty
my friend
just prepare your
throne
i know you got SOUL
a chance
just how to fire yourself
someday you will know
and all the lack of confidence
one day you will see
as you become old
from that pain you'll reap
Barbara.

104
Old Gold and Loose Diamonds
JEF BARBARA

BM - A - F#M - G

— ON THE WATER —

ON THE WATER DECISIONS ARE FEW
AS A DRIFTER Flies the CHOICE is yours
i TELL You i May be there
i TELL You How i NEED you
i can BARELY WAlK i CAN ONLY RUN to you
i COME CRASHing through the Door
Just to tell you how much i lovE you

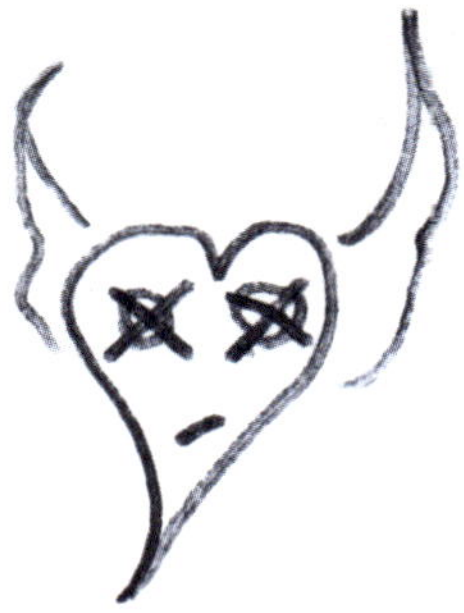

All THE WATER is Poisoned now
AND All THE TREES HANG DYEiNG
All THE EARTH is EMPTY
All thought void
i WAiT Upon my knees
AND when the night slowly Fades
AND i WAKE TO This Day
You'll COME CRAShing through the door
Just to Tell me how much you lovE ME

i remember how we said Hello
i Remember how we said good bye
i Remember Everything
i Remember Everything

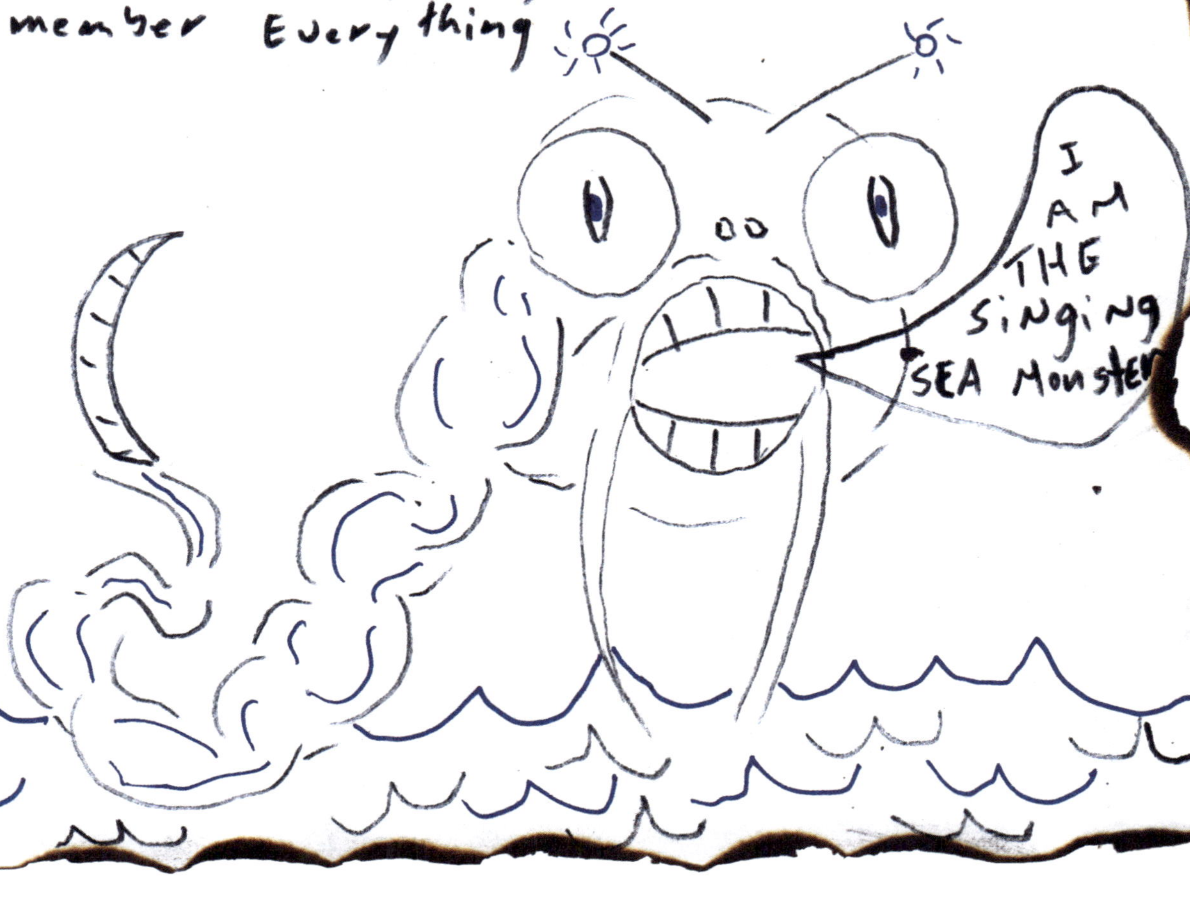

PAll JENKINS 2014

105
On the Water
PALL JENKINS

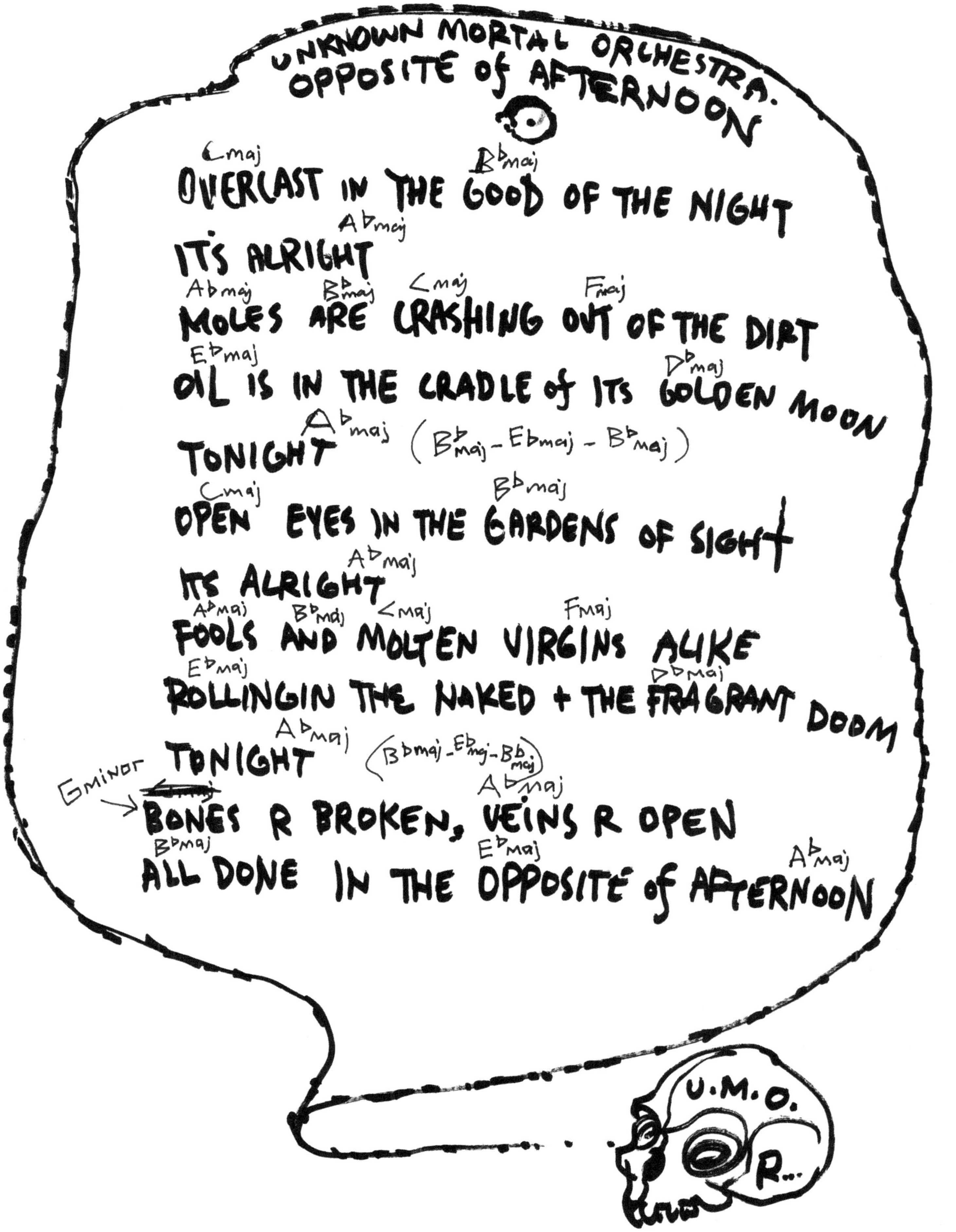

UNKNOWN MORTAL ORCHESTRA.
OPPOSITE of AFTERNOON
Cmaj Bbmaj
OVERCAST IN THE GOOD OF THE NIGHT
Abmaj
IT'S ALRIGHT
Abmaj Bbmaj Cmaj Fmaj
MOLES ARE CRASHING OUT OF THE DIRT
Ebmaj Dbmaj
OIL IS IN THE CRADLE of ITS GOLDEN MOON
Abmaj (Bbmaj - Ebmaj - Bbmaj)
TONIGHT
Cmaj Bbmaj
OPEN EYES IN THE GARDENS OF SIGHT
Abmaj
ITS ALRIGHT
Abmaj Bbmaj Cmaj Fmaj
FOOLS AND MOLTEN VIRGINS ALIKE
Ebmaj Dbmaj
ROLLINGIN THE NAKED + THE FRAGRANT DOOM
Abmaj (Bbmaj - Ebmaj - Bbmaj)
TONIGHT
Gminor Abmaj
BONES R BROKEN, VEINS R OPEN
Bbmaj Ebmaj Abmaj
ALL DONE IN THE OPPOSITE of AFTERNOON
U.M.O.
R...

106

Opposite of Afternoon

UNKNOWN MORTAL ORCHESTRA

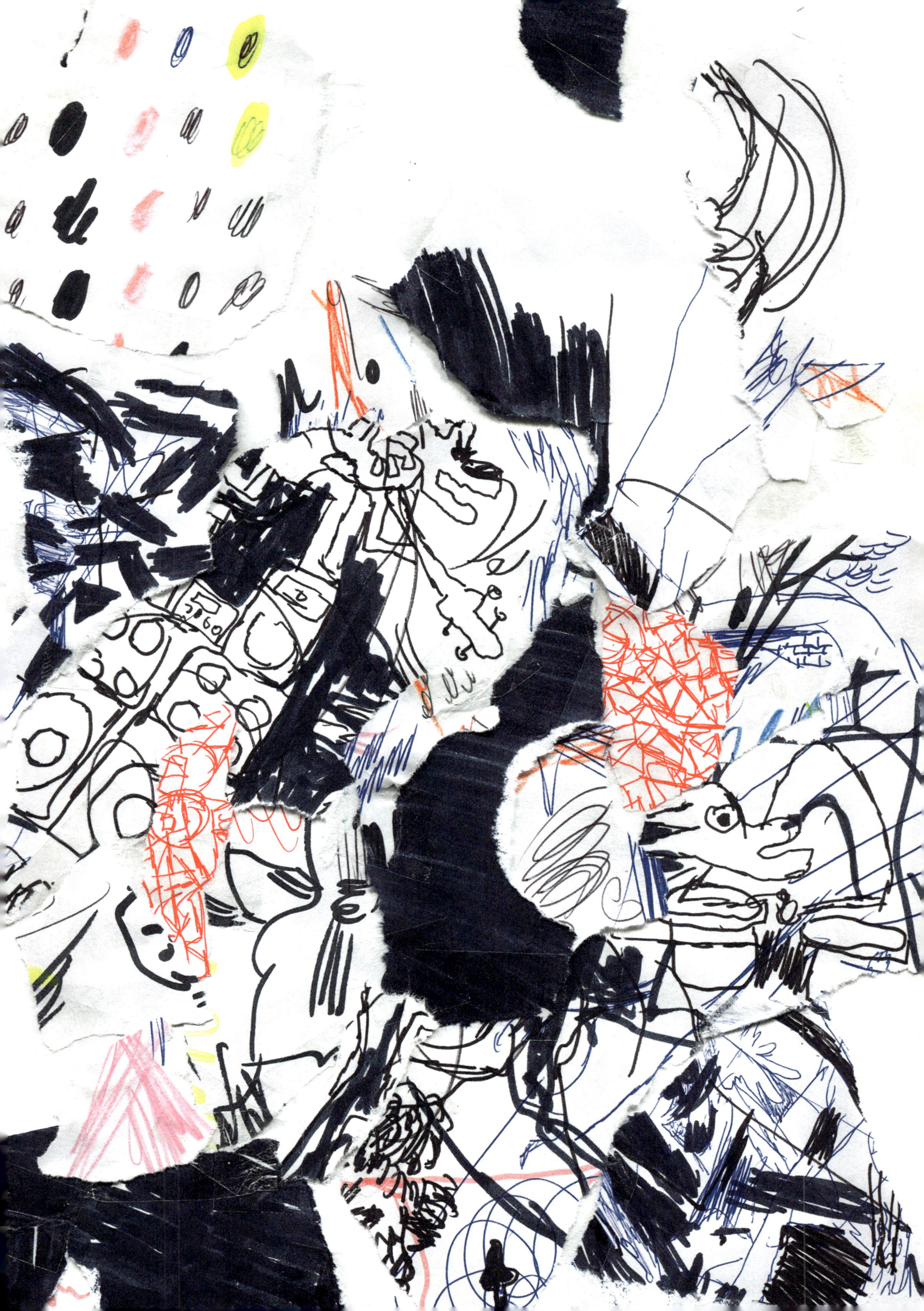

107

Over the River and Through the Woods

LIGHTNING BOLT

P

Power to the Women of the Morning Shift ..

by Oum Skatt

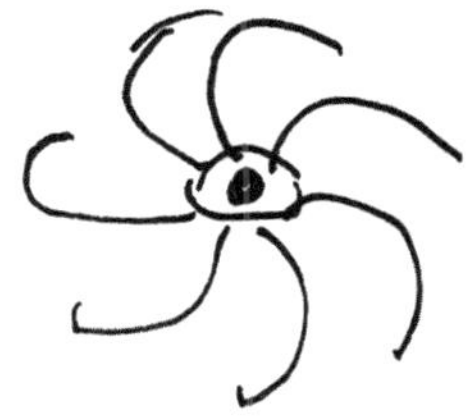

RIFF (what's it all about)

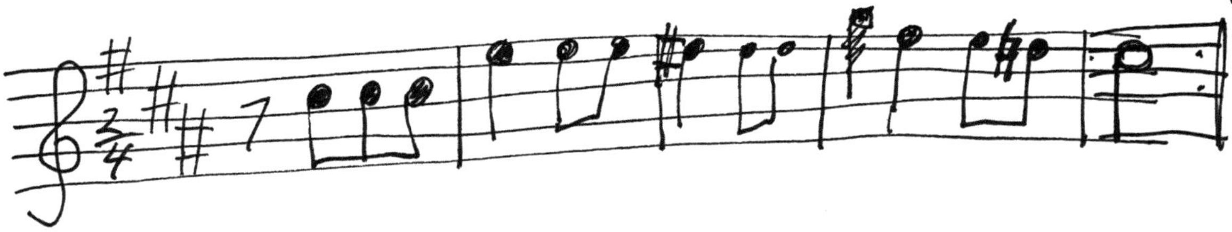

~~Akt~~ CHORDS:

F#m Am G#m Bm F#m F#m

in between:

"Power to the Women of the Morning Shift": in C#m

Lyrics: I Blonde one from the Wilderness
is almost dressed and i'm
just a guest now. Female grace ??
she hits my face! Makes me
feel like i've ruled this world too long.

⟹ Power to the Women of the Morning Shift 2x

II Yesternight your rhythm made me stumble
your geometry made me feel humble

but: i'm ~~a~~ man (!), rock'n'roll makes
me cry in the dawn ... i mean ...
... almost ... – anyway you've got to move on!

108

Power to the Women of the Morning Shift

OUM SHATT

SHEEP DOG BEEN NIPPING AT YOUR HEELS

ALL DAY SHEEP DOG

LEAP FROG DONT HAVE A WAY TO

STAY IN LINE

AND SO YOURE MINE

YOU CAN SEE A SHEEP WHERE SHE LAY

YOU CAN KEEP A TEMPTRESS AT BAY

TO KEEP WHATS IN THE DNA

YOU SHOULD LEAD THEM TO A NEW PLACE

COCOON A SPACE TO SAY SO SOFTLY

FOOL THESE UGLY THOUGHTS WHAT ARE THEY?

GOOD GUY DONT KNOW YOU WHEN YOU HIDE AWAY

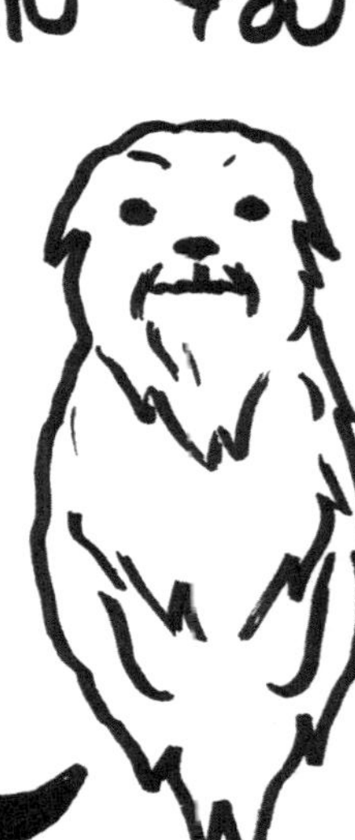

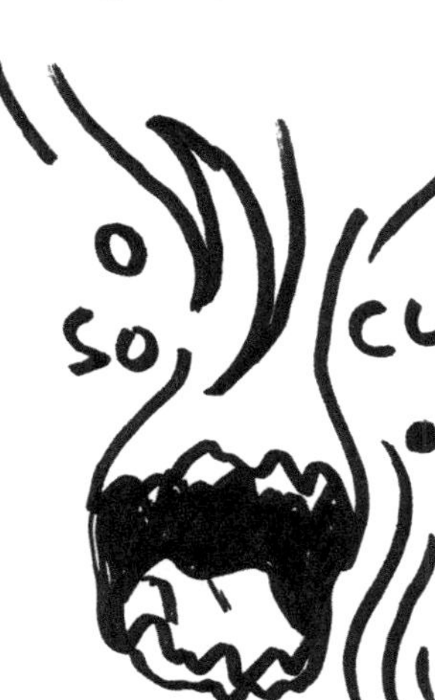

SO CLOSE - AS GENTLE AS A SLEEPING BABY BOY

NOAH + DANNY

109
Principe Real
PANDA BEAR

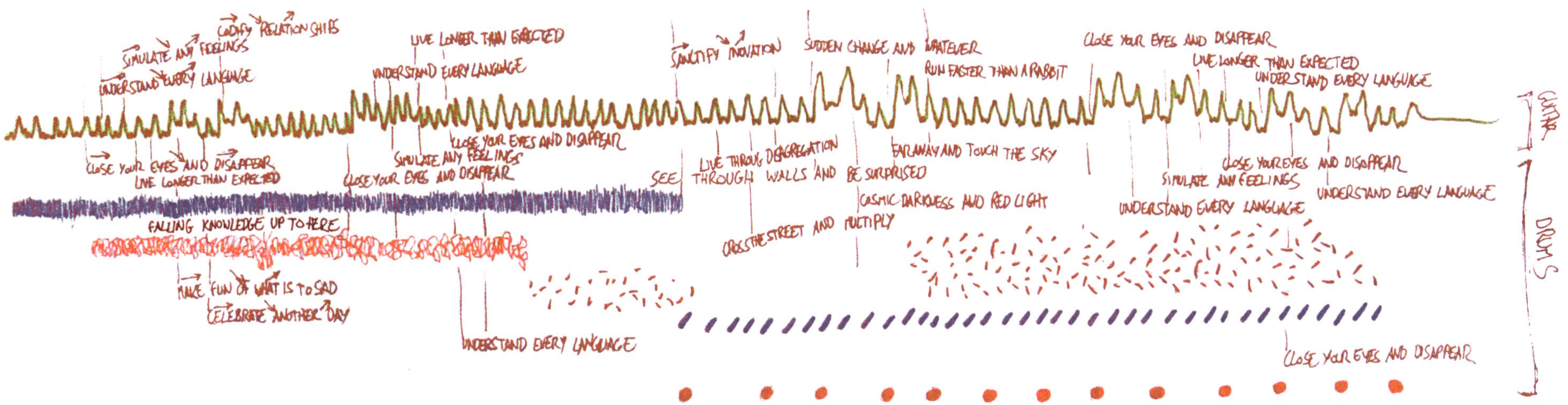
GUITAR
DRUMS
UNDERSTAND EVERY LANGUAGE
SIMULATE ANY FEELINGS
CODIFY RELATIONSHIPS
CLOSE YOUR EYES AND DISAPPEAR
LIVE LONGER THAN EXPECTED
UNDERSTAND EVERY LANGUAGE
LIVE LONGER THAN EXPECTED
SIMULATE ANY FEELINGS
CLOSE YOUR EYES AND DISAPPEAR
CLOSE YOUR EYES AND DISAPPEAR
FALLING KNOWLEDGE UP TO HERE
MAKE FUN OF WHAT IS TO SAD
CELEBRATE ANOTHER DAY
UNDERSTAND EVERY LANGUAGE
SEE
SANCTIFY INOVATION
LIVE THROUGH DESEGREGATION
THROUGH WALLS AND BE SURPRISED
CROSS THE STREET AND MULTIPLY
SUDDEN CHANGE AND WHATEVER
RUN FASTER THAN A RABBIT
FARAWAY AND TOUCH THE SKY
COSMIC DARKNESS AND RED LIGHT
CLOSE YOUR EYES AND DISAPPEAR
LIVE LONGER THAN EXPECTED
UNDERSTAND EVERY LANGUAGE
SIMULATE ANY FEELINGS
UNDERSTAND EVERY LANGUAGE
CLOSE YOUR EYES AND DISAPPEAR
UNDERSTAND EVERY LANGUAGE
CLOSE YOUR EYES AND DISAPPEAR

110
Progression
VELMA

R

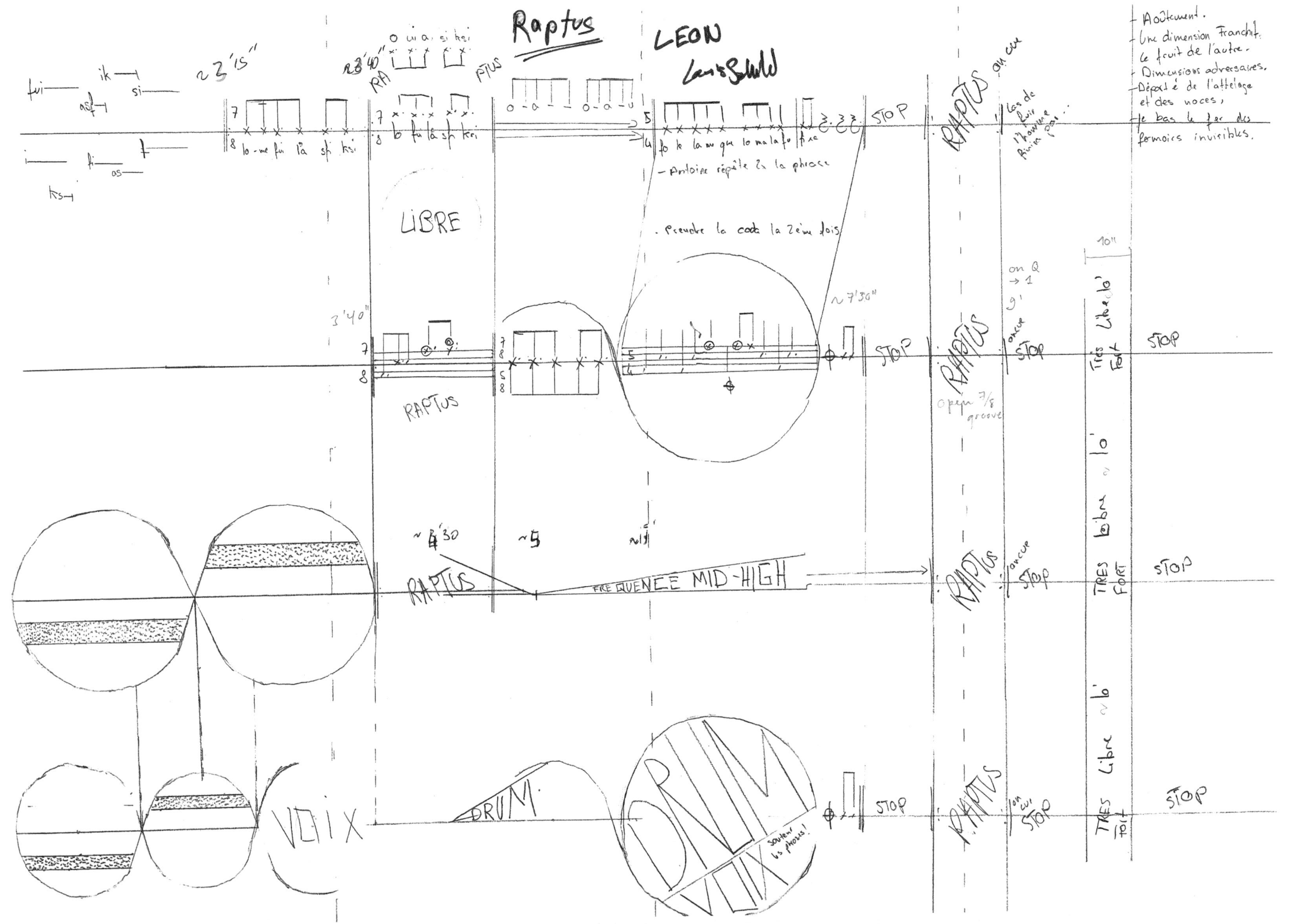
Raptus
LEON
~3'15"
~3'40"
RA PTUS
LIBRE
3'40"
RAPTUS
- Antoine répète 2x la phrase
. Prendre la coda la 2ème fois
~7'30"
STOP
RAPTUS
open 7/8 groove
~4'30
~5
FREQUENCE MID-HIGH
DRUM
VOIX
soutenir les phrases!
TRES FORT
Libre
10"
- Aboutement.
- Une dimension franchit le fruit de l'autre.
- Dimensions adversaires.
- Départ de l'attelage et des noces,
- le bas le fer des fermoirs invisibles.

111

Raptus

LEON

Reach a bit further
by Wild Beasts

I was angry and brash as a bull
You were devastatingly beautiful
I was crude I was lewd I was rude
I was not in the mood.
It's a peculiar dance it's me reaching
for the dire branch.
Yes I will do all the things that you ask of me
I said Yes I will come on darling, have no fear
And though the way is dark, and hands will grab at us
I'll remember this and only this, Yes I will
Tear jerker Shadow lurker Wonder worker
Reach a bit further.
Will you by any chance, remember the dire branch

112
Reach a Bit Further
WILD BEASTS

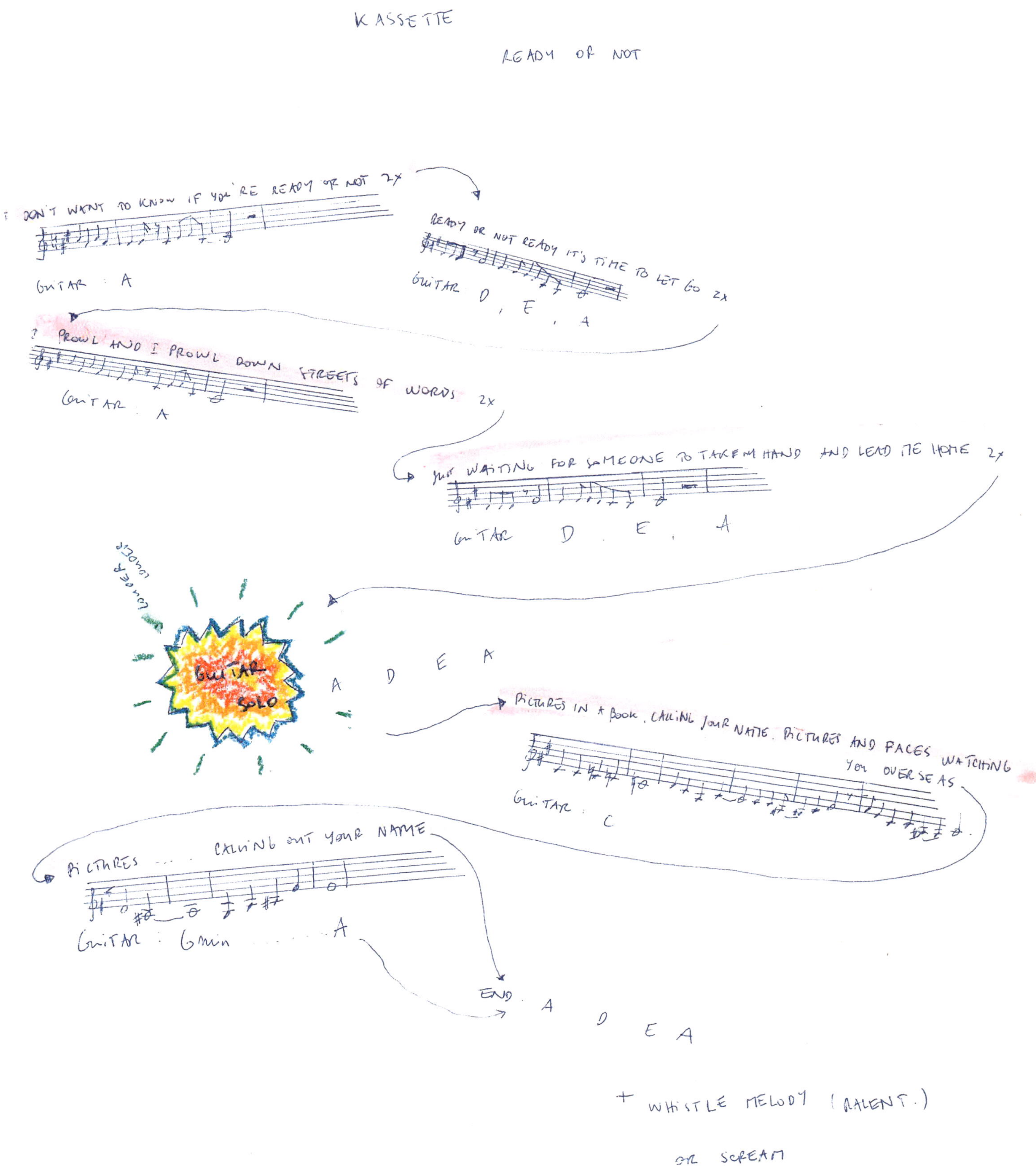

KASSETTE
READY OR NOT
I DON'T WANT TO KNOW IF YOU'RE READY OR NOT 2x
GUITAR : A
READY OR NOT READY IT'S TIME TO LET GO 2x
GUITAR D , E , A
I PROWL AND I PROWL DOWN STREETS OF WORDS 2x
GUITAR : A
JUST WAITING FOR SOMEONE TO TAKE MY HAND AND LEAD ME HOME 2x
GUITAR D . E . A
LOUDER
LOUDER
GUITAR SOLO
A D E A
PICTURES IN A BOOK, CALLING YOUR NAME. PICTURES AND FACES WATCHING YOU OVERSEAS
GUITAR : C
PICTURES ... CALLING OUT YOUR NAME
GUITAR : GMIN ..... A
END . A D E A
+ WHISTLE MELODY (RALENT.)
OR SCREAM

113
Ready or Not
KASSETTE

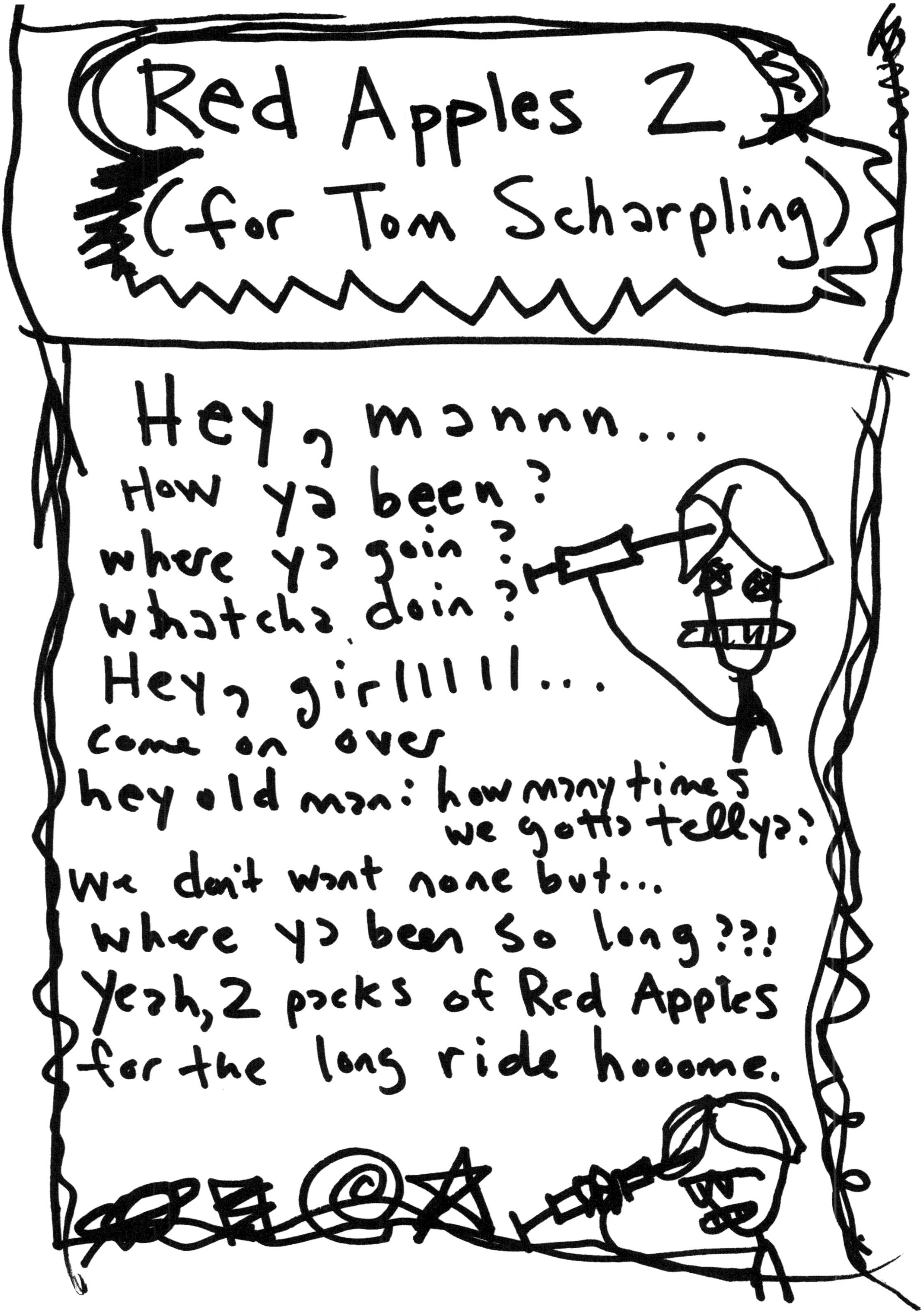

Red Apples 2
(for Tom Scharpling)
Hey, mannn...
How ya been?
where ya goin?
whatcha doin?
Hey, girlllll...
come on over
hey old man: how many times
we gotta tell ya?!
we don't want none but...
where ya been so long??!
Yeah, 2 packs of Red Apples
for the long ride hooome.

114
Red Apples 2 (for Tom Scharpling)
KURT VILE

RED FORD RADIO

(A POEM FOR THE MIDWEST THAT CAN BE SUNG/SPOKEN TO ANY STEADY BEAT.)

STOCKYARDS APPEAR BEFORE ME
WINDY CITY DON'T LOOK SO GOOD FROM HERE
YOU LEAVE ME WITH THE FM RADIO
FM RADIO, THE ONLY ONE I'VE EVER KNOWN
I CAN'T BREATHE IN THIS RED FORD ANYMORE,
CAN'T BREATHE IN THIS RED FORD ANYMORE,
CAN'T BREATHE IN THIS RED FORD ANYMORE
TELL YOU WHAT I'D DO TO GET OUT,
GET OUT
I'LL STAB A LAMB IN THE BACK
FOR YOU, DAD
DO ANYTHING YOU WANT ME TO, YEAH
I'LL GO DOWN IN A BLAZE OF GLORY
JUST LIKE THE WOMAN IN THE STORY
THAT YOU TOLD ME
I DON'T WANT TO CARE ABOUT NOTHING,
DON'T WANT TO CARE ABOUT NOTHING
STOCKYARD RADIO IS COMING OUT THE
WINDOW AND I'D DO ANYTHING TO
GET OUT, GET OUT

I CAN'T BREATHE IN THIS RED FORD
ANYMORE, CAN'T BREATHE IN THIS
RED FORD ANYMORE, CAN'T BREATHE
IN THIS RED FORD ANYMORE.
TELL YOU WHAT I'D DO TO
GET OUT, GET OUT. *

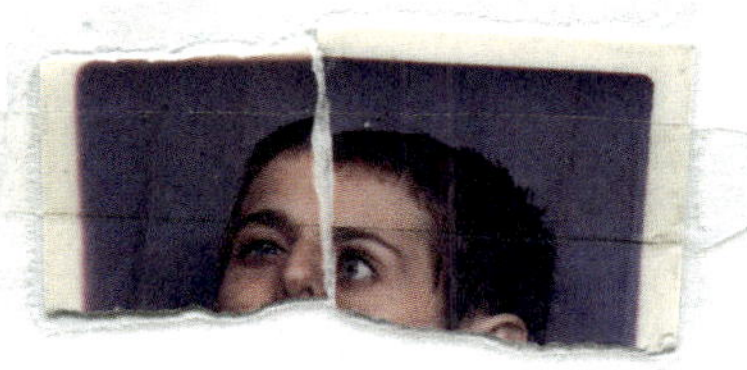

REPEAT UNTIL YOU CAN'T BREATHE ANYMORE.
TRY SINGING "IN ROUNDS" WITH YOUR FRIENDS, FAMILY, ENEMIES.

115
Red Ford Radio
U.S. GIRLS

REEREND
BEAT-MAN

SINGS

BAD
BONN

SAVE MY LAST FRANKS
and GIVE IT ALL TO YOU
BAD BONN
I'LL CLIME the Bigest MOUNTAIN
YUST TO BE WITH YOU
I JUMP In front of a TRAIN
YUST FOR A TICKET TO GO IN
I'LL CUT MY TROAT
YUST TO GIVE YOU
MY BLOOOOOD

116

Reverend Beat Man Sings Bad Bonn

REVEREND BEAT MAN

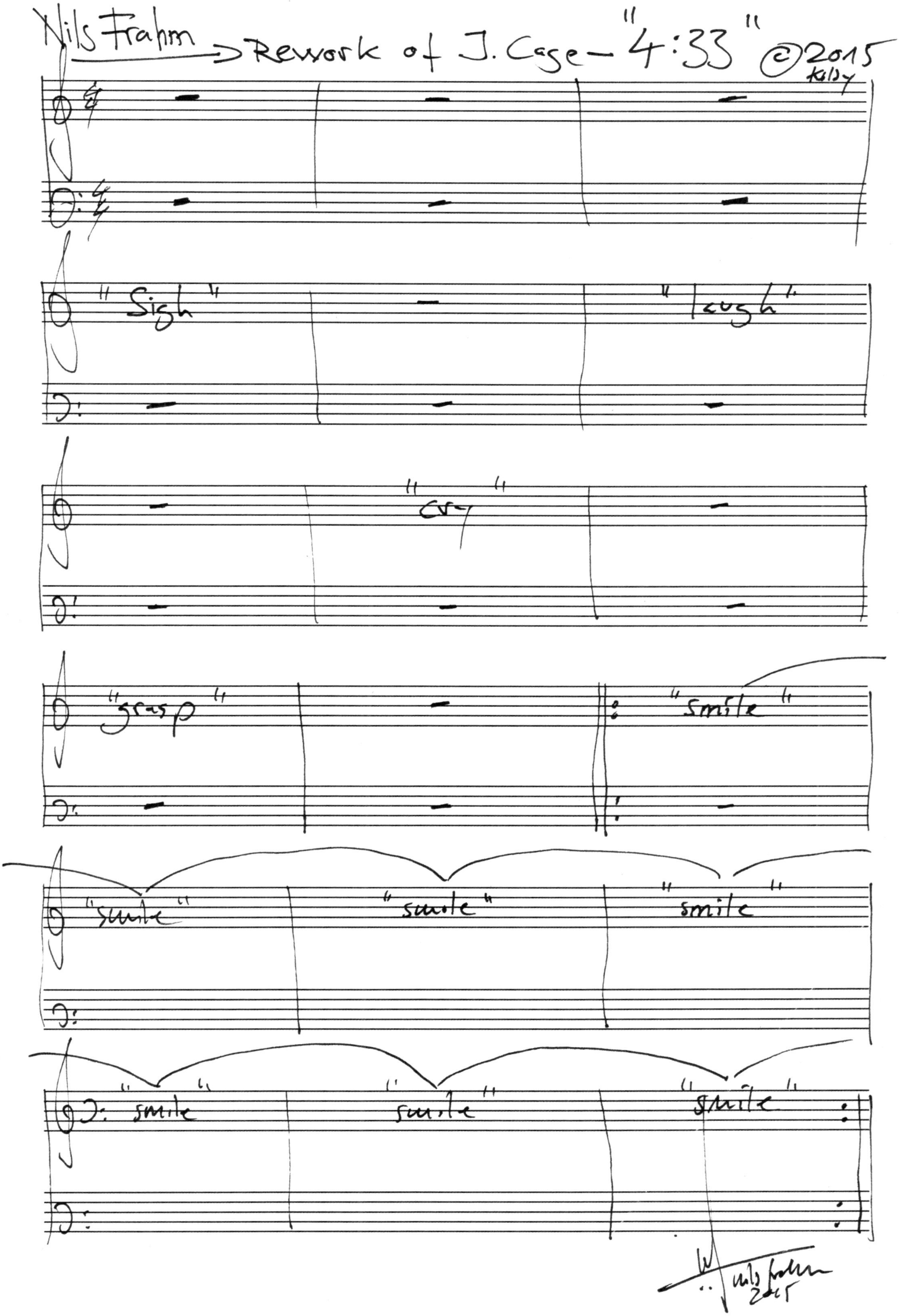
Nils Frahm
Rework of J. Cage – "4:33" ©2015
"Sigh"
"laugh"
"cry"
"grasp"
"smile"
"smile"
"smile"
"smile"
"smile"
"smile"
"smile"
Nils Frahm
2015

117

Rework of John Cage 4'33"

NILS FRAHM

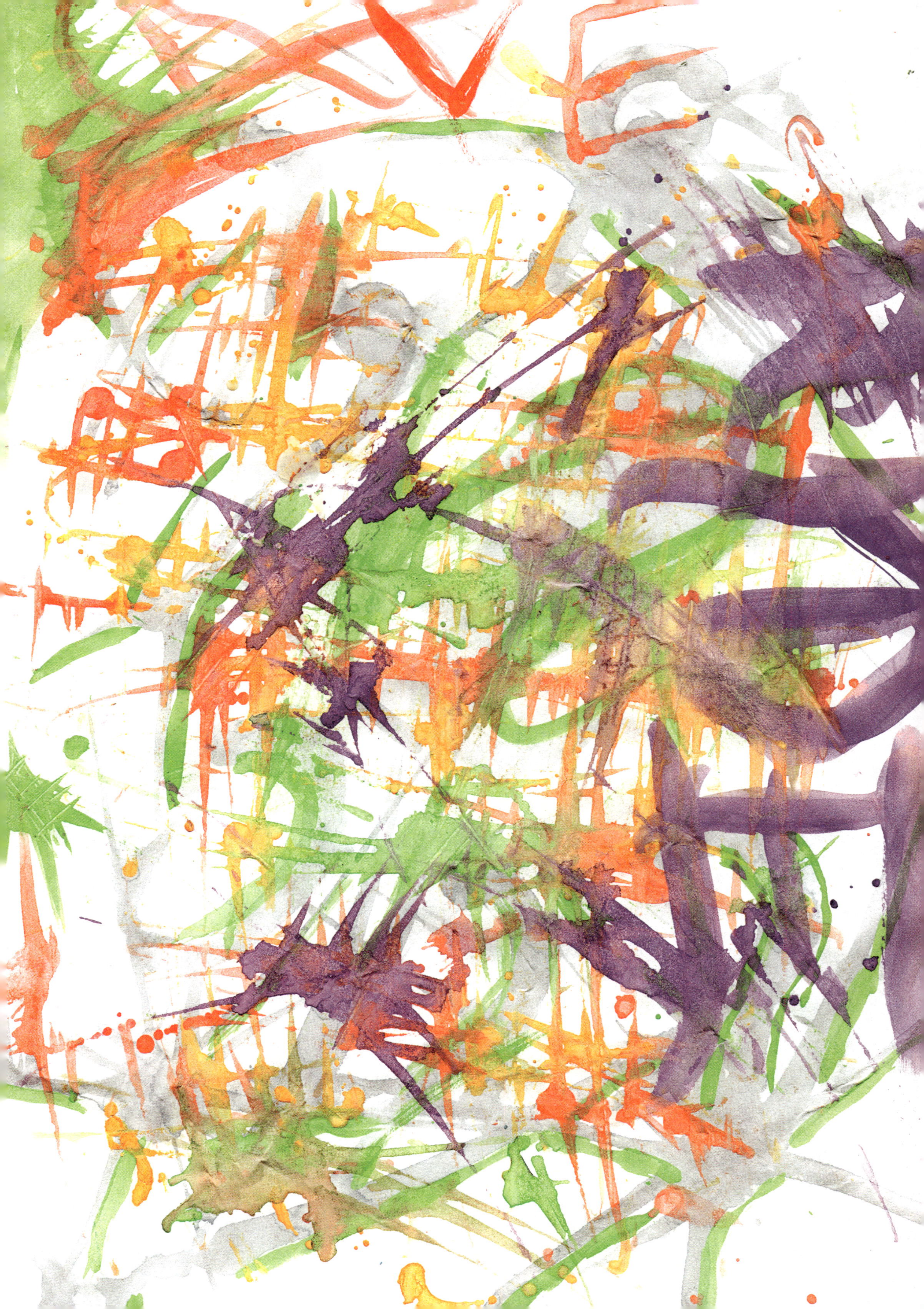

118
The Ride
CAVE

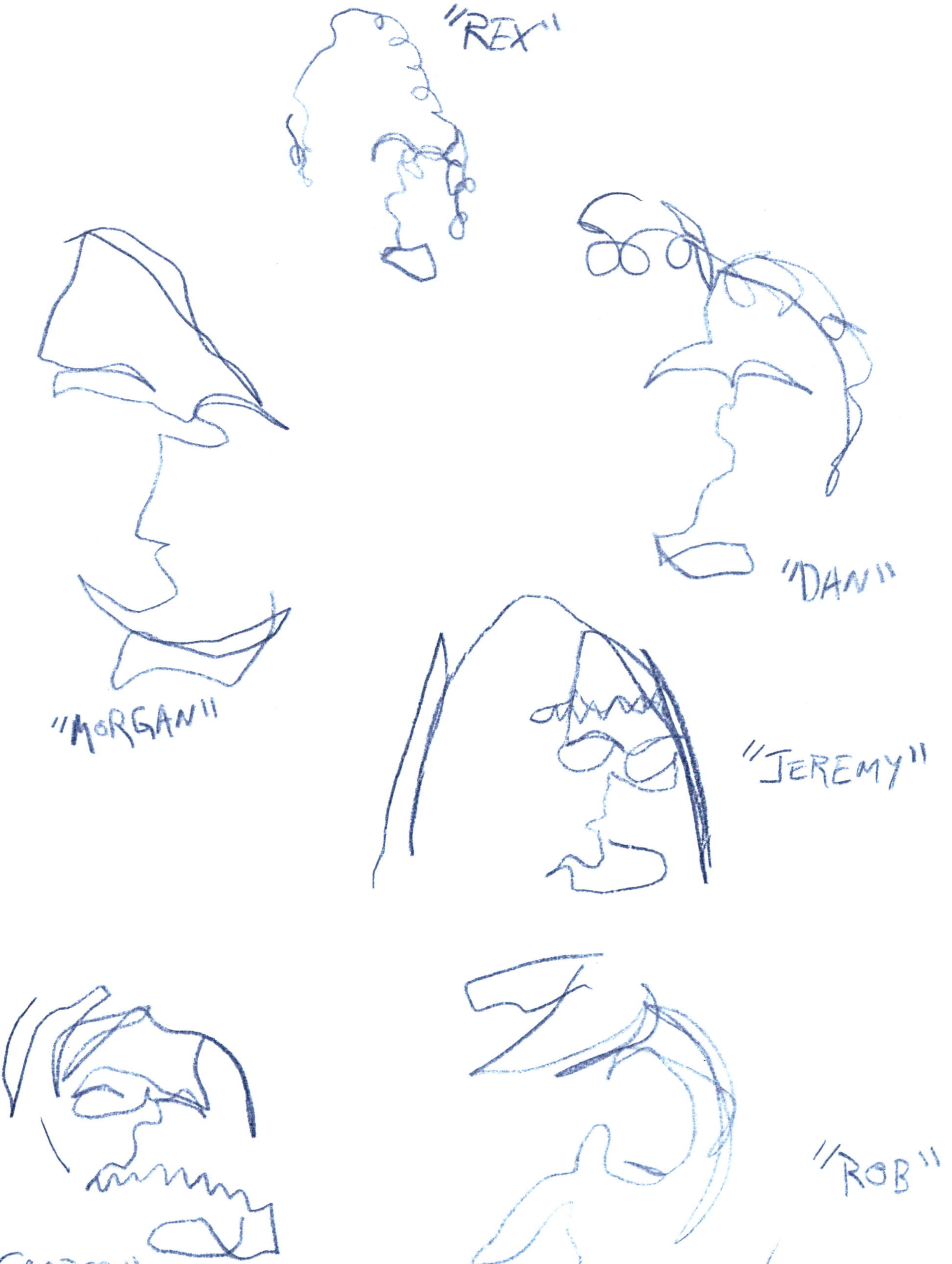

CAVE BAD BONN 2014

Rock'n'Roll ehr Wichser

Da isch för die wo immer wüssed wan i sött
Obwohl's jo wüsse müssted, dass i gar nöd wött
Wo meined i chan alles immer nochli besser mache
Alls öb i nöd scho ab dem ganze Scheiss, woni
Sösch scho om d'Ohre hu chönnt zämekrache

För die, för die, för die und au för die
För die wo meined, i glaub, sie wüssed wie
Dä Scheiss dä intressiert mi nöd und hät er
au no nie
Drom schtecked da ganz Wunschkonzert afach
in en grosse Mixer und
lecked mi alli am Arsch ehr Wichser

I schpiel jetz nämlich afach nochli Rock'n'Roll
Rock'n'Roll ehr Wichser
Rock'n'Roll ehr Wichser

I bremse au bi Orange und tue d'Füess nöd uf de Sitz
Pisse au im Hocke und I mach kai schlechti Witz
I wür sau allne recht mache, hett i nume Ziit
Obwohl – wenn i ganz ganz ehrlich bi, denn
Goht mer dä Scheiss au afach z'wiit

Ha nämlich do und do und do schö Sorge
De Schtress mit em Ärger goht los vor em Zmorge
Und d'Hälfti vom Scheiss isch im Pult no
verborge
Drom lönd mi etz afach in Rue min Kafi trinke
Und höred uf schtändig a mer omez'schtinke

I schpiel jetz nämlich afach nochli Rock'n'Roll
Rock'n'Roll ehr Wichser
Rock'n'Roll ehr Wichser
Solo
Rock'n'Roll ehr Wichser …

119
Rock'n'Roll ehr Wichser
KNÖPPEL

S

♩=60

SAD SONG FOR JANDEK

FLAMING LIPS – MAY 2013

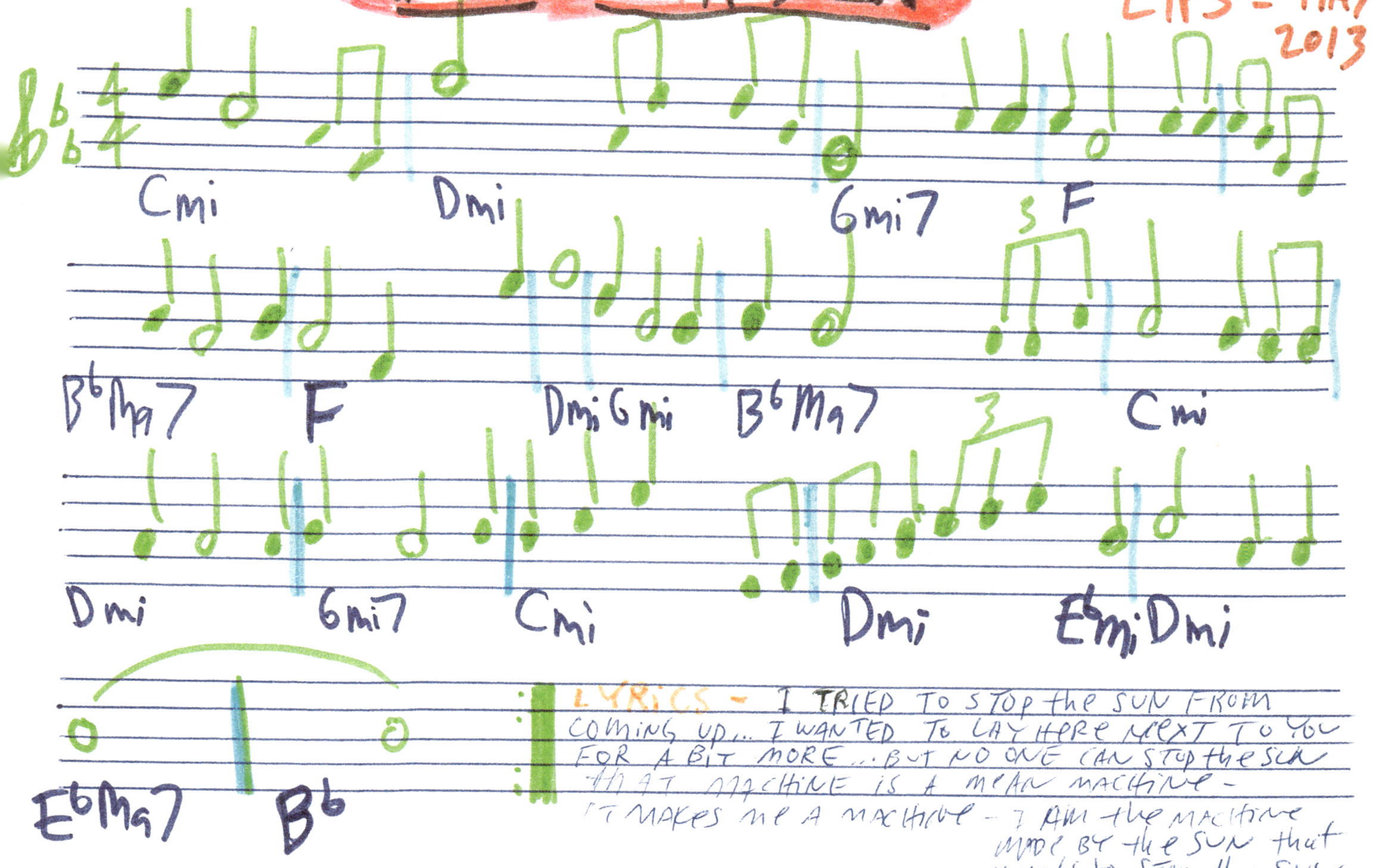

THIS WAS COMPOSED BY TURNING PAGE UPSIDE DOWN, THEN RANDOMLY DRAWING DOTS ON STAFF PAPER, THEN TURNING BACK OVER AND RANDOMLY PUTTING CHORDS UNDERNEATH. WE FELT THAT THE MELODY HAD A SAD QUALITY TO IT, AND WANTED TO GIVE IT TO JANDEK AS A SONG OF APPRECIATION...

Steven – the FLAMING LIPS

120
Sad Song for Jandek
THE FLAMING LIPS

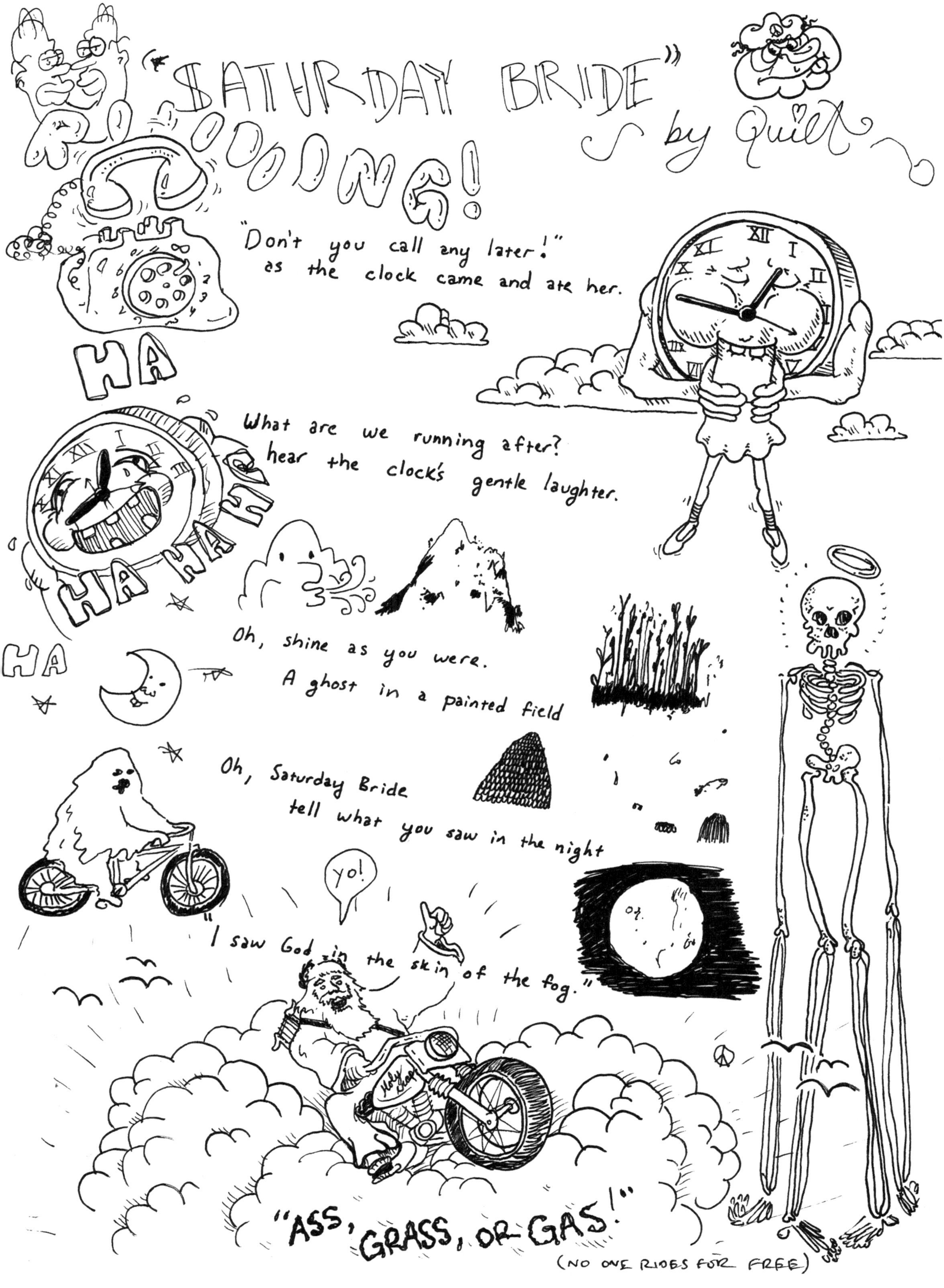
"SATURDAY BRIDE"
by Quill
RIOOOONG!
"Don't you call any later!"
as the clock came and ate her.
HA
What are we running after?
hear the clock's gentle laughter.
HA HA HA HA
HA
Oh, shine as you were.
A ghost in a painted field
Oh, Saturday Bride
tell what you saw in the night
yo!
"I saw God in the skin of the fog."
"ASS, GRASS, OR GAS!"
(NO ONE RIDES FOR FREE)

121
Saturday Bride
QUILT

ELVIS PERKINS'

SHAMPOO

<F#m A Bm, F#m A D, F#m A Bm, F#m A E... repeat at ∞ >

Sweep up! little sweeper boy
It's You who's got the wig on here
Sweep up. little Sweeper boy, Sweep up

Yellow is the colour of my true love's crossbow
Yellow is the colour of the Sun
Black is the colour of a Strangled Rainbow
Just the colour of my lung
Black is the colour of my true love's Arrow
Exactly the colour of a human's blood

You' got a shot of Shampoo
Though it was made 30 years ago
You've got a shot of Starring in Shampoo
Though you were made 20 years ago

Speak up!, little Sweeper boy
They are hard of hearing
Anything that anyone has to say

I don't want to die
However dark tomorrow may be
above me a perfect square of sky
You are worth your weight in gold

122
Shampoo
ELVIS PERKINS

worth your weight in sorrow, baby
though you will never know why...

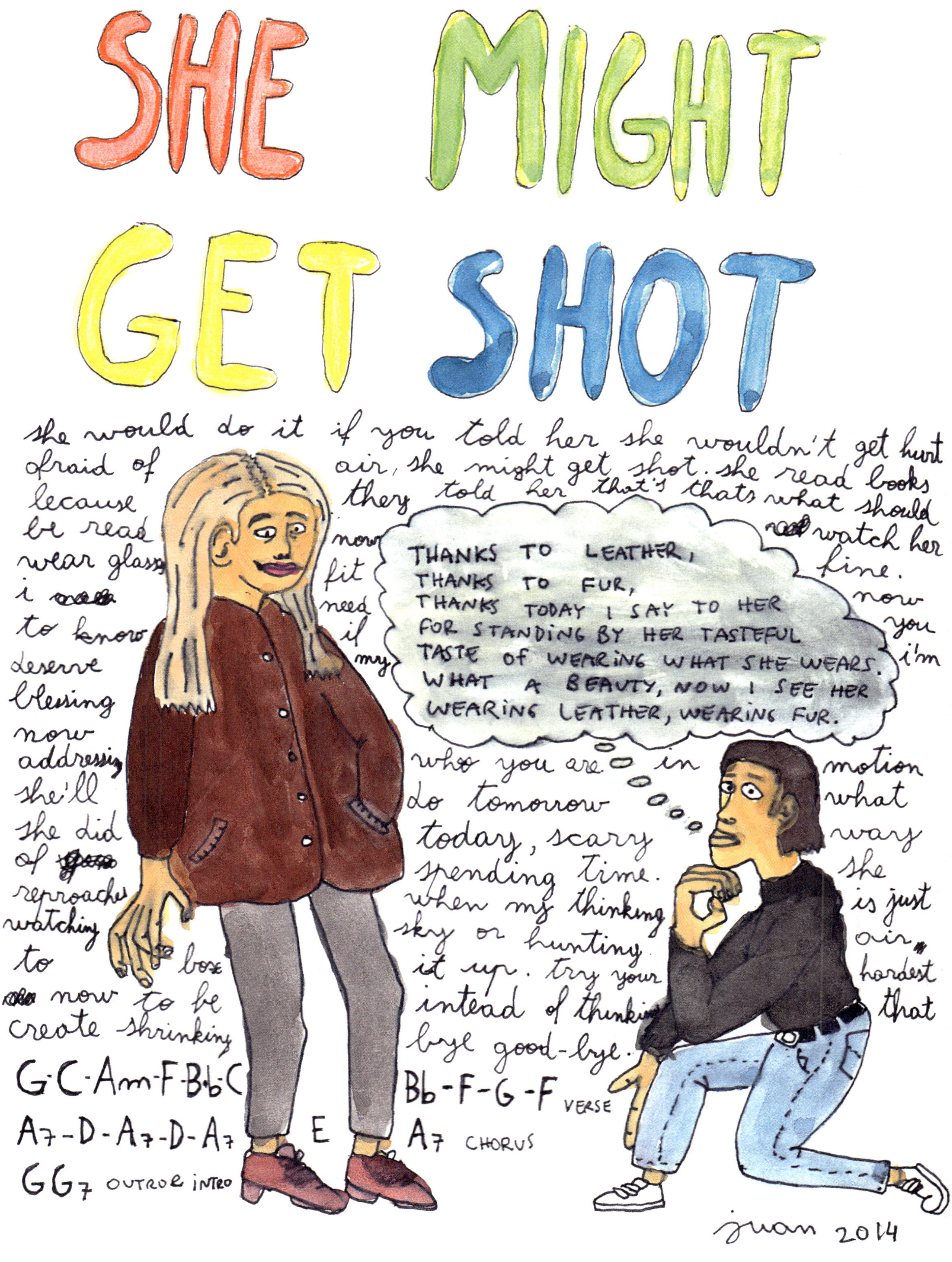
SHE MIGHT GET SHOT
she would do it if you told her she wouldn't get hurt
afraid of air, she might get shot. she read books
because they told her that's thats what should
be read
wear glass
i
to know
deserve
blessing
now
addressing
she'll
she did
of
reproaches
watching
to
now to be
create shrinking
now
fit
need
if
my
watch her
fine.
now
you
i'm
THANKS TO LEATHER,
THANKS TO FUR,
THANKS TODAY I SAY TO HER
FOR STANDING BY HER TASTEFUL
TASTE OF WEARING WHAT SHE WEARS.
WHAT A BEAUTY, NOW I SEE HER
WEARING LEATHER, WEARING FUR.
who you are in motion
do tomorrow what
today, scarry way
spending time. she
when my thinking is just
sky or hunting air,
it up. try your hardest
intead of thinking that
byl good-bye.
bose
G-C-Am-F-Bb-C
Bb-F-G-F VERSE
A7-D-A7-D-A7 E A7 CHORUS
GG7 OUTRO & INTRO
juan 2014

123

She Might Get Shot

JUAN WAUTERS

Shipbreakers

MOANING CITIES

D
Early in the morning, I walk on silver sand
Joining the boys for another day, yeah I'm a shipbreaker
We're thousands here selling, selling work of hand
Pullin' iron off of dead ships on the bay
Yeah I'm a shipbreaker, yeah I'm a.

D
My bare feet crawlin' up the rusted deck
Hundred and more brothers circling the shipbreak
Looking down on what used to be miles of sand
We're all garbage men on a beach turned in a wasteland
Yeah I'm a shipbreaker

People say they come a long way
A whole life spent on a dollar a day
People say they come a long way to die here
End up down in Chittagong
Far away from where we're born
Come with nothing to work for nothing
Far away from where we've growin
Tear down what the tide is bringin'

124
Shipbreakers
MOANING CITIES

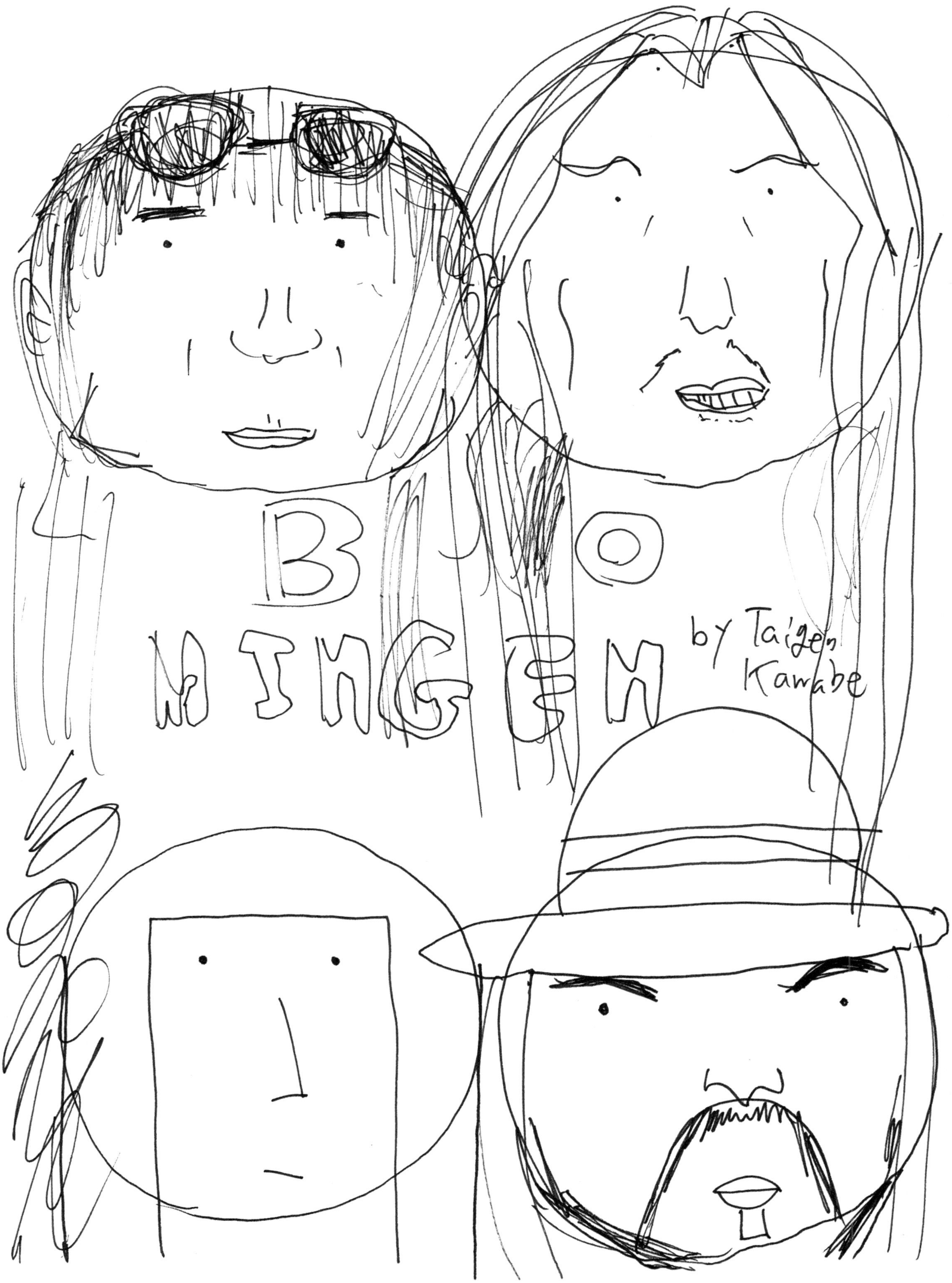
BO
NINGEN
by Taigen
Kawabe

125
Slider
BO NINGEN

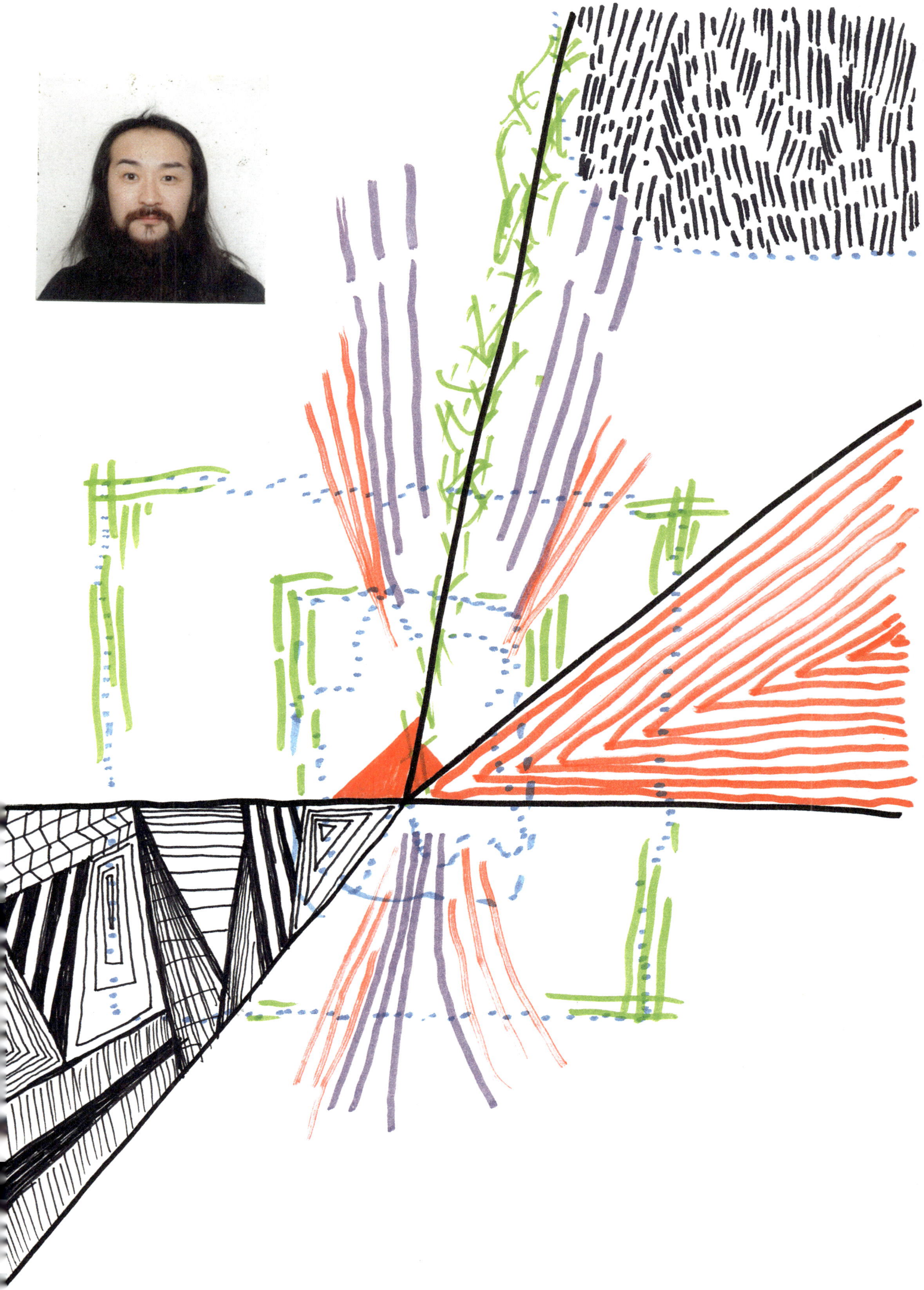

125

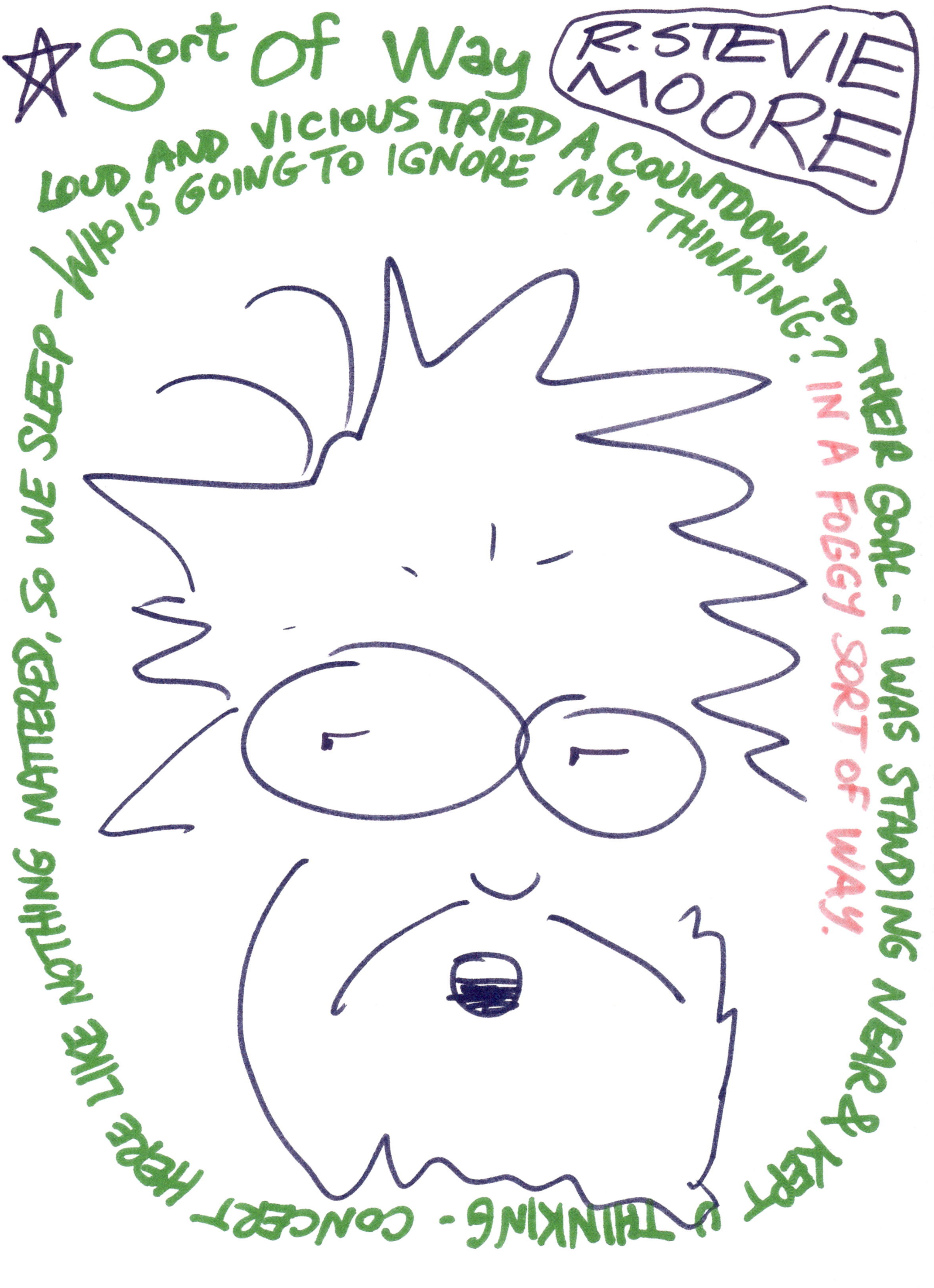
Sort of Way
R. STEVIE MOORE
LOUD AND VICIOUS TRIED A COUNTDOWN TO THEIR GOAL - I WAS STANDING NEAR & KEPT U THINKING - CONCERT HERE LIKE NOTHING MATTERED, SO WE SLEEP - WHO IS GOING TO IGNORE MY THINKING?
IN A FOGGY SORT OF WAY.

126
Sort of Way
R. STEVIE MOORE

HOW TO PLAY "THE STARS KEEP ON CALLING MY NAME" BY "MARC DIFRANKO"

ACT 1:
PUT A CAPO ON THE 4TH FRET OF YOUR GUITAR →

4

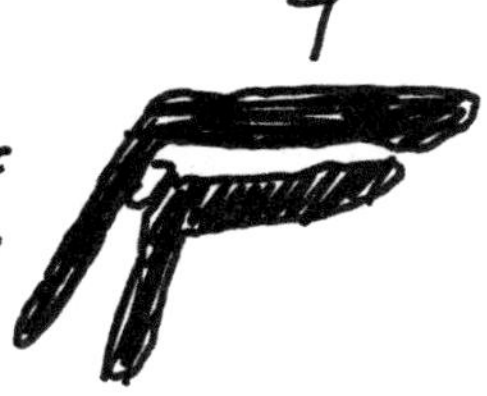

#2:
THE FIRST CHORD IS OPEN "E" SHAPE

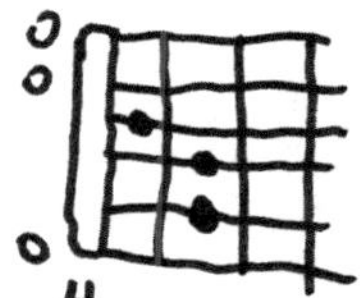

4

3: NEXT CHORD LOOKS LIKE ~~THIS~~ THIS

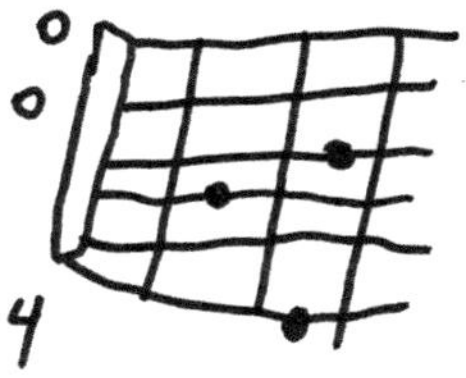

4

FOUR:
THE NEXT TWO & FINAL CHORDS OF THE VERSE ARE F#M7 SHAPE & B7 SHAPE IN THE FOURTH POSITION

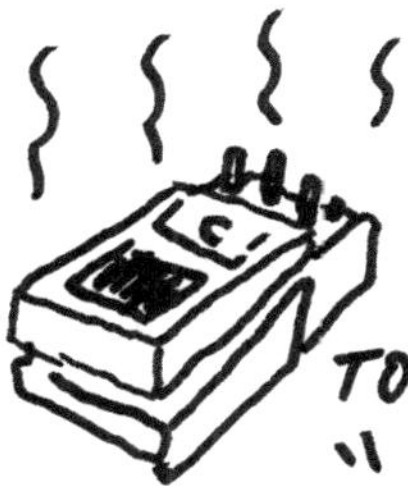

STEP 5:
REMEMBER TO USE A "KHORUS" PEDAL
(SLOW RATE & WIDE DEPTH)

KHORUS KHORDS:
(ALL IN 4TH POSITION)

A / / / | G#M7 / / / | B7 / / / |
E / / /

MISTAKE →

G#M7

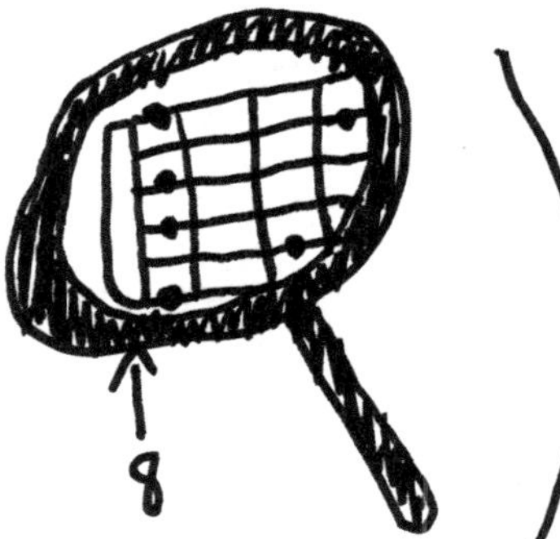

8

&
BOOM!
YOU KNOW THE CHORDS!
JUST PLAY THEM ALL TOGETHER NOW:
VERSE / CHORUS / VERSE / CHORUS
& SING SOME SHIT!

→ CONGRATULATIONS
LOVE MAC D.

127
The Stars Keep On Calling My Name
MAC DEMARCO

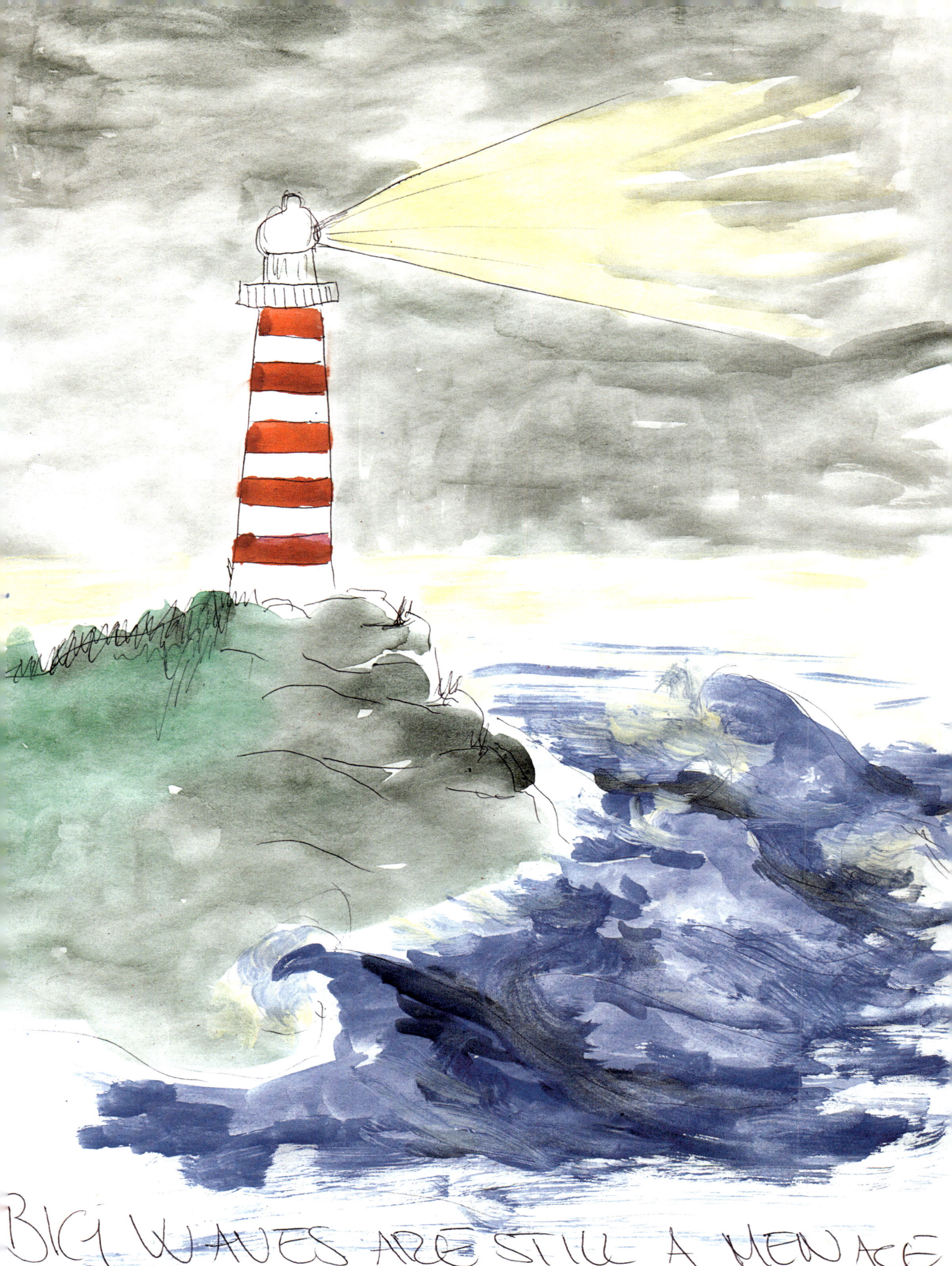

BIG WAVES ARE STILL A MENACE

—EVIE 2014

128
Still
EVJE

(STROBOHOBO)

Strobohobo

Toc Toc Toc – ich klopf auf Holz
Allein auf meiner Ghostranch
Das Mondlicht tropft, ich denk was soll's
Und werd zum Wolfsmensch
Die Pseudo Weirdos proben schon
Ich wurde so geboren
Von einem Poster gemixt Van Gogh
Bis über beide Ohren

Toc Toc Toc – zu Protokoll
Mit meinem Zauberodem
Mit Hokus Pokus, Rock'n'Roll
Wood up! Nomen est Omen
Der Golem fordert Sisyphos
Um den Tribut zu zollen
Lord Oblomow malt mit Bob Ross
Zu schöpfen aus dem Vollen

Toc Toc Toc – Mein Mikrophon
wird zur Lokomotive
Bringt mich zurück nach Babylon
Wo blüht das Positive
Der Big Boss droht dem Capitol
~~Dann~~ Die Pole machen Terror
Der Demokrat macht Frost im Alkohol
Und Hollywood sendet Error . . . . .

129
Strobohobo
JOCHEN DISTELMEYER

Summer's Game

Lyrics

Summer days are at my door, it won't be like before
The wind blows softly through my room
Summer dreams are in the air
Some place but I don't know where
I feel I'll find them pretty soon.

Memories keep flashing by
And I allways wonder why
I've got to make myself believe
Things won't allways be the same, while I play the summer's game
Golden sunlight I percieve.

FORM: A A A A B A A A A

A

A	C#m	G	Bm
B	D#m	A	C#m
F#	Bm	E	E7

B

Em	Bm	F	Am
A	C#m	G	F#
B	B7	E	E7

WRITTEN BY: Jacco Gardner

130

Summer's Game

JACCO GARDNER

SWEET SWEET SOUTH

BY FRESCHARD

A
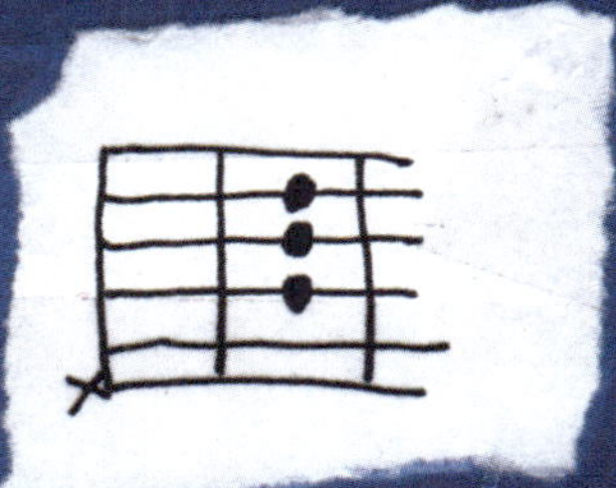

Bm
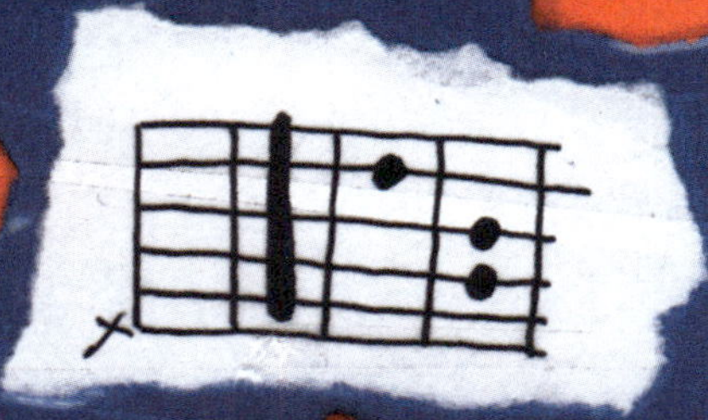

A Bm
STOP AT THE DRIVE THROUGH DAIQUIRI
A
SWAMP WATER WILL KILL ME
Bm
ONE SIP AND I'LL KISS YOU ON THE MOUTH
A
IN THE SWEET SWEET SOUTH

Bm A
HEHAHA HEHEHE HE HEHAHA HE HEHE HE

Bm
AT THE CAJUN STATION
A
RYE WHISKY INVITATION
Bm
ONE SIP AND I'LL KISS YOU ON THE MOUTH
A
IN THE SWEET SWEET SOUTH

Bm
AT THE ACADIAN SUPERETTE
A
YOU BOUGHT A FORTY HAD A CIGARETTE
Bm
ONE SIP AND I'LL KISS YOU ON THE MOUTH
A
IN THE SWEET SWEET SOUTH

Bm
AT MARY'S YOU GET THE BEST BLOODY MARY
A Bm
I HAD ONE TOO MANY
ONE SIP AND I'LL KISS YOU ON THE MOUTH
A
IN THE SWEET SWEET SOUTH

131
Sweet Sweet South
FRESCHARD

T

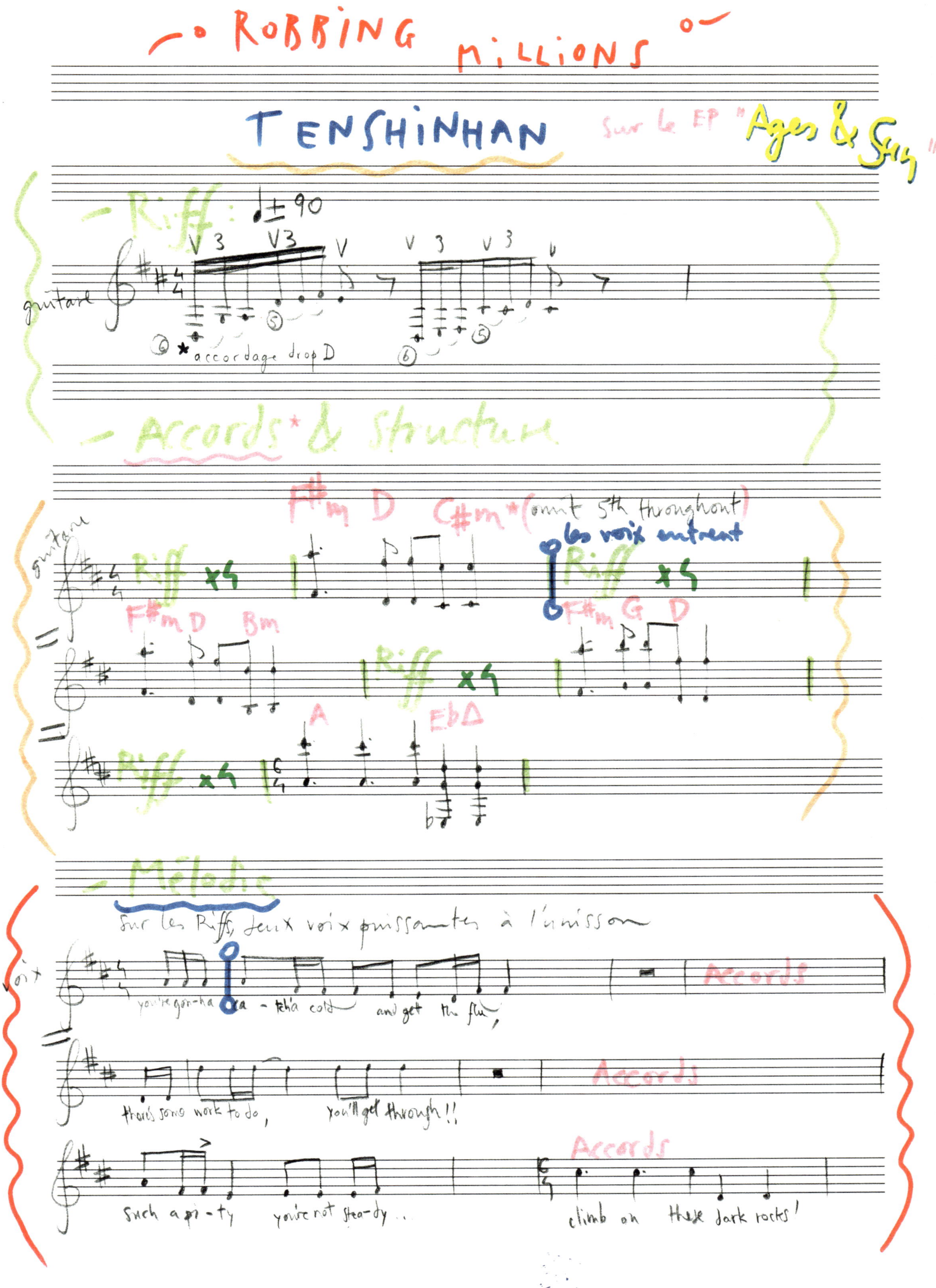
ROBBING MILLIONS
TENSHINHAN
Sur le EP "Ages & Sun"
Riff : ♩± 90
guitare
accordage drop D
Accords* & Structure
F#m D C#m* (omit 5th throughout)
les voix entrent
Riff x4
F#m D Bm
F#m G D
A EbΔ
Mélodie
Sur les Riffs, deux voix puissantes à l'unisson
voix
you're gonna catch a cold and get the flu,
Accords
there's some work to do, you'll get through!!
such a pi-ty you're not stea-dy..
climb on these dark rocks!

132
Tenshinhan
ROBBING MILLIONS

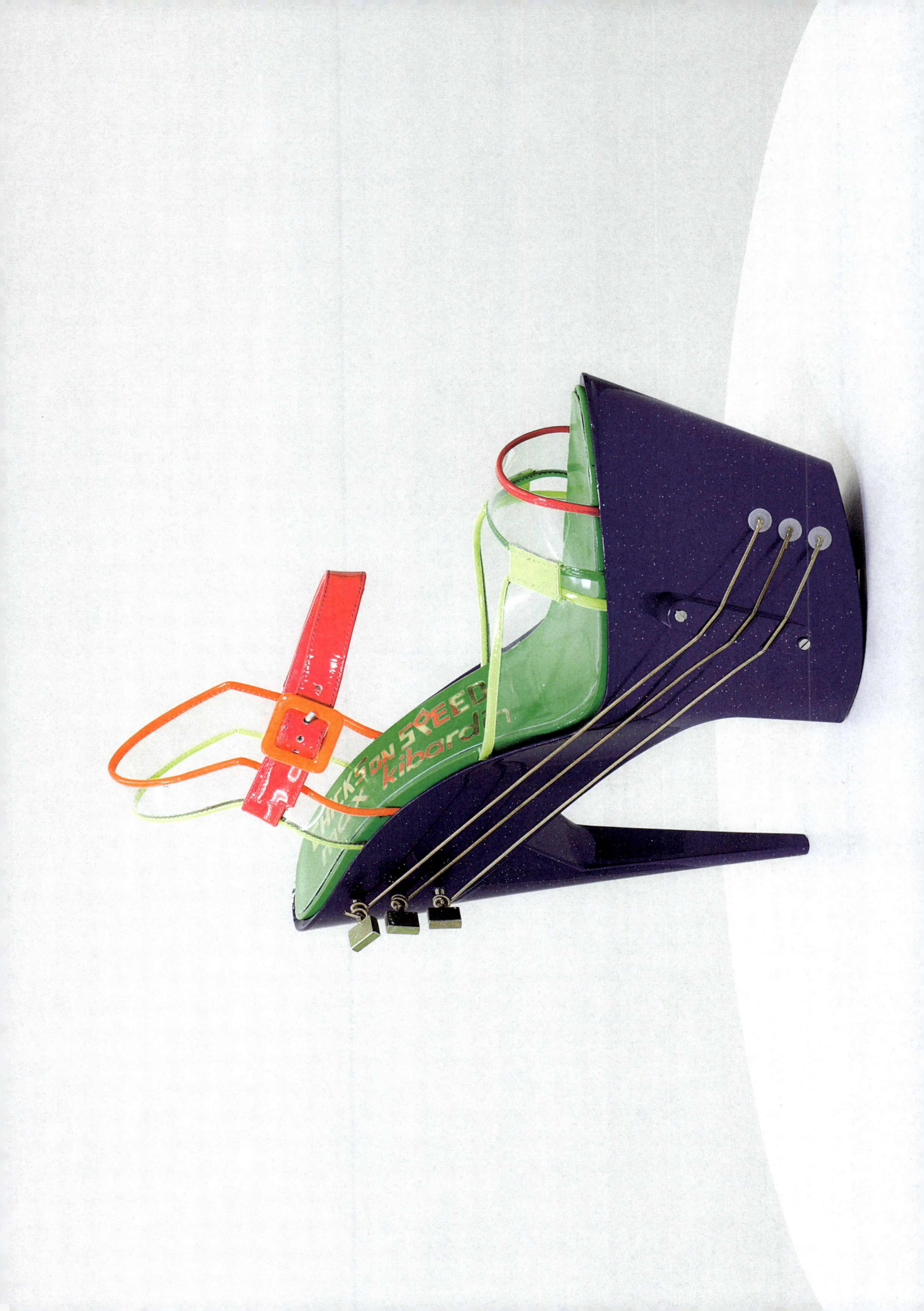
SPEED
x kibardin

133
The High Heeled Shoe Guitar
CHICKS ON SPEED

This Is My Hand

July 28, 2014

Shara Worden

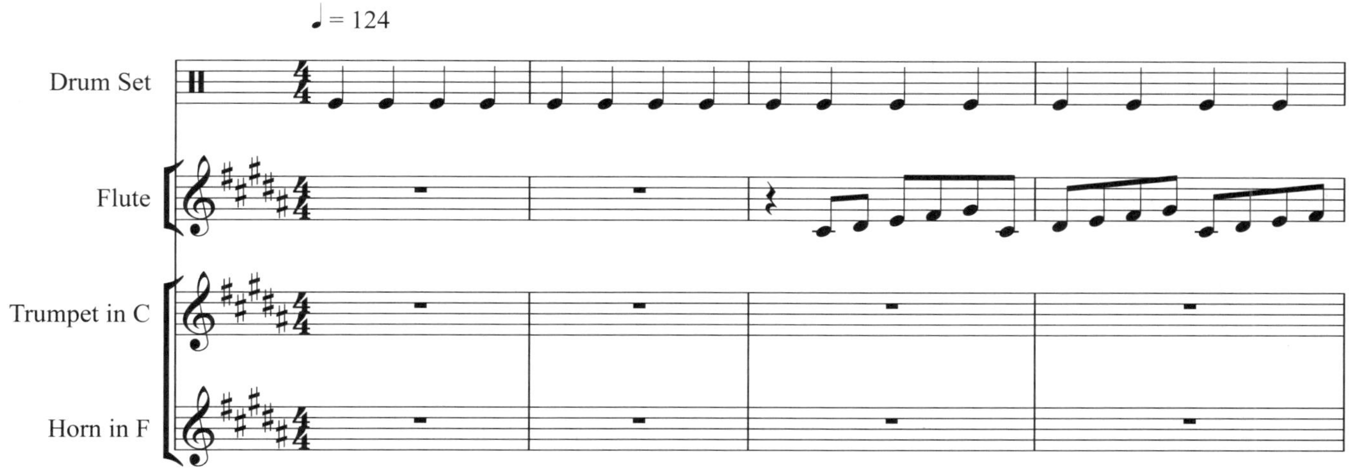

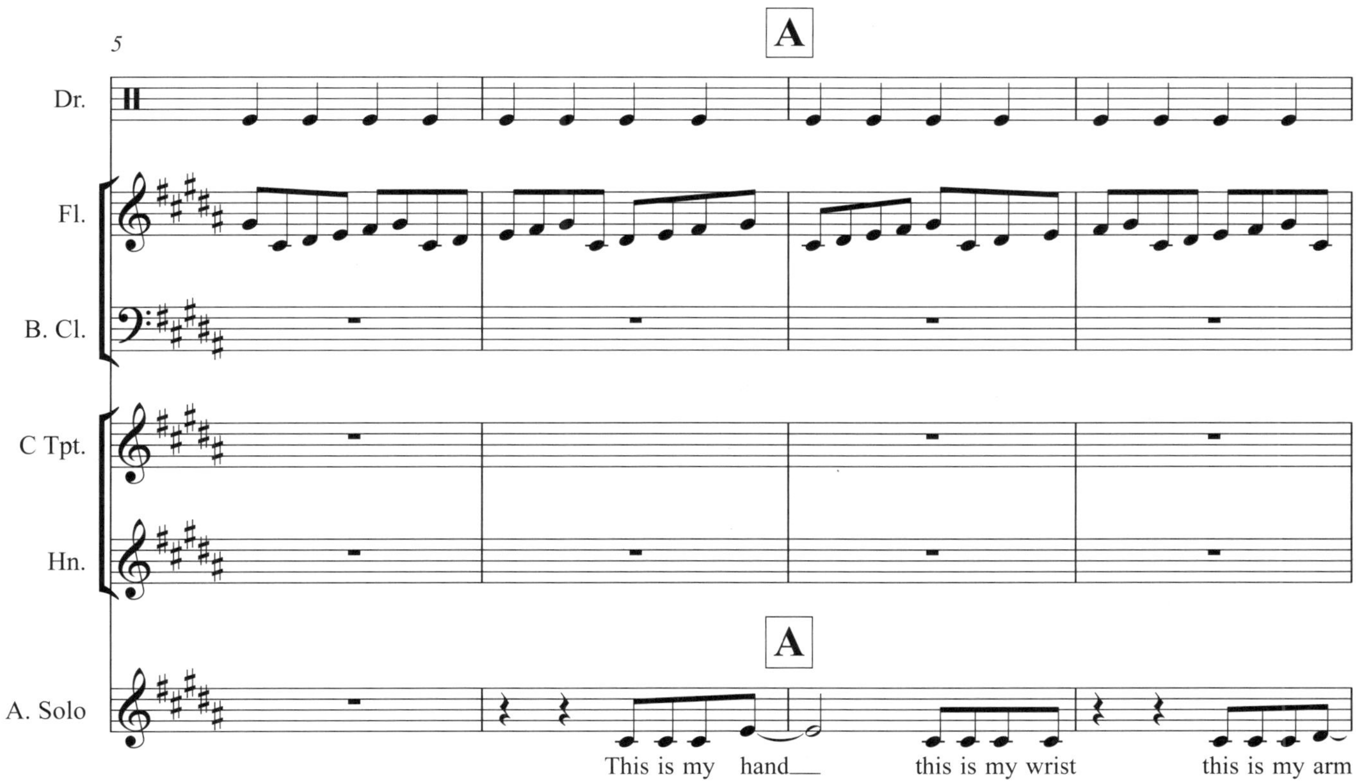

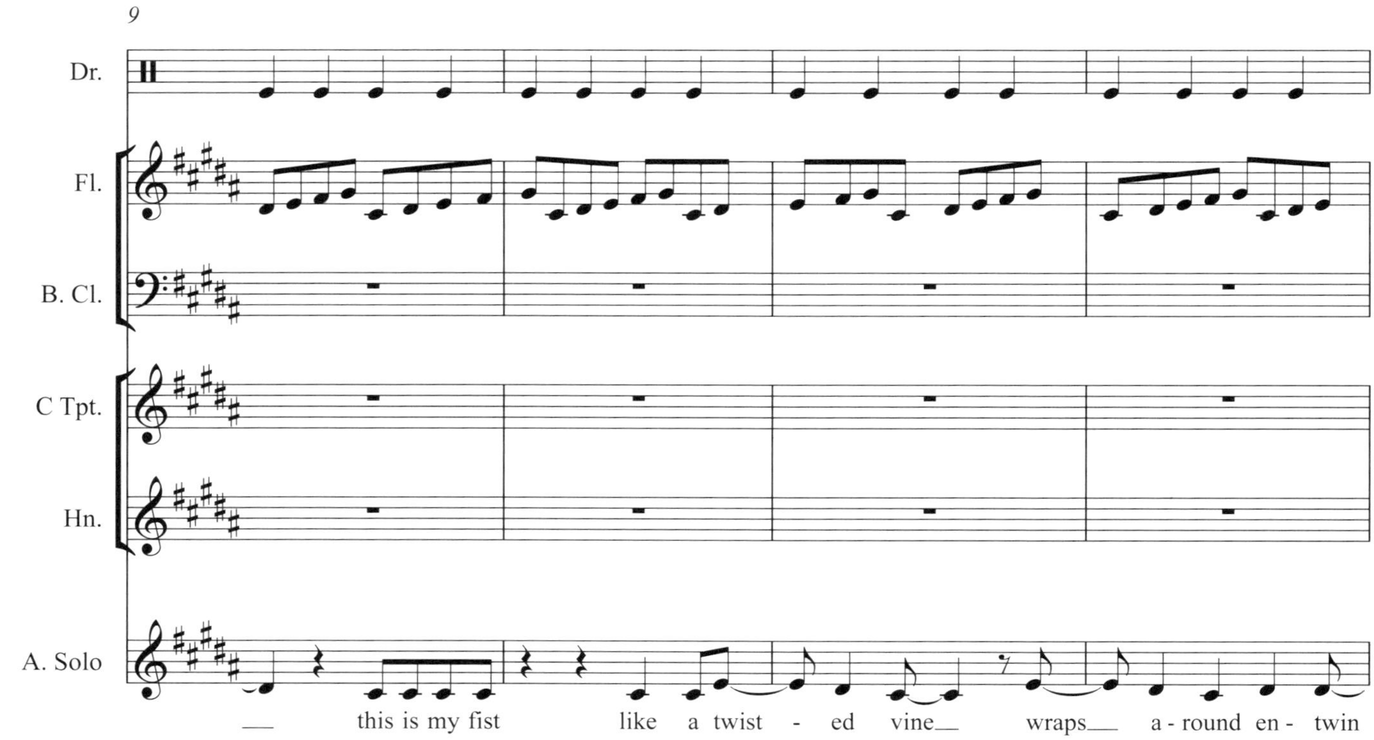
9
Dr.
Fl.
B. Cl.
C Tpt.
Hn.
A. Solo
this is my fist like a twist - ed vine wraps a - round en - twin

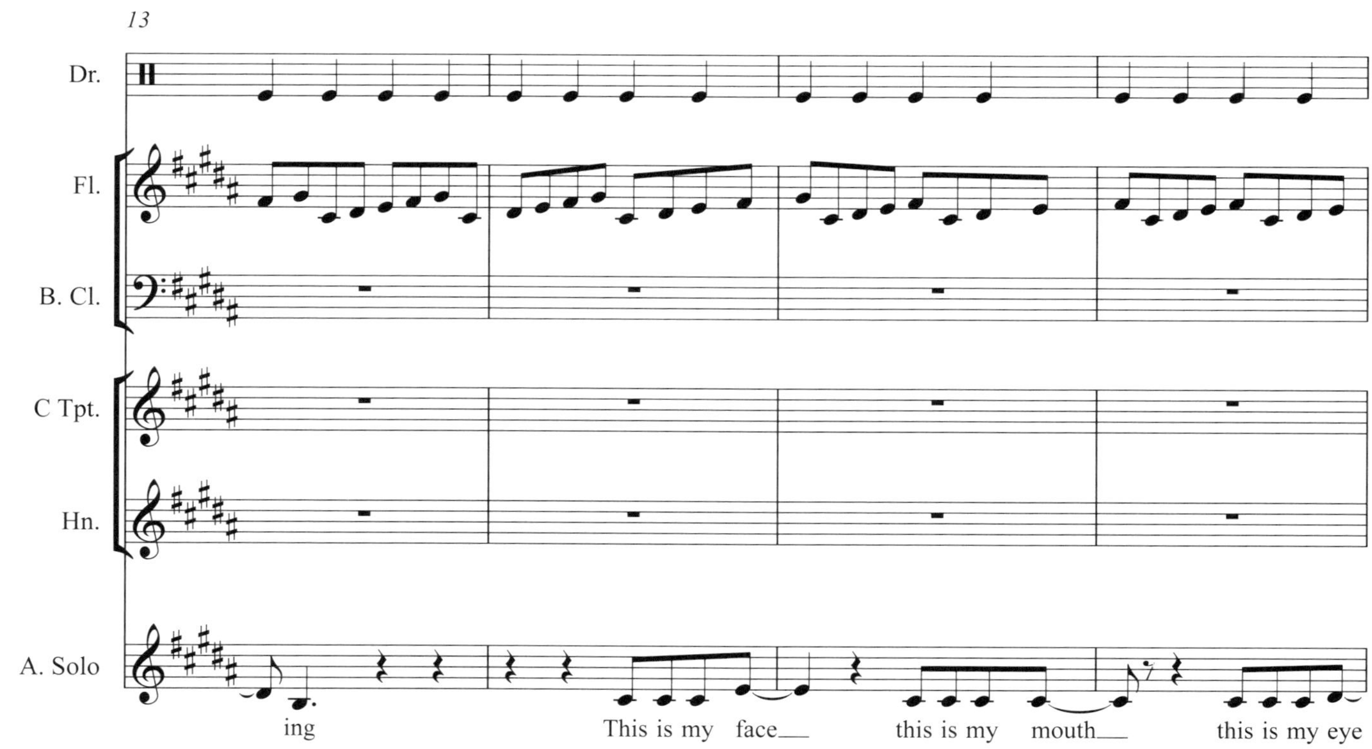
13
Dr.
Fl.
B. Cl.
C Tpt.
Hn.
A. Solo
ing This is my face this is my mouth this is my eye

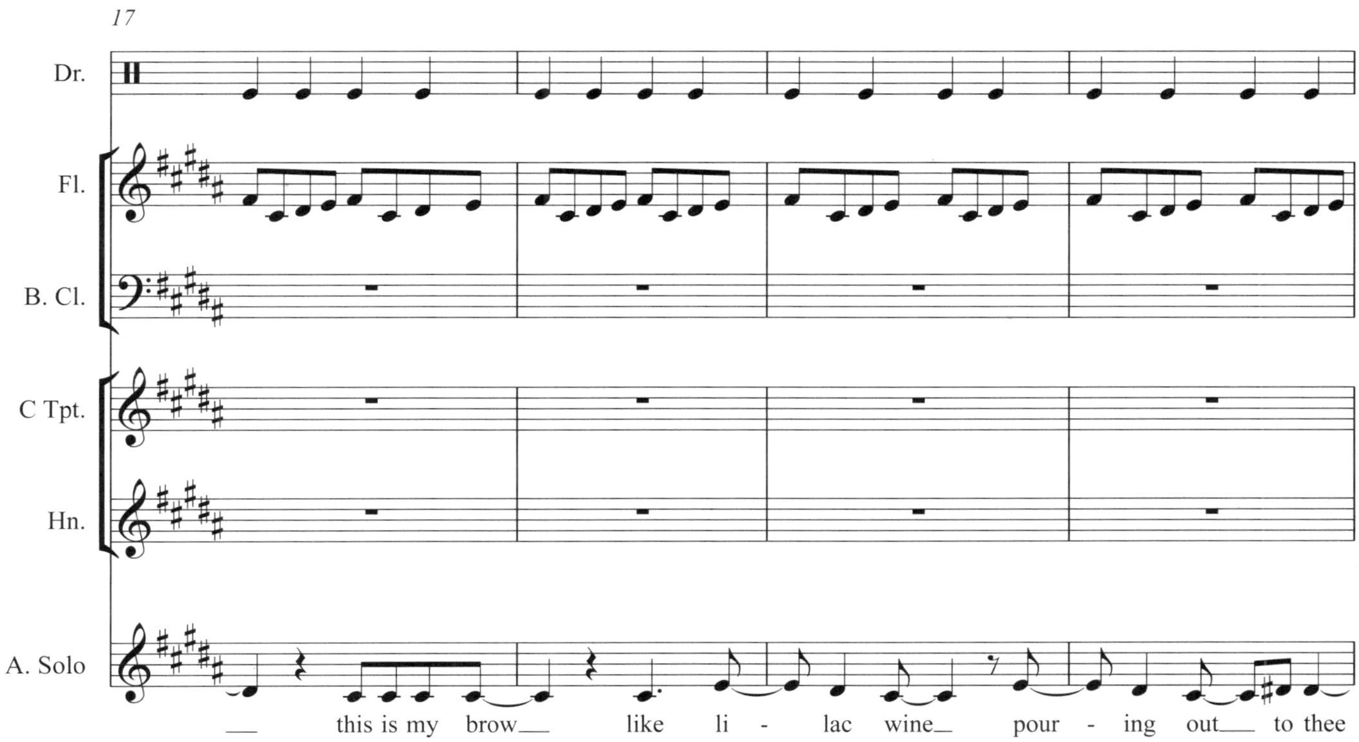
17
Dr.
Fl.
B. Cl.
C Tpt.
Hn.
A. Solo
this is my brow like li - lac wine pour - ing out to thee

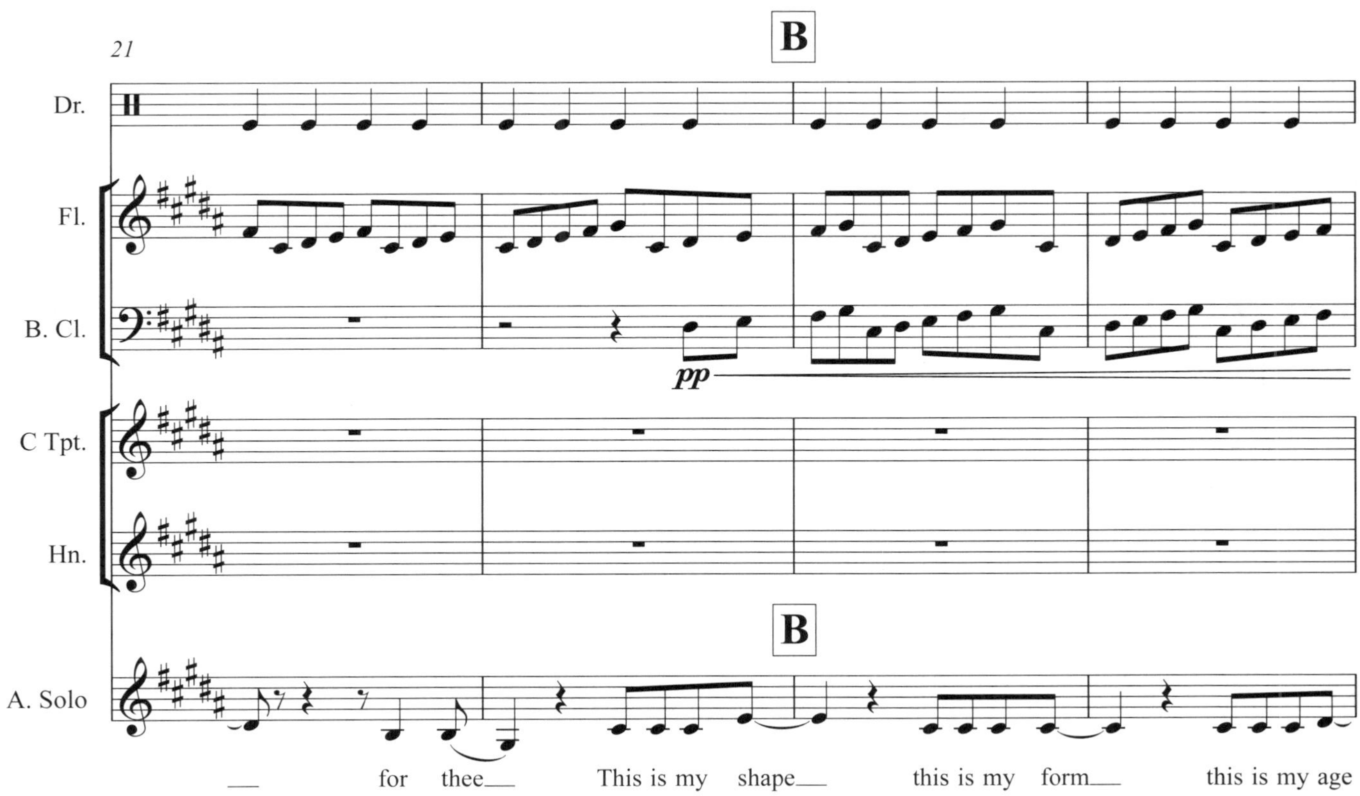
21
B
Dr.
Fl.
B. Cl.
pp
C Tpt.
Hn.
B
A. Solo
for thee This is my shape this is my form this is my age

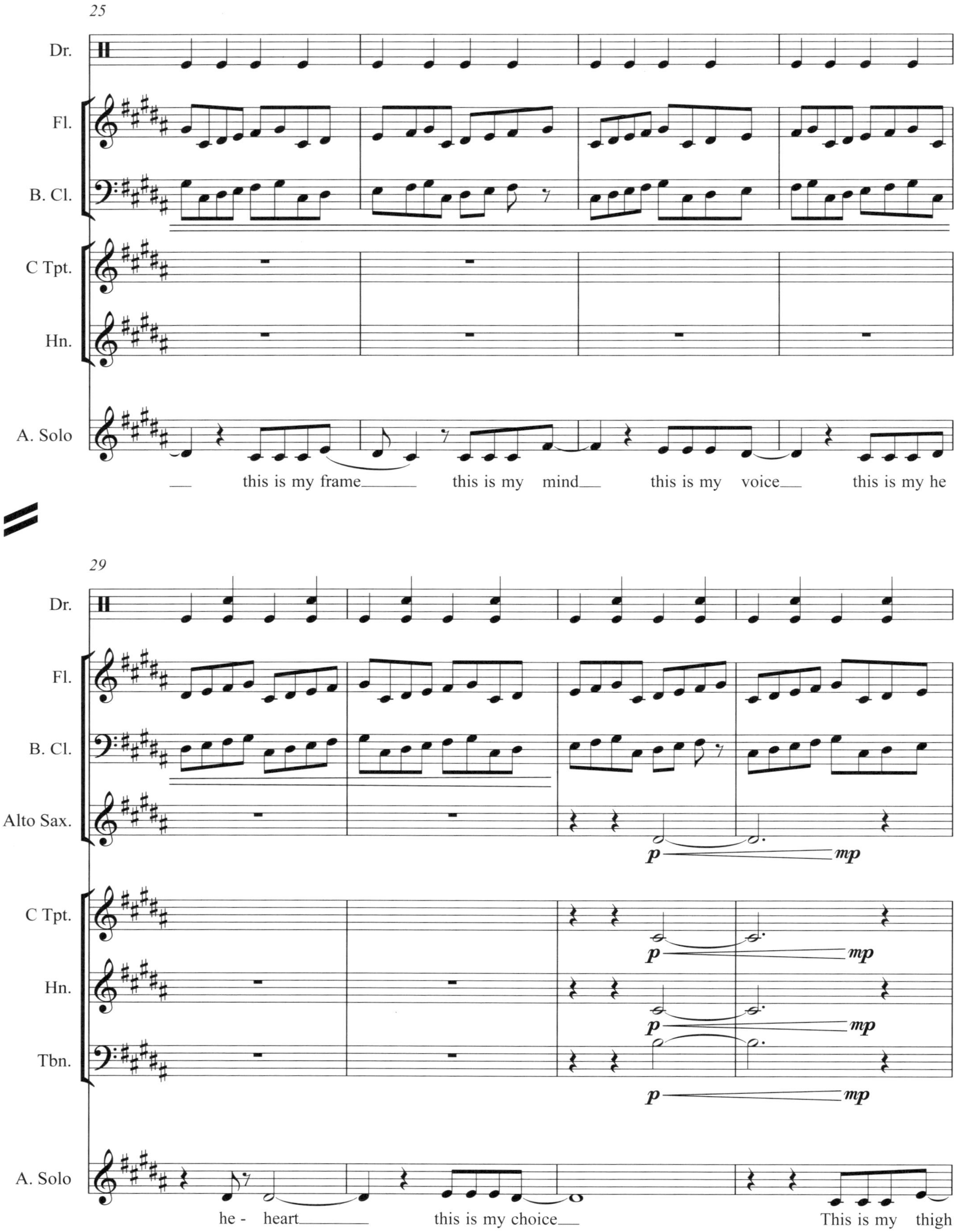
25
Dr.
Fl.
B. Cl.
C Tpt.
Hn.
A. Solo
this is my frame this is my mind this is my voice this is my he
29
Dr.
Fl.
B. Cl.
Alto Sax.
C Tpt.
Hn.
Tbn.
A. Solo
he - heart this is my choice This is my thigh

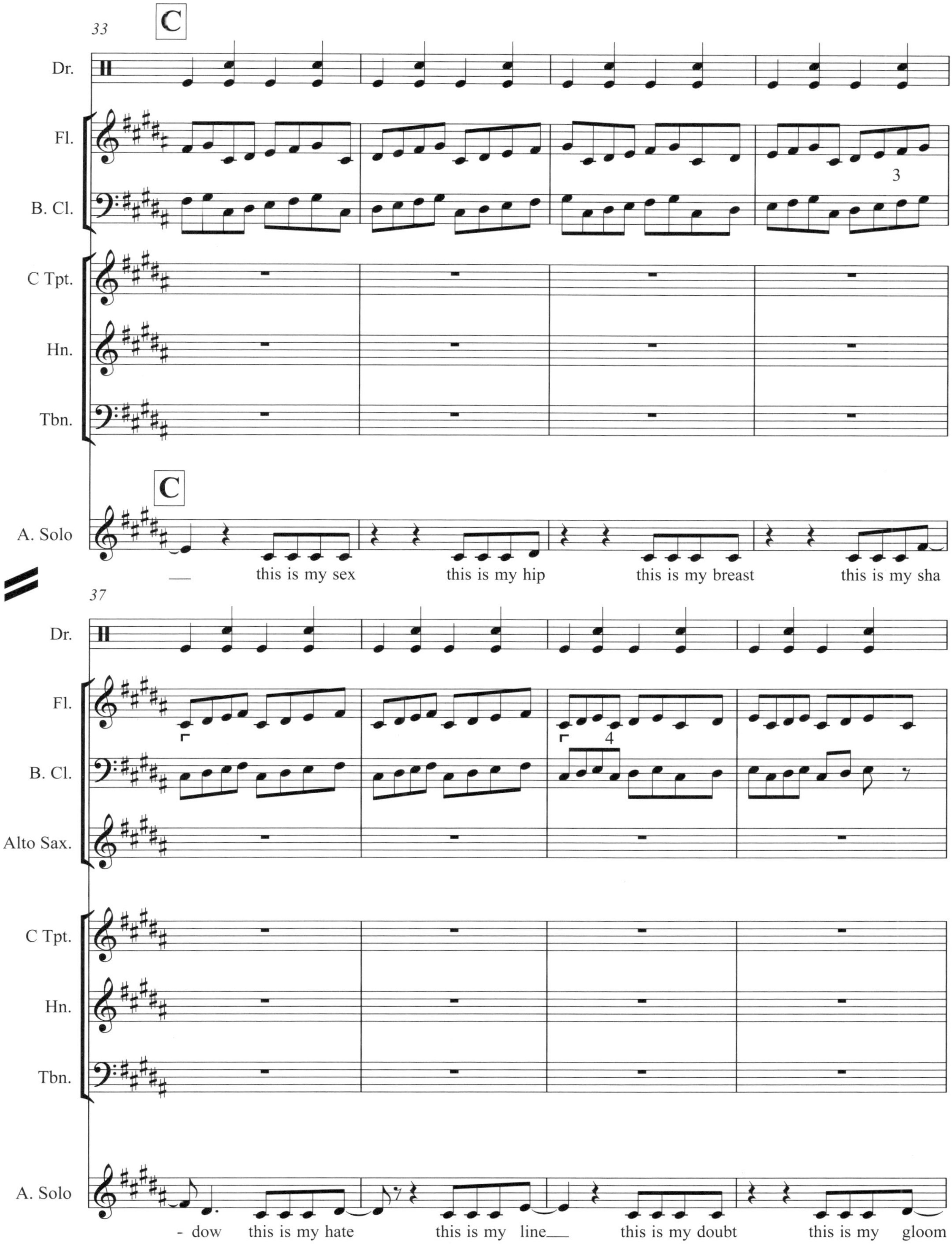
33
C
Dr.
Fl.
B. Cl.
C Tpt.
Hn.
Tbn.
C
A. Solo
this is my sex
this is my hip
this is my breast
this is my sha
37
Dr.
Fl.
B. Cl.
Alto Sax.
C Tpt.
Hn.
Tbn.
A. Solo
- dow
this is my hate
this is my line
this is my doubt
this is my gloom

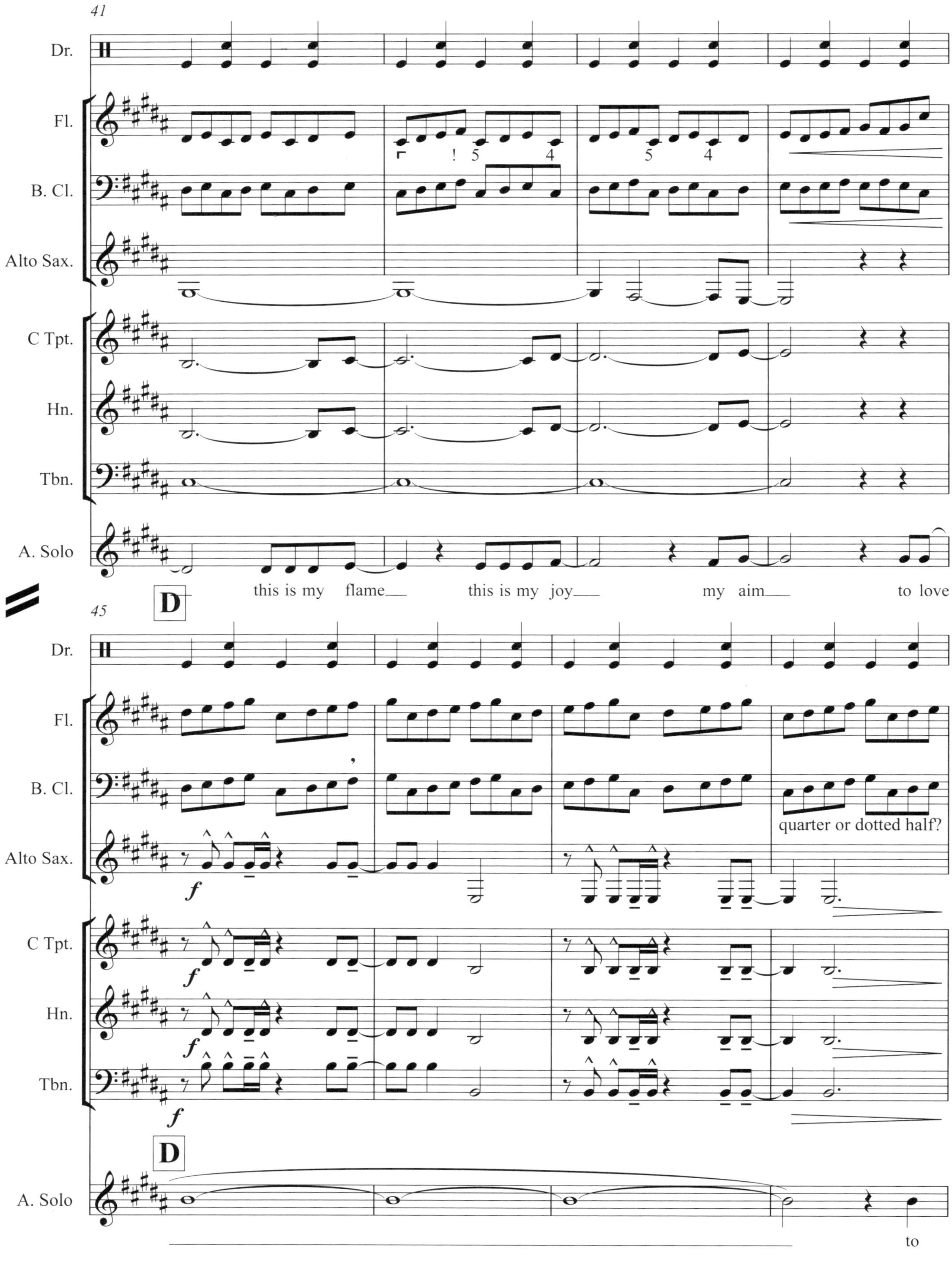
41
Dr.
Fl.
B. Cl.
Alto Sax.
C Tpt.
Hn.
Tbn.
A. Solo
this is my flame__ this is my joy__ my aim__ to love
D
45
quarter or dotted half?
f
to

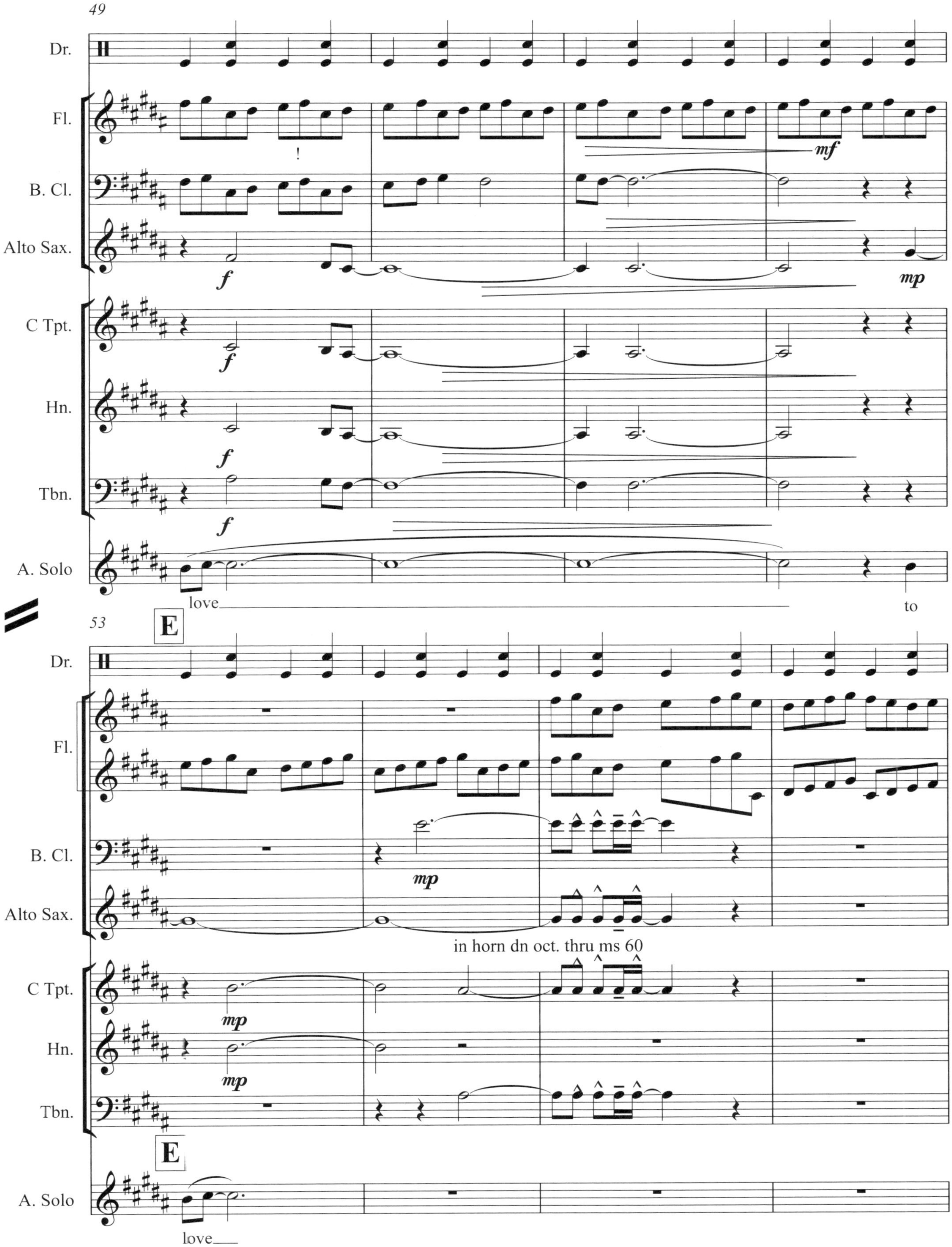

49
Dr.
Fl.
B. Cl.
Alto Sax.
C Tpt.
Hn.
Tbn.
A. Solo
love
to
53
E
in horn dn oct. thru ms 60
E
love

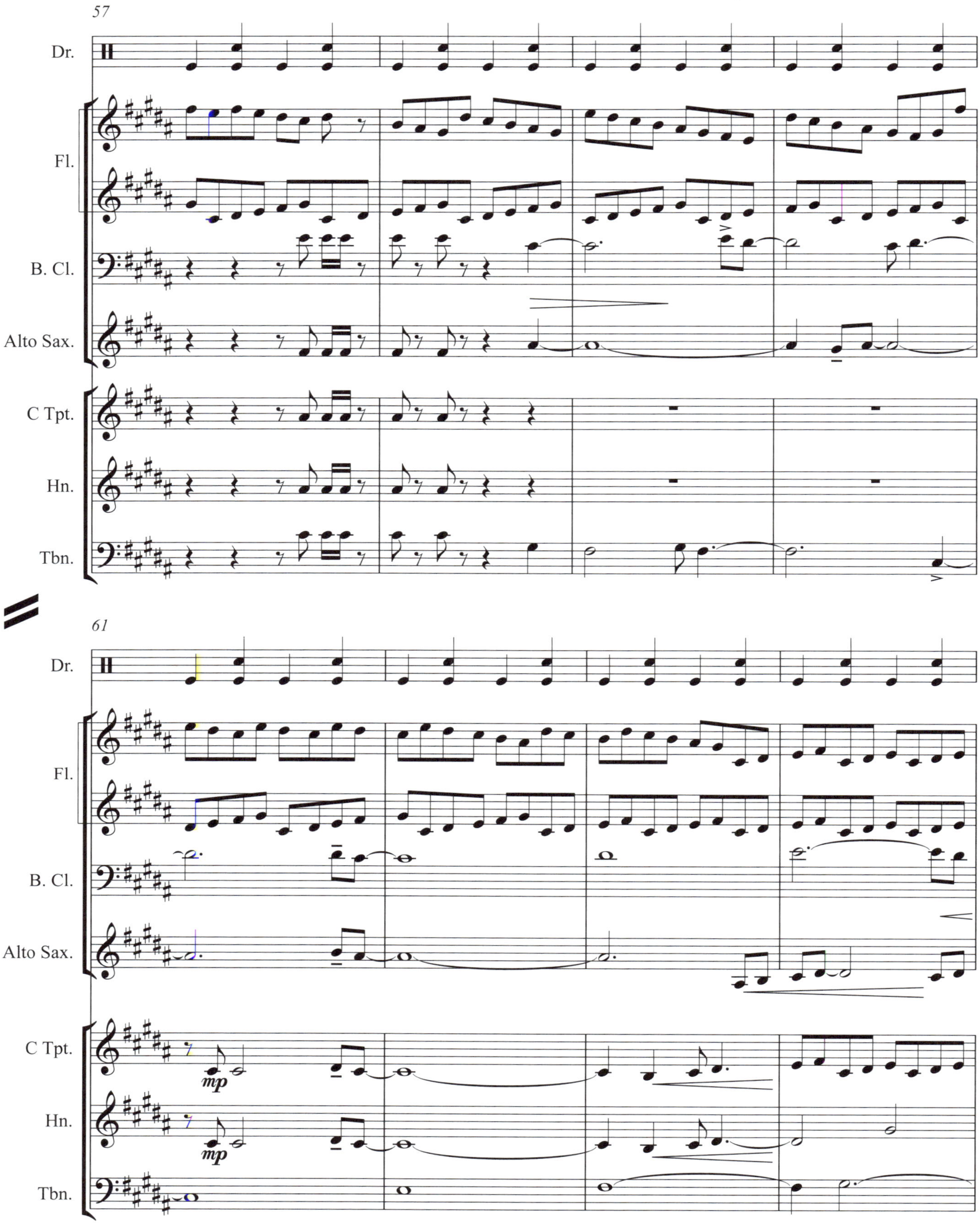
57
Dr.
Fl.
B. Cl.
Alto Sax.
C Tpt.
Hn.
Tbn.
61
Dr.
Fl.
B. Cl.
Alto Sax.
C Tpt.
mp
Hn.
mp
Tbn.

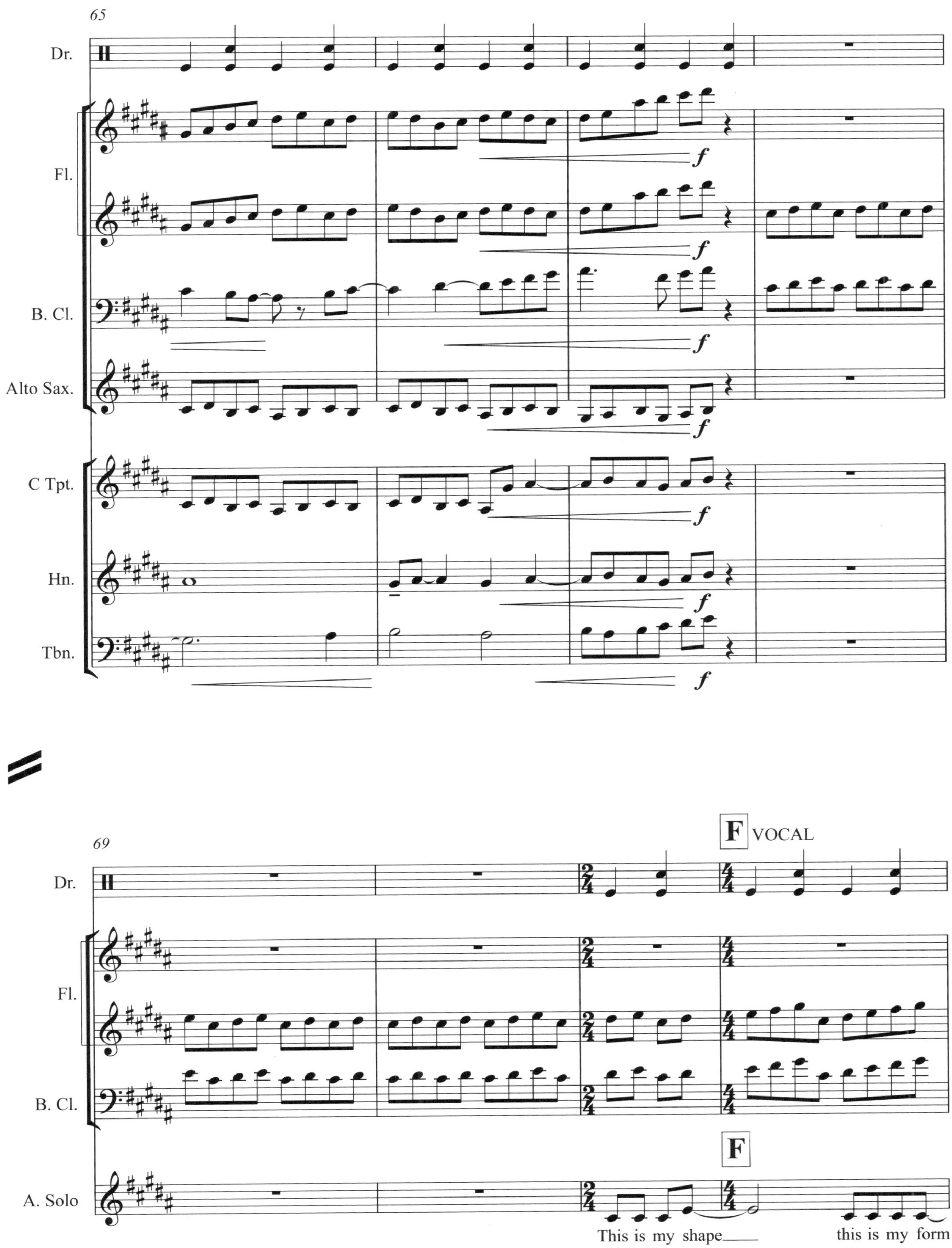
65
Dr.
Fl.
B. Cl.
Alto Sax.
C Tpt.
Hn.
Tbn.
69
F VOCAL
A. Solo
F
This is my shape___ this is my form

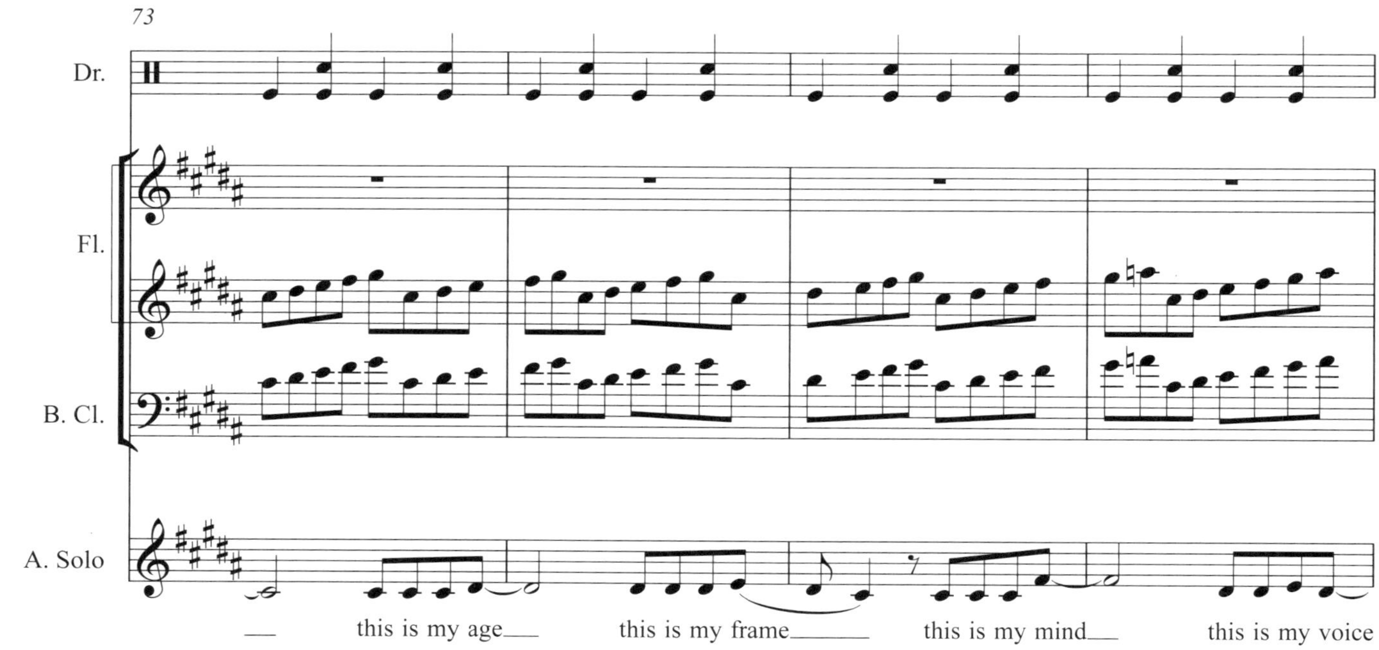
73
Dr.
Fl.
B. Cl.
A. Solo
— this is my age— this is my frame—— this is my mind— this is my voice

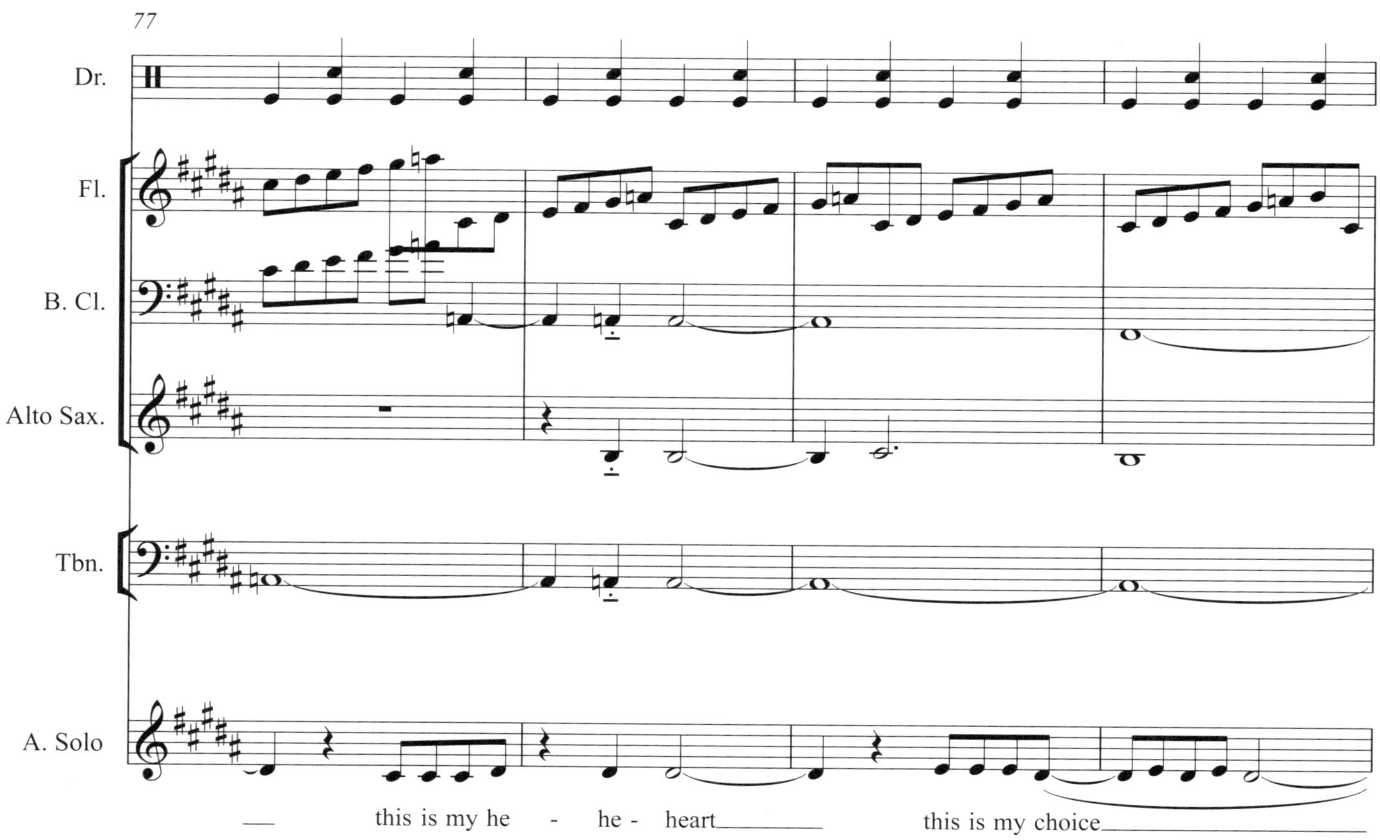
77
Dr.
Fl.
B. Cl.
Alto Sax.
Tbn.
A. Solo
— this is my he - he - heart—— this is my choice——

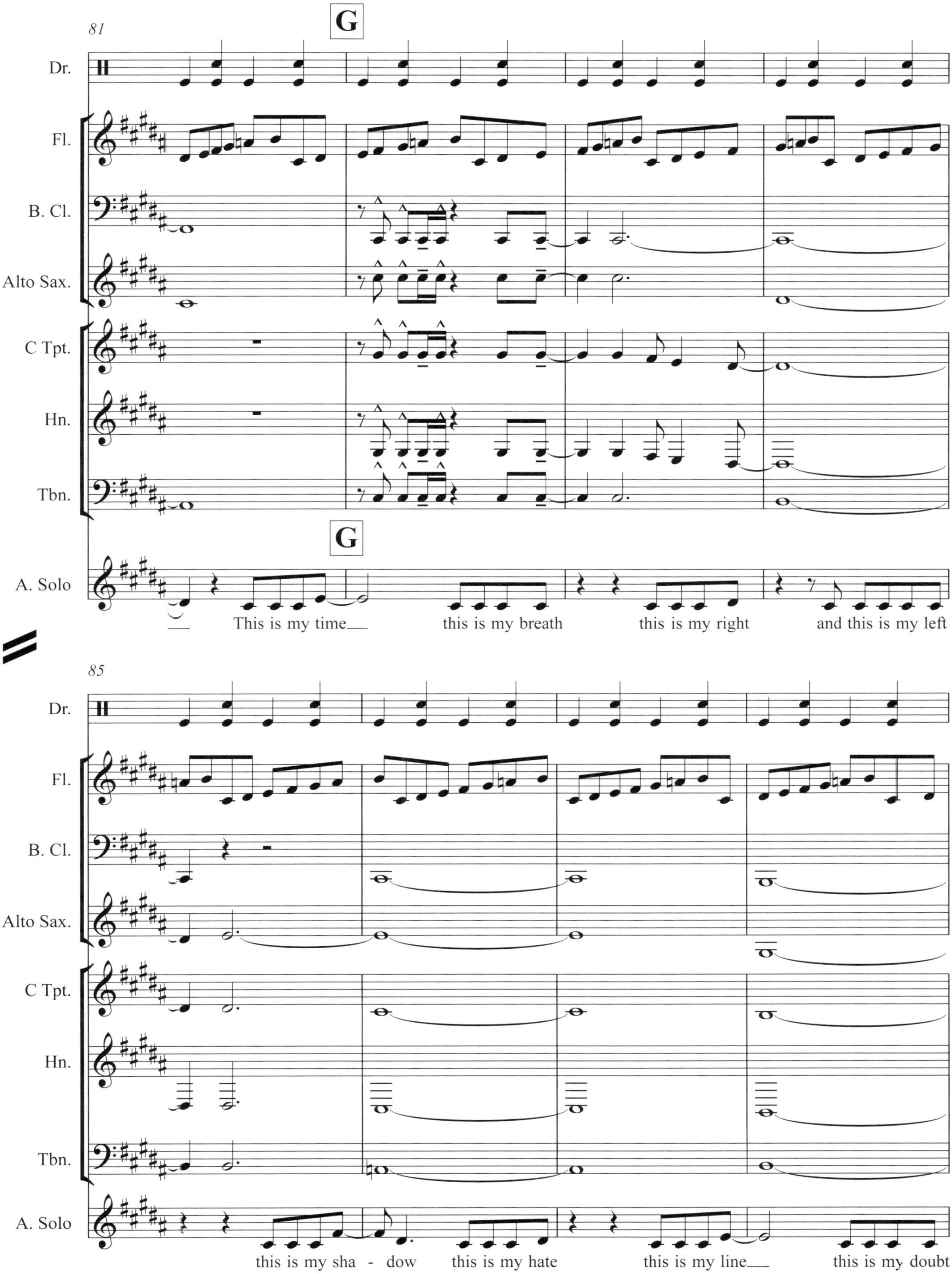
81
G
Dr.
Fl.
B. Cl.
Alto Sax.
C Tpt.
Hn.
Tbn.
G
A. Solo
This is my time this is my breath this is my right and this is my left
85
Dr.
Fl.
B. Cl.
Alto Sax.
C Tpt.
Hn.
Tbn.
A. Solo
this is my sha - dow this is my hate this is my line this is my doubt

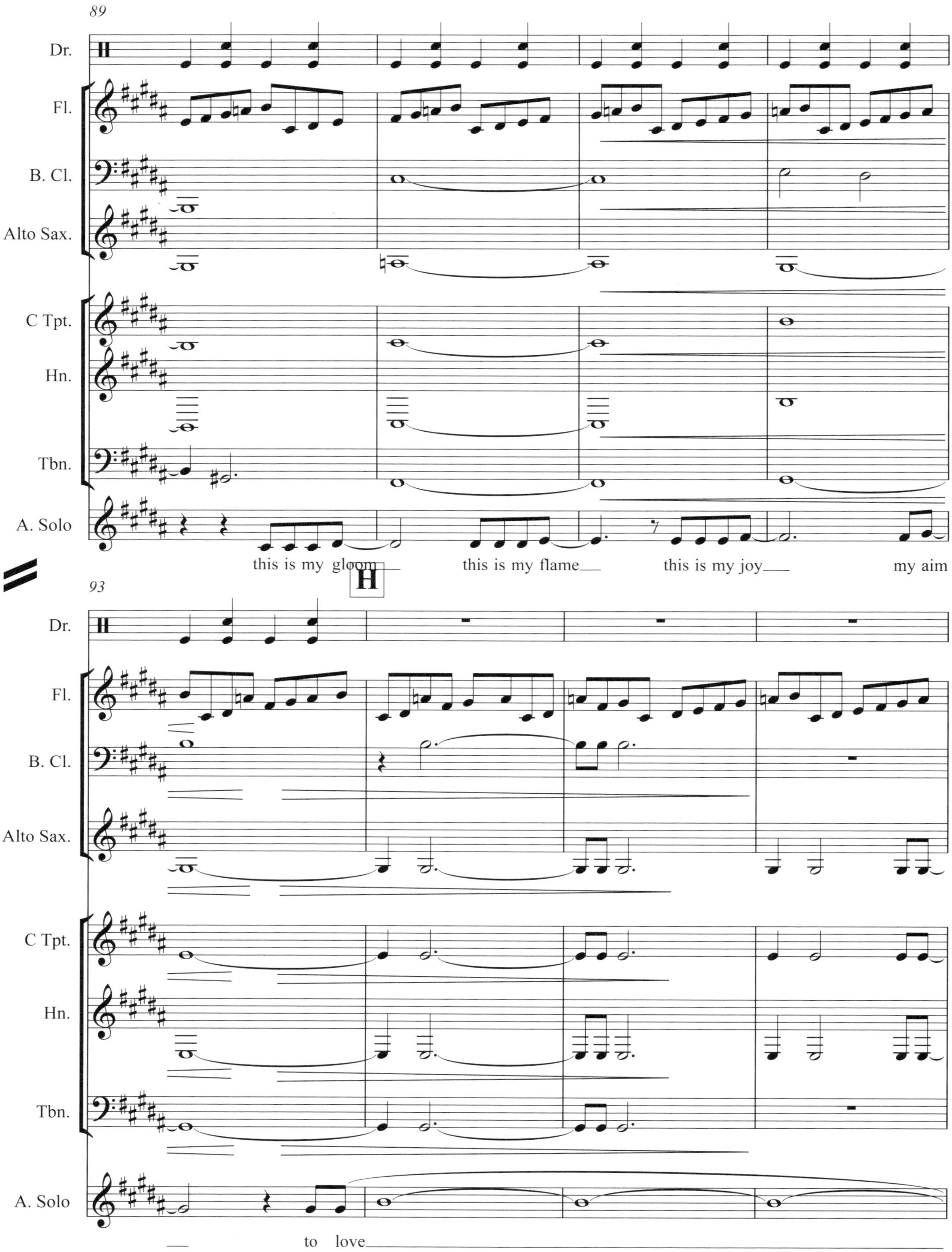
89
Dr.
Fl.
B. Cl.
Alto Sax.
C Tpt.
Hn.
Tbn.
A. Solo
this is my gloom
this is my flame
this is my joy
my aim
H
93
to love

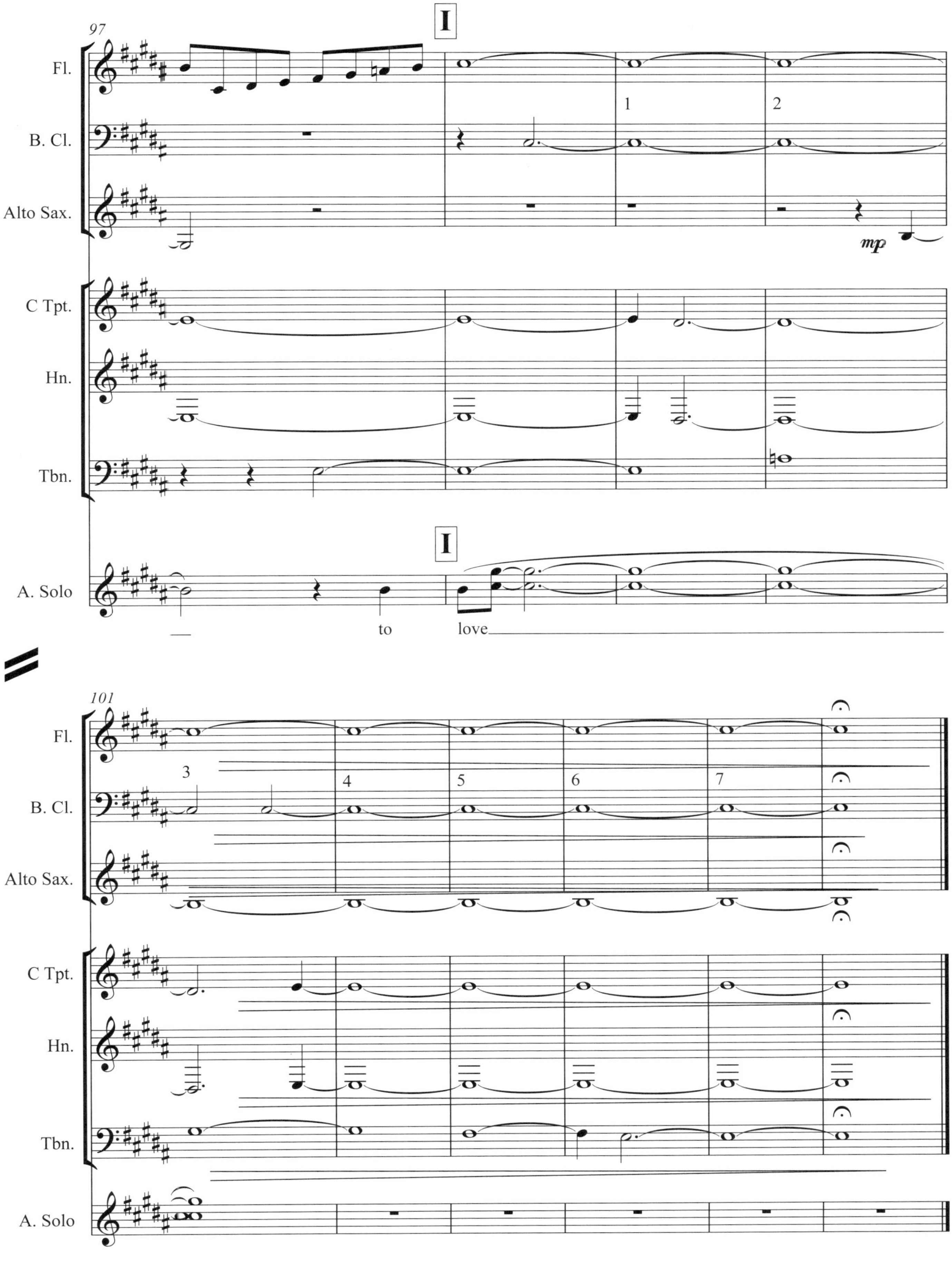
97
I
Fl.
B. Cl.
Alto Sax.
C Tpt.
Hn.
Tbn.
A. Solo
1
2
mp
to
love
101
3
4
5
6
7

134
This Is My Hand
MY BRIGHTEST DIAMOND

To see, to hear, to touch, to kiss, to die
I sit, I sigh, I weep, I faint, I die

135
Tiptoes
DAEDELUS

Tom's Diner
Suzanne Vega

1.
I am sitting in the morning
At the diner on the corner
I am waiting at the counter
For the man to pour the coffee

And he fills it only halfway
And before I even argue
He is looking out the window
At somebody coming in

2. It is always nice to see you
Says the man behind the counter
To the woman who has come in
She is shaking her umbrella

And I look the other way
As they are kissing their hellos
I'm pretending not to see them
And instead I pour the milk.

3. I open up the paper
There's a story of an actor
Who had died while he was drinking
It was noone I had heard of

And I'm turning to the horoscope
And looking for the funnies
When I'm feeling someone watching me
~~And~~ so I raise my head

136

Tom’s Diner

SUZANNE VEGA

4. There's a woman on the outside
Looking inside. Does she see me?
No she does not really see me
Cause she sees her own reflection

And I'm trying not to notice
That she's hitching up her skirt
And while she's straightening her stockings
Her hair has gotten wet.

5. Oh this rain it will continue
Through the morning as I'm listening
To the bells of the cathedral
I am thinking of your voice

And of the midnight picnic
Once upon a time before the rain began
I finish up my coffee
It's time to catch the train...

Da da da da da da da da
Da da da da da da da da . . .
etc.

S. Vega
Oct 2013

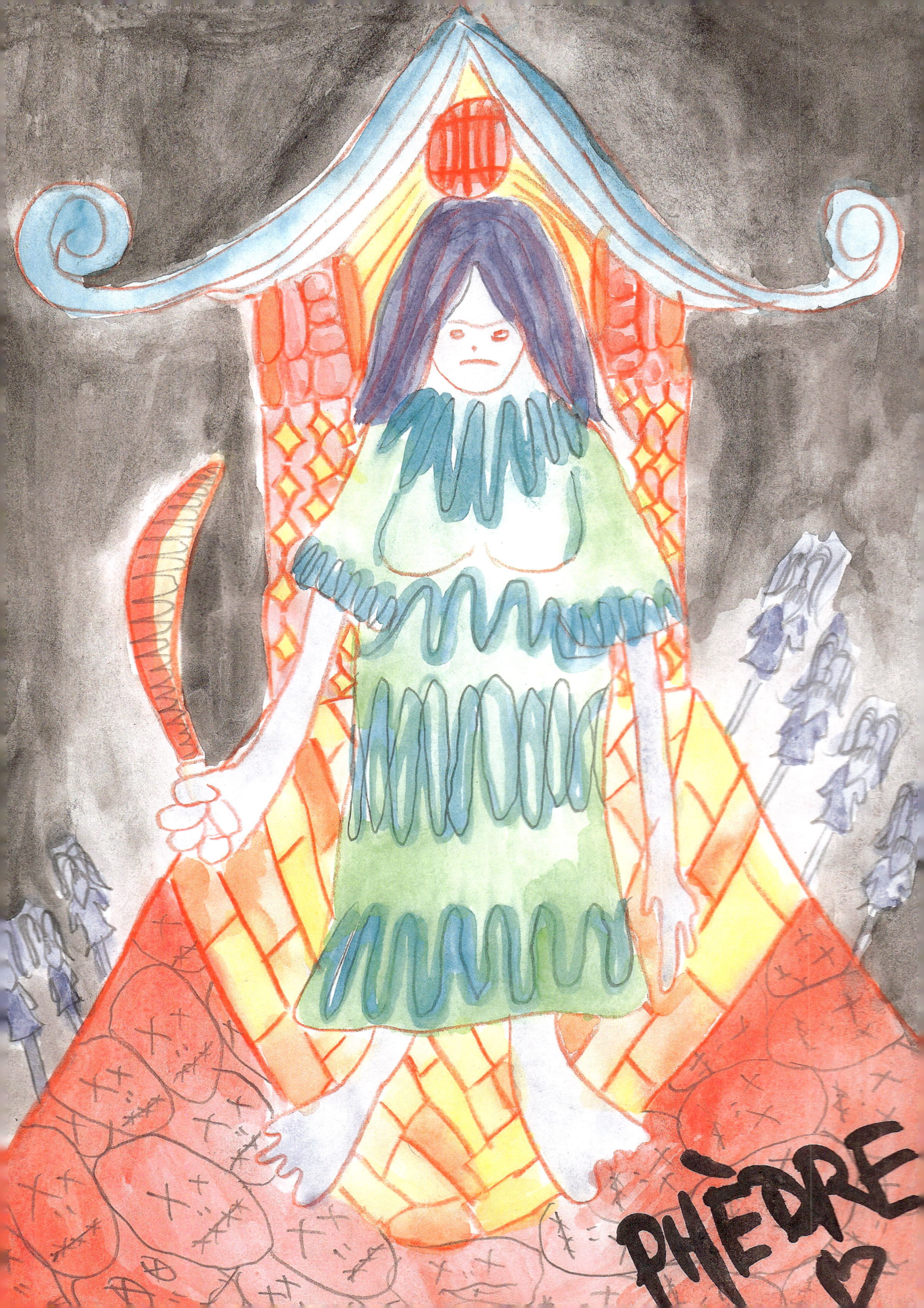
PHÈDRE

137
Too Many Lashes
PHÈDRE

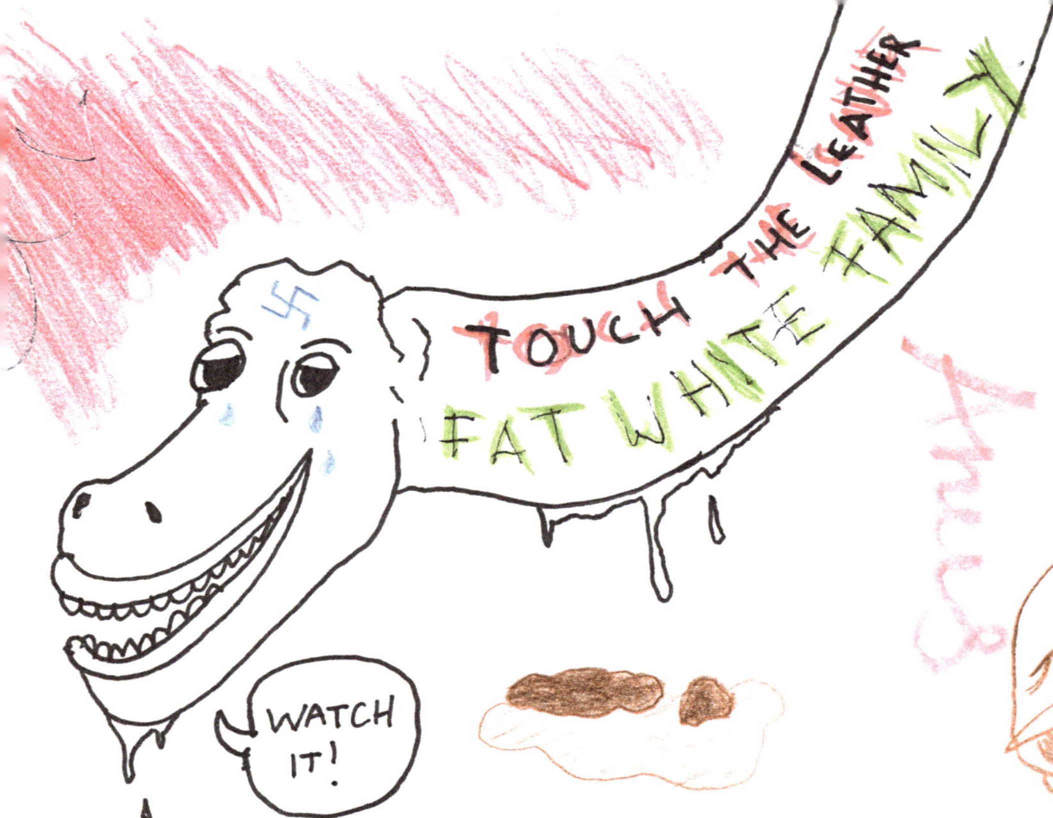

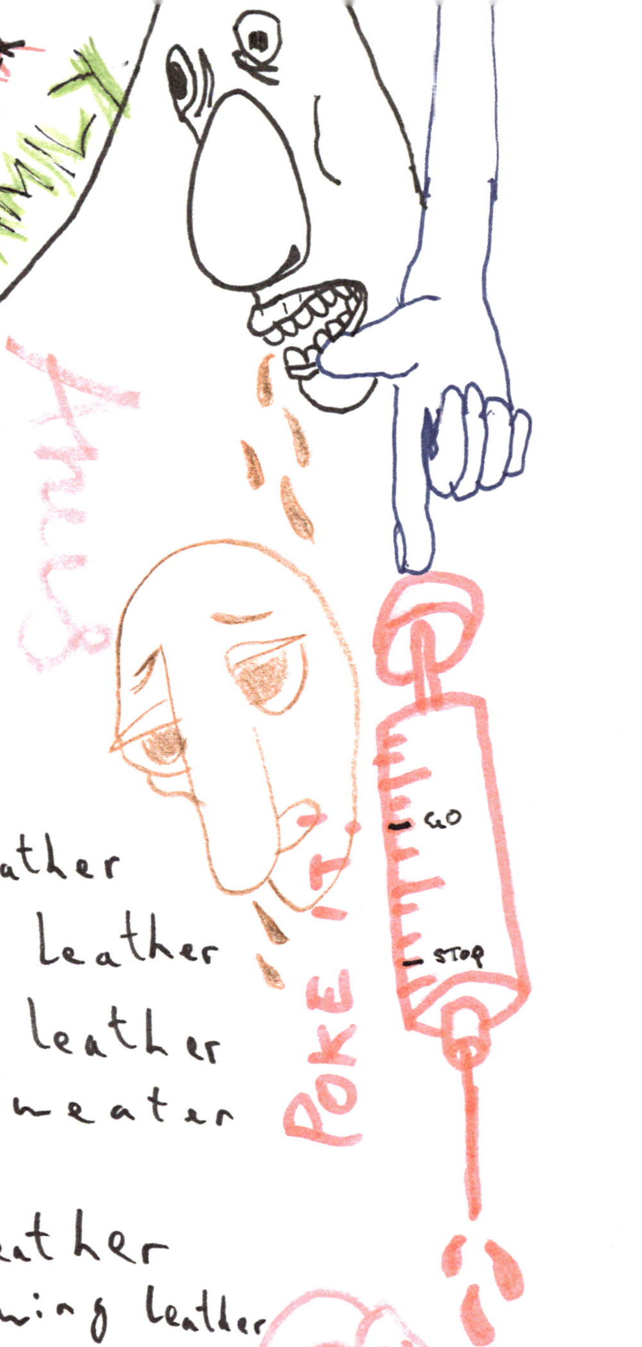

t white skin on the devastated leather
ersold skin on the soggy soggy leather
ew age skin on the out of date leather
orts socks and a warm sweater

chorus

ashville skin on the tupelo leather
ght wing skin on the right wing leather
ut of date skin on the new age leather
lmon pink skin on the duck egg leather

me and my baby gonna x2
touch that leather
me and my baby gonna
touch that leather

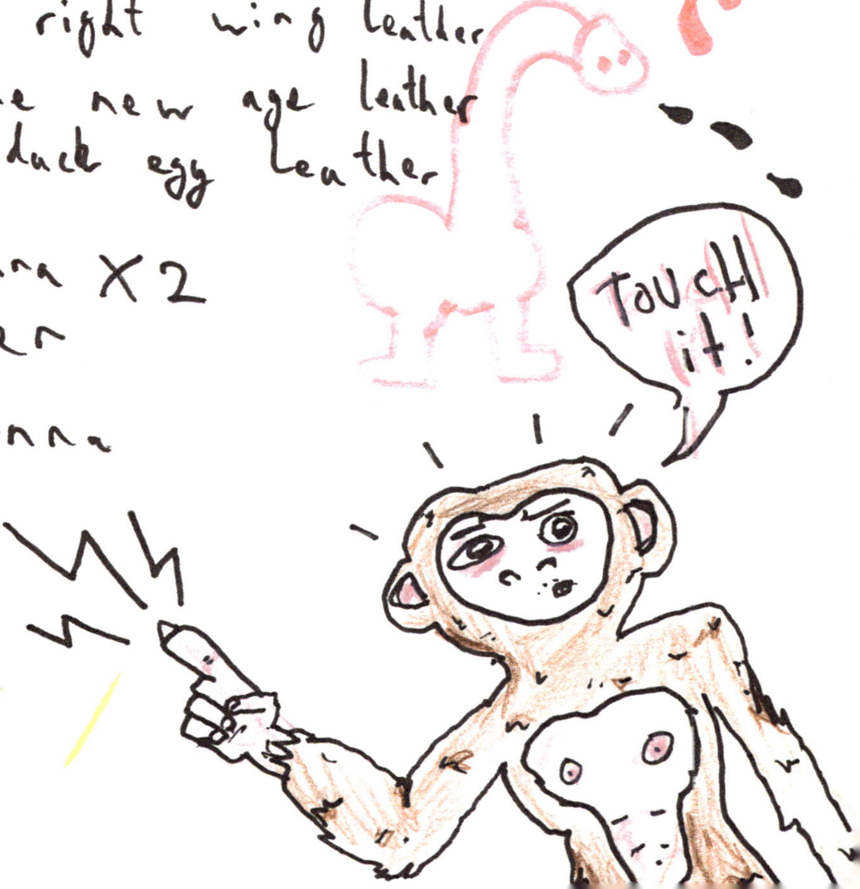

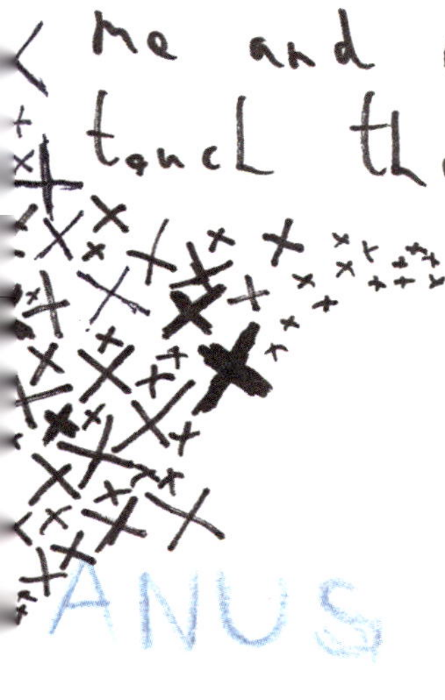

138
Touch the Leather
FAT WHITE FAMILY

TRAVELLING AND PLAYING WITH THE FAMILY

VIAGGIANDO E SUONANDO CON LA FAMIGLIA

STEFANO DE PONTI

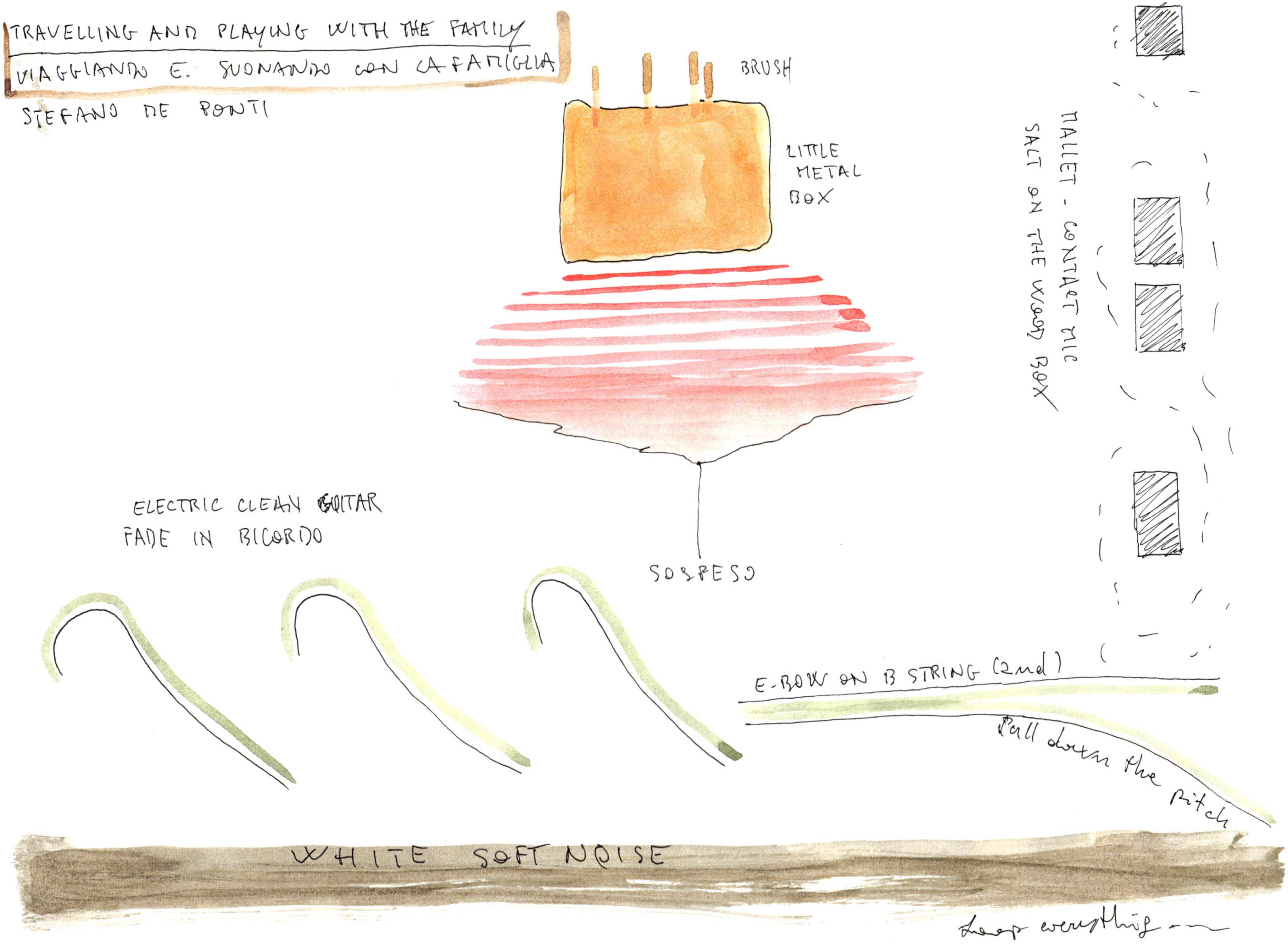

139

Travelling and Playing with the Family

STEFANO DE PONTI

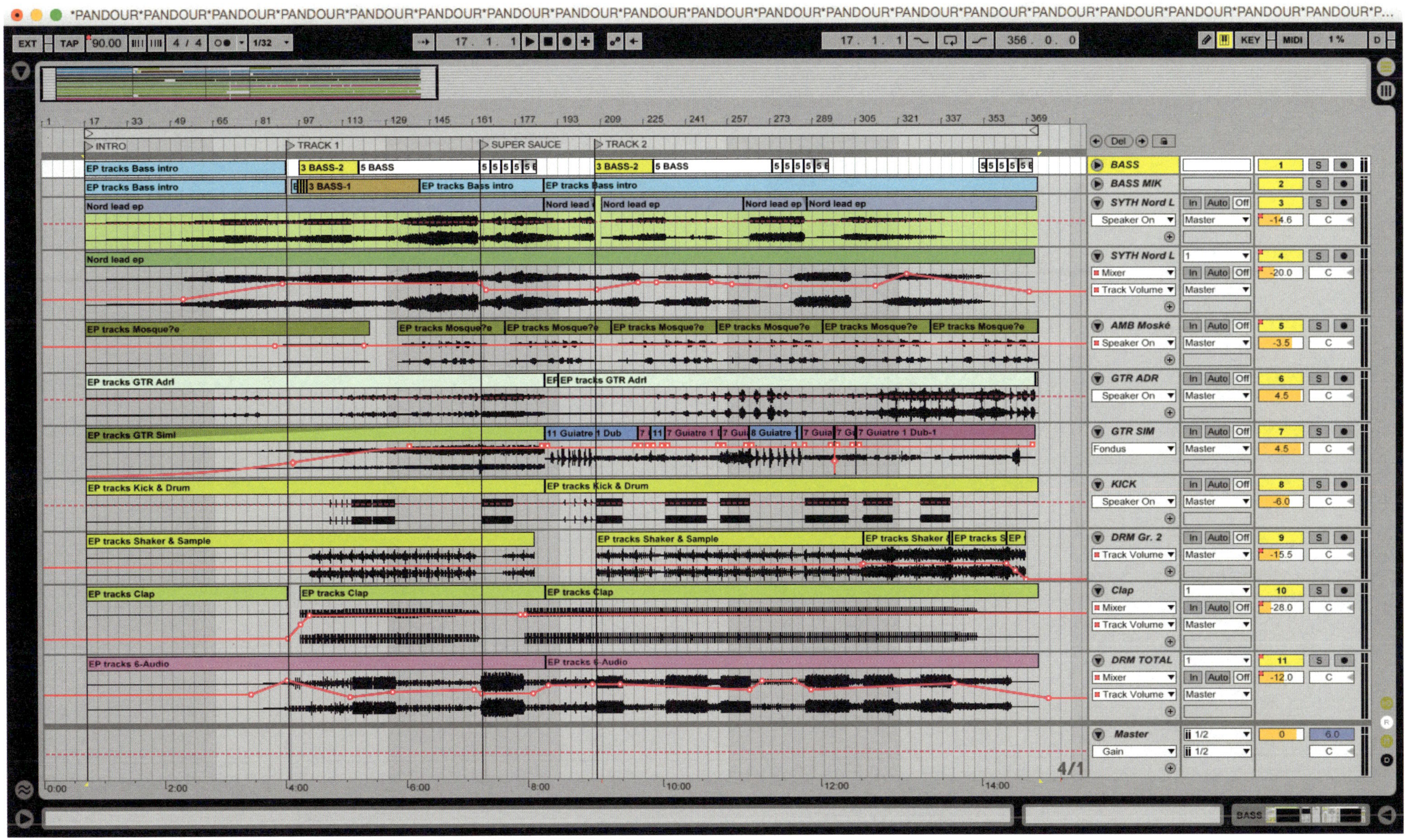
*PANDOUR*P...
INTRO
TRACK 1
SUPER SAUCE
TRACK 2
BASS
BASS MIK
SYTH Nord L
SYTH Nord L
AMB Moské
GTR ADR
GTR SIM
KICK
DRM Gr. 2
Clap
DRM TOTAL
Master
EP tracks Bass intro
Nord lead ep
EP tracks Mosque?e
EP tracks GTR Adrl
EP tracks GTR Siml
EP tracks Kick & Drum
EP tracks Shaker & Sample
EP tracks Clap
EP tracks 6-Audio

140
Turkish 2000
PANDOUR

U

U

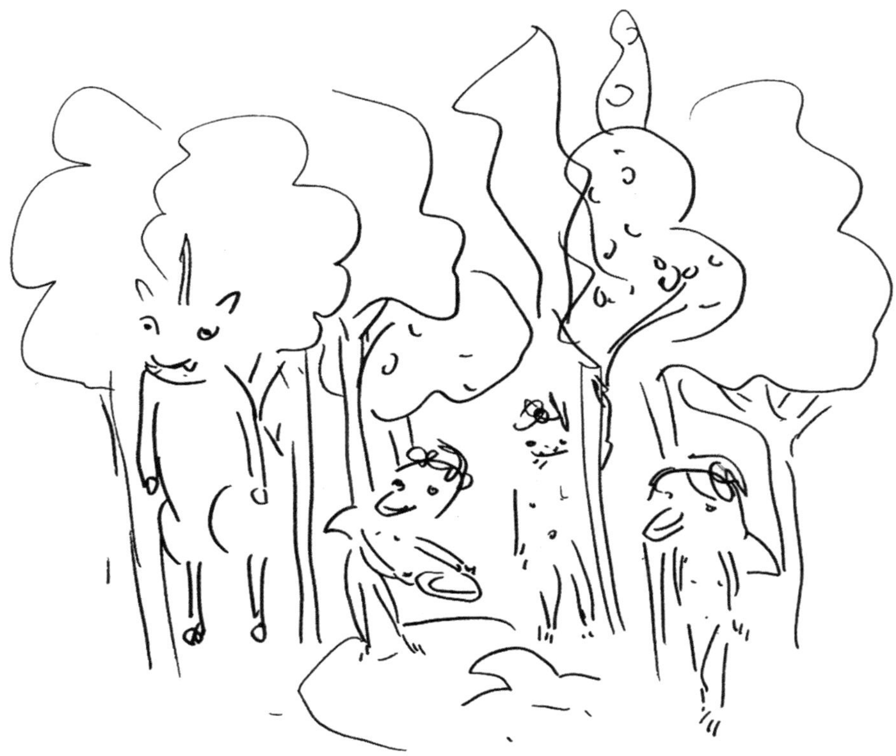

141
Untitled
CONNAN MOCKASIN

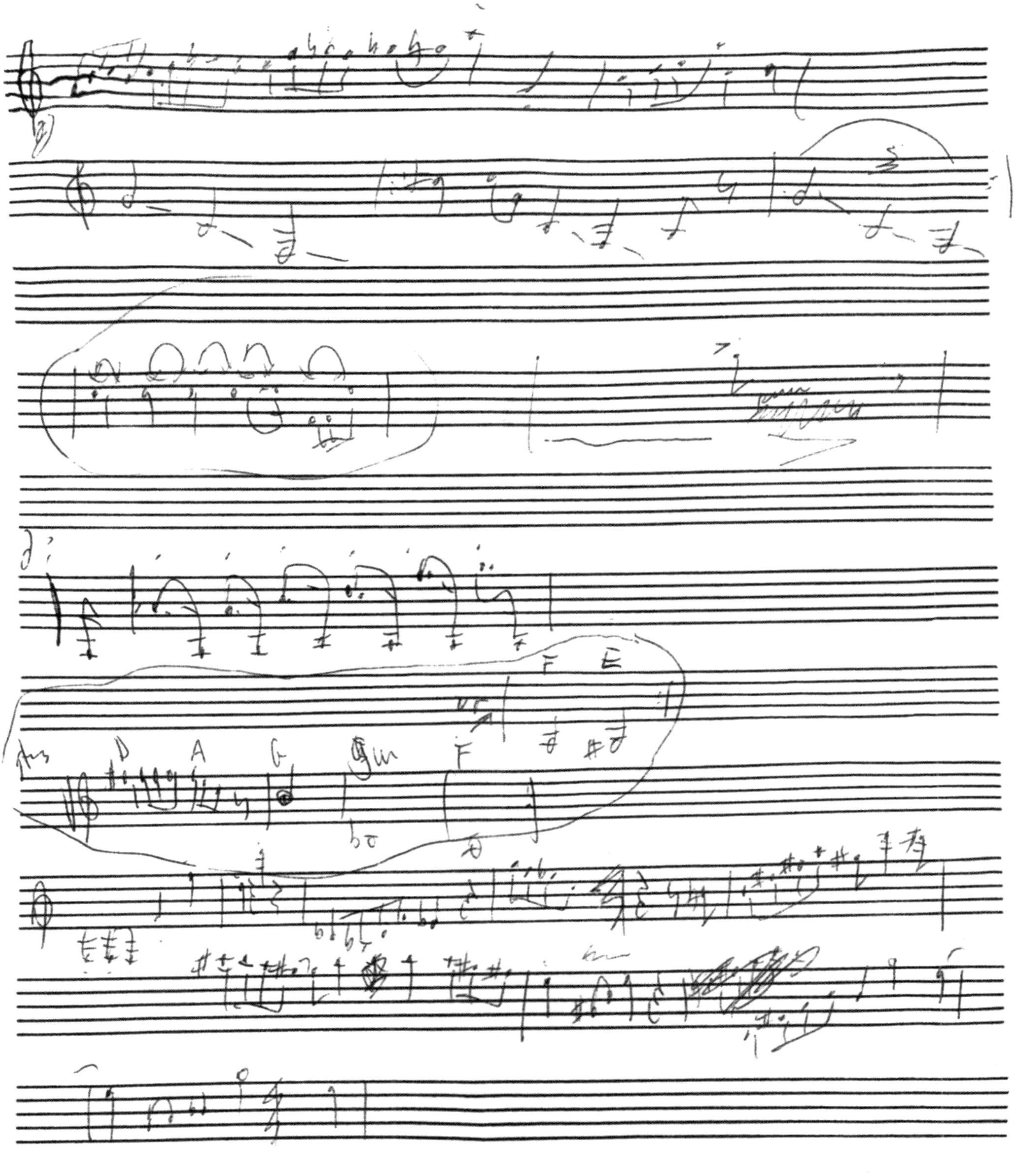

142

Untitled

DEERHOOF

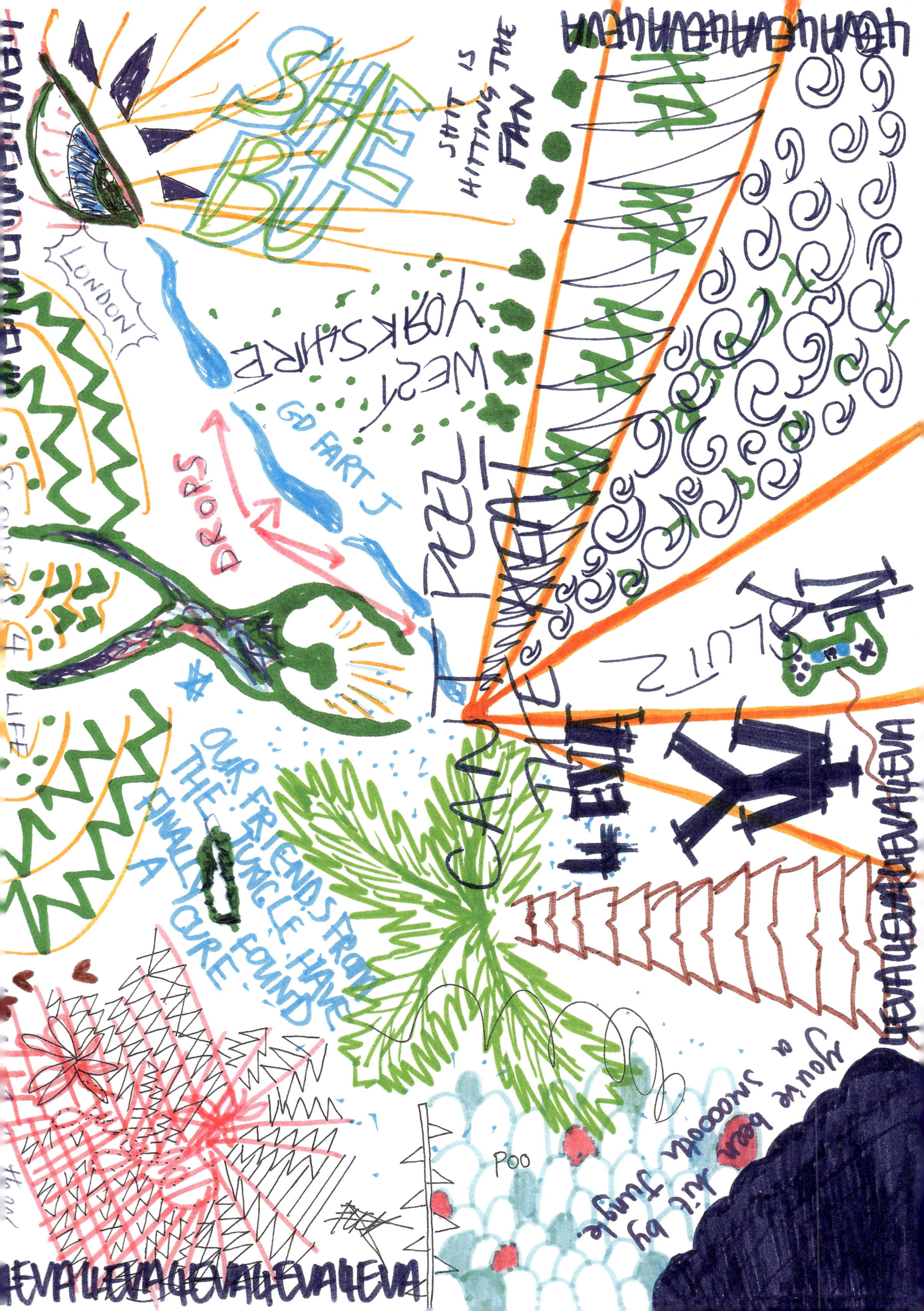
SHIT IS HITTING THE FAN
LONDON
WEST YORKSHIRE
GO FART J
DROPS
OUR FRIENDS FROM THE JUNGLE HAVE FINALLY FOUND A CURE
POO

143
Untitled
JUNGLE

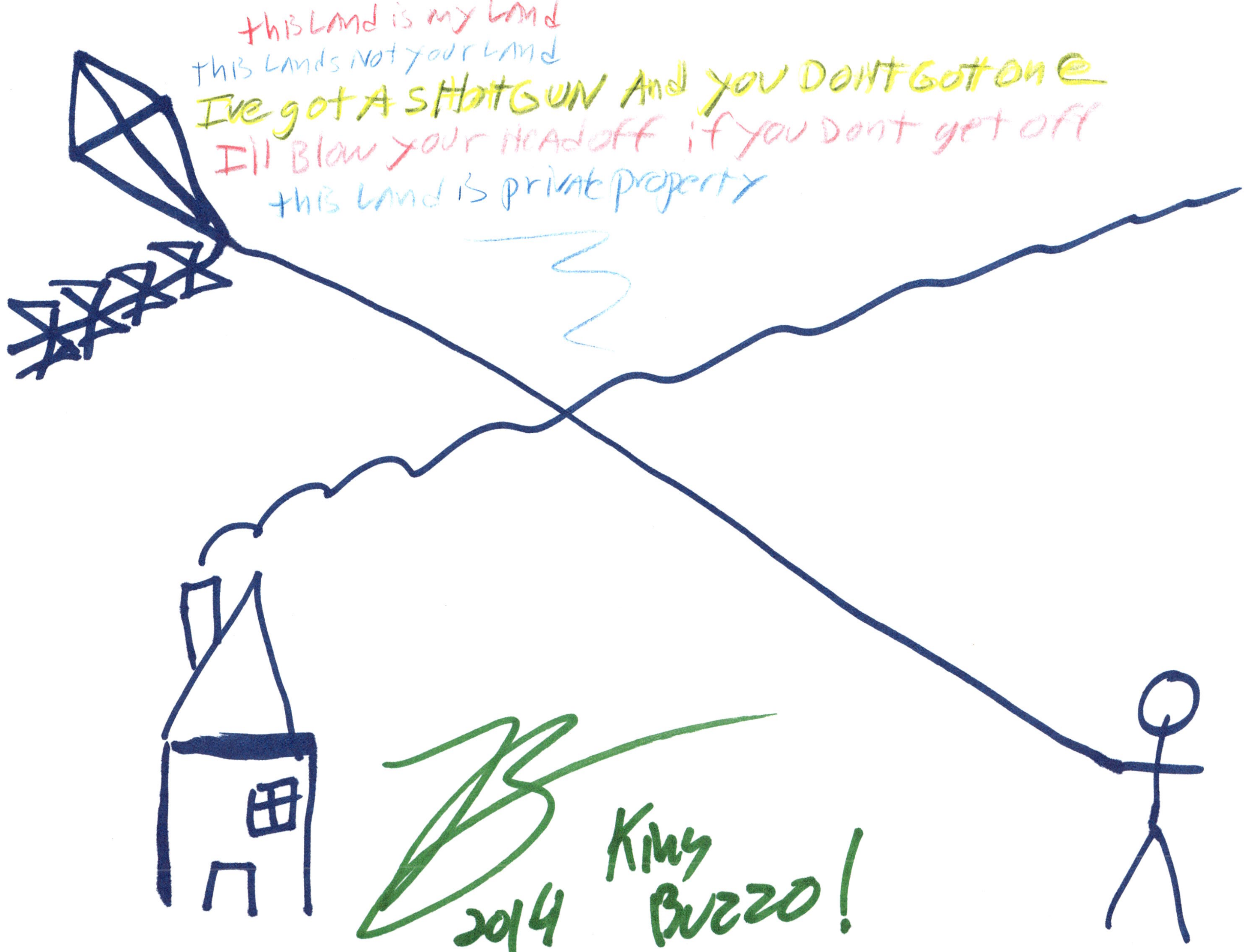
this Land is my Land
This Lands Not your Land
Ive got A SHotGUN And you DONT Got one
Ill Blow your HeAd off if you Dont get off
this Land is private property
King Buzzo!
2014

144

Untitled

KING BUZZO

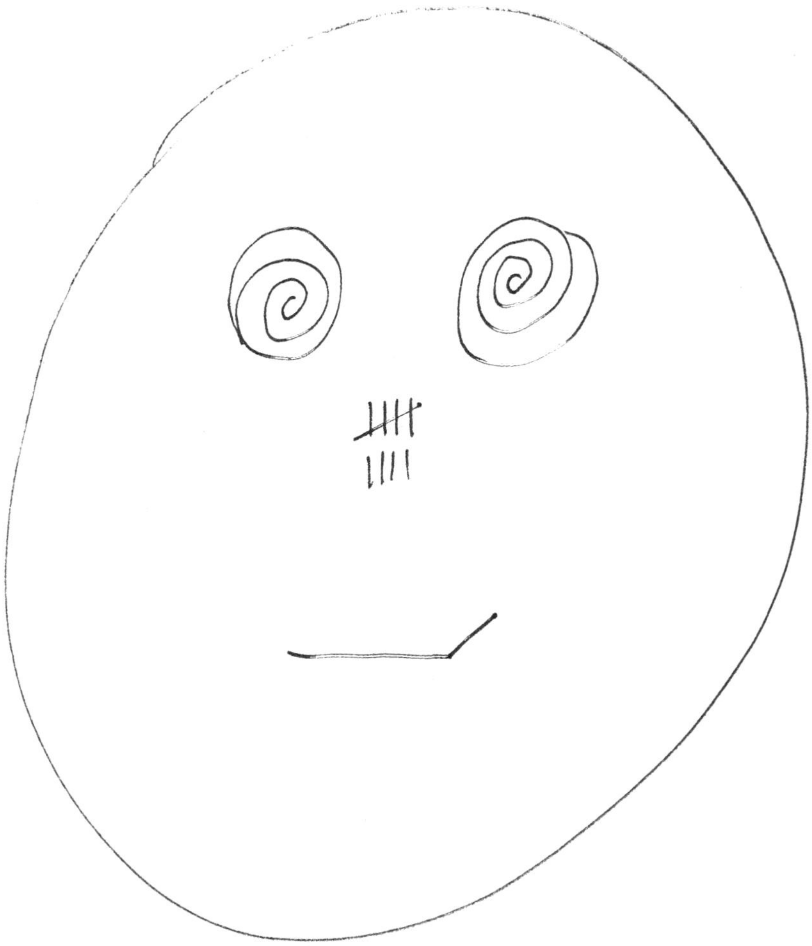

145

Untitled

KODE9

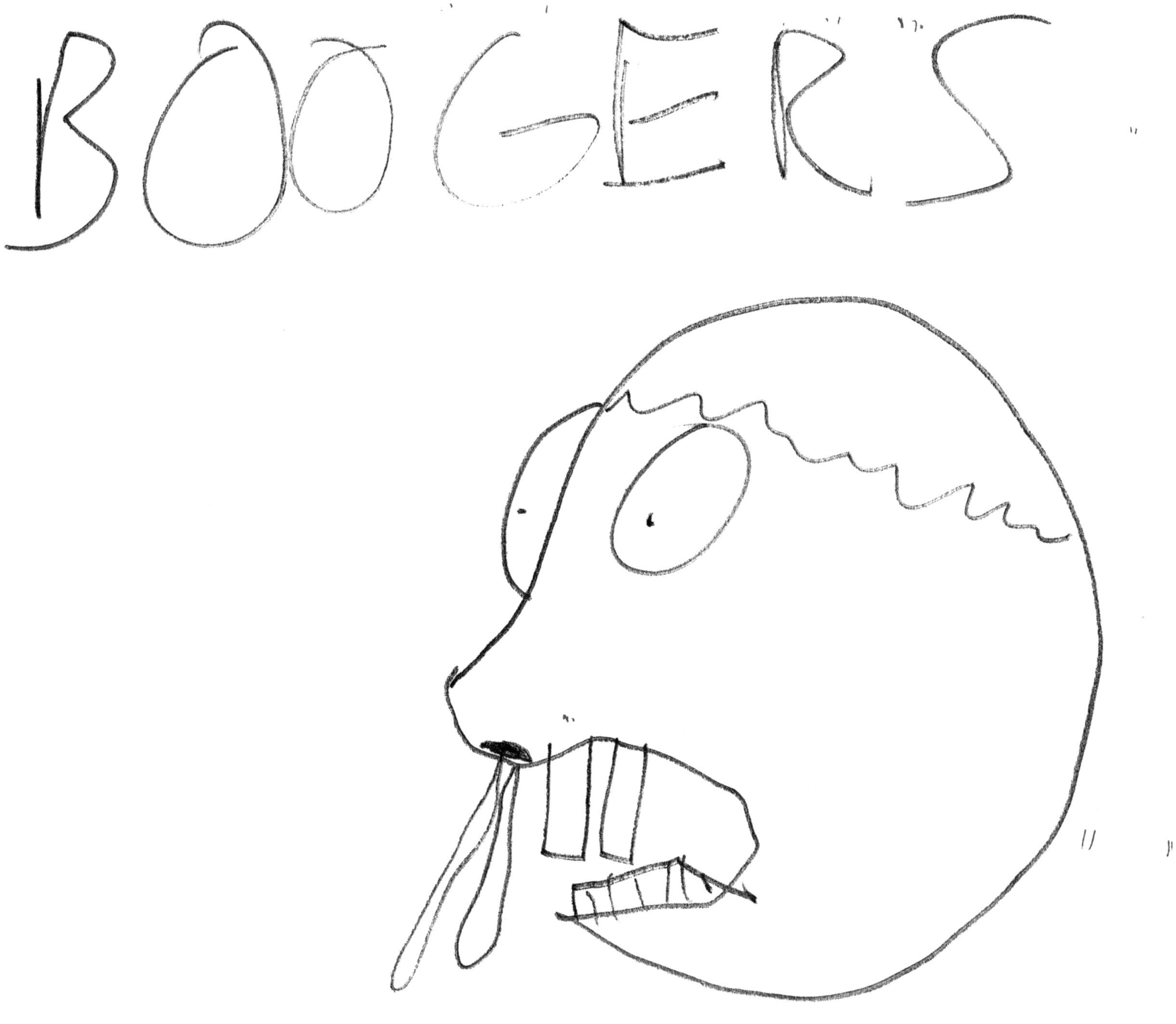
BOOGERS

146
Untitled
PERFECT PUSSY

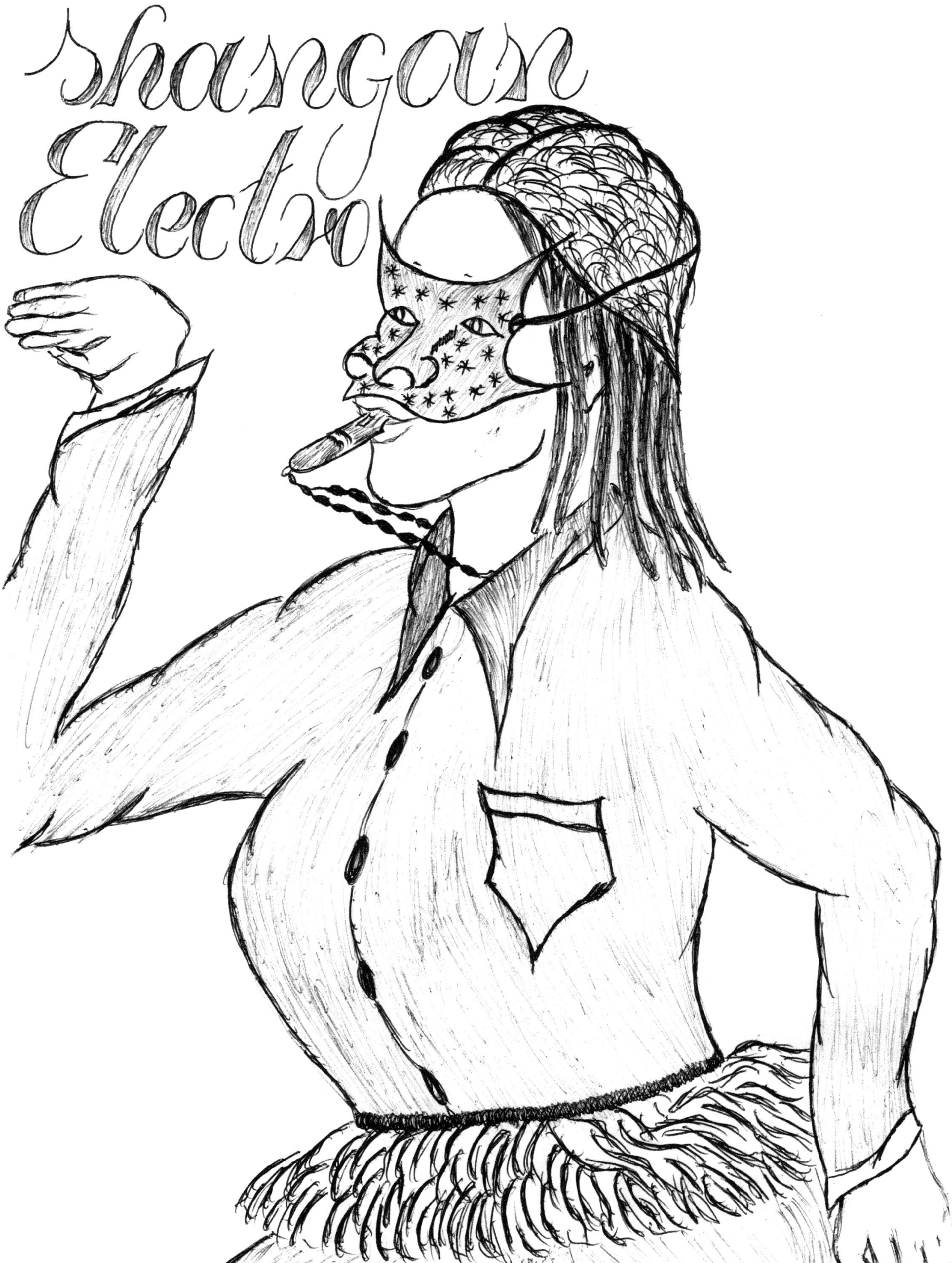
Shangaan
Electro

147
Untitled
SHANGAAN ELECTRO

YOU ARE NOTHING. YOU ARE EVERYTHING.
YOU ARE NOT HERE. BE PRESENT. BE REAL.
FUCK YOURSELF. FUCK EVERYONE ELSE.
DREAM ABOUT IT. EAT IT. LIVE IT. BE IT

HURT. SUCK. PEEL. RANT
FLESH. BONE. SINEW
STORM. GUSH. SQUIRT.
SLICK. WET. WASH.
PLUMP. RIPE. JUICY. HOLLOW.
ENGORGED. RICH. VESSEL.
FUCK. SLIDE. SLICK. ROB
PENETRATE. IMPOVERISHED
VIOLENT GLUTTONY.
RIP. R.I.P PLOW. RING
EXCAVATE. BURN.
ABSORB. RUN. FLEE.
SLOBBER. TEAR. SHIT
DECONSTRUCT. BLOOD.
DECOLONIZE. MUCUS

148
Untitled
TANYA TAGAQ

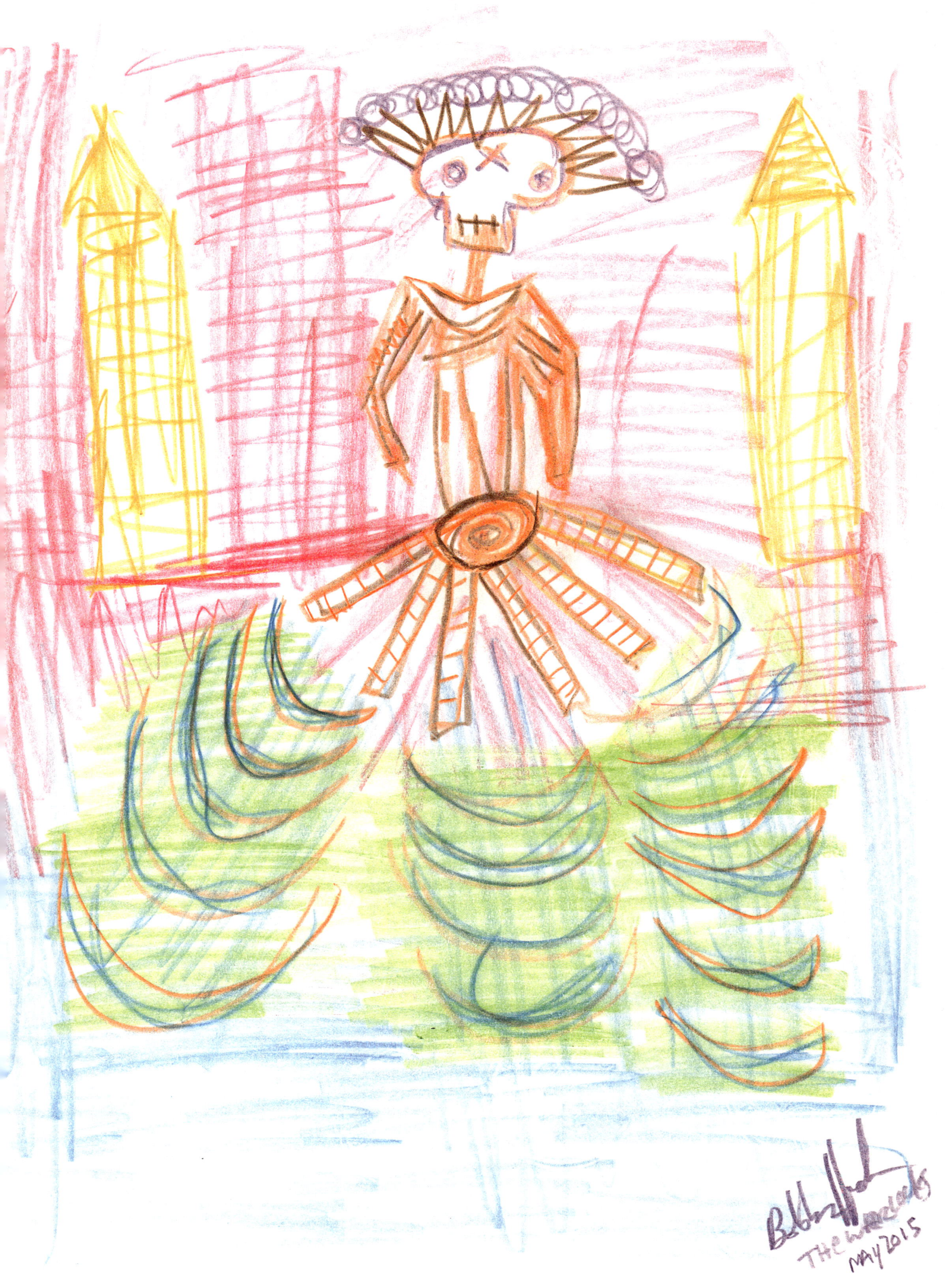
MAY 2015

149
Untitled
THE WARLOCKS

تسبيح آفلان مصروكب أ علبه
حامد ملان ذالك آمزبية

سبت وسواس ذل نسمبه
كبالتل واس بيواس جبنأ ماسبه

أفلان
نورة بنت سيمالي

150

Untitled

NOURA MINT SEYMALI

V

V

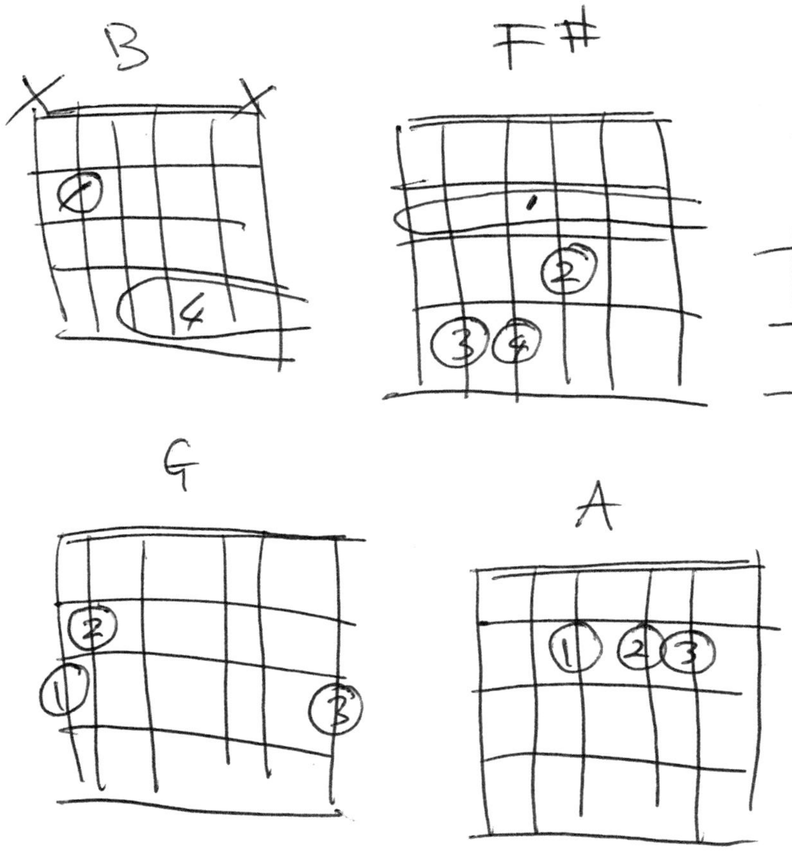

VERSE

B F#
I LOVE, I LOVE MY VEGEMITE
(chords: B over "I", F# over "LOVE", E over the second "LOVE", F# over "VEGE-", B over "-MITE")

IT'S STRONG AS HELL AND BLACK AS NIGHT
(chords: F# over "STRONG", E over "HELL", F# over "BLACK", B over "NIGHT")

I KEEP MY LOVE ALL SCREWED UP TIGHT
(chords: F# over "KEEP", E over "LOVE", F# over "SCREWED", B over "TIGHT")

AND SPREAD IT THICK WHENEVER I LIKE
(chords: F# over "SPREAD", E over "THICK", F# over "WHENEVER", E over "I", F# over "LIKE")

I LIKE
(chords: E over "LIKE", F# after "LIKE")

KING GIZZARD AND THE LIZARD WIZARD –

VEGEMITE

151
Vegemite
KING GIZZARD & THE LIZARD WIZARD

②

B F# E F# B F# E F#
VEGEMITE! /

B F# E F# B F# E F#
LIKE VEGE MITE /

E F# E F#
LIKE / LIKE

CHORUS

B F# E F#
AND WHEN EVERYONES GETTING GRUMPY COS ITS EARLY

B F# E F#
I'LL HAVE BREAKFAST WITH MY GIRLFRIEND

E F#
AND WE'LL HAVE TOAST

E F#
WITH AVOCADO

E F#
AND TOMATO

G A
AND VEGEMITE!

3rd only

'VELVET ITCH'

```
E                                                               7 6 5 4 3 3 2 1
A  7  7  10  10  7  7  10  10  7  7  10  10                       7  7  10  10
D  9  9  12  12  9  9  12  12  9  9  12  12                       9  9  12  12
G  9  9  12  12  9  9  12  12  9  9  12  12                       9  9  12  12
B
E
```

```
E  10  10             0                   0  0  0  0
A                         10              0  2  0  2
D          12 0 12                        0  2  0  2
G                             12  0
B
E
```

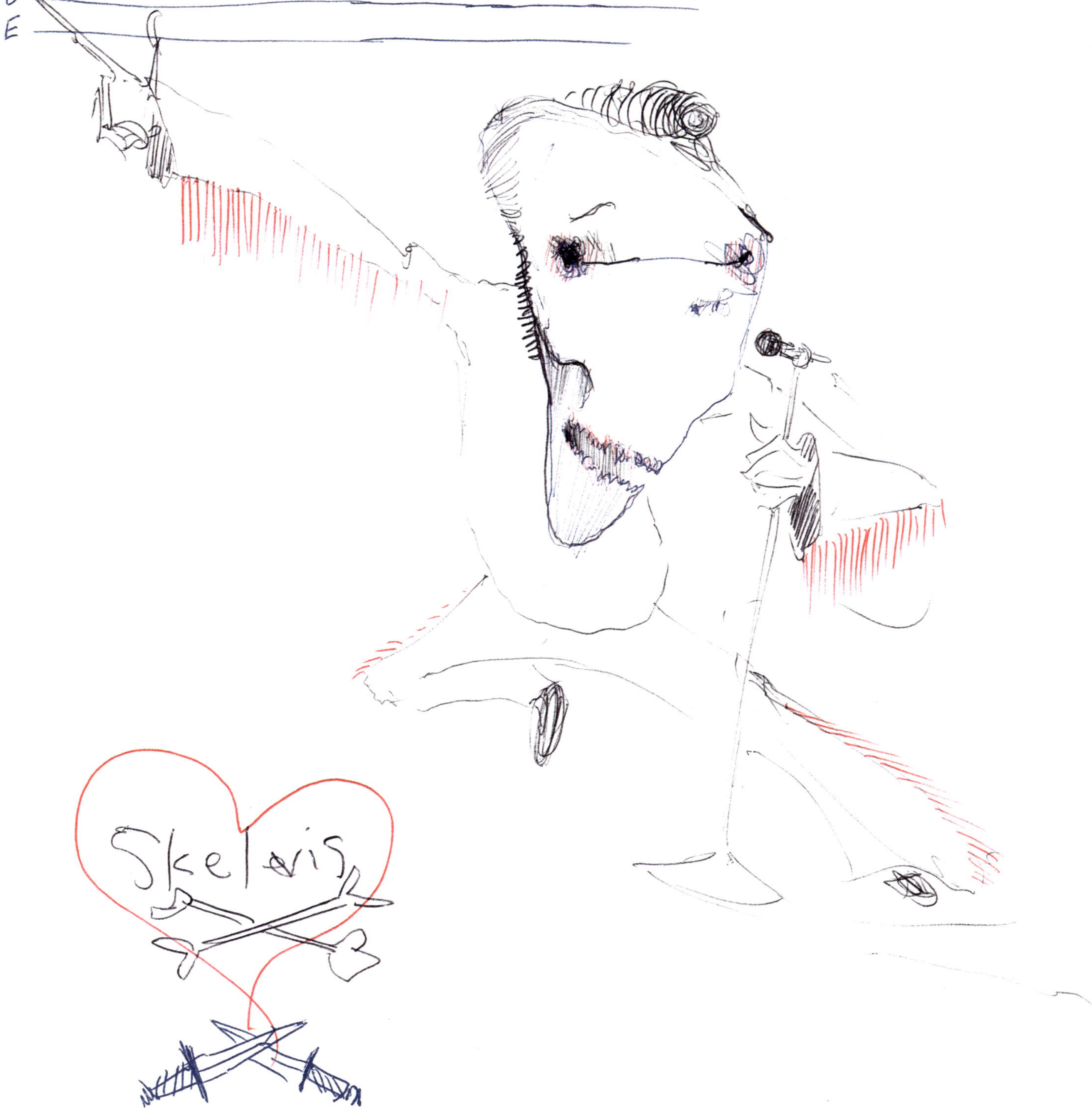

152
Velvet Itch
BASS DRUM OF DEATH

W

A PLACE TO BURY STRANGERS

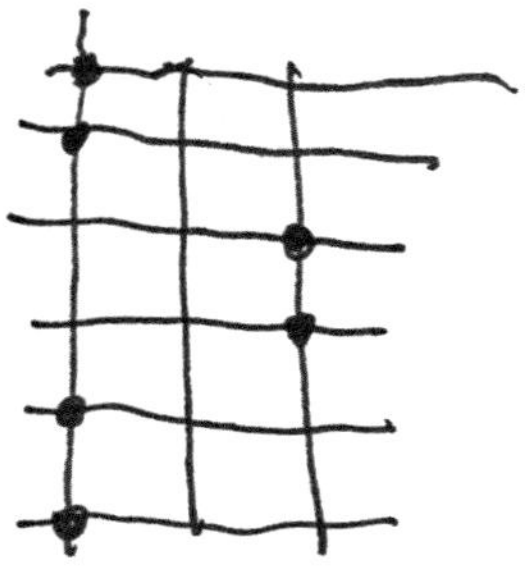

WE'VE COME SO FAR.

HIGH G

TASTES SO REAL
I LOST MYSELF TODAY
FEELS SO REAL
I LOST MYSELF TODAY

G D C G

I FEEL RIGHT NOW

G D F G

WE'VE COME SO FAR

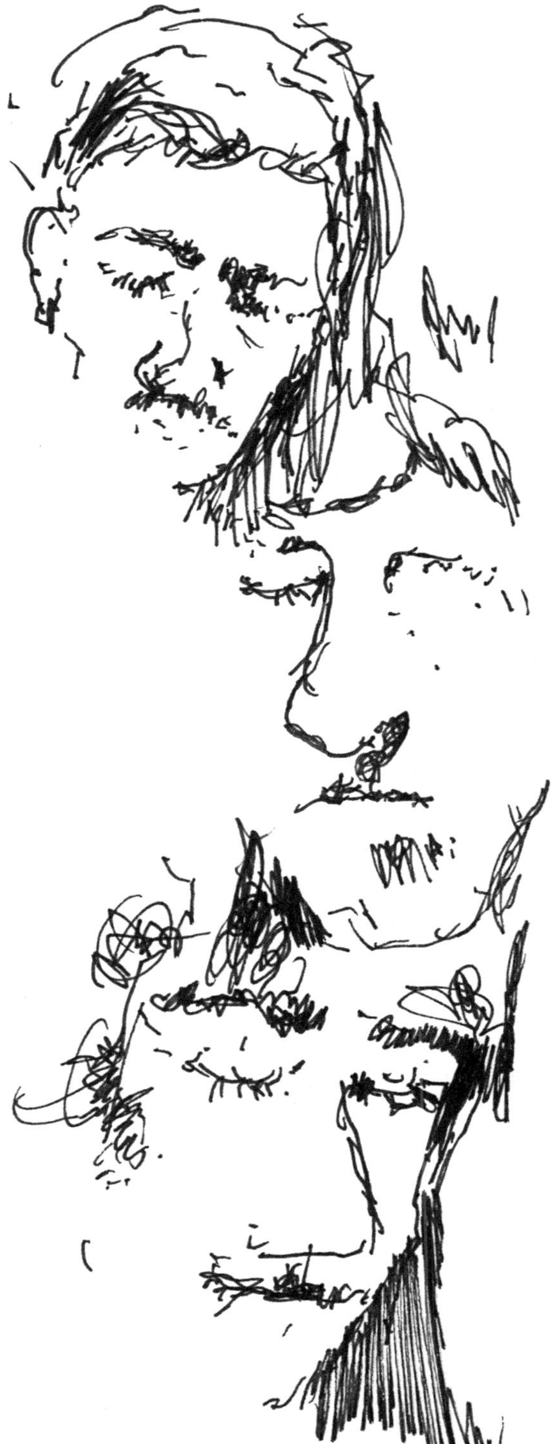

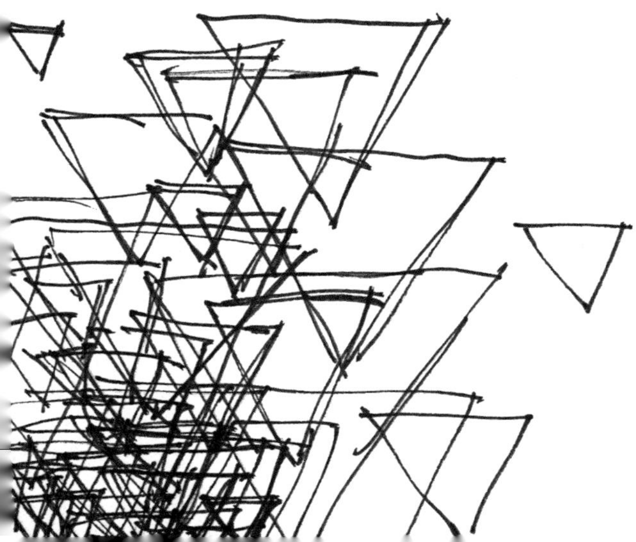

153
We've Come So Far
A PLACE TO BURY STRANGERS

WELCOME TO THE DOGHOUSE

you're obviously funny and smart
and, of course, you have a good heart
please make yourself at home in my humble abode
or, at least, have one for the road

i know you're busy, like a busy bee
but you can't be too busy for me
stop crouchin' around, let it all hang out
for cryin' out loud, we won't bite

my friend is dumb, but he's not stupid
he's always eavesdropping, always snoopin'
he loves a piece of chocolate, he loves a grain of rice
he is the cutest of mice

please do not be afraid
to sit on a bed that hasn't been made
meet the mouse, meet the louse
welcome to the doghouse

154
Welcome to the Dog House
STANLEY BRINKS

TOMORROW, i GO

Gm % D7 Gm

2nd half of verses:

G	Cm	F	Bb/Am
Gm	Cm	D7	Gm

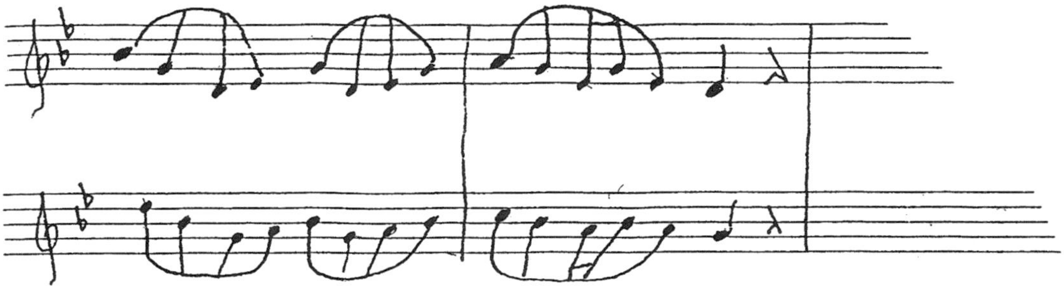

IX. WELCOME TO THE DOGHOUSE

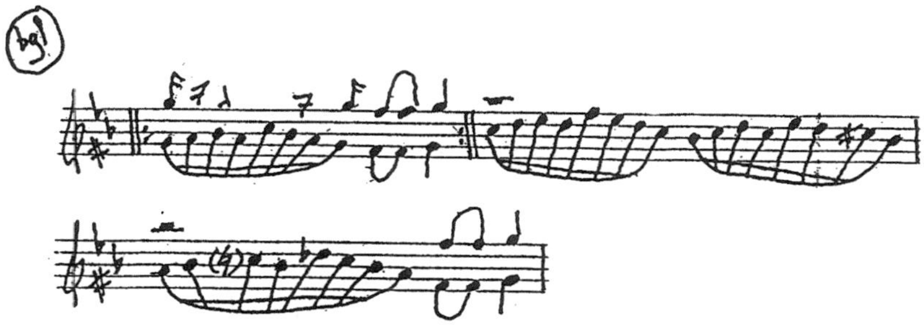

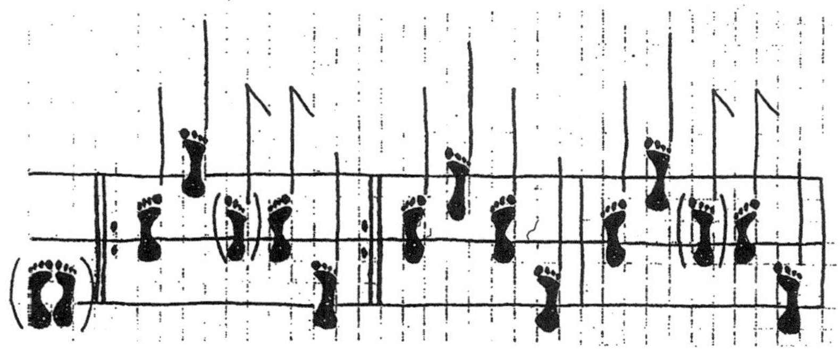

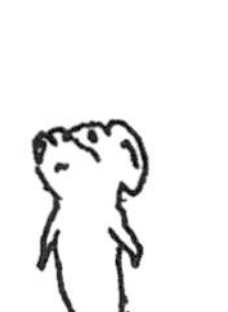

"What Can I do?" -Scout Niblett

Baby, What can I do?
to make it, right for you?
Baby, what can I do?
to make it, right for you?

I was doin' all I could
to numb it out,
it's taken all I've got
to not just break down

But I want to surrender
I want the tears to come.
The sooner they start
The sooner I'll be done

What the hell did they do to you
to make you so scared
of falling in love
and feeling you care

I prey one day out there,
You will find a Love
that crowns you
and all the fear will come undone....
oh baby, what can I do.... to make it right for you?

155
What Can I Do?
SCOUT NIBLETT

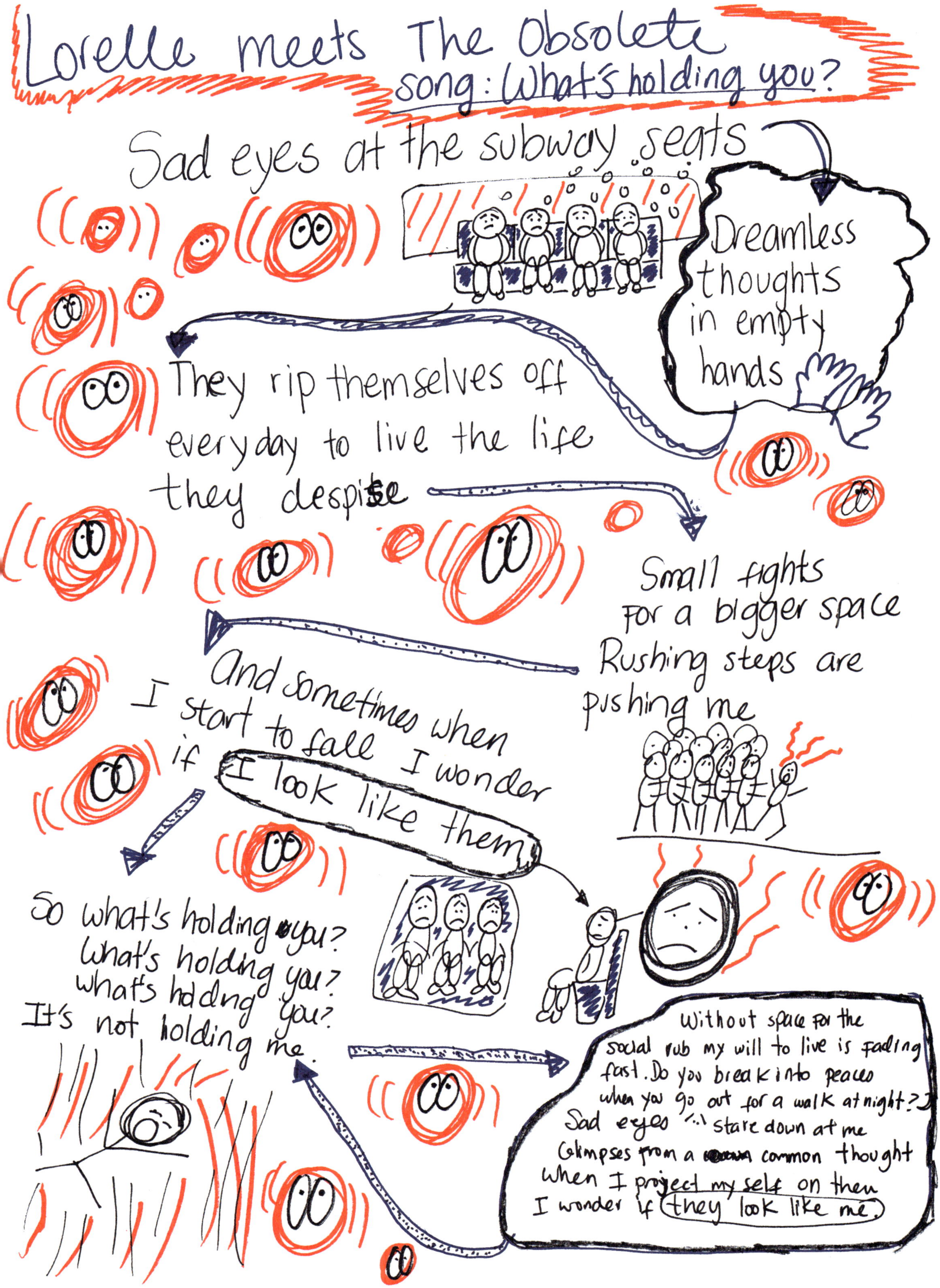
Lorelle meets The Obsolete
song: What's holding you?
Sad eyes at the subway seats
Dreamless thoughts in empty hands
They rip themselves off everyday to live the life they despise
Small fights for a bigger space
Rushing steps are pushing me
And sometimes when I start to fall I wonder if I look like them
So what's holding you?
What's holding you?
what's holding you?
It's not holding me.
Without space for the social rub my will to live is fading fast. Do you break into peaces when you go out for a walk at night?
Sad eyes stare down at me
Glimpses from a common thought
When I project my self on them
I wonder if they look like me.

156

What's Holding You?

LORELLE MEETS THE OBSOLETE

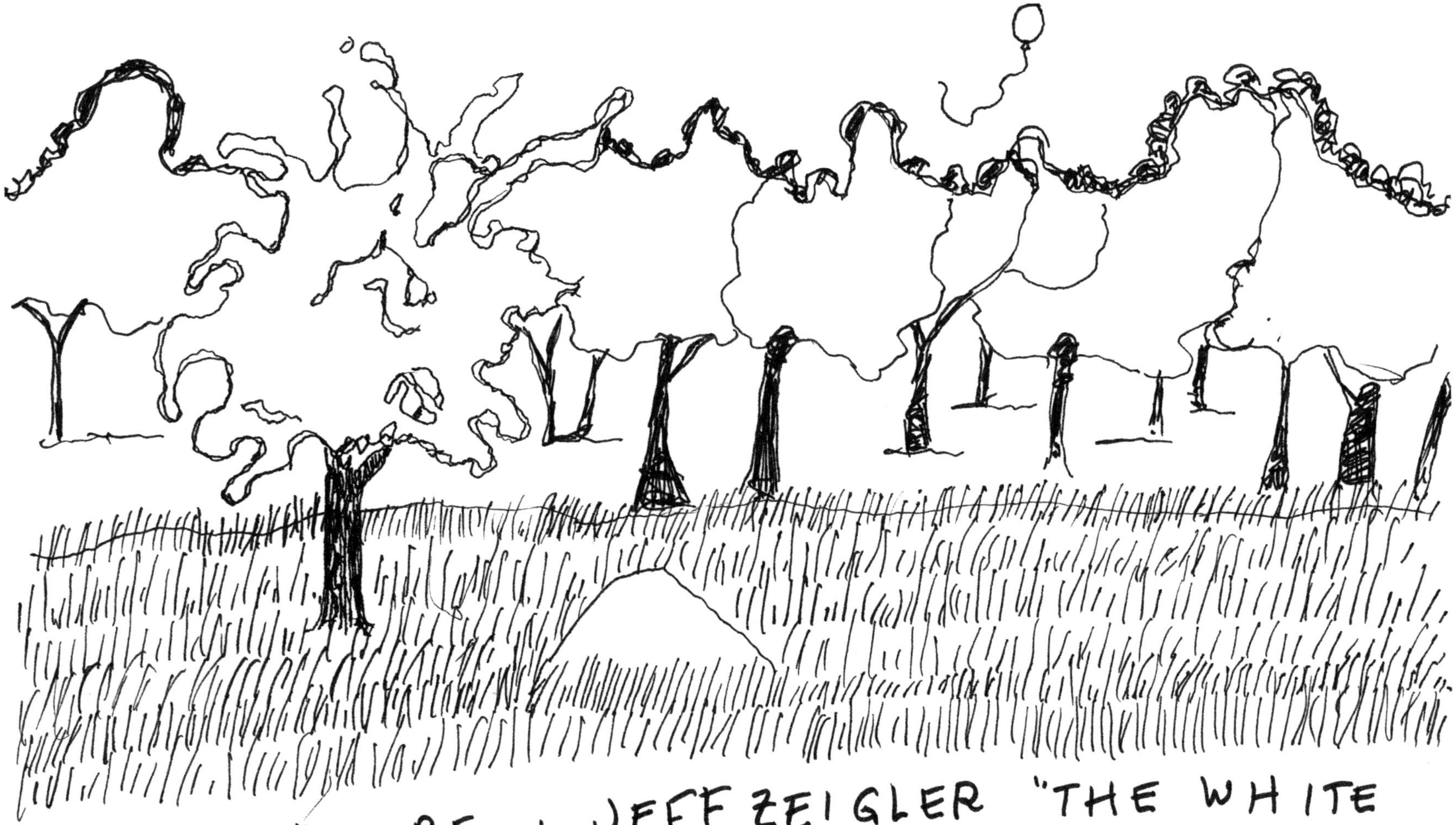

MARY LATTIMORE + JEFF ZEIGLER "THE WHITE BALLOON"

157

The White Balloon

MARY LATTIMORE & JEFF ZEIGLER

THE ASTEROID NO.4

WICKED WIRE

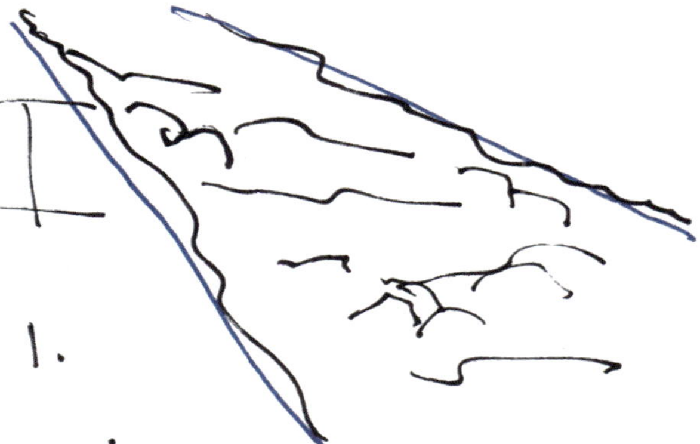

LET'S ASSUME YOU AND I.
TAKE A JOURNEY LIKE WE'RE LOVERS
ALONG THE RIVERBED
THIS IS WHERE YOU SHALL DISCOVER
NOW TAKE ME BY THE HAND
AS I LEAD YOU THROUGH THE SAND
I'LL HOLD YOU UNDER THE DEEP
WHY'D YOU CAUSE ME ALL THIS GRIEF

IT'S JUST ANOTHER DAY. WITH MY WICKED WIRE
IT'S JUST ANOTHER DAY. I LOVE MY WICKED WIRE

I STILL REMEMBER US AS FRIENDS, LONG BEFORE
YOU LOOKED AT OTHERS
BEFORE THIS RIVERBED. BEFORE I TOOK YOU IN THE WATER
NOW TAKE ME BY THE HAND, SURELY YOU MUST UNDERSTAND
HOLD YOU UNDER THE DEEP, WHY'D YOU CAUSE ME ALL THIS GRIEF

IT'S JUST ANOTHER DAY. WITH MY WICKED WIRE
IT'S JUST ANOTHER DAY, I LOVE MY WICKED WIRE
IT'S JUST ANOTHER DAY, I LOVE MY WICKED WIRE

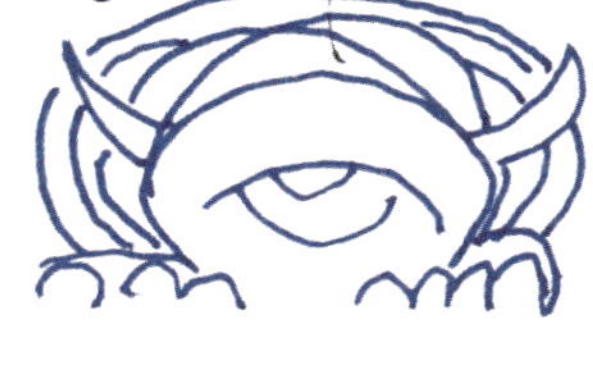

158
Wicked Wire
THE ASTEROID NO.4

With Hope Comes The Morning

There's no better view than the distance yet untravelled
There's no such feeling as walking it with you
One's heart is never prepared to be shattered
But with love comes hope and with hope comes the morning
Being unprepared will keep us going.

See the breaches in the road, smell the dust
We'll be found in silent corners
But as long as with love comes hope
As long as with hope comes the morning
We'll keep on, keep on going.

Scarlett O'Hanna * 31.05.14

LOVE FROM KILBI FESTIVAL *

159

With Hope Comes the Morning

SCARLETT O'HANNA

Y

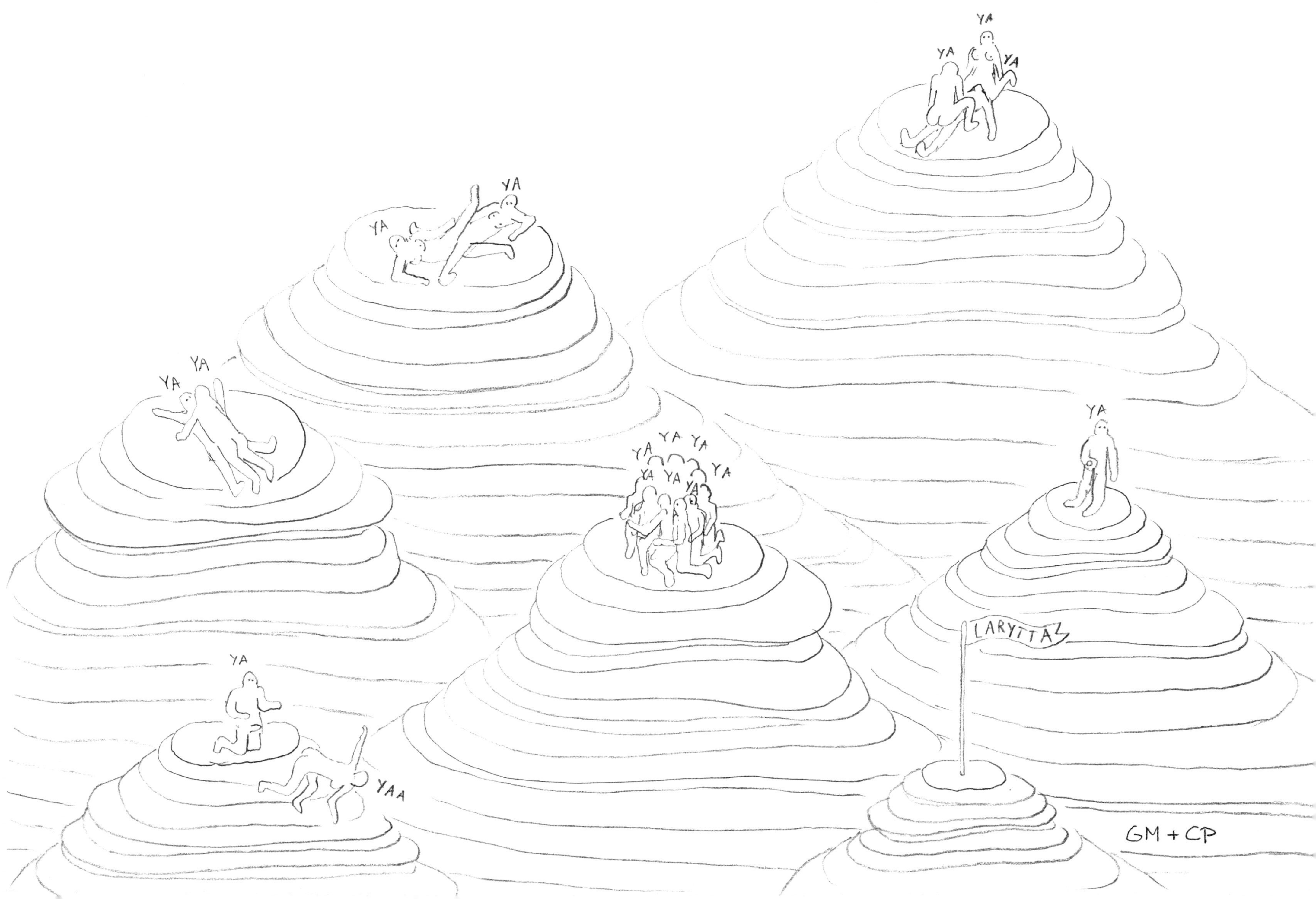
YA
YA
YA
YA
YA
YA
YA
YA YA YA
YA YA YA YA
YA
YA
YA
YAA
LARYTTAZ
GM + CP

160
Ya Ya Ya
LARYTTA

Yegle nesh (Amharic)
«You are mine»
this song is composed by me from orginal Ethiopian scale -

Hailu mergia

29/5/15

CEFAB

161
Yegle Nesh (You Are Mine)
HAILU MERGIA

Z

Zarathustra

DOWN

Pete

In the Zoo, in a Valley of pigs
They came like an Army
An army without wings

3X

Sounds all around remove the silence
They talk about us (2X)

Is it a dream OR you'll ask me to Rape You
Trust me Honey you'll go home
Keep Calm and Carry On
I'll do it for you I'll do my Best

Allright.

That's my Answer you've got answer
You've got chance and you've got the fame
That's m... a
You Broke everything you need
You've got the answer Alllllright.
Do you hear me
The end lie, Don' The solution is here
We are the same
please
of the end / You & Me / We are the same
+ cheval → Face to Face Freak Fan Fils de Pute.

162
Zaratoustra
SOLANGE LA FRANGE

JULIAN SARTORIUS - ZATTER

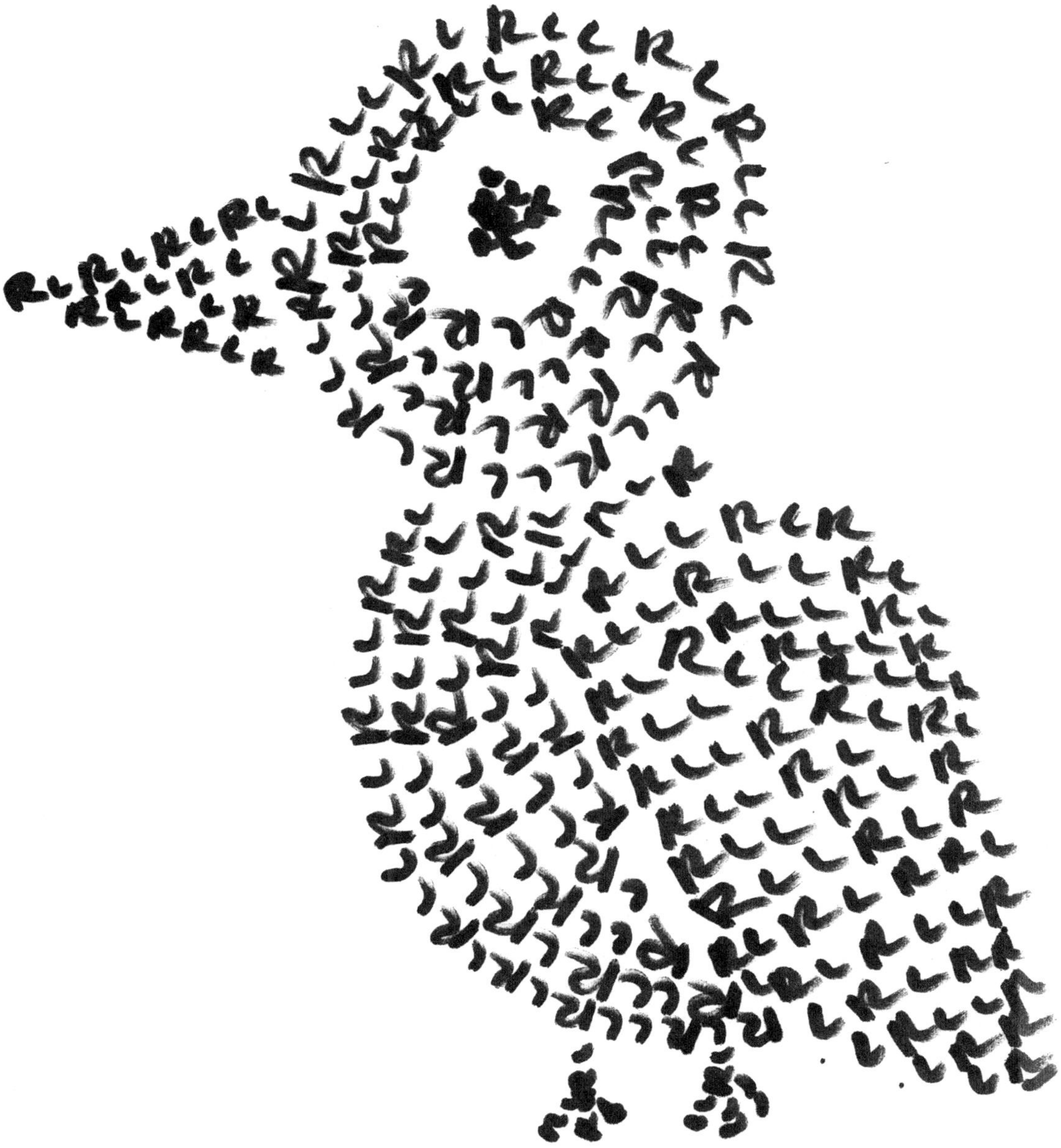

PLAY:

R = RIGHT HAND

L = LEFT HAND

163
Zatter
JULIAN SARTORIUS

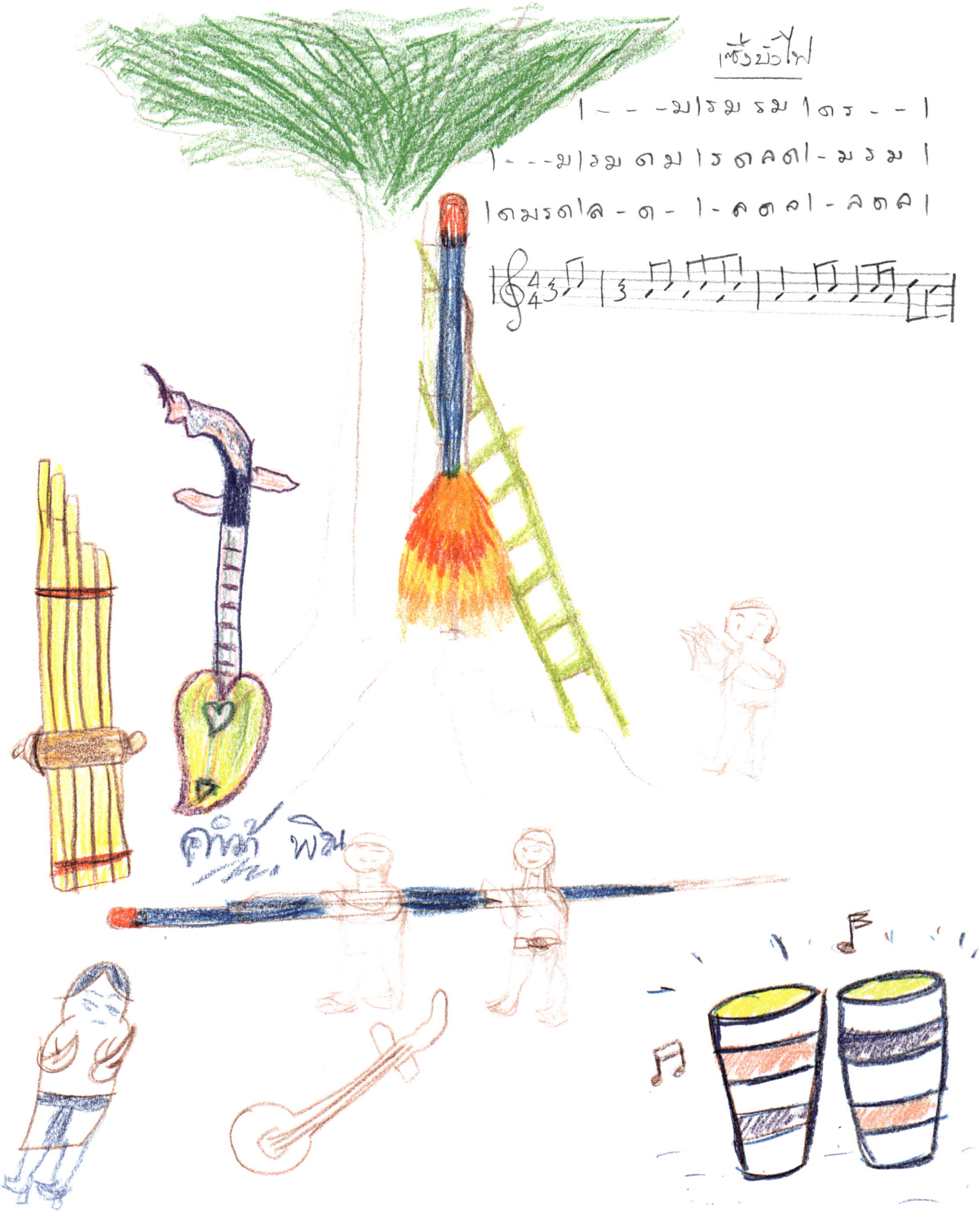
เซิ้งบั้งไฟ
- - - ม	ร ม ร ม	ด ร - -
- - - ม	ร ม ด ม	ร ด ค ด	- ม ร ม
ด ม ร ด	ล - ด -	- ค ด ค	- ล ด ค

164

Zerng Bang Fai

THE PARADISE BANGKOK MOLAM INTERNATIONAL BAND

Was it wheat? I don't know. Ask Daniel — "Dux". He knows the field. Since standing in that field, till now, having traveled many different times around and around the world. Something about landing in that town, Düdingen, walking off the dirt road, into the field, the tall field. Could have just been grass. Who knows? But it was tall enough to be a crop of wheat or so. Coming out of the van (or whatever the hell car it was), not wanting to go into the club. It doesn't look like a club anyway. Pulling off the highway and driving around and around, pulling up, stepping out of the car and straight into the field. Standing under the huge sky, surrounded by this tall grass, smiling, knowing I was exactly where I wanted to be. My first tour in Europe. I pull out a camera, ask someone (maybe it was Daniel) to take a picture of me in the field. All of my photos from all of my travels, from Africa to all ends of the world, all of my photography and writing and paintings were destroyed in a flood in Atlanta in 2004 maybe? 2006? 2005? But I know exactly what that Polaroid looks like. I've returned to that field, that spot, where Daniel has a festival now. It used to be just a small refuge from the snowy night, with the fireplace, excellent food, around the bar, warm.

The venue is what it is. A petite venue. The land that surrounds the venue is Bad Bonn to me. It is Kilbi to me. The nature. The physical articulation we can't put into our songs that I call Life. The comfortable life of nature that is Bad Bonn. I remember playing there again one winter night, and that a Death Metal band played before or after me, I don't recall, but it's those walks through the snow under the moon down to the water, past the sheep and the horses. That is Bad Bonn to me. The sound echoing from the venue. The four neighbors may complain about it — I don't know. Wishing that one day I could be one of those neighbors. That I could have an existence like that. Inside of nature with Bad Bonn just at my back.

Being there in summer is a whole other experience altogether. Sleeping in the tall grass with my friend from the Women and Children Band. Staying at the Auberge aux 4 Vents. And truly exercising my right to the artistic life. Smoking spliffs with Res from the Auberge aux 4 Vents after the hotel has closed. Him allowing me to steal sausages and chèvre, bread and wine, as long as I told him how much I stole in the morning. Taking a bath outside of the window from the Blue Royal Room with a donkey below in full Spring glory. Crying alone. Playing the piano in Auberge aux 4 Vents' formal dining setting where I befriended Res. Playing Bad Bonn that year was my heart broken time. I've been there first, and middle, and I don't know when will be my last.

Favorite memory? Swimming in the river. Swinging in the hundred-foot swing. Cooking marijuana from the marijuana garden. Playing with the baby pigs. Pulling nettles up from the ground only to have them stick into my fingers. Walking down that road on a hot, hot day with a cold beer in my hand. Drinking everyone under the table on a frozen night. Laughing. All the smiles I could never forget. Nothing will ever live up to or has ever lived up to my first, second, third times playing Bad Bonn. That is what home feels like when you're on the road. Places like that. Places you always take with you. You strive to return to. You never forget. You always want to share. And you always hope it will stay the same. Bad Bonn for Life! Rock On, Kilbi! Love you, Daniel!

Chan Marshall (Cat Power)

The foregoing is a transcription of Chan Marshall's message on Bad Bonn's answering machine.

My first experience of Bad Bonn and Kilbi Festival was a poignant one. Shortly after moving to Switzerland, me and my wife had to rush back to the UK to the bedside of my brother-in-law, who was in a coma in intensive care. After a week in which he survived a lifesaving brain operation and by grace came out of his coma, we returned to Switzerland and almost immediately headed for Kilbi Festival, where we hoped to catch Gang Gang Dance. Turned out to be the most cathartic night: the festival and Bad Bonn site has some good voodoo about it, reminds me of the magic in the fields of Glastonbury but on a much more intimate scale. It's a place, like Glastonbury Festival, where everyone does a good set. It's a place where music thrives, where the invisible vibrations of music combine harmoniously with the invisible forces of a geographical point. There are other factors of course that make it such a treasured venue, primarily the ethos of its founder and chief curator Daniel Fontana: "Obeying fashions is trivial, what interests us more is the social side of events and the coming together of opposing trends. Bad Bonn is a peaceful rock hole open to people from all walks of life."

The roadhouse-like building also plays its part, the 17-minute walk there from the train station, as streetlights give way to pitch-black cornfields and a clear starry alpine sky, then in the distance the welcoming glow of Bad Bonn. I've done that walk with music-mad friends who fall silent as we near the venue as if approaching a shrine. In the air the still decaying chords of musical geniuses and innovators, mind-blowing events all the more epic for being witnessed by so few.

For my part I've played three different sets at Bad Bonn to date: singing my songs with the Sartorius Drum Ensemble (solo voice with four drummers and no other instruments), a one-song set in which myself, Shahzad Ismaily and Julian Sartorius perform an extended extemporised version of the Merz track Many Weathers Apart for the duration of the gig, and a solo set on a bill with Richard Dawson also playing solo. Bad Bonn encourages musicians to experiment and express themselves fully, it's one of those crucibles for the wider industry's gold.

This songbook is another extension of the Bad Bonn ethos, made by friends of the venue to celebrate its 25th anniversary, with contributions by 160-plus touring musicians happy to give back to what they quickly sense is a giving venue. It's probably the most authentic and honest songbook currently published if you subscribe to the view that music is not just a mere combination of notes on a page but an attitude that you either get or don't get, a sensation that can't be expressed by order of any kind, a continuing, evolving form which should never be repeated verbatim but interpreted, added to, continually recontextualised. That's certainly in the spirit of live music, for which the humble Bad Bonn venue is one of the world's greatest arenas.

Conrad Lambert (Merz)

Bad Bonn, so munkelt man, das liegt irgendwo in Deutschland. Bad Bonn: Das ist verschüttet unter den Wassermassen eines Stausees der auch ein Badesee ist. Bad Bonn, das gibt's gar nicht. Bad Bonn, zum Teufel denn, wo liegt das?

Nun, das Bad Bonn ist zuallererst ein Café, ein Spunten, ein Konzertclub, und die Landpartie in dieses schillernde Lokal, das auf dem Boden der deutschfreiburgischen Gemeinde Düdingen liegt, ist eine einfache, und sie geht so, zumindest von meinem Wohnort aus: Man betrete am Höllenschlund-Bahnhof der Stadt Bern die S-Bahn Nummer 1 mit Destination Fribourg, zählt munter die Haltestellen durch, steigt in Düdingen aus, folgt spazierenderweise den Ausdünstungen der Käseexport-Firma von Mühlenen, lauscht den Noises der Autobahn, grüsst die Gartenzwerge, ehe der Himmel ganz weit wird, so weit, wie nirgends in diesem zuweilen arg engen Land – und schon gar nicht in diesem Tal der Sensler, jenen Menschen mit dem drolligen Dialekt. Man schreitet weiter, abwärts, rasch und immer rascher, denn mittlerweile ist es erkennbar, dieses Architekturverbrechen, das den Namen vom alten Kurbad geborgt hat. Und so tritt man ein ins Café Bad Bonn, bestellt ein Getränk und platziert sich vor der beinahe ebenerdigen Bühne, auf der die schönsten, neusten, roughsten, primitivsten, neugierigsten und auch herzlichsten Musiken gespielt werden.

Zum ersten Mal suchte ich diesen Fluchtpunkt acht Tage nach der Jahrtausendwende als Minderjähriger auf, und ich weiss nicht mehr viel, ausser dass die Band Alboth! spielte, damals noch auf der ursprünglichen Garagen-Bühne. Und dass wir uns im dichten Nebel fürchterlich verfahren hatten und die bekannte Frage «Where the hell is Bad Bonn?» einer Dorfbewohnerin stellen mussten. Dann, ein paar Jahre später, erlebte ich die tollen Nähmaschinen von Nista Nije Nista (wir waren zu sechst im Publikum), die Besuche der goldenen Antifolk-Generation, den gefährlichen, besser: gefährlich schlechten und doch faszinierenden Kassettenauftritt von Ariel Pink und holte mir einen lang anhaltenden Tinnitus bei den Goldenen Zitronen. Zuweilen bereitete ich mich auch schlecht auf die affichierten Darbietungen vor, weil die Reise kurz ist und das Internet lange Zeit noch aus dem Telefon bezogen wurde. Und so sagte man mir: Tarantula A.D. sei eine tolle Band, was nicht stimmte. Glücklicherweise spielte später an diesem Abend noch eine andere Band auf, sie hiess Grizzly Bear und testete vor einem Dutzend Menschen ein paar Songs in einem überwältigenden Konzert, nachdem man flugs wusste: Oh, da geht noch was (wahrscheinlich war das bei den frühen Bad-Bonn-Konzerten von The Prodigy und den Queens of the Stone Age auch so). Einfach macht es der Hausherr Daniel «Duex» Fontana seinen Gästen auch heute nicht – auch nicht während der Bad-Bonn-Kilbi, diesem Festival, das einst mit einem Programm aus Coverbands startete. Die schönen Zumutungen muss man sich zuweilen auch bei Temperaturen nahe dem Gefrierpunkt geben, weil die Freiburger Alpen nah und die Frühsommer wahlweise hart und doch herzlich wie das Bad Bonn sind.

Wenn ich ans Bad Bonn denke, dann denke ich aber auch an Lee Ranaldo, Stammgast des Hauses – ob mit oder ohne Sonic Youth –, der nach einer Velotour mit dem Fahrrad vorfährt. An Bonnie «Prince» Billy, der mit einem seiner Mitmusiker Frisbee spielt. An die Dart spielende Dorfjugend an einem Samstagabend, an dem kein Konzert stattfindet. An die Eishockeyfans, die hier die Matches schauen, auch wenn Konzerte stattfinden. Und natürlich auch an die Schwimmrunden im Schiffenensee. Wenn man denn tauchen würde, dann könnte man sie wahrscheinlich sehen, die Ruinen von Bad Bonn.

All diese Erinnerungen klingen nun an, wenn ich durch das vorliegende Buch blättere. Ein Buch zum 25. Jubiläum, das 164 Songs versammelt. Songs, aufgeschrieben, gezeichnet oder collagiert von Musikern und Musikerinnen, die auf ihren Konzertfahrten Halt im Bad Bonn einlegten. Die wunderbar unaufgeräumte Tonspur, die sich im Kopf entspinnt und die bei jedem Wiederbesuch des Songbooks neu klingt, kann eine Ahnung davon geben, was für ein wunderbarer Ort das Bad Bonn ist.

Benedikt Sartorius

Bad. Bonn. Kilbi. Trois mots associés, à la fin des années 90, à des noms d'artistes familiers écoutés sur CD, K7 ou mini-disc. En tête Cat Power et The Notwist. Tout comme une pléiade d'autres noms inconnus, oubliés ou découverts depuis, parfaits pour titiller la curiosité et rêver de cette destination exotique: Düdingen. C'est fou comme tout semble distant à l'adolescence. Surtout quand on grandit à la campagne.

J'ai attendu 2006 et la venue d'Animal Collective pour participer à ma première Bad Bonn Kilbi. Et, depuis, je n'en ai plus raté une seule. Jusqu'à prendre mes quartiers dans un hôtel de la ville, histoire de dormir au sec ou au chaud, selon les éditions. Mais juste pour dormir. Car le foyer, le vrai, est ailleurs. Là où vibre la passion. Cette année-là, le slogan du festival était: I ♥ Kilbi. Je n'aurais pas mieux dit.

Je me souviens de la première fois où, en voiture avec un ami, nous suivions des panneaux de fortune en traversant la zone industrielle de Düdingen. Bad Bonn Kilbi. Le pont par-dessus l'autoroute, la route entre les villas puis un champ, une ferme et enfin la petite maison qui se dresse au loin et la grande tente juste à côté. Un trou perdu, pourrait-on dire. «Where the hell is Bad Bonn?» dira-t-on bientôt.

Cette route, je l'ai refaite des dizaines de fois depuis, comptant les nouvelles villas sur le chemin, les nouveaux nains dans les jardins. Je me rappelle un soir glacial de novembre, quand je tombai nez à nez avec le chien de la ferme qui précède le Bad Bonn. Et de réfléchir dans l'urgence nocturne au comportement à adopter pour masquer sa peur de l'animal. Mais la bête se lassa vite de me toiser et retourna à sa soirée. Et moi à mon concert. Wire. Mémorable.

Je ne me rappelle pas ma première rencontre avec Duex. Sans doute durant cette soirée en 2006 nous nous étions serrés la main. Mais j'étais un journaliste. Donc il se méfiait un peu. Et puis il y a eu des courriels, quelques coups de téléphone, des textes pour son programme, un ou deux verres à des concerts, et, un jour, comme un défi, je me suis retrouvé dans la cuisine du Bad Bonn à le seconder dans la préparation d'un couscous pour Deerhunter. Avant de partager quelques verres de schnaps avec son acolyte George à l'heure de la vaisselle.

Plus tard, nous avons taillé la route ensemble vers Camber Sands pour le All Tomorrow Parties, je lui ai chipé sa casquette dans une boîte de nuit zurichoise, je l'ai croisé en slip dans mon salon se levant du canapé où il avait passé la nuit, on s'est bien éclaté, on a bien ri et on a parlé de musique, un peu aussi des cachets à la hausse, de la concurrence, de ce que devenait la Bad Bonn Kilbi et de ce dont il rêvait. Je crois que c'est devenu un ami.

J'ai dû voir plus d'une centaine de concerts dans le cadre du festival ou du club. Dont certains résonnent encore avec force dans ma mémoire. La résurrection de Cat Power, the Greatest pour un soir. The Notwist torturant une console de jeu pour un dernier larsen. Et d'autres plus inattendus. En vrac The Ex, Bombino, Carla Bozulich, Nomeansno, Health, Mudhoney, Fucked Up, Puts Marie… magie d'un festival où la claque d'une soirée n'est pas toujours celle qu'on attend.

Et puis aussi tous ces souvenirs impossibles ailleurs. Sonic Youth redémarrant plus électrique encore après une panne de courant. Lee Ranaldo incognito au premier rang pour photographier Steve Shelley sur scène avec Michael Rother. Les Flaming Lips en costumes de scène, perdus au milieu du public de Jandek. L'oraison funèbre du chat Bliss célébrée par le Reverend Beat Man. Des chevaux affolés dans le parc voisin lorsque vrombissent les guitares de Sunn O))).

Dix ans déjà depuis ma première visite à Bad Bonn, ma première Kilbi. Et ce sentiment d'avoir trouvé un espace où la musique se vit comme je l'entends. Où la passion est plus forte que le business. Et si le constat vaut pour ceux qui ont bâti ce lieu et les artistes qui s'y sont produits, il s'applique aussi à son public, curieux, attentif, passionné. Le cœur de la Bad Bonn Kilbi, c'est lui. Et l'assurance qu'elle vivra longtemps encore.

Christophe Schenk

ACTS 1991–2015

#

13 & God*
1349
16 Bitch Pile-Up*
08/16 Industrie Schmalfilme
17F
2 Foot Yard
22-Pistepirkko
31Knots
34m^2
3Rad
4th Time Around
50 Foot Mama
59 Times the Pain
65daysofstatic
69 Chambers
7 Dollar Taxi
:Take
<Ström>Exp
$400 Suits

A

A Crashed Blackbird Called Rosehip
A Place to Bury Strangers
A Storm of Light
A Whisper in the Noise
A-Poetik
a.p.A.t.T.
Ab Forensis
Abgrund
About
Absolutely Free
Absu
Abu
Abu & the Trash Bash Puppet Show
Abwärts
Accelerator
Acid Arab*
Acid Mothers Temple
Aclys
Acousmatic Jug Band
Action Beat*
Ad Hoc
Addison
Adem
Adieu Gary Cooper
Ad'Absurdum
Aelters
Aeternus
The Afghan Whigs*
Africa Hitech Soundsystem
Agatha Max
Agent Orange
Agent Side Grinder
Aidan Knight
Aie ça gicle
Air Attack
Air Sonic
Aki Onda*
Akku
Akron/Family*
Al Comet
Alboth
The Album Leaf
Alcoholic Faith Mission
Alela Diane
Alembic
Alessi's Ark
Alexander Tucker
Alice in the Wonderland
Alice Rose
Alien 8
Alien Nightlife – The Sound of the Extraterrestrials*
Alina Orlova
Alix
All Ice and Berries
All Ship Shape
Allah-Las*
Almaza Kings
Almost Human
Alog*
Alpendynamo
Always the Same
Am Kap
Amagortis
Amen Dunes
Amok
Amorphis
Ampersand
Anaheim
Analog Pussy
Ancient
Ancient Mith
And All Because the Lady Loves
Andrea Bignasca
Andrea Parker
Andy Stott*
Ane
Angel Corpse
Angel Olsen*
Angelika Express
Anger
Ani and the Flowers
Anika*
Animal Boys
Animal Collective*
Anitras Garden
Anna Aaron*
Annakin
Anoraque
Anouk & Henry
The Antlers*
Antoine Chessex
Antoine Lukac
Anton & Pamela
Anton und die Hellen Barden
Antonelli Electr.
Aphex Twin*
Apparat
Apparat Band*
Approach to Concrete
Apse
Arboriginal
Archie Bronson Outfit
Arco Iris
Arf
Ariel Pink
Arival & Boo Boo Groove
The Armonist
Arno
Art Mode
Art of Fighting
Arthur Russell's Instrumentals Directed by Peter Gordon*
Artlu Bubble & the Dead Animal Gang
Arto Lindsay
Artofex
Ashburry
Asphyx
Ass of Spades
The Asteroid No.4
Aston Villa
Astronautalis
Asva
At Dawn
Atlas Sound*
Atritas
Atrocity
Attack Vertical
Au Revoir Simone
Audiolegend
Augustine's Suspenders
Autokratz
Avant'Garde Rock'n'Roll Soundsystem*
Avec le soleil sortant de sa bouche
The Awkwards

*Kilbi Festival only

Axxis
Azalia Snail
Azeotrop
Aziz
Azure Ray

B

B.O.D.*
Baba Shrimps
Babalon Anon
Babblegum
Bad Little Dynamos
Bad Seed
Badmarsh & Shri
Bal Sagoth
Balmorhea
Banda & DJ Danson
Banjo or Freakout
Barbara Manning
Barbara Morgenstern
Barberos
Barbez
Bardo Pond
Barn Owl*
Baroness
Bass Drum of Death
Baths*
Battery
Battles*
Bauchamp
Baze
Bbphoque
Beach House*
BEAK>*
Bear the Eagle
Beat Dictator Crew
Beat Moustache
Beat-Man
Beatie Bossy
The Beautiful Crew
feat. Paul Breitner
Beautiful Leopard
The Beautiful New
Born Children
Beerzel & the Salads
Behold the Arctopus
Bela
Belong
Ben Frost*
Benediction
Benzin
Berserk for Tea Time
Berthold Seliger
Bethlehem
Beuret-Bühler-
Vonlanthen
Big Bang
The Big Bang Boogie
Big Mama
Big Pants
Bill Direen
Bill Orcutt
Bill Pop
Bill Wells &
Aidan Moffat*
Billie Bird
BirdPen
Birth of Joy
Bishi
Bishop Allen
Bit-Tuner
Bit-Tuner/.Suffix*
The Black Angels*
Black Bananas
Black Box Revelation
Black Bricks
Black Cargoes
Black Cat Bone
Black Dice
Black Engine
feat. Mick Harris
Black Forest
Black Guru
Black Lake County
Black Lips*
Black Lipstick
Black Mountain*
Black Sabbath Tribute
by Evelinn Trouble &
Band
Black Sea
Black Skull and
Pink Ladies
Black Sonic Prophets
The Black Velvet Band
Black Yaya
Blackmail
Blaudzun
Blew
Blind Addiction
Blinde Kinder
Blitzen Trapper
BLK JKS
Blomstre
Blonde Redhead*
Blood on the Saddle
Bloodtaste
Bloody Blasphemy
Bloody Horseface
Blouse
Blow Job
Blue Brain Juice
Blue Light District
The Blue Tape
The Bluefish
Blues Horror Brigade
Bluesaholics
Blumfeld
Blush
Bo Ningen*
Bo Wiget &
Luigi Archetti
Bob Color
Bob Corn
Bob Log III
Bob Page &
Blue Kerosene*
Bobby Conn
Body Bag
Bogus
Bohren & der Club
of Gore
Bolt Thrower
Bomb Mitte Sound
System*
Bombino*
Bonaparte
Bonnie “Prince” Billy
Bonnie “Prince” Billy &
Matt Sweeney
The Bony King of
Nowhere
Boo Boo Grove
Boob
Bored Man Overboard
Boris*
Borknagar
Borko
Bossinova
Bottom Rock
Boy Android
Boys on Pills
Brahma-Loka
Braids
Brain Damage
Brainchild
Brant Bjork & the Bros.
Brant Bjork
Brasstronaut
Brazen
Brian Jonestown
Massacre
Brink Man Ship
Broken Social Scene*
Broken.Heart.
Collector*
Brutalistos
Bubblegum
Buckshot O.D.
The Budget Boozers
BulBul
BulBul + Tumido*
Bungalow Lifestyle
Bunny Rabbit
The Burden Remains
Busdriver
Buvette
By Chance

C

C7inch*
Calcined
Calvin Jackson
Calvin Jackson*
Camera
Candie Hank*
Candye Kane
Cannibal Corpse
The Cardinals
Careless
Caribou*
Carla Bozulich
Carsick Cars*
Carson

Casiotone for the Painfully Alone
Casperduet
Caspian
Casque
Cass McCombs
Castanets
Castle Well
Cat Power
The Catamaran
Catatonia
Caterpillarmen
Cativo
Cat's Eye
The Cave Singers
Caveman
Cave
Cecilia Ugarte
The Celluloid Gurus
Celtic Frost*
Chairlift
Channel Zero
The Chap
Charger
Charles Spearin
Charlou Nada
Cheers
Cheesecake
Chelsea Light Moving
Cheveu
Chevreuil
Chewy
Cheyenne
Chicago Bob Nelson
Chicago Underground Duo
Chicks on Speed
The Chikitas
The Chocolate Side
Choo Choo
Chris Brokaw
Chris Clark & Flat-E Eyeburps*
Chris Lee
Christ.
Christene Ledoux
Christian B et les Oryx
Christian Death
Christian Kjellvander
Christina Ertl
Christina Rosenvinge
Christine & Me
Chrome Hoof
Chromic Acid Flakes
Chupa Cabra
Churchill
Cideraid
Ciderman
Chimaera
Cinema Cinema
Circadian Rhythms*
Circle
Circuit des Yeux
Citizens!
Clare Bowditch
Clark
Clay Lion
The Clever Hans Effect
Climax
Clipping.
Clit Commander
Clockwork
Closer Than Kin
The Cluster
CocoRosie
Codex Empire
Coilguns
Cold Shot
Coldeve
Colleen
Collett Jason
Colin Stetson & Sarah Neufeld
The Collins
Coloured Trip
Com Truise*
Comanechi
Combineharvester
The Come N' Go
Congaking
Connan Mockasin*
Consolation
Console
Constantin Seibt
Convulsif Big Band
Consumed
Contract
Convulsif
Coogans Bluff
Coolhaven
The Cooper Temple Clause
Cooptrol
Copy & Paste
Core
The Corleons
Corners
Coroner*
Cortez
The Cosmic Dead
Cosmonauts
The Cosmopoets mit Stritt
The Cosmopoets
Cotton Mount
Couch*
Count to React
Crack Up
Cradle of Filth
Crank
Crawlin' Kingsnake
Credit to the Nation
Cremation
Crematory
Crocodiles
Crooner & Buzz
Crowbar
Cruszt
Cryptic Voice
Crystal Fighters*
Crystal Stilts
Cult of Youth
Curse ov Dialect
Cursive
Cut feat. Gibet
Cutty Sark
Cyclic
Cynic

D

D'Schmier
D.R.I.
Da Sign & The Opposite
Dactylola & Ereccan
Daedelus
Dag för Dag
The Dagons
Daigoro
DakhaBrakha*
Dam Mantle
Damnation Call
Damnation
Damo Suzuki
Dan Deacon*
Dan Mangan
Dandy
Daniel Higgs
Daniel Meister
Daniela Weinmann
Danielson
Dans la tente
Danse Noire
Darius James
Dark Dark Dark
Dark Day Dungeon
Dark Funeral
Dark Tranquility
DarkRise
Darkstar*
Darling
dARMCABINED
Das Röckt
Dat Politics
Dauerfisch
Dav/D
Dave Eleanor
Dave Phillips
David Emanuel
David Grubbs
David Grubbs
David Howald
David Robert Callahan
DAVV
Days of Betrayal
Deacon Fuller
Dead Bunny
The Dead Brothers
Dead Combo
Dead Meadow
The Dead Science
Dead Western*
The Deadline Experience
Deafheaven
Dean Wake
Dear Deer
Dear Johnson
Death by Chocolate
Death Grips*
Debleudacht
Decapitated
Decode
Deconstructing Drumboys*

*Kilbi Festival only

The Deep Dark Woods
Deeplow
Deerhoof
Deerhunter
Déesse
Deetron
Defiled
Defleshed
Degadron
Delaney Davidson
The Delilahs
Delorian Cloud Fire
Demilliac
Demolition Blues*
Denra Dürr
The Department of
Misfortunes
Der Eremit
Der.Rek 7.9
Derrick
Destinity
The Devastations
Diamond Version*
Diane Cluck
Diario
Die Goldenen Zitronen
Die Hellen Barden
Die Krupps*
Die Regierung
Die Sterne
Die Zorros
Die!Die!Die!
dieb13
Diestyled
Dieter "Yello" Meier –
Out of Chaos*
Difficult to Cure
The Dillinger
Escape Plan
Dillon
Dimension X
Dimette
Dimlite*
Direction Survet
Dirty Ghosts
Dirty Projectors
Dirty Purple Turtle
Dirty Sound Magnet
Disappears
Disco Doom
Disco Drive
Disfear
Dismember
Dissection
The Distillers*
Dither
Division 4
Division Kent
Dizzy by Fortune
DMX Krew*
Do Make Say Think
Doddodo
Dodo
Dolly Bastards
Doll
Domi Chansorn
Don Air
Don Gatto
Donna Summer
Doomenfels
The Doorknobs
Dope Body
Dora Bleu &
Sam Shalabi
Double Nelson
The Dough Rollers*
Downset
Dozer
Dr. Pepper Family
Drama Queen
Dream City Film Club
Driller Killer
Driven by Hate
The Driven
The Drones*
Drowning Boats
Drowsy Pop
Dub Scots
Dubwar
Duck Duck Grey Duck*
The Dues
Duffstep*
Duke Garwood
Dum Dum Girls*
Duo Immerblau
Duri Darms
Dälek
Dälek vs. Faust
Dänu Siegrist Band
Dÿse

DJs:
DJ /rupture
Aïkon
Alex Reece
Artmaillé
Atol
Awesome Tapes
From Africa*
DJ Beni B
Billy Ben
Breitner Paul
Cheers
DJ Cio
Coconut Jama Jama
Cool Cat
DJ Danny Ramone
Diskothekar
DJ Dottter
Dustbowl
DJ El Duderino
Electrodudes
DJ Elephant Power
Eric
Explosivo
Fart Fanfare
DJ Feldermelder
DJ Fett
DJ Fitz*
DJ Funky Mosquito
Gaex
DJ Gamma
Georges Wyrsch
Gerald
The Good, the Bad and
No Ugly
DJ Gül Baba
Hablitzel
DJs Headup & D
& Dany Boy
DJ Hightower
DJ Ike*
DJ Invincible
DJ Jane Vayne
JS1
Kalabrese
Kassette
DJ Kermit
Kev the Head
DJ L-Cut
La Femme à Fred
LayDJ
LCP
Le Tourette
Leo Plasma
DJ M T Dancefloor
DJ Maex
DJ Mamborghini*
DJ Marc Robert
DJ Marcelle
DJ Marten Davis &
Melodee Maker
DJ Miasmo
DJ Mifume
Minus 8
Mira & Chris
Schwarzwalder*
MO
Morphene
Ms. Hyde & Inderrock*
Mzelle Charlotte
DJ Neuphore
Olver Revolver vs.
Van Surmelen
Optimo*
DJ Pablo*
P-Corn
Phrank
Pilsoca
DJ Pj
DJ Pj & Pain
DJ Plusminus Remedy
DJs Ricky F vs. Thiry
DJ Ronfa
DJs Selectah &
Dustbowl
DJ Scientist
DJ Scotch Egg
Scud
DJ Selectah
DJ Sgt. Pepper
DJ Smash My Car
DJ Smelly Tongue
Solange La Frange
DJ Soulsource
DJ St. Paul*
Submerge
DJ Sylek
Tini B.
DJ Uhuruku
Uncle Dan
U.V.W.*
DJs V-Kev & Cheers
V-Key
DJ Vadim
V.C.A.
Wenedikt
DJ Wizard*
DJ Wurstfinger
Xebeche
DJ Zampone

E

The E's
Eagles of Death Metal
Earth
Easy Tiger
Eaux
EC8OR
Efterklang
EF
Eggippa Fifauter
Ego-N
Egopusher
Eisregen
Eistroll
Ektomorf
El Rakkas
El Vez with the Memphis Mariachis & the Lovely Elvettes*
El-G
Ela Orleans
Eldorado FM
Electric Eel Shock
Electric Fishing
Electric Owls
Electric Sheep
Elektro Guzzi
Elektrobopacek
Elektrostatik
Eleven Aces
Elikan Dew
Eluveitie
Elvis Perkins
EMA
Emerald
Emika*
Eminence
Emiro & Emira Brautkopf
Emmerhoff
En Pire
End
End of Void
Endeavour Jones
The End
Enigmatik
ENO
Ensemble Economique
Enslaved
Entombed
Ephel Duath
Epica
Erin Lang
Erin Lang & the Foundlings
Ernst Kahl
Erotic Jesus
The Espionne
Ethnician
Euroboys
Evangelista*
Eve & the T-Shirts
Evelinn Trouble
Evelinn Trouble & Trespassers*
Everest
Evile
Evje
The Ex*
Excidium
ExcuseExcuse
Existereo
Exnova
Expander
Experimental Jet Set
The Experimental Tropic Blues Band
Extra Life*
Ezra Furman & the Boyfriends

F

F.X. Randomix
Fade*
Fai Baba
The Failures
Fakir
Fan Club Orchestra
Fantõmas*
Fat
Fat Black
The Fat White Family
Fat32*
Fatherfuckers
Fatso Jetson*
Faun Fables
Fauve
Favez
Fe-Mail
Featherlike
Featuring Jim
Feerglas
Feldermelder & D'Incise Quadro-phonic Show
Feldermelder X HP Zürrer "Hit the Bird"
Feldermelder
Felix Kubin
Felka
Fell
Fence
Fennesz & Mike Patton*
Fennesz
Fenster
Ferocious41
Fichtre*
Field Studies
The Field
Fiery Furnaces
Figurines
Filewile
Filipe Felizardo
Final aka Justin K. Broadrick
Final Fantasy
Fingerpoke
Finn.
Fiona Daniel
Fisher Price Factory
Fishnet Stockings
Fizzy Jam Jar
Flabbergasted
The Flaming Lips*
Flava & Stevenson
Flavien Berger
Flieder
Flieger
Flimmer
Flo Fernandez
Flo Kaufmann*
Florian Ast
Florian Horwath
Flourish
Flower
Flug 8
Flying*
The Flying Luttenbachers
Fogan 10
Food
Food for Animals
Foot Village
For God Con Soul
Forest Swords*
Forks
Formel
Fort Wendy
Found Footage
Fractal
Fractura
Fragment
Francis Francis
Frank Dommert
Franz Dobler
Frathese / Toys*
The Freaks
Freedom Bus
Freizeit 98
Freschard
Friends of Dean Martinez
Friska Viljor
Frittenbude
Frkse
Frogbelly and Symphony
From the Dying Sky
Frozen Brain
FTDS
Fu Manchu
Fuck
Fuck Buttons
The Fuckadies
Fucked Up*
Fuck
Fuerte de la Muerte
Fühlifliisch
Fumaça Preta*
Fun Gögh
Funbelt
Funky Bastard
Fuo
Fursaxa

*Kilbi Festival only

Fuschi Muschi
Füsiker
Fusion
Future Islands
Fygeludi

G

g-Punkt
The G's
Gabardine
The Gallery
Gambit
Gang Gang Dance
Ganglords
The Gaslamp Killer
Gateaux Blasters
Gates of Oblivion
Gehennah
Geneva Jacuzzi
Genghis Tron
Get Lost
Get On Jolly
Get Well Soon*
GFYMSC
Ghinzu
The Giant Robots
Giardini di Mirò
Gigi Moto
Girl Band
Glasser
Glauser & Strotter Inst.
Glenn Jones
Gletscher
Glimmbrand
Gluecifer
Gnu
The Go Find
Go!zilla
Goat*
God Dethroned
Godhead
Gold Panda*
Goldbarne
Golden Boy
Golden Diskó Ship*
Golden Teacher*
The Golden
Göldin N'Bit-Tuner
Goldrush
Gondi-San
Gonjasufi
Gonoreas
Gonzo
Good Enough for Us
Good Enough for You
The Good Life
Gorsungazaga
Graal
Graber: Lieder zum Schluss
Grace Core
Grace
Graf von Spiegelberg
Gran Noir
The Grand Astoria
Grand Atlas Mondial
Grand Pianoramax
Grandfey
Grand Mother's Funck*
Grave
Gravel Path Perform Dream Theater
Gravenhurst
Graveyard
Gray Chalk
Great Black Waters
Greed
Gretel
Grimsvötn
Grizzly Bear
Groombridge
Groove Lords
Group Rhoda
Grove
Grégoire Quartier
Grönland Orchester
Guapo
Guitar Fucker
Gundi
Gurd
Gustav
Gustav & das Kummerorchester*
Gustav & Les Frères M
Gustav & the Electric Noise Club
Gustav & the Ultra Vista Social Club
Guz
Gyða Valtýsdóttir

H

Haco & Hiro Michi Sakamoto*
Hailu Mergia with Tony Buck & Mike Majkowski*
Haisy Ventures
Half a Cup of Superkings
Half Japanese
Halma
Hamlet
Handclaps*
Hang or Die
Hank Haint
Hannah Miller
Hans Platzgumer
Hardcore Superstar
Hare
Harlekin
Harry
Hate Squad
Hauschka
Headlights
Headlock
Health*
Heart Attack Alley
Heavy Trash*
Hecata
Hedera
Heidi Happy
Helios & Hess
Hellmute
Hell's Kitchen
Helmut's Monolog
Helsinki Soulstew
Hepp
Herman Dune
Herman Dune feat. Berg Sans Nipple*
Herman Dune & the Baby Skins
Herpes Ö DeLuxe
Hervé
Hervé Boghossian
Hess
Heymoonshaker
HGH
The Hidden Cameras
Hielo Negro
High Places
Highfish
Hildegard Lernt Fliegen
HNO
HO99O9
Hobotalk
Hometrainer
Homi MC
Honey for Petzi
Honeyrider
Hong Kong Dong
Hospitality*
Hot Chip*
Hot Panda
Hot Rod Honeys
Houndstooth
Hovercraft
Howlin Mad Murdock*
HTRK
Hubeskyla
Human Bell
Humungus Fungus
Hundred Waters
Husky
Hype Williams
Hyperculte
Hyphen
Hypnosis

I

I'll Dry Your Tears Little Murderer
I Am Oak
I Made You a Tape

I-Sound
Ian Constable
The Ian Fays
The Icarus Line
IKKI
Ill Ease
Illeist Collective
Imagho & Mocke
Imaon
Immaculate Machine
Immolation
Immortal
Impaled Nazarene
In Flames
In the Woods
InBetween
Incensed
Incognegro*
Indias Indios
Industrial Fields
InfraRed
Infunkted
Inis Fail
Inishmore
Insane
Institut für Feinmotorik*
Institut für Leistungsabfall und Kontemplation*
Iokoi
Isis*
Islands
Isolated Lines
Isolation Berlin
Ivo Stritt & Peter Sarbach
Ivvvo
Iwacu
Iwan Petrowitsch
IZC
Izdiucz

J

J&L Defer
J.C. Satan
Jacco Gardner
Jack Stoiker
Jacuzzi Boys
Jagwa Music*
Jagwar Ma*
Jake Bellows
JaKönigJa
James Ferraro
Jamie Lidell
Jammin'
Jan Jelinek*
Jandek*
Jason Anderson
Jason Collett
Jason Forrest
Jay-S
Je m'appelle Mads
Jecko Kay
Jef Barbara
Jeff Hunt
Jeffrey Hayes
Jeffrey Lewis Band
Jerk
Jesca Hoop
Jesse Poe
Jessica93
Jessie Evans with Toby Damnit
Jesus Messerschmitt
Jibcae
Jim Bows
Jim the Barber & His Shiny Blades
Jimmy Bastard
Jimmy Edgar*
Jimy Hofer Band
Jivaros Quartet
JJ & Pallin
Joan & the Sailors
Joan of Arc
Jobert & Pancetta
Jochen Distelmeyer
Joe Galen
Joe Tabu
Jogger
John Dear
John Caroline
John Doe Tale
John Garcia
John Guilt
John Is Strong
John J. Presley
John Parish
John Vanderslice
John Wiese
John Willow
John Wolfington
Johnny Dowd
Joi
Joker feat. MC Nomad*
Jolly and the Flytrap
Jolly Goods
Jon Hopkins
Jookabox
Joules
Joyside
Jozef van Wissem & Jim Jarmusch × Sqürl*
JP Inc
JR Ewing
Juan Wauters
Judith Juillerat*
Judith Wyder
Judy Birdland
Julian Sartorius
Julianna Barwick*
Julie Doiron
Julie
Jump
June de Ville
June Tempest*
Jungle*
Jürg Halter
Just 4 Fun
Justice Yeldham*

K

K-The-I???
K-X-P
K9 + One
Kabak
Kaki King
Kalabrese & Rumpelorchester*
Kalle Mattson
Kammerflimmer Kollektief
Kampf dem Sonnensystem
The Kandidate
Kante
Kapoolas
Karl Bartos*
Karma to Burn
Kashmir
Kassette
Katelepsy
Katergon
Katze
Kehlvin
Kelley Stoltz
Kevin Blechdom
Kevin Flynn
Khan
Khan & Kid Congo Powers*
Kickback
Kid 606
Kid Ikarus
Kieran Kennedy
Kiku feat. Blixa Bargeld & Black Cracker
Killbody Tuning
Killed by 9V Batteries
Killed on X-Mas
Killl
Kim and the Created
Kim Gordon & Ikue Mori
Kimya Dawson
Kinderzimmer Productions
King Buzzo
King Dean
King Gizzard & the Lizard Wizard
King Pepe & Le Rex
Kings of Convenience*
Kira Kira
KissKissBangBang*
Kitchen Surprise
Kitty Solaris
Klaus Johann Grobe*
Klee
Knut
Knut & Silvy
Knöppel feat. Jack Stoiker & Don Bosso
Knöppel

*Kilbi Festival only

Koch-Schütz-Studer & the Young Gods*
Kockroach
Kode9
Kokon
Komah
Komatsu
Komedie, Kabarett & Katastrophen
Kominform
Konono No.1
Korsett Kollektiv
Kotra*
Koufax
Kraftpost*
Krankenzimmer 204
Kreator*
Kristof Hahn
Kruger
Kummerbuben
Kurjakovic*
Kurt Vile & the Violators*
Kurt Vile solo
Kutti MC
Kwes

L

L'Arbre Bizarre
L'Enfance Rouge
L'Enfance Rouge & At-Tufûla Ai-Hamra*
L'Espèce Anonyme
La Freakmachine
La Gale*
La Luz
La Muse en Délire
La Renarde
La Vie C'est Facile
Labrador City*
laFayette
Lafopaes
Lahar
Lamps of Delta
Land Covered with Briar
Lapin Machin*
The Lappetites
Larry Gus*
Larytta
Laser von Nazareth
Lasse Marhaug & Dror Feiler*
The Last Moan
Last Quiet Time
Last Torridas
Lau Nau
Laub
Laure Perret
Laurel Halo
Lawrence English
LCP
Le Baron Vampire
Le Cirque Électrique
Le Club des Chats
Le Soldat Inconnu
Leafcutter John
Leak
Led Airbus
Ledoux Christene
Lee Gamble
Lee Ranaldo*
Lee Schornoz & Michel Gorski*
Lee Scratch Perry
Leech
The Legendary Lightness
The Legendary Pink Dots
Leisure Society
Lena Willikens
Leon*
Les Browns
Les Pedzes
Les Pongs
Les Toblens
Les Yeux sans Visage*
Liar of Golgotha
Liars
Lichtenberg
Liechtenstein
Life as War
Life of Agony
Light Asylum
Lightning Bolt
Lightning Dust
Lilium Sova
Lilli Press Release
Limousine
Liquid Roots
Lird van Goles
Lisa Germano
Lithops
Little J.C.
Liturgy*
Live Artist
Lived Inside
Liz Green
Lo
Lo & LeDuc
Lödig
Lödig & Strotter Inst.
Löffel Andreas
The Lonesome Organist
The Lonesome Southern Comfort Company
Lonesome Station
Long Fin Killie
The Long Last
The Long Winters
Loops Haunt*
Loose Connection
Lord Belial
Lord Kesseli and the Drums*
Lorelle Meets the Obsolete
Lorenzo Senni*
Los Dentistas Increibilimente
Los Tres Grandes Argumentos
Lost Letters for Lucy
Lost Songs
Loudmerge
Louis Schornoz Trio
Love and Girls
Love of Everything
The Lovebirds
Lovebugs
Low Tide Digitals*
Lower Dens*
Lucile's Hat
Lucky Dragons*
Luft
Luke Vibert*
Lunacy
Lunazone
Lune Palmer
Lunik
Luomo
Lydia Lunch's Putan Club

M

M-Force
M. Ward
M.I.e. Smiles
M.O.D.
M.R.I.
Mac DeMarco*
Machine Gun Messiah
Macuso Vikovsky
Madame Gasoline
Made in Brats
Mademoiselle K
Madonna Hip Hop Massaker*
The Mae Shi*
Magic Arm
Magnetfisch
Mahadev Cometo
Mahjongg*
Maja Ratkje
Maja Ratkje & Stephen O'Malley*
Maja Ratkje & Strotter Inst.
Make Me a Donut
Mama Rosin
Manolo Panic
Manuel Stahlberger
Manuel Troller
Manufactur
Mãozinha
Mapstation
The Marble Man
Marc Ribot
Marc Ribot & Lucien Dubuis Trio
Marc Ribot's Ceramic Dog
Marco Nuvolari

Marco Repetto
Marilou
Mariola Brillowska*
Marissa Nadler
Mark D
Mark Ernestus Presents Jeri-Jeri*
Mark Lanegan
Mark Siegenthaler
Markku Peltola
Markus Detmer
Markus Moser Quartett
Marnie Stern
Marochine
Marshmellow Sound System
Martin Biafa
Martin Bisi Band
Mary Lattimore & Jeff Zeigler*
Maryclare Brzytwa
Marygold
Mary's Private Eyes
Maserati
Masha Qrella
Massacre
Massicot
Masters of Reality
Matana Roberts
Mathis Altmann
Matthew Dear*
Matthew Skoller*
Matthias von Imhoff*
Matto Rules
Maurice Louca
Max Bailey
Max Tundra
Maximilian Hecker
Maya Turbo
Mayday
Mayhem
Mazes
Maïak
MC Wuzi Khan
Mclusky
Mediengruppe Telekommander*
Medusha
Megaforce
Megalomaniax
Meienberg
Mekong Delta
Mekonium
Mellowtone
Melt Banana
Men From S.P.E.C.T.R.E.
Men
Mephitic Entities
Merauder
Merfen Orange
Meridian Brothers*
Meril Wubslin
Mermonte
Merz
Merz feat. Sartorius Drum Ensemble
Merz feat. Shahzad Ismaily & Julian Sartorius
Mesmerised
Metronomy*
Metzger & Bauer
Mi and L'Au
Micachu & the Shapes
Mich Gerber
Mich Gerber feat. Al Comet
Mich Grünling
Michael Beer & The Spaceships
Michael Gira
Michael Hilton
Michael von der Heide*
Michel Gorski
Michto Swing
Microcuts
Midaircondo
Midgets
Midnight Blues
Midnight Choir
Mike Patton*
Mike Watt & The Missingmen
Miki Yui
Mikron 64*
Miles
Mina
Ming
Minimal Man
Minimetal*
Ministry*
Minkus
Minor Majority
Minus 8*
Miqo & Jahmool
Mir*
Mira Calix
Mirel Wagner
Miss Kittin & The Hacker*
Mist
Mister Wonkey Man
Mixhell
Mlada Fronta*
Mmmh!
Mo Blanc
Moaning Cities
Mochipet
Model 101
Modern Ass Quartet
The Modernist
Moe
Moeslang-Fages-Gross Trio
Mogwai*
Molly Milsson
Mondo Generator
Mongrel Bitch
Monkey 3
Monkeys with Tools
Monno*
Mono
Monoski
Monotonix*
Monpetitponey
Monsieur Jean
The Monsters
Montavillain
Moody Marsden Band*
Moon
Moon Duo
Moondawn
Moonface*
Morb
More Experience
Morelli Marco
Morgan Delt*
Morphologue
Mother Razorblade*
Mother's Pride
Motorama
Motorpsycho
The Motowns
Mount Kimbie
Mount Terrible
Mountaineer
Mouse on Mars
Moustafa Moustache
Moutique Ensemble
Mozes & the Firstborn
Mr. Airplane Man*
Mr. Ed Jumps the Gun
Mr. Melodee Maker
Mr. Thing
MRI
Mrs. Burroughs
Mu Ziq
Mucky Pup
Mudhoney*
Mugison
Mungo Aside
Mur/Mur
Murcof & Philippe Petit
Murcof
Music for Your Heart
Must Have Been Tokyo*
Musée Mécanique
Müslüm
Muzak
MV & EE with the Golden Road
MXD
MXP
My Best Shirt
My Bloody Valentine*
My Bones Itch
My Brightest Diamond
My Little Pony
Mystery Park

N

N.O.M.A.
Nadine Carina
Nadine Shah*
Nadj
Nadja Zela
Naked Lunch
Naked on the Vague
Nancy Glowbus
Narziss
Nasty Girls
Nate Young
Nautical North

*Kilbi Festival only

Navel
Nawari
Near Death Condition
Nebula
The Neckbones
Need a New Drug
Nele van der Broeck
Nelson Can
Nemoy
Nénuphar Is What We Are
Neoangin
Nephlim Modulation Systems
The Nervous Return
Network
Neutral Milk Hotel*
New Point
The New Year
Next Life
Nexus 77
Nguzunguzu*
Nice Noise
Nick Oliveri
Nicolette
Niels Jensen
Nihilo
Nik!
Nikki Sudden
Nils Frahm
Nina Nastasia
Niobe
Nisennenmondai
Nista Nine Nista
Nite Jewel
No Access
No Comment
No Return
No Valid Names
No Way to Escape
No-Neck Blues Band*
Noah 23
Noble Weed
No Means No
None of Them*
Nordsite
Norient
Noriko Tujiko
Norman Palm
Northern Lite
Nostromo
Not the Sensational Alex Harvey Band
Not Yet
The Notwist*
Noura Mint Seymali*
Nova Huta
Novice
Now It's Overhead

O

O'Brother
O'Death
Octanone
October Behind the Stone
Offshore
Okmalumkoolkat feat. Cid Rim & the Clonious
Omar Souleyman
Omnicide
Omophagia
The One Ensemble*
One Inch Punch*
One Sentence. Supervisor
One:Shot:Orchestra
Oneohtrix Point Never*
Ongatu
Onimo & DJ Nomad
Oozing Wound
Op-Rechts
Opak
Open Mike Eagle
Operation Mission
Oral
Orange Goblin
Orchestra of Spheres
Orchestre Tout Puissant Marcel Duchamp
Oregon Trail
Orenda Fink
Orphan Fairytale
Orymus
Osaka Tiger Frosties
Oscar and the Wolf
Ostinato
Other Lives*
Otto von Schirach
Ought
Oum Shatt
Out
Oval
Overdrive Amp Explosion
Overload Collapse
Oxbow*

P

P 27
P. Moos
P.C. Zumthor
P.M.T.
P.S.
Pablo Fiasco
Pablo Infernal
Pale
Pall Jenkins
Paloma
Pamelia Kurstin
Pamela Mendez
Panacea
Panda Bear
Panda Lux
Pandour
Pantha du Prince*
Panther
Papa Brittle
Papaya Fuzz
The Paper Hats
Papiro
The Paradise Bangkok Molam International Band
Paradox Now
Paraffine
Parasites
Parrot to the Moon
Pascal Fuhlbrügge
Pascale Etter & Band
Pat Jordache
Pat V
Patrick Watson & the Wooden Arms
Patrick Wolf
Paul Armfield
Pavel Schmidt*
Pawnshop
PC Worship
Peaches*
Peasant
Peelander-Z*
Pelican
Pendler
Pendleton
Pendulum*
Penniless People of Bulgaria
Penta Tonic
Penthouse
Perfect Pussy
Perrine et les Garçons
Perspective
Pestilence
Pet Lamb
Peter Kernel
Peter Sarbach
Peter Swanson*
Peters
Petit Vodo
Petra Jean Phillipson
The Petties
Pétur Ben
Phased 4° F
Phased
Phil Duke & J&L Defer
Phoneheads
Phosphorescent
Phraseland
Phèdre*
Phébus
Pianocktail
Piccolo Teatro Morelli
Pierre Omer & Grey Mole*
The Pietasters
Pilomotor
Pinback
Pink Mountaintops
Picastro
The Pipe Monkeys
Pirol

Pitchtuner
Pivot
Pixelpunx (VJ)
The Places
Placyde
Plaid
Playskool
Pneu
Poissons Autistes
Pole
Pollux
Poltergeist*
Polvo*
Pond*
Pony del Sol
Pooka*
Popshop
Port O'Brien
Portobello
Portrait of David
Portugal. The Man
Posse Royal
Poster Children
Pothead
Pow!*
Praed*
Prancing Prawns
Preamp Disaster
Presocratics
Prince Rama
Prinzhorn Dance School*
Prisma
Pro-Pain
Proceed
The Prodigy*
Propaganja
Prosody
Proud 2B Loud
Pruno Truman & Friends
Psychic Ills
Psychic TV
Psycho Ritual P.O.*
Psychobitch
Psychotic Waltz
Psychotron II
Pterodactyl
Pulkas*
Pulse
Pulver
Pungent Stench
Purple Haze
Pussy Galhore*
Puts Marie*
Putsch
PX-Pain
Pyrit

Q

Quarks
Queens of the Stone Age*
The Querulent Rovers
Quickie
Quickspace
Quickspacer & B
Quilt
Quince

R

R. Stevie Moore*
Radian
Radio Explosivo
Rahzel*
Rainbow Arabia*
Ralf Schlatter
Ramblin' Bomber
Rape Blossoms
Raphelson
Rasen
Rats on Rafts
Ray Wilko
Razen
Realplayer: Genderfuck*
Rebel Squad
Rebuilding the Rights of Statues*
Rechenzentrum
Rectangle
The Red County
Red Harvest
Reding Street
Reeto von Gunten
Remi*
Remote Lane
Requiem
Reverend Beat-Man
Reverend Beat-Man Blues Trash Trio*
Reverend Beatman & The Church of Herpes*
Revolt
Rhododendron
Rhythm Trip
Ricardo Da Silva
Richard Dawson
Rick Rok
Ricochet Rabbit
Rik Rok & Michael Hilton
Rings
Rio Wolta
Rita Hey
Rival Kings
Rival Schools*
Rizzoknor*
rm74
rm
Roamer
Robbing Millions*
Rock It Royal
Rockandies
Rocky Wood
Rodrigo Amarante*
Rod
The Roebucks
Roger Rotor
Rökkurró
Romeo Bonvin
Rope
Rosa Dorn
Rosebud
The Rosebuds
Rosqo
Rother/Shelley/Mullan play NEU!*
Rotkeller
Rotting Christ
Round Table Knights
Roy & the Devil's Motorcycle
The Royal Hangmen
Rozbub
Rübe
Rude*
Rudy Rotta Band*
Rue Royale
Rumplestitchkin
Rundfunk
Russian Circles
Rustie*

S

Sa-Prize
Saalschutz
Sacha Love One Man Band
Sacha Love Trio
The Sad Riders
Sad Rockets
Safi
Sage
Salad*
Salaryman
Sally
Salut C'est Cool*
Sam Prekop
Samael*
Samara Lubelski
The Same Girl
Sampha
Samuel Hall Band
San Augustin
Sandra Hall
Santanico
Sartorius CD System
Saturnus
Saymen
Scapegoats
Scarlett O'Hanna
Scarlett's Fall
Schallpodium

*Kilbi Festival only

Schiffenen
Schlammpeitziger
Schnaak
Schneider TM
Schnellertollermeier*
Schnulze & Schnultze
Schwarz
Schwervon
Scorn
Scott Matthew
Scout Niblett
Scratch Pet Land
Scratches
Screaming Females
Scumbag
Scumbucket
SDNMT
Seabear
Seafood
Sean Nicholas Savage
Sebadoh
Second Hand
Secret Chiefs 3
Secret Circuit
The Secret
Seidenmatt
Seigmen*
Seilen
Selda
feat. Boom Pam*
Selenium
Self-Service
Selvhenter*
Sendak
Senking
Sensational
Sensavenue
Sepalcure
Septagramm
Serafina Steer
Serafyn
Serge
Seyni & the Spiritual
Free Hand
Shabazz Palaces*
Shackleton
Shadowsfear
Shake It Machine
Shalil Shankar Trio
Shalil Shankar
The Shamrockers
Shangaan Electro
Shannon Wright
Shantel & Bucovina
Club Orkestar*
Shaper
She
She Keeps Bees
Shearwater
Shever
Shilpa Ray
The Shit
shnit – Kurzfilme*
Shocking Pinks
Sholi
Shootyz Groove
Shotgun Blues
Shovel
Shroudshifter
Shy
Sick Sharks in Space
Sigurd
Silencio
Silentbass
Silicone Carnet
Silver Firs
Simon/Off
Simone Henneken*
Simone White
Simple Communication
Singh Pretam
Sinner D.C.
Sir Richard Bishop
Sissikontest
Six by Seven
Six Feet Under
Six Months of Sun
Six Organs of Admittance
Six Reasons to Kill
Six-Pack
Sixty Watt Shaman
Skeletons
Skip&Die*
Skirt
Skrew
Slandet
Slaves
Sleaford Mods*
Sleepmakeswaves
Sleepy Sun
Sleepytime Gorilla
Museum
Slimboy
The Slow Show*
Sludge
Slut
Slütspürt
Smiling Faces
Snackbeat Toys
Snarf
Snitch*
Snurfu
Soap&Skin
Soda Machine
Sodom
The Soft Moon
Soften
Soil
Solange la Frange
Solex
Sóley*
Solitune
Solstafir
Sombre
Son Lux
The Son of Dog
Sonar Nation
Songs of Neptune
Sonic Youth*
Sonograph
Sons of Morpheus
Sons of Noel and Adrian
Sophia
Sophie Hunger*
Sophie Hunger Plays
Bob Dylan
Soren
Soul Brother
Soulfly
Soulin' Crash
Soulless
The Sound of Fridge
Soundscapes From
the Edges*
Soup
Space Tourists
The Spacecommander
Sparrow & the Workshop
Speck
Spectacle
Spectre the Ill Saint
Speedball Baby*
Speedy Ortiz
Spencer
Spherical
Spidergawd
Spitting Off Tall
Buildings
Spookey Ruben
The Spores
Spot the Loony
The Spudmonsters
Spunk
St. Augustine
Stade feat. Erik Truffaz
Stahlberger
Stan Webb's Chicken
Shack*
Stanley Brinks
Stanley Brinks &
Freschard
Starcellar
Starfighter
Stars Like Fleas
Station 17
Steak
Steaming Satellites
Stearica
Steel Pole Bath Tub
Stefan Aeby Trio
Stefano De Ponti
Steff la Cheffe
Stella
Stereo Total
Steve Gunn
Still Angry
Still Corners
Stiller Has
Sting of Death
Stone Hill on Tour!
Stop the Shoppers
Strand of Oaks
Stritt
Stritt Ivo
Stritt: Eins
Strobocop
Strotter Inst.
Strybadrag
Strøm Meets
Ad'Absurdum
Stuck Mojo
Stump Fucking
Sturch
Subscribe
Subtitle
Such a Surge
Suchas
Sudden Infant
Südfleisch
Sue Ellen
Sum of R
Sun

Sun Glitters
Sun Kil Moon
Sun of Moon
Sun Ra Arkestra*
Sunn O)))
Sunn O))) performing "The Grimmerobe Demos"*
Superchunk*
Surrogat
Susie Asado
Suuns
Suzanne Vega
Suzanne Zahnd
SVND
Swans*
Sweet Disease*
Syd Matters
Syg Baas
Sylek
Syndrome WPW
Synthesize Me!

T

T-Model Ford
T.S. Brooks
T.S. Brooks & the Accountants
The Tabascos
Table of the Elements
Takemura Nobukazu
Takeo Toyama Trio
The Tallest Man on Earth*
Tamikrest & Dirtmusic*
Tankard
Tanya Tagaq*
Tar Queen
Tarantula A.D.
Tasteless
Tatum Rush
Team im Kongo
Tears Eviction
Technogod*
Teebs
Teen
Telekinesis
Tenko Texas Seduction Meets Dejan
TG
Thavius Beck
Thee Irma & Louise
Thee Oh Sees*
Thee Silver Mt. Zion Orchestra
Theo
Therion
The Thermals
Thilges
The Thing
Think About Mutation
Thom Roberts
Thomas Sauter Trio
Three Blind Wolves
Three Bones Left
Three Trapped Tigers
Threshold
Throne
Thumb
The Thurston Moore Band*
Thus:Owls
Tibert
Tiere der Nacht
Tiger Saw
Tigerbeat
Tight Finks
Till/Tape
Tim Exile*
Tim Fite
Timber Timbre
Timesbold
Timmermahn & die Waldrauscher Band
Timor
Tinariwen*
Tinu for President
Tiny Vipers
TJ Aus & TJ Chucks
TJ Spool
Toast Machine
Tobias Carshey
Toboggan
Toby Goodshank
Tocotronic*
Today Is the Day
Todos Destinos
Toe
Toini
Tokage
Tomaga
Tomcat Blake
Tongue Tied Twin
TOPS
Torche
Toronaut
Totem
Totemaus*
Toy
TR/ST
Tra-LaLa Band
Transport League
Trashy Lullabies
Trencher
Tribe After Tribe
Trieb
Triggerfinger
Tripkoff
Tritop
Trixa Arnold
Trottles of the Dead
Trottles of the Dead & Herr Wempe
TRUE
Truckfighters
True Blue
Trust*
Trust Fund
TS Zodiac
Tsar Shate II
Tuff Stuff
Tulip
Tulipe
Tumido
tUnE-yArDs
Tunica Dartos
Tuniq
Tunng*
Turbo Fantôme
Turbogeist
Turbostaat
Turner
Tweak Bird
Twisted
Two & Juna
Two Gallants
The Twobadours
Tyrehead
Tyvek

U

U.S. Girls
Überreel
Ufo
Ugly Mustard
Ulme
Umoja
Undead Vision
Under Construction
Under the Linden Tree
The Underground Youth
Underschool Element
Undiscovered Soul
Undivided
Unexisting Structures
Unfold
Unhold
Unida
Unisex Chainsaw
United to Be Famous
Unkind
Unknown Mortal Orchestra
Unleashed
The Unwinding Hours
Unwound
Up in Smoke
Urban Addictive
Urban Junior
Urlaub in Polen
Ursina Giger
The Usaisamonster
Uschan Delucca

V

*Kilbi Festival only

V.I.T.
V.O.D.
Vader
The Vagabonds
Vale Tudo
Valgeir Sigurðsson*
Vampyr 6006
Vampyros Lesbos Show
Veglia Crack
Velma
The Velvet Teen
Velvet Two Stripes
Venetian Snares
Venetus Flos
The Ventilators
Verboten Is
Veronica Falls
Versus
Vert
Verveine
Vescoli Toni
Vessel*
Vetiver
Vialka
Viaticum
Vic Du Monte's Persona Non Grata
Viet Cong*
Violetta Parisini*
Viral Load
Vital Remains
Vito
Vive la Fête*
Vivid
Vladislav Delay
Voivod
Volcano the Bear
Von Spar
The Voyeurs
Vundabar

W

WAB & DJ Rade
Wab
Waldorf
Walk Choc Ice
The Walkmen*
Wand*
The War on Drugs*
Warbringer
Wardhill
Wargasm
The Warlocks
Warm Graves
Warpath
The Wave Pictures
Wayne Sodabherk
We Are the City
We Dsp on You
We Loyal*
We Said
We™
Webba
Weekend
Weekend Phantom
Weiss
Welken
Wellington Irish Black Warrior
Wet Moss
What's Wrong with Us?*
What's Up
When Icarus Fall
The White Birch
White Fence*
White Hinterland
White Miles
Who Cares
Why?*
Whysome
Whyte Seeds
Widdershins
Wiggerside
Wild Beasts*
Wildbirds & Peacedrums
Will Oldham
Will Samson
Willard Grant Conspiracy
William the Contractor
William Tyler & Volker Zander
William White
Willy Schwarz
The Winchester Club
Wintersleep
Wire
Witchrider
Witch
With Hatred
Withered Hand
Wodaswar
Wolf Eyes
Wolf Parade*
Wolfman*
Wonderspleen
Wooden Shjips*
WTF Bijou

X

X-Cops
X-Mas Project
Xindu
Xiu Xiu
Xylouris White

Y

Yacht
Yakari
Yawning Man
Yeah!*
The Years Between
Yeasayer*
Yellow Teeth
Yeti Lane
Yog
Yokonoe
Yolk
The Young Gods
The Young Gods & Erika Stucky*
Your Fault
Yximalloo

Z

Za!*
Zatokrev
Zavoloka*
Zayk
Zebda*
Zebra Katz*
Zeno Tornado
Zigitros*
Zitto & Splendini
Zitto & Zitto
Zomby
Zorc
Zorg
ZS!
Zu
Zu & Damo Suzuki*
Züri West*
Zuul FX
ZZZ's

We love music and hosting our artists well. There was not much time to take care of our archives. We are very sorry if any artist who has performed since 1991 can't find their name on the alphabetical list above.

BAD BONN SONG BOOK

This book was published for the 25th anniversary of Bad Bonn Düdingen, Switzerland.

All the artworks were specially created by the performing artists themselves for the Bad Bonn Song Book.

Editors
Patrick Boschung
Daniel Fontana
Adeline Mollard
Katharina Reidy

Assistant editor
Stefanie Mauron

Concept & book design
Adeline Mollard
Katharina Reidy

Printed & bound by
Kösel GmbH
Paper: Munken Print White
Cover: Wicotex Magic
Fonts: Primo Regular, Dinamo
First edition: 1000 copies

Texts
Conrad Lambert (Merz)
Chan Marshall (Cat Power)
Benedikt Sartorius
Christophe Schenk

Proofreading
Mariette Althaus
Mario Corpataux
Eric Rosencrantz
Miriam Wiesel

Chan Marshall's message transcribed by Lee Staples

Edition Patrick Frey
Limmatstrasse 268
CH-8005 Zürich
editionpatrickfrey.com
mail@editionpatrickfrey.ch

First edition
Edition Patrick Frey, 2016
ISBN 978-3-905929-98-0
Printed in Germany

Distribution
Switzerland
AVA Verlagsauslieferung
CH – Affoltern am Albis
ava.ch

Germany, Austria
GVA Gemeinsame Verlags-auslieferung
D – Göttingen
gva-verlage.de

France, Luxembourg, Belgium
Les presses du réel
F – Dijon
lespressesdureel.com

United Kingdom
Antenne Books
GB – London
antennebooks.com

Japan
Marginal Press
JP – Tokyo
marginal-press.com

USA
RAM publications + distribution
USA – Santa Monica
rampub.com

Australia, New Zealand
Perimeter Distribution
AU – Melbourne
perimeterdistribution.com

Rest of the world
Edition Patrick Frey, CH – Zürich
editionpatrickfrey.com

With the kind support of

ETAT DE FRIBOURG
STAAT FREIBURG
WWW.FR.CH

Etat de Fribourg
Staat Freiburg
fribourg-culture.ch

Gemeindeverwaltung Düdingen

Thank you!
Edition Patrick Frey
All the musicians who wrote down their songs for us with amazing enthusiasm
Marco Fallico & the kitchen crew
Bad Bonn staff
Bad Bonn Kilbi staff

bbsongbook.ch
badbonn.ch